METHODS AND PERSPECTIVES IN URBAN MUSIC EDUCATION

Edited by

Charles E. Hicks
James A. Standifer
Warrick L. Carter

UNIVERSITY
PRESS OF
AMERICA

Copyright © 1983 by

University Press of America, Inc.

P.O. Box 19101, Washington, D.C. 20036

Library of Congress Cataloging in Publication Data
Main entry under title:

Methods and perspectives in urban music education.

Includes bibliographical references and indexes.
1. Music--Instruction and study--United States--
Addresses, essays, lectures. 2. Education, Urban--
United States--Addresses, essays, lectures. I. Hicks,
Charles E. II. Standifer, James A. III. Carter,
Warrick L.
MT1.M46 1982   780'.7'2973   82-16105
ISBN 0-8191-2760-4
ISBN 0-8191-2761-2 (pbk.)

198871

FOREWORD

THE CONTINUING CRISIS OF URBAN EDUCATION

During the latter part of 1970, the book **Crisis in the Classroom** presented a massive study authored by Charles E. Silberman, and funded by the Carnegie Coroporation. Silberman elucidated the problems of education in America and recommended strategies for changing unexciting educational structures into schools that are not in conflict with the nurture and development of children. Silberman and several other social reformers began laying the format for educational change during the end of the sixties. Unfortunately, the once balloning concept of the "Great Society" was being gradually deflated by an administration that adopted regressive social policies. The framers of the "Bring Us Together" concept effectively disembowled any further attempts to rebuild and revitalize the large urban centers and their institutions.

Undoubtedly, one of the crucial issues facing public education today is how to meet the challenge of the urban learner effectively. The urban learner includes such racial minorities as American Blacks, Mexican-Americans, Puerto Ricans, American Indians and a substantial number of poor Whites. Data now available to most parents and administrators provide testimony that the state of public education within urban areas, particularly the inner-city, is at a virtual standstill for most participants. Comfice, the dullness and rigidity of curricula and the ineptness of teachers. The most common complaint is the one that suggest that students are not as bright as they used to be. Schools have historically placed the responsibility for failure on the product--the student--and not on the institution which develops the product. The case, bluntly stated, suggests that education is the only industry in which the consumer-- the child--is held responsible for the quality of the product.

The general response from superintendents to this charge has been a plea for more money to revamp their programs. And, of course, this is a valid request. School systems definitely require more money to operate, but the method of operation is, in many cases, questionable. For example, we have watched school

iii

budgets rise with no comparable rise in educational effectiveness.

One of the most pervasive problems in urban education is that present day curricula in ghetto schools are not meeting the educational needs of racial minorities who inhabit the inner-city. These curricula are often watered down versions of educational programs that have a middle-class orientation. Little attempt has been made to tailor-make the curricula to fit the specal needs of the inner-city child and to build upon the strengths of these children.

Teachers, administrators and most of the components of the educational establishment have generally classified urban inner-city students as being "slow," "dull" .and "non-verbal," "culturally disadvantaged" as well as being "generally disinterested in education." These characteristics, generally, are described as inherent to the child. This classification is not entirely borne out by Frank Riessman and others who suggested that "deprived" children are slow for reasons other than inherent deficiencies. Professor Riessman stated that:

> A pupil may be slow because he is
> extremely careful, meticulous or
> cautious. He may be slow because he
> cannot understand a concept unless he
> does something physically, for example,
> with his hands. The disadvantaged
> child is typically a physical learner,
> and the physical learner is generally a
> slower learner.[2]

In addition, Riessman points out that the disadvantaged child may also appear to be a slow learner simply becase his is a "one track" learner who persists in one train of thought and cannot easily adopt the teacher's middle-class frame of reference. He further states that "very often this single-minded individual has considerable creative potential, much of which goes unrealized because of lack of reinforcement in the educational system".[3] Unfortunately, Riessman and others use the terms" culturally deprived" and/or "culturally disadvantaged" to account for the academic failure of children in the urban inner-cities. These terms imply that the culture of the child is deprived, or in some way, inferior. The labels,then, infer inferior status of ethnic minorities, and this places the responsibility for the deprived condition on the oppressed (the children of the inner-city) rather than on the **institutions that oppress** (the school). This point of view does not suggest that Riessman has not identified some important issues, but it does suggest a revision in the labels that are applied.

Bernard Mackler and Morsley Giddings, writing in **The Urban R's: Race Relations as the Problem in Urban Education,** indicated that" . . . an adequate theory of deprivation must eventually explain why certain pupils succeed and others do not, given the same social background."[4] As yet, there is no such theoretical formulation.

The mis-education of children continues to prevail in urban America. Instead of correcting this corruption of education, one proposed solution is to displace the urban consumers to the outer fringes of the inner-city or its adjacent suburbs. Anthony Downs, in his book **Opening Up the Suburbs,**[5] suggests that the urban poor be moved to the suburbs in order to facilitate revitalization of urban inner-cities. Downs, however, makes it clear that the suburban middle class must retain control of these "open" suburbs. There is no mention of the dynamic of shared power. Thus, it is suggested that a significant segment of the urban population that has developed marginal political power should become the powerless migrants of the suburbs.

W. E. B. Du Bois made a rather candid observation regarding urban (Northern) education. Writing in the July 1935 issue of the **Journal of Negro Education,** Du Bois said:

> . . . I know that race prejudice in the United States today is such that most Negroes cannot receive proper education in white institutions. . . There are many public school systems in the North where Negroes are admitted and tolerated but they are not educated: they are crucified.[6]

Du Bois continued by developing his thesis for overcoming the process of mis-education.

(This book, the first of its kind offers some special insights into the problems and needs of education in the whole urban educational community. Although it is primarily directed towards teachers in music education and teacher training, I hope that its message - especially on multicultural education in music will be transmitted to those who make decisions concerning curricula in **MUSIC**.)

Charles A. Martin

FOOTNOTES

[1]Charles E. Silberman, **Crisis in the Classroom** (New York: Random House Publishers, 1970).

[2]Frand Riessman, **The Culturally Deprived Child** (New York: Harper and Row, 1962), p. 64.

[3]Ibid.

[4]B. Mackler and M. Giddings, "Cultural Deprivation: A Study in Mythology," in **The Urban R's**, Robert A. Dentler, Bernard Mackler and Mary Ellen Warshauer (eds.) (New York: Praeger, 1967), p. 211.

[5]A Downs, **Opening Up the Suburbs, Urban Strategies for America** (New Haven: Yale University Press, 1973).

[6]W. E. B. Du Bois, "Does the Negroe Need Separate Schools?" **The Journal of Negro Education**, IV (Summer 1935), 328-335.

BARBARA WESLEY BAKER chairs the music department at Eleanor Roosevelt Sr. High School in Greenbelt, Maryland, where she has developed a reputation for outstanding gospel, concert and chamber choirs. While completing her Ph. D. at the University of Maryland, she was selected as an American Association of University Women Research Fellow. In addition to her extensive research in Black gospel music, she is well regarded as an author, clinician and lecturer in Black gospel music.

ED BLAND is a composer, arranger and musical consultant who specializes in music career option clinics across the country. He was formerly executive producer for Vanguard Records and a member of the Presidential Commission for the White House Record Library. John Hammond of CBS Records said of Ed; "very few people in music have as much expertise in so many aspects of the music business today." Ed maintains his own business in New York and continues to write, arrange and produce on the side.

TILFORD U. BROOKS is Associate Professor of music and Chairman of the Music Department at Washington University, St. Louis, Missouri. Dr. Brooks received his B.A. in Music Education at Southern Illinois University, M.A. in Music and Education and Ed. D. in Music at Washington University. He has had extensive experience as an instrumental teacher in the public schools of East St. Louis, Illinois and served as director of Music for that school district from 1971-1973. He is a specialist in instructional media and Black Music. He has published numerous articles in leading research journals and is a frequent reviewer for the book review section of the **Journal of Research in Music Education**. He was also a special consultant for the Silver Burdette Book Company; the author of **Afro-American Music and Its Toots**: 1976 general music series.

REGINALD T. BUCKNER is Assistant Professor of Jazz Studies and Afro-American/African Studies at the University of Minnesota (Minneapolis). He received his Bachelor and Master of Music Education degrees from the University of Kansas and his Ph.D. in Music from the University of Minnesota. He was a classroom teacher for five years and a junior high school instrumental music teacher for three years in the Kansas City, Kansas Public Schools. He is a jazz pianist and organist. He was the host, writer, interviewer, bandleader and pianist on **Jazz: An American Classic,** a television credit course produced by the University of Mid-America and the University of Minnesota. His research interests include the psychology of jazz (how it is learned and perceived) and jazz history.

WARRICK L. CARTER holds a Doctor of Philosophy degree from Michigan State University with a major in music and is currently coordinator of Music Programs and Professor of Music in the College of Cultural Studies, Governors State University, Park Forest South, Illinois.

Dr. Carter lists among his curriculum specialities such subjects as A Survey History of Afro-American Music, Arranging and Orchestration, Black Composers of the European Tradition, History of Jazz, Instrumental Conducting, Jazz Ensemble and Jazz Materials for Teacher Education.

A widely published author, Dr. Carter, has to his credit a number of authoritative articles dealing with jazz education in the college curriculum, indigenous American music, music in the black studies program, black composers of the European tradition, and music education for the culturally different student.

He is a much sought after speaker and panelist and has served a number of leading colleges and universities in a consulting capacity.

Warrick Carter is a composer and recording artist as well as a featured performer and soloist. His performance schedule has literally taken him around the world and includes featured appearances at the Montreaux International Jazz Festival, the Illinois-Sao Paulo Centennial Celebration in Sao Paulo, Brazil and military bases in Korea, Japan, Gaum, the Phillipine Islands, Okinawa and Tiwan.

EFFIE T. GARDNER is Associate Professor of Music and Supervisor of Music Education at Hampton Institute, Hampton, Virginia. After teaching high school choral music in the Chicago Public Schools for twelve years, she received her Ph. D. from Michigan State University in Music (1979). She serves as state advisor to the student chapters of the Virginia Music Educators Association and teaches courses in choral techniques, elementary and secondary methods of music, vocal jazz ensemble, and piano.

BARBARA A. HICKS is presently a Job Specialist with Jobs for Missouri Graduates, Inc.. A former full-time instructor of Business Education at Hickey Business School and part-time instructor at Forest Park Community College, St. Louis, Missouri. She has had extensive experience teaching in schools of large urban populations; having taught in Detroit from 1967-1976. A graduate of Tennessee State University, she holds a M.S. degree in secondary education from the University of Missouri-St. Louis.

CHARLES E. HICKS, is currently University Professor of Instrumental Music and directs the concert band at Governors State University, Park Forest South, ILL. Dr. Hicks began his career as a high school band director in 1960 and has spent sixteen of those years as an effective music teacher in schools of large urban populations (Detroit and Chicago). He received his Ph. D. from Michigan State University in 1976 where he also served as a teaching associate in the Music Education Department. He has lectured in Afro-American Music and Jazz History at both Lansing and Wayne County Community Colleges. His present research is concerned mainly with teacher training and minority testing in music. He has published articles in leading music journals dealing with teacher-student interaction and learning processes in instrumental music.

JIMMIE JAMES, JR. is presently serving as professor of music and director of musical activities at Jackson State University. He directs the Brass ensemble, Announcer/Publicity Director for the Marching Band, and has served as Director of the Concert Band and Assistant Director of the Marching Band. Dr. James' experience in church music includes six years as Director of Music and Director of the Sons and Daughters of Allen Choir at Pearl Street AME Church, Jackson, Mississippi. He is music editor of the **AME Christian Recorder**, where he has received nationwide acclaim for his column, "The Musician's Corner." Dr. James is author of the handbook **Organizing and Administering the AME Church Music Program** and presently serves as Director of Music of the AME Church's Eighth Episcopal District, having been appointed to this newly created position in August of 1976 by Bishop Frank C. Cummings.

A versatile musician, Dr. James serves as a member of the Board of Directors and Principal Tuba for the Jackson Municipal Band. Elected President of the College Division of the Mississippi Music Educators Association. He is also a member of the Music Educators National Conference, the National Education Association, Phi Delta Kappa Educational Fraternity, and several other professional, social, and civic organizations, including Omega Psi Phi Fraternity, Inc.He was named Omega Man of the Year for the 1978-79 term.

He served as the Director of the First AME Church Music Workshop which was held in cooperation with Jackson State University in July of 1977 and attracted more than 100 participants from thirteen different Episcopal Districts. Dr. James has also conducted workshops in the following places: New Orleans, Louisiana; Columbus, Ohio; Mobile, Alabama; Andalusia, Alabama; Kansas City, Missouri; Wilberforce, Ohio; St. Louis, Missouri; Wheeling, West Virginia; Los Angeles, California and Slidell, Louisiana.

DONALD J. JONES is Dean of Students at Southwestern High School, Detroit, Michigan. He was a high school instrumental music teacher and supervisor for fifteen years in the Chicago and Detroit Public Schools Systems. In addition, he has been an adjunct lecturer at Wayne County Community College and is presently a member of the Music Advisory Board of the Michigan Council for the Arts. He has authored numerous articles dealing with the arts and urban education in leading journals throughout the country. His bachelors an masters degrees in music education were received at Tennessee State University and the University of Illinois; and doctorate in educational administration from the University of Michigan.

ROBERT H. KLOTMAN is Professor of Music and Chairman of the Music Education Department in the School of Music at Indiana University. Prior to coming to Indiana he was the Divisional Director of Music for the Detroit Public Schools. He has also served as Director of Music for the Akron Public Schools giving him a wide variety of experiences in urban areas. He received his Ed.D. from Columbia University, Teachers College in

1956. He is the author of the text, **THE SCHOOL ADMINISTRATOR AND SUPERVISOR: CATALYSTS FOR CHANGE IN MUSIC EDUCATION** and has co-authored **LEARNING TO TEACH THROUGH PLAYING** (with Ernest Harris). Dr. Klotman is a Past President of the Music Educators National Conference and is currently the contributing editor for the string column in the magazine, The INSTRUMENTALIST.

LAWRENCE MCCLELLAN, JR., a native of Knoxville, Tennessee, received the undergraduate degree from Knoxville College, a M.S. degree in music education from the University of Tennessee, and a Ph.D from Michigan State University. During his studies he served as a graduate assistant at both The University of Tennessee and Michigan State University. He has taught music at the elementary, junior high, and high school levels in Atlanta, Georgia and Knoxville, Tennessee. A musican of note, Dr. McClellan made his debut as a trombonist with the Oak Ridge (Tennessee) Symphony Orchestra prior to performing with such recording artists as Nina Simone, Tennessee Ernie Ford, Bettye Swann, Glen Campbell, and Nancy Wilson. Marching bands and jazz ensembles throughout Georgia, Tennessee, and Michigan have performed his arrangements. Dr. McClellan is presently Director of Music at The College of the Virgin Islands in St. Thomas.

WILLIAM T. MCDANIEL is presently Professor of Jazz and Afro-American Music at the Ohio State University. A graduate of Morehouse College, he holds the M.A. and Ph.D degrees from the University of Iowa. He is a specialist in Jazz and Afro-American music and has performed and lectured extensively on the subjects.

E. O'HARA SPEARMAN is presently serving as Assistant Professor of Music at Southern Illinois University at Edwardsville-East St. Louis Center. Dr. Spearman was formerly a band director in the St. Louis Public System and from 1974-1979 was superviosr of instrumental music for that same district. He is a Jazz Saxophonist of exceptional talent, has performed with many of the giants of Jazz; among some notables are the "Cannonball" Adderly Qunitet, and Clark Terry to name a few. An outstanding instrumentalist and musician, he developed superior school bands both in Florida and St. Louis. He received his B.M. in music at Florida A & M University, his M.M. and Ph.D. at Washington University in St. Louis.

JAMES A. STANDIFER, Chairman of the Music Education Department, joined the faculty in 1971 after having taught in the public schools of Cleveland, Ohio, and at Morristown College and Temple University. He teaches courses and conducts research projects in curriculum and multi-cultural music education. A specialist in general music for secondary schools, he is called upon nationally as a consultant in problems of urban school music education and for projects asssociated with music instruction in Public Television. He is a member of the advisory board of the Council for Research in Music Education. He is also the author of several articles on general music, curriculum, and teacher education and of The Source Book of African and Afro-Afro-American Materials for the Music Educator, and the American Book Company's Secondary Level New Dimensions in Music Series. Standifer is Director of the University of Michigan School of Music's Eva Jessye Collection of Afro-American Materials, and lectures nationally on this and other projects related to Multi-Cultural Arts Education.

WARREN C. SWINDELL is Director and Professor of Afro-American Studies, the Center for Afro-American Studies, at Indiana State University. Prior to assuming his current position, he served as chair of the department of Fine Arts, and Professor of Music at Kentucky State University, Frankfort, Kentucky. He has taught music in grades K-12, including general music, choir, band, and orchestra in both urban and rural settings. His Ph.D. was earned at the University of Iowa where he studies with Edwin Gordon and specialized in music literacy learning theory and music achievement testing. He has held MENC and other professional organization offices at the state, regional, and national levels.

ACKNOWLEDGEMENTS

My sincere thanks is extended to all of the contributing editors to this book for their ideas and assistance. Special thanks is also extended to the National Black Music Caucus, Mr. Camille C. Taylor and Dr. Yvonne Cheeks for their assistance in the promotion of this manuscript. To Dr. Richard Graham, Dr. Dominique-Rene de Lerma, and Professor Marian T. Brown my thanks to them for their excellent critique and suggestions for revisions and improvement of the book. To Dr. John Hylton for his reading and editorial comments of chapter 3. Special thanks go to Bill Banker for his expertise in completing the index of the book.

To the clerical staff in the Music Department of the University of Missouri-St. Louis--Linda Callies and Mary Rank -- and the manuscript typists -- June E. Hilliard and Melody Newsom -- from the dean's office of the College of Arts and Sciences special thanks is extended for their many hours of devotion to the completion of this project.

To my wife Barbara and my son Christopher my deepest appreciation goes for their patience, love and understanding throughout the duration of this project.

To Joan Coleman Special thanks is extended for her research assistance with chapters 2 and 12.

The following publishers and companies have given permission to use their copyrighted materials:

"I'm Goin' Up North", **Negro Songs From Alabama** - Secular, Vol. I, Side 1, Band 6, Ethnic Folkways Library, FE 4417, recorded and edited by Harold Courlander. "I Must See", Negro Songs from Alabama - Ring Games Songs and Others, Vol. VI, Side 1, Band 8, Ethnic Folkways Library, FE 4474, recorded and edited by Harold Courlander. The PUBLICATION: NEGRO SONGS FROM ALABAMA, collected by Harold Courlander, Published with the Assistance of the Wenner-Gren Foundation for Anthropological Research, copyright 1960 by Harold Courlander. Reprinted with Permission.

PUBLISHERS' LICENSING CORPORATION, for the use of printed excerpts from Thad Jones' CONSUMMATION

PREFACE

METHODS AND PERSPECTIVES is a book which consists of three sections. Part I represents articles focusing on the demographics, sociology and some perspective about the peoples and their institutions. Part II provides an overview of the urban crisis in music education. Some contemporary problems faced by music educators, i.e. discipline, violence, vandalism, drugs, poverty, finance, curricula and competency testing are presented in a probing and sensitive manner. Part III presents an arrey of practical prescription programs as possible solutions to the problems faced by many music teachers in urban America today.

The prescription programs are offered in several areas: (1) The classroom setting - practical strategies designed for immediate use by teachers, (2) approaches to comprehensive musicianship, (3) other methodologies, and (4) perspectives on teacher preparation for urban schools. Specifically, the text is a source of methods and materials which provide designs for learning: means for constructing learning centers for urban schools, general music classes, and performance programs. Some special emphasis will be given to commercial music studies as currently manifested in urban schools with implications for consumer and career education.

This book is a definitive handbook that is aimed at **ALL** music educators. It includes some special insights for those involved with education in and teacher preparation for urban environments. Finally, this book can serve as a handy source for organizations and institutions who are endavoring to see that music education be taught from a truly multicultural approach.

C.E.H.
J.A.S.
W.L.C.

LIST OF TABLES

CONTENTS

PART 1

Chapter 1

INTRODUCTION AND OVERVIEW/THE URBAN SETTING

Charles E. Hicks and Donald J. Jones

Music education in large urban centers today face the very serious problem of becoming extinct. The problem of music education is but a part of the larger problem called the **URBAN CRISIS** which continues to worsen year after year. According to the Kerner Commission's Report, "American cities face a fourfold dilemma: (1) fewer tax dollars available as middle income taxpayers move out and property values, business, and commerce decline; (2) more tax dollars are needed for essential services to meet the needs of low-income groups; (3) increasing costs of goods and services, resulting in dwindling tax dollars buying less; and (4) increasing dissatisfactions with services provided as needs, expectations, and living standards increase."[1]

Beginning in the early sixties, urban schools have been in a state of inbalance and change. Most of this change has come from the growing discontent from forces within. This discontent represents every sector of society; the young, the old, the local community, the teaching staff, the political and business community. So loud have been the voices of criticism that those who are in the policy making decisions have begun to change every aspect of the educational process. Most of these changes represent new and innovative programs designed to meet the needs of every group within the urban population.

URBAN PROBLEMS

Ask anyone, what's the number one problem facing the urban school systems in our large cities today and eight out of ten responses would no doubt be, MONEY. President Carter stated that "changes in education must begin with the methods of financing...a major overhaul of the revenue-sharing concept is needed. Funds for local government should be greatly increased, and the prohibition against using these funds for education must be eliminated."[2] For the last ten years or so the leaders in our public schools and others have

1

complained of the present formulas used for disbursing funds to states and local school districts. These formulas do not take into account the special needs of the urban poor. According to the Urban Education Task Force, the formulas are based on two factors: (1) "the financial ability of the local school district and (2) the educational needs of the local school district."[3]

The most serious threat to local support to education in inner-city areas is not just finances, but neglect and the continuous eroding tax base. This situation is caused by what urban experts called population migration. The constantly shifting of people from the core of the city to the outlying areas. Along with this population change has been a mass exodus of business from the cities to the suburbs because of greater tax benefits. Many whites also flee to the suburbs because of better schools and better housing. Those that remain are there because they cannot afford to leave, and are labelled the "urban poor" of which the largest percentage is black. In 1967 the median family income for those in the inner-city as compared to those of outlying areas were $7,813 to 9,367. Because of the lower income and lower educational levels, the cities are faced with higher costs for educational services and fewer tax dollars from its citizens.

The deteriorating tax base suggests that if quality education is to become a reality for the nation's poor, a fair way of determining education expenditures must be found. More money is needed to remedy the inequities of the past and to respond with vigor to meet the challenge of the future. The National Education Association (NEA) reports the foremost need of urban cities are for funds to correct the existing deficiencies of the past and upgrade the regular educational program to the level of the best practices of contemporary education.

CURRICULA

During the last fifteen years the problems of urban cities and educating the poor has been the center of much controversy and debate. Out of this rhetoric, commissions and task forces have invented new acronynms, concepts, and cliches. Through research and deliberations these groups have introduced into the educational jargon words, such as culturally deprived, inner-city, programmed instruction, compensatory

2

education, open classroom and career education to name a few. Because the curricula in most large urban schools are primarily structured to meet the needs of those students who seek a college education, many inner-city students are not so inclined to follow a college preparatory curriculum. Since a large percentage of the graduating seniors in urban schools do not continue or plan to attend a four-year college many students find it difficult to follow this type of regime. Consequently, many become disinterested and drop-out of school completely, and others enter the job market unprepared, while the majority end up as tax liabilities.

LOSS OF CREDIBILITY

Harry S. Broudy states, "our educational systems are suffering from "a loss of consensus, loss of mission, and loss of credibility...and are in need of a new voice to speak for the schools." This new professional voice must speak with "intellectual and political authority." The most serious harm the old voices have caused is that of having told the public and tricked them in believing that:

> If teachers were competent, the school could get rid of crime on the streets, solve the drug problem, diminish sexual promiscuity and pornography, and restore faith in American institutions. The schools have been told to enforce discipline, but cautioned that if they do so, they will be liable to court suits. But the most serious is the general belief that the cost of schools as measured by per capita expenditures is the cost of student instruction.[4]

Dr. Broudy is suggesting that administrative costs, staff salaries and non-instructional activities eat up a large portion of the school budget, and that the remaining funds go for actually educating students.

ACCOUNTABILITY

During the mid 1970's accountability became a top priority in educational circles. This circumstance came about not from what the schools have or have not done; rather from the social conditions of the times. According to dictionaries "accountability is defined

3

as the condition of being accountable, liable or responsible." Accountability as used in current educational literature is described as "when resources and efforts are related to results in ways that are useful for policy-making, resources allocation or compensation"[5] and "the guarantee that all students without skills necessary to take advantage of the choices that accrue upon successful completion of public schooling."[6]

Klotman states "the citizenry is becoming increasingly concerned with **accountability**. Basically this implies holding educators responsible for what children actually learn in a classroom or, more specifically, for achieving their educational goals."[7] Parents are beginning to file suits against school districts because their students do not achieve an adequate education. Historically, teachers have always been held accountable for their work, but not in terms of the outcomes of his students. Competency-based teacher education is a step in that direction. Some twenty-five or more states have enacted legislation concerning accountability and many more will have some type of law soon. Whatever emerges in this regard, the signal is clear for educators. If nothing is done to improve the performance of its students, one could be held liable.

Glass has listed six plans which have been used to describe accountabilty. They are behavioral objectives, performance contracting, voucher systems, economic input-output analysis accreditation, and community participation."[8] Educational accountability is a multi-dimensional relationship which consists of the state, city, board of education, building adminis-trators, teaching staff, paraprofessionals, parents and students. At every level in this cooperative relationship accountability must be built in. Unless this is done, equal educational opportunity for all students will remain a dream for most of the urban poor.

DECENTRALIZATION

Public education in big cities has been the target of much criticism during the decade of the sixties and continues to the present day. There are those who say the systems are too large and filled with poor adminis-tration, inefficiency, red tape, and duplication of services. This is especially true with those urban

4

system who decided to decentralize the total system because of politics, and pressure from parent organizations and community groups. The proponents of decentralization are naive enough to believe that this change will improve urban schools, and this will ultimately affect the quality of education. There are some who say, well it can't hurt. The desirable outcomes of decentralization are listed below:

1. More community involvement.
2. Improved conditions within present system.
3. Altered present power structure.
4. Increase minority participation in decision making positions.
5. Modified curricula to meet local needs.

During the early 1970's, decentralization of The Detroit Public Schools by the legislature as a means of desegregation and a transition from a white majority to a black majority school board was undertaken. Some years later, this system finds itself close to bankruptcy. It is believed by many politicians, educators, and community persons that decentralization is partly responsible for the system's financial decay. As of 1977, the Michigan House voted 79-11 to end decentralization in the Detroit Public Schools and swift action in the Senate is expected. Today Detroit is going throught its last school year under decentralization.

A sample of opinions from almost every segment of the Detroit community suggests that decentralization (the regional concept) is an impediment not an aid to quality education. Not many of the desirable ends of decentralization have been realized. In fact, the complaints of "too many chiefs", duplication of services, material waste, and red tape still exist. A cursory look at the massive administrative structure of the Detroit system staggers the imagination as to just how efficient and effective this large a system can be administered in the traditional "loose way" urban schools are being administered.

Some idea of how the local print and electronic media felt about this issue, some of their comments were taken from the November 23rd issue of the official publication of the Detroit Federation of Teachers, **THE DETROIT TEACHER**. They are as follows:

Editorial Viewpoints on Decentralization

Lining minds, not pockets
The Michigan Chronicle, April 30, 1977

"In the past year, we've watched an already eroded city school system slash even further into an embattled budget by almost completely eliminating arts and music programs as well as eliminating spring sports programs.

"At the same time, however, we've seen increasing examples of capital expenditures to keep the highly developed region board system intact.

"...we would still advocate the abolition of the regional board system simply because the final analysis is that we are expending massive amounts of money to the regional structure at the expense of our children's education.

"Education, after all, should be about lining minds instead of lining pockets."

Never achieved its goals
WWJ Opinion by James F. Clark, Editorial Director, May 5, 1977

"...we believe decentralization is a costly failure that created an unneeded layer of administrators who have added nothing to the quality of education.

"Decentralization was started with high ideals of bringing the school system closer to the people of a particular area, or region. But with busing and high administrative costs, it never achieved its goal. So, we still think Detroit should dump decentralization."

Regional boards cost too much
Detroit News, May 10, 1977

"Whatever the figure (for annual costs), regional boards are no longer worth the cost. Regional boards are the "frills" - not music and art education.

"Rep. Morris Hood, (D-Detroit) bluntly labels regional boards 'a ripoff - a waste of time'. 'School systems are for the education of youngsters.' Hood says, 'and not to provide ego trips for adults!'

"We agree completely."

"The boards have become frightfully expensive sounding boards no longer needed with changing times and needs."

"The school system needs less bureaucracy and more dollars going into education."

Use funds to improve schools
Detroit Free Press - May 4, 1977

"When it was imposed upon the city by the state Legislature, decentralization offered a necessary and effective safety valve that provided the transition from a white majority to a black majority school board."

The Detroit Public Schools is an example of what has become the rule instead of the exception in finding solutions to the problem of education in large urban areas. The strategy includes realizing a mistake, making the necessary changes, and moving on; also, being able to profit by errors made and learning from the errors of others. Detroit, almost the last of the large urban cities to end decentralization on the eve of bankruptcy might indeed be on their way to solving its problems and providing quality education for all of its students.

It must be stated here that law makers should leave the crucial decisions concerning quality education to those best qualified. The educators should consult with law makers in seeing that they provide the necessary laws that make it possible to

7

achieve quality education for its citizens. And both groups should not kindle the hopes of the urban population by having them believe that any one program will be a panacea for the urban school woes.

URBAN ADMINISTRATOR

During the chaotic days of the sixties when student protest, especially in the big city schools was at its highest level, many black educators were promoted to administrative positions and given the job of "keeper of order" in the schools. But regardless of this description of their duties, inner-city schools need educators who are sensitive, concerned, decisive, and above all capable administrators. Today's schools need educators who respect the worth of each individual regardless of race, religion, or academic background. Most of all, the urban schools need administrators who are themselves secure. In a recent study Bentzen stated, "a principal cannot be all things to all men. He must walk the middle road between what others expect and leadership demands."[10]

The black administrator must constantly deal with additional forces or expectations from a variety of sources. All principals struggle through a bramble of education, training, hard-won experience, and pure happenstance. Roye goes on to state that:

> black administrators and principals in addition must overcome sophisticated patterns of discrimination and manage the multi-world living required of blacks in such positions. They must often endure the suspicions of several communities; the white, the black, the poor, the powerless, and the enraged. They must overcome many personal, racial, and personality dilemmas.[11]

Though viewpoints may vary, one certainty appears definite that joint effort by all concerned will prove effective. Each facet of this operation must consist of dedicated and hard-working professionals if solutions to the problem of urban city schools are to emerge.

TEACHER PREPARATION

Preparing teachers for the urban public schools is one of the most pressing needs of college and university teacher education programs. During the early sixties the federal government provided funds to support institutes for teachers of "disadvantaged youth," but after this initial thrust, this novel idea has not been continually used by schools and teacher training institutions in helping teachers prepare themselves for teaching in the urban areas of this country. In a recent study the National Education Association (NEA) report showed that teachers lacked preparation for teaching covering three areas as follows: "(1) teaching methods, (2) classroom management routines and discipline, and (3) the use of audio visual equipment and materials."[12] All of these areas are directly related to the type of training that prospective teachers receive in their teacher training institutions.

The teacher must come to grips with the background of his/her students. The urban ghetto youth is a very complex organism about whom we do not have enough information that would enable teachers to deal with, tolerate, or possibly help this student in the classroom. Historically, our educational system has placed emphasis on making all students conform to the middle-class values of the teacher. The urban school system lacks sensitivity in coping with the social problems of the inner-city students. No substantial effort has been made to really understand and provide for the unique differences which the average urban youth bring to the classroom. The middle-class syndrome that permeates our society characterizes the only right way to act, react, and behave in many school situations. By and large, those who do not adhere or conform to this norm are branded as different and in some cases doomed to failure. Research in this area by the Detroit Board of Education reveals the following results concerning teacher expectation and student achievement. Findings of the study seemed to fall into four categories: (1) students, (2) teachers, (3) methods and materials and (4) school factors. Some conclusions from the study are as follows:

> **STUDENTS:** actual success in learning depends a great deal on whether the student expects to succeed and individual differences in learning

9

rates exist not only between children for the same learning task but within the same child for different learning tasks...

TEACHERS: teacher characteristics such as sex, age, and race are unrelated to student achievement, teaching behavior can be changed to improve learning, and the behavior of the teacher in the classroom is the most significant single controllable variable in the teaching situation...

METHODS AND MATERIALS: improvements in learning and skills can be achieved by the introduction of systematic instruction based on diagnosis, prescription, instruction, performance testing, and feedback applied in an individual manner, students can learn from each other, increased variety in instructional approaches and teaching materials will improve overall learning, and a supportive climate enhances motivation and reinforces success experiences which leads to improved student achievement....

SCHOOL FACTORS: pupil achievement tends to improve when the teaching staff is directly involved in the formulation and selection of curriculum content, the quality of schooling affects achievement and is more important to the poor than the middle class, and desegregation of socioeconomic status and race can contribute in some measure to achievement.[13]

Washington (1974) in an article suggests that teachers and prospective teachers alike should focus upon self-concept development of students. The basic question in his discussion was: "what effect does a negative perception of self-concept have on the child's academic achievement?" The conclusion was "that there is a strong correlation between positive conception of self-concept and good academic achievement."[14] The primary responsibility of the teacher, according to

10

Washington, "is to identify the child's strengths and interests, rather than focus on his weaknesses. Teachers who interacted in an affective educational experience were able to internalize at a visceral (gut) level the importance of all children having strong self-concepts."[15] It is highly possible that teachers who are more accepting and less rejecting in their relationships with students and those that use a variety of teaching behaviors will no doubt be better prepared to help students develop better self-concepts and thus facilitate more learning in the classroom environment.

SOLUTIONS

There are as many solutions to the problems stated as there are problems. Much of what has been written concerning possible solutions to correct the problems requires enormous costs that make many of the remedies prohibitive. Others, perhaps, would disarrange completely the present structure of urban educational systems to the extent that the harm might far outweigh the good. Still other recommendations offer some hope for improvements.

Professor Thomas Pettigrew of Harvard University proposes the "Metropolitan Educational Parks" concept, while Professor Donald Erickson of the University of Chicago suggests parents with children of school age be given credits against their taxes and these parents would remain free to send their children to the type of school they so choose. These two novel concepts, while being on the extremes of each other, are suggesting alternatives to the present system of education.

To adapt the school programs so that they will keep pace with the changes in the larger society, the Kerner Commission recommended the pursuit of the following strategies with appropriate programs to deal with each:

PROBLEM

Increasing efforts to eliminate de facto segregation

PROGRAM FOR DEALING WITH PROBLEM

increased financial aid to school efforts to systems seeking to elimi-

11

nate segregation within the system itself or in cooperation with neighboring systems; establishment of major educational magnet schools to draw racially and socioeconomically mixed populations and provided special curricula and specialized educational programs; establishment of supplemental education centers to provide racially integrated educational experiences for white and black students.

PROBLEM

Improving the quality of teaching in ghetto schools

PROGRAM FOR DEALING WITH PROBLEM

year-round education for disadvantaged students; establishment of early childhood programs designed to overcome effects of disadvantaged environment, involving parents and the home as well as the child; provision of extra incentives for highly qualified teachers in ghetto schools; reduction in maximum class size; curricular recognition of the history, culture, and contribution of minority groups; individualized instruction; intensive concentration on basic verbal skills; and development of new patterns of education for students who do not fit into traditional forms.

PROBLEM

Improving community-school relations

PROGRAM FOR DEALING WITH PROBLEM

elimination of obstacles to community participation in the educational process; opening schools for a variety of community service functions; use of local residents as teacher aides and tutors; increasing the accountability of schools to the community.

12

PROBLEM

Expanding opportunities for higher and vocation education

PROGRAM FOR DEALING WITH PROBLEM

expansion of Upward Bound Program; removal of financial barriers to higher education; emphasis on part-time cooperative education and work-study programs through use of released time; elimination of barrier to full participation in vocational education programs; [16]

Certain specialists believe that those administrators, boards of education, teachers, and parents within each local urban school population must be given the mandate to solve their own problems. Dr. Martin Deutsch of the department of psychiatry, New York Medical College, emphatically stated, "society has maintained inequality, second-class citizenship, poverty, and discrimination and society must correct and compensate for what has been done." [17] But in the final analysis, the school itself must lead the way in reaching a needed solution.

Kenneth B. Clark, Professor of Psychology at the City College of the City University of New York and President of the Metropolitan Applied Research Center, Inc., has made a blanket indictment concerning the ability of the public school system to alter the course of urban public education. Clark has lost faith in public schools and says "I'm convinced that the big city school systems will not do the job that is needed." His statements seem to imply that he believes the public school system is incapable of making the reforms that are needed and that the entire system should be replaced with the following alternatives:

1. Regional schools financed by the state -
A "regional" school presumably is one that serves several contiguous school districts, generally in a metropolitan area. This would presumably recruit students on a volunteer basis, with a balanced racial

13

and socioeconomic composition. Arrangements would be made to transport most children to school by bus.

2. Regional schools financed by the federal government -
These would presumably be similar to the state-financed schools, but could serve pupils from two neighboring states and could be established in states that are unable or reluctant to maintain such schools at state expense.

3. Open schools operated by colleges and universities -
These would be laboratory-type schools, open to voluntary enrollment, and balanced in racial and socioeconomic terms. Presumably, these schools would be supported by public funds.

4. Open schools operated by industrial and business corporations -
These would presumably be operated on contract with the school district or another governmental unit. There is a precedent in the form of Job Corps units operated on contract by business corporations.

5. Labor-union sponsored schools -
These might give preference to children of union members, within limits imposed by the requirement of a racial and socioeconomic balance. These would presumably be operated on contract with a governmental unit.

While Dr. Clark's alternatives are well thought out and tend to be rational for most thinking educators, there still remain the unanswered questions of what to do with those millions of dedicated educators who have tried and spent most of their working careers at trying to eliminate the problems. But because of the lack of proper finance, resources and support, could not do any more about this continuous eroding situation. It would seem feasible that, among whatever alternatives were suggested, some would fit within the present school system's structure.

Other specialists view the problem of urban education and the schools as being one that is tied to housing and urban renewal. Robert J. Havighurst, Professor of Education at the University of Chicago and a member of the committee for Human Development, suggests a different type of educational approach. His premise is to rebuild the central city and the population, perhaps, will not leave to find newer or better housing elsewhere.

It is true that as cities grow bigger they become more identifiable as to income, socio-economic status, race and other social characteristics. According to Havighurst, the reason that families move are: (1) "to find better housing, (2) to secure better schools for their children, and (3) an overall better place for the family to live."[19] If we follow this line of reasoning, all that must be done would be for leaders, politicians, and business community to provide decent housing, improve and make equal the quality of education in all schools, and make the cities a safe place to live for all. But such simplistic answers do not adequately cover the questions. The basic of the Havighurst solution is that it is tied to integration. "These problems are not only a threat to the democratic unity, and educational opportunity, but the slum areas of the central cities breed political and social divisiveness and discontent."[20]

What tends to be strange in this whole process of segregation and integration is that the minute a particular school becomes all black or a 30% to 40% minority ratio, the quality of education and educational opportunity diminishes. This suggests that we as a nation are not willing to provide the type of education for minorities, or we do not understand just what is needed for quality education to become a reality except in mono-racial situations. It is difficult for some to accept the notion that quality education lies only in physical integration. Despite the 1954 Supreme Court Decision concerning both de jure and de facto segregation, segregated school districts still exist. This also suggests that the only way the schools will become responsive to their clientele is probably through court mandates. Dr. Havighurst in focusing on the problem of educating the urban poor says any solution must include integration. He stated "at the outset, we must face the fact of pervasive racial and economic segregation of the children in our school system. We must grant that a viable solution of the educational problem in the long run must include integration of pupils of different racial and economic groups in the schools, for their entire period of schooling, or most of it."[21]

It is very difficult for most black educators to accept the premise that the improvement of education for blacks and the rest of the urban poor peoples, must include integration. These educators, realizing full well that society has changed so drastically in the last two decades, argue for a change in both educational method and philosophy. However, most people cannot equate the mixing of whites, blacks and other minorities with solving the problem of quality education for the poor. The major problem seems to be one of not enough money to support the kind of diversified school system that's represented by the many different cultures in our society today. The all black schools in the South up until 1954 is an example of a segregated school system. Students graduated, had high self-esteem, and could compete adequately in colleges and the world of work. And for the most part the schools did a good job with less than adequate finances and resources. Is this really the problem? Or is it another excuse for the lack of action and support?

The key to the success of blacks and minorities in the South during the period of segregated education was parental support and highly motivated self-determined students. Those students were no doubt very much concerned about their destinies. The black institutions were the guiding light for these students and continue to be a viable force in the education of all its students. The critics, perhaps, are correct when they say, "the schools have taken on too much responsibility and as a result are doing everything except that of educating students." The call for "back to the basics" may bring a stabilizing force to the confused and chaotic state of urban education.

IMPROVED MATERIALS

The educator and teacher must be involved in the planning, writing, and research phases in order that appropriate kinds of materials will be introduced into the curriculum that will highlight the ethnic heritage of groups in our society. A large portion of the instructional materials should provide for the special needs of the students. The instructional materials should be highly motivational in content. These materials should involve the student's tactical sense and cause the student to participate physically. The learning climate should be non-threatening and focus on only things that are positive. Audio visual materials tend to involve the student in a total learning experience, the educational media phase should be expanded and improved.

DIFFERENTIATED STAFFING

This type of staffing is an alternative to the traditional way of using school personnel that incorporates the component of team-teaching. This concept allows a group of teachers to be responsible for the education of a particular number of students. This new responsibility includes: planning, implementing a curriculum for this specific group of students. This concept recognizes the different learning styles of students and provides many different instructional approaches. Differentiated staffing places the teacher in a new role--instructional facilitator with other personnel available to perform administrative functions not related to teaching.

The HEW Urban Education Task Force recommended the problems of urban areas be considered a priority item for our national administration during the decade of the 1970's. The task force, while recognizing a need for a carefully constructed long-term comprehensive program, views the situation as being urgent and requiring immediate and long-range solutions. The Task Force report called for the following:

1. Money--significantly increased levels of funding are needed for urban education far exceeding what current appropriations and authorizations now make possible.

2. Concept of Urban Education--the educative process must be expanded in its focus to the whole individual at all educational levels...including his health, his emotional well-being, his intellectual capacities, his future employment, and self-realization.

3. Master Plan for Urban Education--development and implementation of a master plan for urban education, tailored to the specific needs of a particular urban area, that deals with causes and symptoms, within a framework of over-all urban problem-solving rather than education per se, and must encompass all educational levels, i.e., from early childhood through higher and adult education.

4. Institutional Changes--Among the areas of concern for such sequence should be: (1) local neighborhoods; (2) curriculum and instructional programs; (3) social agencies; and (4) the staff that will perceive and teach the students.

5. Community Determination--direct participation in decision-making by community residents, including priorities for spending the available monies, design of curriculum and implementation of program components, and employment and evaluation of key personnel.

6. Performance Standards--clearly stated objectives concerning specific knowledges, attitudes, and skills which the students

themselves are expected to demonstrate.

7. Assessment--this should be continuous and designed to assure rapid feedback on the program's strengths and weaknesses and should allow for swift modifications and adjustments when needed.

8. Racial and Ethnic Integration-- should be a major element in ALL planning and implementa- tional phases of urban education programs and should be clearly stated as a major criterion for receiving funds; separatism, local control, and recognized identity are seen as alternate means to the goal of integration.[22]

Dr. Mel Ravitz, Professor of Sociology and Anthropology at Wayne State University, sums up the views of the writers when he characterizes the prevailing attitude of Americans toward urban public school education as "Benign neglect." He writes, "with pious phrases about our children, with endless cliches about the importance of quality education for all, with conference piled atop conference to determine educa- tional criteria, we have simply denied our children the education birthright of a rich, free society. Either out of ignorance or more likely out of a calculated personal acquisitiveness, we have subordinated concern for our children's education to more important matters. However benign our parental intent, the net effect has been massive neglect."[23]

And finally, we must remember that the health of our national economy requires that the schools of America prepare students to be self-supporting, to contribute to the national income rather than the cost of public services. The Task Force on Urban Education stated "the survival of American democracy insures that schools help students become self-respecting and self- determined individuals." This is especially true among the powerless and the poor. As we advance through this decade, America still continues to write a sad commen- tary, that of being the wealthiest nation in the world

19

and after its 200th birthday there are still
approximately 25 million citizens termed as
functionally illiterate.

THE URBAN SETTING

Much has been written in recent years relative to
the plight of urban public schools. To adequately
understand the problems of the schools, one must first
comprehend the communities in which schools serve.
Schools mirror the strengths and weaknesses of the
community. All of the problems characteristic of urban
communities--crime, urban blight, unemployment, and
deprivation--accompany students to the classroom.

Today, our cities, once the envy of the civilized
world, have become objects of scorn and ridicule,
places where people work and conduct their business
during the day and leave when daylight diminishes,
places which exhibit physical, moral, and social
decay.[24]

Demographic information reveals that since 1950
there has been a great migration of blacks from the
South to the large industrial cities of the East and
Midwest. As the number of poor residents increases,
the demand for city services increases. This entails
higher taxes, which impel more taxpayers to leave the
city. As a result, large numbers of black and white
upper-income residents have fled from the cities,
leaving behind an increasingly poor black and other
non-white population at its core.

Thomas Muller in "Growing and Declining Urban
Areas: A Fiscal Comparison" published by the Urban
Institute (1975) believes that the recent near collapse
of New York City is an indicator of the future fate of
other large central cities. His analysis of factors
affecting the financial well being of 27 urban areas
with populations of 500,000 or more discovered the
following factors at work:

1. The older industrial cities of the Northeast
and Midwest are being drained by migration of middle-
income families while the cities of the South and West
are gaining;
2. The costs of running municipal services are
much higher in the declining cities;

3. Older cities have not enjoyed the ability of annexing or incorporating large areas as part of the inner city.

These factors represent some of the special problems that confront urban areas. Also the quality of education in most urban areas has been dropping steadily, for most reading and math scores are well below national norms. Many citizens are reluctant to support school bond issues because they feel that much of their tax money is being used to support a growing and firmly entrenched oligarchy insensitive to the needs of its inhabitants.

These problems--in addition to widespread violence, truancy and high absenteeism--leave little reason for optimism in many beleaguered urban school systems.

According to statistics compiled by the National Association of Secondary School Principals, absenteeism is the number one problem facing classroom teachers today. The situation has become so grave that there seems to be no clear cut consensus about how the public schools can turn things around.

Statistics from the census of 1980 indicate that more than half of all Black Americans reside in urban areas. Approximately thirty-seven percent of that total live in the twenty-five largest metropolitan areas in this country. While blacks were migrating in increasingly large numbers to the central cities, a reverse migration of white families to the suburbs increased dramatically.[25] The following table graphically illustrates the segregation problem faced by big city school systems today:

Table 1:1 Major School Systems in Which Black Students Comprise at Least Half the Enrollment

City	Percent Black Enrollment
Washington, D.C.	96
Atlanta, Georgia	81
New Orleans, Louisiana	77
Richmond, Virginia	73
Newark, New Jersey	72
Gary, Indiana	72
Detroit, Michigan	70

Baltimore, Maryland	70
St. Louis, Missouri	69
Memphis, Tennessee	68
Oakland, California	62
Birmingham, Alabama	62
Philadelphia, Pennsylvania	61
Chicago, Illinois	58
Cleveland, Ohio	57
Kansas City, Missouri	56
Louisville, Kentucky	52
Shreveport, Louisiana	51
Norfolk, Virginia	50

Source of Table 1:1 "Busing Why Tide is Turning," **U.S. News & World Report** (August 11, 1975), p. 26.

This trend can be expected to increase in the future with the black population in urban areas expected to increase by approximately sixty-eight percent by 1985. Therefore, urban schools will become even more predominantly black. Urban schools also face the problem of not having the resources, the power, or the knowledge to successfully educate students from low-socioeconomic levels. The following table provides further vital statistics relating to education in urban cities.

Table 1:2 Educational Characteristics of the Black Population for Cities with 100,000 or more Blacks: 1970

Selected Cities	Number of Black Children Enrolled in Grades 1-12 (by Thousands)	Black Persons 25 Years and Over	
		Percent High School Grad	Percent High School Graduates
New York, NY	414	41	4
Chicago, IL	316	39	4
Detroit, MI	174	37	4
Philadelphia, PA	173	32	3
Washington, DC	134	44	8
Los Angeles, CA	126	50	6

Baltimore, MD	121	28	4
Houston, TX	86	35	6
Cleveland, OH	81	35	3
New Orleans, LA	78	26	4
Atlanta, GA	66	34	7
St. Louis, MO	72	31	4
Memphis, TN	73	24	4
Dallas, TX	58	37	5
Newark, NJ	58	35	2
Indianapolis, IN	37	36	4
Birmingham, AL	35	29	4
Cincinnati, OH	34	29	3
Oakland, CA	36	43	4
Jacksonville, FL	34	29	5
Kansas City, MO	32	40	5
Milwaukee, WI	33	34	3
Pittsburgh, PA	28	35	3
Richmond, VA	29	26	4
Boston, MA	27	45	4
Columbus, OH	28	41	5

Source of Table 1:2 U.S. Department of Commerce, Social and Economic Statistics Administration, Bureau of the Census.

The growth of non-white populations in our urban cities represents one of the most significant social phenomenon of the twentieth century. Urban schools not only face the problem of educating poor blacks, but must also serve many poor Hispanics, Puerto Rican and Cuban students. Hispanics (browns) constitute the largest minority in America outside blacks. Most Hispanics are concentrated in five southwestern states: Arizona; California; Colorado; New Mexico and Texas. In these five states, Hispanics make up almost 25 percent of the total school enrollment.[26]

In California, the nation's most populous state, the impact of Hispanic students is even more dramatic. In Los Angeles, 38.7 percent of its school children are Hispanic with 55 percent of all kindergarten being of Mexican-American origin. By 1981, the school district estimates that 43.2 percent of its total enrollment will be Hispanic, with Whites constituting 24.4 percent and Blacks 22.1 per cent.

Not only will the impact of this new constituency be felt in Los Angeles, but also demographic studies indicate that if present trends continue, more than half the population of the entire state of California

23

will be Hispanic by 1990. The political, economic and social implications of this dramatic population shift is enormous.

In the Northeastern part of the United States there are almost two million mainland Puerto Ricans, most of whom live in New York City. The public schools have over 300,000 Puerto Rican students enrolled or one-third of its total enrollment. Census data also indicate that there are over 500,000 Cuban Americans residing in Southern Florida. The problem faced by urban schools in educating minorities is not one which can be solved through funding. Rather the problem is a deeply rooted fundamental social problem both in the schools and society.

California State Superintendent of Public Instruction Wilson Riles recently stated the problem in this manner:

> We've had a change in the cities. The poor and the disadvantaged have come to the cities as the other people have moved to the suburbs. The challenge is before us, one that I think we can meet. But we're going to have to come up with approaches that are different.[27]

Until recently, the educational needs of minority students were almost totally ignored in big city schools. If educators are to adequately meet the needs of a culturally diverse student population, drastic reforms in curriculum and ideology are needed. In-service training for teachers must occupy a high priority. Many teachers are totally unprepared to function effectively in a culturally pluralistic setting.

Teachers generally are products of their own environments and educational experiences. Many have little knowledge of minority cultures and often bring to the classroom personal prejudices and biases greatly in need of change. Teacher training institutions must face and meet the challenge of adequately preparing future teachers to understand and teach effectively in multi-cultural settings.

POVERTY AND UNEMPLOYMENT

The urban poor live in an environment characterized by frequent periods of unemployment between low-paying and unrewarding jobs. Obtaining accurate figures relative to how many individuals are employed and unemployed is a very difficult task.

For example, as of August, 1979, the official unemployment rate nationally was 6.0% or 6,185,000 jobless individuals. However, these figures fail to include an estimated 1,060,000 "discouraged workers" (those workers unemployed but not actively seeking work) and another 3,368,000 involuntarily part-time workers. For Blacks and other minorities however, the unemployment rate was 11.0, compared to 5.3 for Whites.[28] These figures undoubtedly are much higher for Black Americans and other minorities living in large urban areas.

Education is a key factor affecting poverty and employment. Although the educational disparity between blacks and whites in terms of years of schooling has been lowered substantially, the differences in terms of quality has not. Many employers blame urban public schools for turning out graduates who are not prepared for the job market.

Many cannot read, write or perform the most basic tasks. Employers not only state that many teenage job applicants are unskilled, but often they demonstrate little understanding of the responsibilities of holding down a steady job. Many have no idea of the importance of promptness, proper dress, suitable language or taking orders from supervisors. This lack of basic educational skills only perpetuates poverty and unemployment.

The "poverty line" for an urban family of four is now $4,800 in annual income. Presently more than thirty-one percent of America's 25 million blacks are below that figure, with the percentage constantly increasing.[29]

Dr. Robert B. Hill, director of research for the National Urban League states that the median black family income of $9,563 is only 57 percent of the $16,740 annual income earned by Whites. This gap in family income increased during the decade of the seventies. The unemployment rate for Black Americans is normally twice as high as that of Whites, and with Black teenagers in urban areas it rises to forty or fifty percent.

These facts are some of the harsh realities which have greatly affected the quality of education and the quality of life in our large American cities. Before the problems of our schools can be solved, first solutions to the dilemmas facing our cities must be found. The problems of our urban schools cannot be appraised apart from the ills of our society.

Noted school psychologist, Kenneth B. Clark, in a recent interview made the following comments on urban public schools:

> My personal opinion is that the quality of education provided for minority children in the segregated urban public schools of the north has deteriorated. These schools for the most part are criminally inferior. They are spawning hundreds of thousands of our young people as functional illiterates each year. The drop-out rate is intolerably high. Even those who finish school are generally so retarded educationally that they are really unable to compete with more privileged youngsters in the area of academic mobility or for jobs. I think that nothing will suffice short of mass organized, mobilized demand for increased quality of efficiency, a return to the basics, where parents would organize themselves not only to demand verbally accountability in the performances of administrators and teachers, but to see that a day-to-day program of increased effectiveness of the educational process is actually in operation.[30]

Black Americans have a special interest in the destiny of our cities, not merely because that is where the majority reside. For if our cities, many presently under black political control, fail, then the development of Black political control will be retarded.[31]

Instant solutions to problems which have taken decades to develop are unrealistic. However, if our urban cities are to undergo a renaissance, then reform of our educational institutions must be a top priority.

If one were asked to point to a single index contributing to the decline of our major cities, it would undoubtedly be the deterioration of the public school system.

The future of our urban schools must be linked to the future of our cities. The trend of new employment opportunities being created in rural and suburban areas must be reversed. Segregated and substandard housing must be eliminated. These forces and others must be improved if we are to shape an effective, comprehensive plan to re-shape the destiny of our schools and our cities.

Chapter 1

DISCUSSION QUESTIONS

1. What are some of the problems facing (inner-city) schools today? How do these problems affect the music programs?

2. Discuss curricula and accountability as they both relate to quality education in urban schools? How does these impact upon programs in urban schools?

3. What is meant by "keeper of order" vs "administrative leader" as is often referred to the urban principal?

4. In terms of teacher preparation, should teachers who teach in urban schools be trained differently?

5. What are the weaknesses in pre-service teacher education programs?

6. Will integration, desegration and bussing affect or improve the quality of education in urban schools? If so, why? If not, why not?

7. List several characteristics that distinguishes the urban setting from other areas of a city. Consider the fiscal, social and economic factors.

8. In terms of racial make-up, who are the residents of the inner-city?

9. What are some possible solutions for improving education in urban schools?

Bibliography of Further Readings

Bommarito, Barbara and Kerber, August, **The Schools and the Urban Crisis**, Chicago, Ill: Holt, Rinehart and Winston, 1966.

Eisenhauer, Ward and Venetoulis, Ted (Eds.) **Up Against the Urban Wall**, Englewood Cliffs, NJ: Prentice-Hall, Inc., 1971.

Heindenreich, Richard R. **Urban Education, revised edition**, Arlington, VA: College Readings Inc., 1972.

Hummel, Raymond C. and Nagle, John M. **Urban Education in American: Problems and Prospects**, New York, NY: Oxford University Press, 1973.

Gentry, Atron, and Jones, Byrd et al, **Urban Education: The Hope Factor**, Philadelphia, PA: W.B. Saunders Company, 1972.

Marcus, Sheldom and Vairo, Phillip, **Urban Education: Crisis or Opportunity?** Metuchen, NJ: The Scarecrow Press, 1972.

Passow, Harry Editor, **Education in Depressed Areas**, New York: NY: Teachers College Press, 1963.

Sigel, Efrem, Quirk, Dantia, and Whitestone, Patricia, **Crisis The Taxpayer Revolt and your Kids' Schools**, New York, NY: Knowledge Industry Publications, Inc., 1978.

Woock, Roger R. **Education and the Urban Crisis**, Philadelphia, PA: International Textbook Company, 1970.

Notes for Chapter 1

1. National Advisory Commission on Civil Disorders. **Report of the National Advisory Commission on Civil Disorders.** New York: Bantam Books, 1968 p. 399.

2. An address by President Jimmy Carter printed in the February 1976 issue of **Change,** New Rochelle, New York.

3. Wilson, C. Riles, **et al, The Urban Education Task Force Report.** Final Report of the Task Force on Urban Education to the Department of Health, Education and Welfare. New York: Praeger Publishers, 1970, p. 49.

4. Harry S. Broudy, "A new Voice for the Schools, " **Today's Education 66:2** (1977): 28-31.

5. Richard Colwell, "Editor's Note," **Council for Research in Music Education** 36 (1974): 2-6.

6. John Cooksey, "An Accountability Report for Music Education," **Council for Research in Music Education** (1974): 6-13.

7. Robert Klotman, **The School Music Administrator and Supervisor: Catalysts for Change in Music Education.** Englewood Cliffs: Prentice-Hall, 1973.

8. Gene V. Glass, "The Many Faces of Accountability," **Phi Delta Kappan** 13:10 (1972): 636-639.

9. The Detroit Federation of Teachers, **The Detroit Teacher,** 37:6, (November, 1977): 1-8.

10. Mary M. Bentzen, **Conflicting Roles, The Principal and the Challenge of Change,** Dayton, Ohio: Institute of the Development of Educational Activities, Inc. 1971, p. 23.

11. Wendel J Roye, "Black Principals: Vanishing Americans or Out-Flanked Agents?", **National Center for Research and Information on Equal Educational Opportunity** (Tip Sheet #7). New York: February (1972): 1.

12. Hazel Davis, "Profile of the American Public School Teacher, 1966," **National Education Association Journal** 56 May (1967): 12.

13. Detroit Public Schools. Abstract of "Report of the Superintendent's Committee on Achievement," Detroit, Michigan, March (1973): 4-6.

14. Kenneth R. Washington, "Self-Concept Development: An Affective Educational Experience for Inner-City Teachers," **Young Children**, 29:5 July (1974): 305-310.

15. Ibid.

16. National Advisory Commission on Civil Disorders. **Report of the National Advisory Commission on Civil Disorders.** New York: Bantam Books, 1968, pp. 438-455.

17. Martin Deutsch, "Integrating the Urban School," **Proceedings of the Conference on Integration in the New York City Public Schools.** Gordon J. Klopf and Israel A. Laster, editors. New York: Bureau of Publications, Columbia University, 1963, p. 86.

18. Kenneth B. Clark, "Alternative Public School Systems," in **Equal Educational Opportunity,** ed. Harvard Educational Review Editorial Board. Cambridge: Harvard University Press, 1969, pp. 173-186.

19. Robert J Havighurst, "Urban Development and the Educational System," in **Education in Depressed Areas,** ed. Harry Passow, New York: Teachers College Press, 1963, p. 44.

20. Ibid.

21. Robert J. Havighurst, "Public Education for Disadvantaged Urban Minorities," in **Urban Education in the 1970's,** ed. A. Harry Passow, New York: Teachers College Press, 1971, p. 49.

22. Wilson C. Riles, **et al. The Urban Education Task Force Report.** Final Report of the Task Force on Urban Education to HEW. New York: Praeger Publishers, 1970, pp. 9-14.

23. Mel Ravitz, "Urban Education: Today and Tomorrow," in **Urban Education in the 1970's** ed., A. Harry Passow, New York: Teachers College Press, 1971, p. 177.

24. George C. Simmons, "Urban Education Problems, Part I", **About . . . Time**, Vol. 5, No. 4 (April, 1977), 23.

25. Donald Jones, "Analysis of Selected Court Cases Which Have Applied Metropolitan School Desegregation as a Means of Achieving Equality of Educational Opportunity" (unpublished dissertation, University of Michigan, August, 1976), p. 128.

26. U.S. Commission on Civil Rights. **Toward Quality Education for Mexican Americans** (Washington, D.C.: February, 1974).

27. Wilson Riles, "Wilson Riles Speaks Out," **Black Enterprise**, July, 1978, p. 36

28. Brimmer & Company, Inc. From U.S. Bureau of Labor Statistics Data.

29. "Black Entrepreneur Says Minority Gains Are Being Eroded," **The Detroit Free Press** (July 17, 1977), p. 6B.

30. William Moore, Interview with Dr. Kenneth B. Clark, "Are Black Children Being Educated today?", **Dawn Magazine** (October, 1977), pp. 4-8.

31. Bayard Rustin, "Black Leader Calls for an Urban Policy of Optimism," **American Teacher** (December, 1976), 17.

Chapter 2

MUSIC EDUCATION FOR THE CULTURALLY DIFFERENT STUDENT:

MYTHS VS. REALITY

Warrick L. Carter

Unless it is considered whimsical or completely arbitrary, the decision that one child has a higher mental ability than another, made solely on the basis of IQ tests, presupposes that the measuring object is equally reliable for both children in question. The comparison between culturally different children and dominant culture children, solely on the basis of IQ tests, frequently indicates that the latter's IQ are considerably higher than the former. However, this indication cannot be considered a fact until further investigations are made.

Recent investigations (Erickson, 1964; Maynor, 1968; Carter, 1970; et al.) indicates that a similar approach can be taken in teaching music to culturally different children. The teacher of music has to be aware that the approaches and materials used in affluent neighborhoods will not, and in some instances, cannot provide for similar achievement in culturally different areas.

In order to deal more effectively with culturally different children, the teacher must understand the history, traditions and social structure of the particular area in which he is working. Further, the teacher must comprehend that the children's unique culture patterns, their status in American society, the frustrations which they experience, and their life perceptions are all reflected in the music of their community. In addition, the music teacher should not feel he is introducing music to the child. In most ethnic groups, music already exists as an important part of the culture, history, and environment of the community.

> One logical way to begin a general music class would be to start with music that is indigenous to the group. This is a valid approach because the students can become immediately involved with

familiar music; they can sing it
expressively and can understand the
idiom when they hear it because it is
actually an extension of their own
language and culture.

In order to use the music of an ethnic group, the
teacher must first become familiar with the music;
second, develop an understanding of this music. It is
at the latter point where most educators fall short.
They either fail to realize the intrinsic value of
ethnic music, or else approach the music as "trite,"
"vulgar," and/or "lacking in musical substance," when
compared with "classical music" or "music of the
masters." However, the value of ethnic music has
proven to be unsurpassed if used as the starting point
in the music education of culturally different children
(see Carter, 1970; Klotman, 1968,; and Diog, 1965). As
the use of Hungarian ethnic-related materials (folk
music) has proven successful in the music education of
Hungarian children, so too can American ethnic music
prove successful in the music education of all American
children (see Richards, 1966).

The field of music education has been slow in
recognizing that culturally different children need
different materials and/or different instructional
approaches. Hence, the first developments of new
materials and teaching methods for the culturally
different, are to be found in other disciplines. Two
of the first disciplines to investigate new instructional methods for culturally different children were
Language Arts and Mathematics.

LANGUAGE AND MATH

In teaching language skills to culturally
different children, Newton stressed the technique of
synonymity. Synonymity is the teacher's restating of a
difficult word, term, or idea in many different and
familiar ways. For example, when a passage contains
reference to the "extreme amount of enjoyment one can
receive from a particular job," the teacher should
immediately paraphrase the original passage to "how hip
or groovy a certain gig might be."

Newton's work is closely related to a program
developed at Howard University in 1965. The Howard
program approached the study of English as a foreign
language, without, however, devaluing language skills

33

or systems of communication previously developed by the students. The underlying rationale of the program appears to be two-fold:

1. Black students, because of their culture, history and environment, have developed a language which is foreign to the majority of the white race and that this language is a valid system of communication which does not have to be replaced.
2. English was offered as a foreign language because it is the language of the dominant American society in which the black student must work and live, but English does not have to be the main language of the black student. Rather, black students should be bilingual in much the same way as the Spanish-speaking Americans are bilingual.[3]

An approach differing from that of Newton's and Howard University's has been applied by Ashton-Warner in her teaching of Maori children in New Zealand. Ashton-Warner used the "key vocabulary" of the children as a bridge to "organic" reading and writing. She defined key vocabulary as "the one word illustrations seen by the inner eye".[4] The researcher used these one-word organic illustrations of each child to teach reading and writing. These one-word illustrations were frequently the first English words spoken by the children. She felt that

First words must mean something to the child. First words must have intense meaning to a child. They must be part of his being...Pleasant words won't do. Respectable words won't do. They must be words organically tied up, organically born from the dynamic life itself. They must be words that are already part of the child's being.[5]

Ashton-Warner related that at the beginning of each school day each student was presented with the written form of a word of his choice. "They (the students) ask for a new word each morning and never have I to repeat to them what it is".[6]

After a sufficient number of key words had been learned, the students were asked to construct sentences with their respective words. Reading materials were also provided for each student, constructed from his key vocabulary. Additional words were then introduced by the teacher and the students were asked to share their words with the class. As with the first words, all new words were presented in a written form to each student individually.

Although conceived in New Zealand, this approach of developing language skills has strong implications for the teaching of culturally different children in America. There are several parallel conditions which exist between the Maori and the culturally different: (1) a majority of members from both groups are born into poverty, (2) parents in both groups have been denied the educational opportunities of the dominant society in their respective countries, and (3) the children of both groups speak mainly a dialect or sub-dialect of the English language.

In discussing the development of language skills of Americans' culturally different children, Sawyer offered procedures similar to those of Ashton-Warner. Sawyer believed that the preschool and elementary years should not be concerned with the teaching of a "second dialect" (the English of the more affluent), but that "the purpose of this early language instruction is that of enriching the basic language system which the child already possesses".[7]

In still another experiment with language development, Olson and Larson organized a program of instruction around a combination of pupils and puppets dramatizing well-known stories. They felt that this allowed the children to project their speech without self-consciousness and personal exposure.

Zwier outlined four parts of language learning: stimulation, intake, association and output. She believed that teachers have placed too much emphasis on output (test, etc.). However, with culturally different children, the emphasis should be placed on intake. She stated:

> When the teacher fails to take into
> consideration the form of language
> which the child brings to the school,
> inadequate as they may be from her point[8]
> of view, she has no point of departure.

Zwier concluded that neither the teacher nor the child is disadvantaged if the teacher is able to "match her readiness to teach with the pupil's readiness to learn".[9]

Mathematics instruction is the second subject area common to most programs for culturally different students. Possibly because of the abstract nature of mathematics or these students' need for concrete, physical and/or motoric experiences, culturally different students have often encountered great difficulties with traditional mathematical instruction. In attempt to lessen the abstract nature of the subject, Fremont has suggested several concrete representations (automated programs, commercial aids, mathematical games and puzzles, manipulative devices and flash cards) which may be used.

A year later, Mintz and Fremont (1965) developed a mathematic program for classroom use which applied the instruction to practical everyday use. They used the actual purchasing of an item to teach multiplication and division of decimal fractions, meaning of percent and equivalent percent, conversion of percent to fractions (and the reverse) and general problem-solving techniques. Using order blanks from various large department store catalogs, the students were able to see the practical application of many of the mathematical computations and concepts.

In a similar study of the same year, Graham stressed that all senses of the culturally different child, "particularly his sense of touch," must be utilized to their fullest in learning mathematics. "The disadvantaged child, even more than most, must be exposed to many experiences with concrete materials and perhaps for a longer period of time."[10] Graham offered seven mathematical concepts along with activities which included concrete materials and practical applications of the mathematical concepts. The concepts were: patterns, geometry and measurement, numeration, estimation, budgeting, backing and taxes taught with the use of actual forms. She further encouraged the use of films, film strips, pictures, records and books as "multisensory aids." "Use conversation as much as possible in order to facilitate communication and understanding. Accept his child-like definitions."[11]

CITY-WIDE PROGRAMS

Along with the instructional innovations in English and Mathematics, many cities have organized programs for the culturally different child. The "Higher Horizons Program" (HH) of New York City is a broad-spectrum program which is aimed at raising the educational, vocational, and cultural sights of culturally different children. The HH began in September of 1959, it now has a total population of 50 elementary and 13 junior high schools. The schools are located in Manhattan, Bronx, Brooklyn, and Queens, and are staffed by classroom teachers, supplementary program teachers, and guidance counselors. This program applies the principles of compensatory education, differential utilization of services in curriculum and guidance, and inspirational education. Parental and community involvement and teacher training are most important to the program.

The program offers small-group and "half-class" instruction in reading, mathematics, and other curricular areas where needed. Music, art, and field trips provide cultural enrichment opportunities. The teacher-training conferences involve demonstration lessons by program teachers and methods of group counseling for children and parents. Other services include: publication of the Higher Horizon Newsletter, interaction with local community agencies and cultural resources of the city, workshops, trips, and parental committees.

The Philadelphia "Great Cities School Improvement Program" (GCIP) is a large-scale project which includes an enrichment program emphasizing language arts plus a wide-range community program. The program is designed to raise the achievement and aspiration levels of the students to discover latent abilities among culturally different students and to awaken community responsibility through fostering "home-school ties."

The GCIP began in September of 1960. In 1966, the GCIP had a total student population of 7,447--1,900 students in one junior high school and 5,547 students in seven elementary schools. The student population was predominantly lower SES blacks and Puerto Ricans. Classroom teachers, teacher consultants, arithmetic consultants, language laboratory teachers, school-community coordinators (including two bilingual coordinators), and language arts consultants comprised the staff.

The GCIP provides numerous educational services: once-a-week in-service teacher training and workshops in the use of audio-visual aids; experimental materials and methods in mathematics and language, the latter including "culture free" reading and writing classes; flexible class grouping; and tutorial help for "late bloomers." Extracurricular activities include Saturday and summer field trips, recreational activities, weekly literature enrichment classes, and cultural enrichment trips. The extent of the community services provided are also impressive. These include: special programs to stimulate community interest, understanding and support; parent discussion groups; civic educational associations and special coordinators for Spanish-speaking parents.

The "Detroit Great Cities Project for School Improvement" (DPSI) is a city-wide program designed to promote the development of academic and social competence in culturally different children. The Detroit project began in September 1964. It had a target population of approximately 32,250 pupils and their families in 27 schools throughout the city. The staff was comprised of 1,250 school personnel, including approximately 950 classroom teachers, 27 "coaching teachers," 27 visiting teachers, 27 school-community agents, and a number of language arts specialists.

The Detroit project offered a number of instructional innovations: team teaching, ungraded primary sequences, "block-time" programming with emphasis on developmental and remedial reading, and the use of interracial city-oriented reading materials. Field and camping trips along with comprehensive recreational and enrichment summer programs for remedial work were involved in numerous in-service training and workshops, structured around the various individual problems of the schools. A number of school-community agents were provided to involve parents and other adults in educational and recreational activities. Community personnel, of all ages, were also used as baby-sitters, teacher aides, and after-school assistants in both recreational and educational projects.

The Child Parent Centerprogram (CPC) is one of the most successful of the many Title I funded programs administered by the Chicago Board of Education. Over a six year period (1967-1973), the program annually enrolled over 2,100 children ages 3-9 in eleven centers. Each center offered up to six years of education experiences: two years preschool, one year kindergarten, and primary grades 1-3.

The program was developed to help the "disadvantaged" child build a "strong foundation for cognitive and affective growth." (Stenner/Mueller). The techniques and approaches used in developing this foundation were:

--direct parent involvement in the
    center program and in activities
    designed to meet parent needs;
--elimination of factors such as social
    and health problems that may
    interfere with successful learning
    experiences;
--use of learning materials which
    incorporate a specific learning
    approach with a strong language
    orientation;
--structuring readiness and reading
    programs so that frequent feedback
    is available; and
--a structured, consistent, long-term
    approach. (p. 246)

Each center had a staff comprised of various full and part-time subject-matter teachers, nurses, speech therapists, health aids specialists, social workers, home-economists, community representatives, clerks, principals and custodians. One center also has a team leader and a librarian. Class size averaged 15 in the preschool and kindergarten and 22 in the primary grades.

Materials, approaches and teaching techniques were all uniquely tailored and/or developed for the various centers. Hence, the structure and/or freedom permitted in the language program, for example, differed from center to center. All of the centers, however, "emphasize the use of rewards and praise for pupils when they successfully completed a learning task."[13]

The students were tested in reading, math and on their readiness for the first grade at the conclusion of the first three years (two years preschool, one year kindergarten). Eighty-two percent (82%) of the students scored at or above the nation norms in all three areas. Stenner and Mueller said of the results:

> Growth in readiness and achievement tends to be uniform across classrooms, grades, and centers. The data at this point suggest that the CPC program operates in a manner that uniformly raises the readiness and achievement levels of <u>all</u> children.[14]

The four characteristics which appear to have made the largest contributions to the success of the program were: (1) early involvement of the students; (2) continuity and consistency of programmatic approach; (3) heavy parent involvement; and (4) structured basic skills orientation. "When these four ingredients are present, the traditional gap between disadvantaged students and their more advantaged counterparts can be systematically and substantially eliminated.[15]

During the early 1970's, grants from various state and federal governmental agencies made it possible for most colleges and universities to establish "Special Service Programs." Although the various programs differ in method and practice, they all have the similar goal of providing educational experiences which will help the culturally different student (1) raise his educational and occupational aspirations; (2) develop feelings of "self-worth," "self-pride," and "self-dignity"; and (3) bring the students into the "mainstream" of American life.

All of the aforementioned programs (HH, GCIP, DPSI, CPC, and the Special Service Programs) have been somewhat successful in meeting their stated goals. However, during the past two years (1976-1978) there has been a steady decrease in the number of these kinds of programs. In addition, the 1978 Supreme Court decision on the "Alan Bakke vs. University of California Medical School at Davis case (<u>Newsweek</u>, 1978-B) is seen by many as a reversal in the nation's commitment to the culturally different and hence an indication of future programmatic cuts.

MUSIC PROGRAMS

Underlying many of the special music programs for the culturally different is the realization that music is not a "universal language," but rather a product of each culture, subculture or social class within our complex society. This point was possibly best expressed by DeJager when he stated:

> Each social class has its own standards regarding appropriate ways of spending leisure time, what it considers to be "music," and the functions of music. It teaches its newly-born members what is "good" and "bad" or "beautiful" and "ugly." In this sense, aesthetic emotion is deeply influenced by social factors in that people have learned form other people what to like and what to listen for in musical sounds. Therefore, conceptions of music, as a "universal language" to be understood by everyone, are simply unrealistic. Each social class has its own, more or less distinctive, "style of life," of which music may or may not be a part. It should be stressed that music is not some isolated phenomenon, but that it is integrated with other cultural elements in a style of life. This is one of the reasons, incidentally, which makes it so difficult to transmit music to people who have been raised in another style of life. Members of every social class have been taught to listen to certain kinds of music in certain ways and on certain occasions.[16]

Because of the influence of the work of DeJager and other sociologists (Conyers, 1963; Kaplan, 1966; Miller, 1966; and Finkelsteen, 1957 and 1960), many individual music teachers and even some city-wide music departments have included "indigenous" music as part of these students' music instruction. This segment of the discussion will deal with these developments, either in regard to the use of indigenous musical materials, the use of indigenous musical experiences or programs

41

developed specifically for culturally different students.

Doig reviewed the experiment conducted by Frederick Erickson in the Lawndale Chicago area. The "Experiment in Curriculum Planning" was conducted under a $15,000 grant from W. Clement Stone, president of Chicago's Combined Insurance Company of America and the Jessie V. Stone Foundation. The importance of recognizing the student's cultural heritage clearly formed Erickson's rationale for the experiment. Quoting Erickson, Doig states:

1. Children of the black ghetto should be taught their music, as it derives from the slave-holding South and before, from Africa and the Caribbean.
2. Music should be the focal point in learning and appreciation of their history and culture.
3. Music is an experience had every day.
4. The students need to be shown how their culture and history relates to the world outside the slum.[17]

The program began in October 1964. Weekly sessions of an hour each involving 10 to 15 seventh and eighth graders were held at five different locations in or near the Lawndale area. Voluntary attendance and non-professional teachers helped to distinguish this program from those conducted in the schools. Songs currently popular served as the basis of the instructional material. These songs were used in explaining all musical concepts and in establishing the historical development of these type of songs as a reflection of the history and culture of the black race.

The results of the experiment were so favorable that Erickson ran a second program in early 1965. However, these classes were held in different homes. Instead of using current popular songs, Erickson used those songs popular fifteen to twenty years ago: songs familiar to the students' parents. He felt that this would contribute an important element to family life in the slums by helping to establish the parent as a respected figure of knowledge and authority. The second program was as successful as the first.

42

Like the Lawndale project, the Child Service Association (CSA) in Newark, New Jersey, operated independently of the school system. However, unlike the Lawndale project, CSA was for pre-school culturally different children. In her review of CSA, Foster stated that the primary goal of the program was "to help children build a self-image of themselves as [18] acceptable and adequate individuals". In working toward this goal, the staff of CSA found that music played a large part in attaining this goal. The music period was geared to be more than a scheduled singing period, rather it became an "integral part of the children's living throughout the day". [19] Opportunities were also provided for listening, during rest periods and for playing games. Rhythm instruments were provided for exploration, interpretation and creative response.

Foster found that more than other children, culturally different children respond physically to their inner feelings, thus finding singing and rhythmic movement to be a natural outlet of expression. As an aesthetic experience, she discovered that "music encourages appreciation of this aspect of our cultural heritage at the child's own level" (p. 375). It also contributed strongly to the student's growth in other areas of study. "For some of these children, music seems to be the first, and sometimes the only, group participation which can consistently interest them". [20] In these cases, CSA used music as the starting or focal point for other subject area development.

The program at the Harlem School for the Arts (HSA), New York City, operates similarly to the programs of CSA and the Lawndale project in that it is operated independently of the local public school system. Also, as with the other projects, the Harlem school's organizer hoped that many of the methods, materials and approaches used by the instructors in the Harlem school would be reinforced by the public school music instructors.

The HSA was formed by Dorothy Maynor "in hope that at least a few boys and girls in our area might be given some clue to their own possibilities and selfhood". [21] Maynor did not expect that all the students become outstanding artists, but rather that a student who "seems to have little or no purpose, who has never been taken seriously by his parents, his peers or his teachers, might be taught to dream and to

43

realize that dreams are quite real." Her aim was to give all the students "a view of themselves, a vista" through all types of artistic experiences.[22]

The school enrolled hundreds of impoverished black children from the Harlem area with classes being held after school and on weekends. The courses included painting, vocal music, instrumental music, sculpture, ballet, and modern dance.

One of the conditions insisted upon by the school is a "responsible participation" by the parents in an effort to bring out the best possible responses and musical talents of the child. The aim is toward including both parents; however, the father is frequently missing and/or unable to participate. The school tries to convince the parents that the odds against their child's amounting to anything are "unsurmountable unless the parents take the role of parents with utmost seriousness".[23]

The study of McCoy different from the Lawndale project, the CSA and the HSA in that McCoy's work was performed as part of a school classroom situation. In his junior high school general music class, McCoy's class included black, Syrian, Jewish, Mexican, Chinese and southern white students, all from economically deprived areas. After establishing the goal that "music can and must give culturally disadvantaged youth a sense of identity and belonging",[24] McCoy began using the music of the various ethnic groups as instructional material. Students were first embarrassed to identify with their ethnic groups, but as classes progressed they became proud of their past. McCoy began by showing the class what each ethnic group had contributed to music. Through recordings and actual singing in class, the students were introduced to music from all ethnic groups.

McCoy offered three suggestions for the successful application of his methods:

1. Teach a full unit with emphasis on the cultural contributions to music. Be sure to cite examples and persons.
2. Discuss the background of the "people" (its history) in detail before presenting any music. Try to show how the history of the

"people" enable it to produce its particular contribution to music.

3. Provide for musical experiences with the music, concerts, recordings, companies, etc.[25]

Underlying these three suggestions was McCoy's belief that: "If a person knows his cultural heritage, the accomplishments of his people and the different personalities of his race who have made substantial contributions, his self takes on a new image".[26]

The participants of the **Tanglewood Symposium** (1968) offered many suggestions for the structuring of music courses for the culturally different, which might be instituted on the national level. The article which seems to best articulate these suggestions is the "Minority Report" of David McAllister. For this reason, the McAllister report is included in its entirety.

The MENC has become increasingly aware that the entire Music Establishment is the perpetrator as well as the victim of a hoax. Ralph Ellison has identified it best in **The Invisible Man,** where he points out that the controlling middle class in the United States does not "see" the lower classes and the poor among them. Such euphemisms as "the inner city" (slums), "the disadvantaged" (the poor), "institute for living" (lunatic asylum) are linguistic evidence that the middle class is profoundly unwilling to face the invisible culture.

Most of the establishment is unaware, or unwilling to admit, that the invisible culture has a rugged vitality of its own. When social workers and crime commissions consider the invisible culture at all, they mistake invisibility (their own inability to see) for emptiness.

In a democracy, class barriers are uncomfortable. The Establishment seeing that its entertainments, customs, and values are not shared by everybody, makes a limited effort through the schools to impart the love of Shakespeare, T.S. Eliot, and Schubert to the poor. This endeavor is a failure because these great expressions of the cultural heritage of the Establishment have little to do with the cultural heritage of the poor. This endeavor is a hoax because in the name of communication and the elimination of class barriers we insist that only one cultural language be spoken and that the natives on the other side of the barrier do not, in fact, really have a language at all.

We of the Music Establishment believe that there must be real communication, especially in the arts, between all sectors of a democratic society, if it is to remain healthy. The evidence of a crisis in the health of our society is clear enough. In Dorothy Maynor's words: "It would be tragic indeed if, while we are striving to weave a cloak of democracy for Vietnam and the rest of the world, the fabric of Democracy were torn beyond repair right here within our own borders."

In view of these matters, we affirm that it is our duty to seek true musical communication with the great masses of our population. While we continue to develop and make available, to all who are interested, the great music of the middle class and aristocracy, we must also learn the language of the great musical arts which we have labeled "base" because they are popular.

When we have learned that any musical expression is "music," we hope to be able to reduce the class barriers in our schools and our concert halls. The resulting enrichment of our music will, we hope, give it a new vitality at all levels, and provide a united voice that can speak, without sham, of our democratic ideals.[27]

Along the lines of McAllister's suggestions, Nicosia (1965) offered a three-fold discussion for providing the musical experiences needed to balance the culturally different child's total development. These are: "(1) the acculturation and socialization of the child through music; (2) linguistics, literature and music; and (3) the basic music concepts" (p. 200). Nicosia defines acculturation as "the group's taking on elements from the culture of another group" and socialization as "the progess of building group values into the individual".[28] Therefore, the first experiences should be those which "ease" the new student into a strange environment, and those which assist the student in creating a positive "self-school-community image." She offers the following three suggestions to build these positive images: (1) use of a specially composed welcome song for each new student to help minimize the feeling of strangeness which should enhance self-image; (2) a student-composed school song to build the school image; and (3) a play or musical written and directed by the students, based on positive events or "happenings" of the community, to build the community image.[29]

Nicosia believed that the Orff-Schulwerk approach is very helpful in providing meaningful experiences in language and music learning, and also recommended the use of echo games, chanting of the roll call, intoning proper names in rhythm, and the use of rhythmic patterns and tonal patterns in rhymes, riddles, and ballads in conjunction with the Orff approach.

In regard to the basic musical concepts taught to culturally different children, she stated that "the objectives of the music curriculum for the culturally disadvantaged should be kept to a minimum of feasible concepts predicted by the student's potential and the teacher's capabilities".[30] Two objectives were offered by Nicosia:

1. Build a repertoire of worthwhile songs, singing games, and dances:
   a. For relaxation and enjoyment.
   b. For development of an understanding and an appreciation of other cultures (use both foreign and English texts).
   c. For development of tone

quality, diction and musical
interpretation.
2. To develop specific musical
    concepts
    a. Pitch recognition: the tune
       goes up or down or remains the
       same; the tonal pattern is high
       or low
    b. Rhythmic recognition:
       (1) metric pattern--the song
       swings in 2's or 3's
       (2) rhythmic pattern--the
       notes are even or uneven; long
       or short.
       (3) tempo--the music is fast
       or slow
    c. Phrasing: recognize number of
       phrases; kind of phrases--
       identical, almost alike or
       different.
    d. Dynamics: the mood and tonal
       quality are related to the
       degree of loudness or softness
       as well as tempo.[31]

Nicosia's idea of a "minimum number of feasible
concepts" was completely rejected by Reimer. Reimer
argued that the same aims, objectives and concepts
should be used in the music education of all children,
regardless of social class, economic situation or race.
These considerations should not be ignored, "but should
be taken as opportunities for developing musical
sensitivity applicable to any and all music."[32]

With specific regard to the music education of
"black ghetto" children, Reimer suggests that although
including music from the black culture is important,
there are two dangers which exist in doing so. The
first is a tendency to abandon musical consideration in
favor of social or political considerations. He felt
that the music used in teaching black children should
be of the same musical value as that used for other
children. Consequently, the music used should be
chosen without consideration of its ethnic
affiliation. The second danger is the assumption that
all black children identify equally with all music of
the black culture. He stated: ". . . while some Negro
children will respond to nothing but what they can
identify as 'black music,' others are offended by the
very notion that there **is** such a thing."[33]

Reimer rationalized that because of these inherent dangers in the use of music from the black culture, the teachers of these students must develop strategies applicable to all children and all subjects, "but particularly relevant for ghetto children and general music". These teaching strategies should take the form of "attributes of excellent education" which should apply for all children. The attributes for general music education are outlined in the ensuing manner:

1. Materials of excellent musical and pedagogical quality that bring children into contact with the best music of common Western heritage, of their own social group, of the many groups in America. . .

2. Music teachers are required who are musically mature, personally secure, accepting and loving of children as individuals rather than as so many peas in a racial pod, expert in helping children grasp musical processes, and capable of adapting themselves and their teaching to different situations as they are faced with them.

3. The school as a whole. . .must be supportive of musical learning, providing an environment in which musical opportunities are rich and varied and in which the physical conditions for taking advantage of the opportunities are present in abundance.

4. The attitude surrounding the entire enterprise must be one of respect for the music regarded as important by the children, of respect for their ability to widen their views of what music can be shared by them, of high expectations that they can and will succeed in musical learning, and of devotion to the job of fostering their growth as musically sensitive individuals.[34]

In conclusion, Reimer stated that the effective general music teacher for ghetto students "must be willing and able to transform indigenous manners and mores into opportunities for musical learning and musical enjoyment."[35]

Along with these individual efforts, a few city systems, federally or locally supported, have developed special programs and materials for the music education of culturally different students. Some of these programs are operated in conjunction with the local Job Corps and the school system, while others are housed independently of the school system but operate closely with the school or schools within the area.

Three of the latter type of programs (the Watts Towers Art Center in Los Angeles; the Arts-for-Living Program in New York City; and the Santa Fe, New Mexico Boarding School Project) were reviewed at the Gaitherburg, Maryland, Conference in 1966 (Murphy and Gross, 1968). The first two programs are for black youth, while the third is geared toward American Indians. All three are built upon a rich curriculum of experiences in art and music of all kinds and keyed, but not limited, to the student's respective heritage. From these experiences, it is hoped that the students will "blossom into individuals, develop self-esteem and pride, and gradually transfer their new-found confidence to mastering the routines of arithmetic and English and the other standard school subjects."[36]

Utilizing the accomplishments and practices of the previously mentioned programs, the members of the conference began a discussion of the specific uses or contributions of the arts to the culturally different child. Out of this discussion emerged a statement of purpose that became one of the principal themes of the conference: "that the arts, unlike other school subjects, can engage the whole person in an experience of unusual depth and delight, with effects that are complex, multiple, and powerful"."[37] The conference's participants were able to identify uses of the arts that are geared to help the student to:

1. Have a continuing experience of accomplishment and achievement, and thus acquire the confidence necessary to develop a sense of worthiness.

50

2. Develop greater refinement of taste and sensibility--the ability to discriminate the fine and true from the coarse and false.
3. Appreciate a wide range of sensory, intellectual, emotional, and aesthetic experiences.
4. Acquire an understanding of the importance of work and discipline in order to achieve desired ends in life.
5. Learn how to cope with hostile environments as the result of new understanding, attitudes, and skills.
6. Express himself without the need for words so that teachers can better understand the student's feelings, thoughts, and behavior.
7. Increase the capacity to manage effectively verbal and symbolic nonart tasks, like the three R's.
8. Improve in general mental and emotional health and provide, thereby, for more adequate personality growth and role functioning.
9. Enter various new kinds of reciprocally invigorating relationships with other people.
10. Relate more easily and rewardingly with members of other groups, thus fostering more productive and humane societies.
11. Develop perceptual skills which might contribute to the more complex and subtle view of reality that culturally disadvantaged children often fail to develop.
12. See possibilities for constructive social action.[38]

During the "Music in the Inner-City Schools Symposium" held at **Ohio State University** in June of 1968, Katherine McGill identified four Ohio cities that had developed special programs for inner-city music instruction. The common element of all the programs was the existence of federal funds. However, each of the programs was quite unique and offered a variety of music opportunities. The cities discussed were Akron, Cincinnati, Columbus, and Toledo.

In Akron, the program was divided into three different activities: (a) a summer cultural arts center, (2) a special class of xylophone instruction, and (3) community school activities. The six weeks' summer arts center, designed for fifth and sixth grade students, included singing, music appreciation, music theory, folk dance, creative dance, creative drama, the use of instruments, the history of music, and art.

The xylophone instruction was a special experiment being conducted in seventeen elementary schools. Along with the xylophone instruction, the elements of music and appreciation were also included. Sufficient funds had been provided enabling students to have individual instruments. The community schools offered informal courses in piano and art crafts for both students and adults.

Cincinnati offered an elementary string program in five of the inner-city schools. Other instruments and materials included in the program are Orff instruments, recorders, Kodaly charts and audio-visual material. Saturday enrichment programs during the regular school year and a six-week summer enrichment program which includes art and music instruction by "teaching teams" provide additional musical experiences. The city also had art and music activities in "open studios," and supports art and music classes for talented performing arts students of the inner-city.

Columbus had established a number of regional centers throughout the inner-city area. Art teachers, music teachers, physical education teachers and resource teachers at each center provided instruction for four days and had the fifth day free for research, planning or other activities that would help in their teaching in the inner-city.

Music instructions were provided in band and orchestra instruments, vocal, Orff instrument, and rhythm instruments. Language development is also stressed, with art, music and physical education working together as a team.
Toledo had received an unusually large amount of federal funds. Basically, the program is the same in all areas of the city, but the federal funds have made

possible six harp centers for grades two through five. Two of the harp centers are located in inner-city schools. Three of the eight pre-school violin centers are located in inner-city schools. Special ability classes involving choir, orchestra and band are offered for the inner-city junior and senior high school students. The city supports a piano mobile unit that tours five inner-city schools providing for free piano instruction. Also, during the summer the mobile piano unit tours five of the inner-city recreational facilities.

The grants provided under the auspices of various federal, state and local agencies, have been responsible for a great number of school systems providing special music materials, teachers, and programs for their culturally different students. However, as with other programs for the culturally different, the most recent history (1976-1978) has seen a decrease in the level of funding for many of these music programs. There also appear to be two (2) additional reasons for the declining interest in music programs for the culturally different: (1) a decrease in the total number of school music positions and (2) a return to what may be considered the racial attitudes, fears, and prejudices of the fifties. * An example of the former is the decrease in the number of music teaching positions in the cities of Chicago, New York, Detroit and Los Angeles over the past four years (1974-1978). Because the programs for the culturally different were the most recent to be established, the persons associated with these programs were the first to be released as music positions were cut.

For the latter, a case in point is the recent (1978) passing of the "Jarvis-Gann" initiative ("Proposition 13") in California. This initiative is viewed by many black leaders (see **Newsweek, 1978-B)** as being racial in nature because most of the services, programs and facilities adversely affected by its passing will be those created to help the culturally different. At this writing, the future of special music programs in Compton, Los Angeles, Oakland, San

---

*It is this writer's opinion that during the late 70's the lack of assertiveness (as compared to that of the 60's) on the part of the culturally different must also be considered when discussing the various cutbacks.

Francisco, San Diego, as well as other California cities is uncertain.

CONCLUSION

Over the past twenty years (1958-1978), we have observed a three-staged development in regards to the music teaching of culturally different students: (1) the early period (1958-1965) is characterized by benign and neglect. During this period no special materials, teaching, programs or approaches are felt to be needed for the culturally different. (2) It is during the middle period of assertive attention (1965-1975) that most of the programs, new materials, special teacher education programs, and new approaches are developed and established. (3) In the present period (1975-1978) we have witnessed a decline in many of these programs and an overall attitude of this decline.

The strides made during the second period are most impressive. For the first time in American music education we see a positive attempt to include music of non-European culturals and American popular music; of introducing innovative teaching approaches; the rapid development of ethnic-related teaching materials by the music industry, and the development and implementation of workshops, in-service training programs and special college and university courses for teachers of the culturally different. It is therefore hoped that music educators and administrators realize the importance of these accomplishments and not discontinue them as funds become scarce, but rather incorporate them into the ongoing music learning situation.

DISCUSSION QUESTIONS

1. Why is it unrealistic to predict the success of culturally different students with those of the dominant culture solely on the basis of IQ tests?

2. What steps must one take before they use the music of vaiours ethnic groups in an educational setting?

3. What implications for music instruction can be drawn from the various programs in language skills

and math for the culturally different?

4. What has been the success results of the city wide programs for the culturally different? Wat are the forecasts for the future of these types of programs?

5. What effect, if any, will the Regan budget cuts have on programs of this nature?

6. What music programs have been developed for the culturally different? What has been their success?

7. How can the methods of these special music programs be adopted to general classroom music instruction?

8. What is the outlook for special music programs in the future? What steps should be taken to advance the cause of special music programs for the culturally different?

NOTES FOR CHAPTER 2

1. Naomis Armstrong. "Music Education for Culturally Deprived High School Students" **HIGH SCHOOL JOURNAL.** (November, 1968), pp. 67-68.

2. Eunice Newton. "Verbal Destitution: The Pivotal Barrier to Learning," **Journal of Negro Education.** 29:4 (Fall, 1960), 111-113.

3. Ibid.

4. Sylvia Ashton-Warner. **Teacher.** New York: Simon and Schuster, 1963.

5. Ibid.

6. Ibid.

7. Janet Sawyer, (ed.). **Language Programs for the Disadvantaged.** Champaign, Illinois: National Council of Teachers of English (1965).

8. Marcia D. Zwier. "The Disadvantaged Child or Teachers," **Education.** 88:2 (November, 1967) pp. 156-159.

9. Ibid.

10. Kathryn Graham. "Mathematics for the Disadvantaged Child," **Teaching the Culturally Disadvantaged Pupil**, ed. J. Beck and R. Saxe. Springfield, Illinois, Clarks C. Thomas Publishing, 1965.

11. Ibid. pp 160-161.

12. A. Jackson Stenner, and S.G. Mueller, "A Successful Compensatory Education Model," **Phi Delta Kappan.** December, 1973, pp. 246-248.

13. Ibid.

14. Ibid.

15. Ibid.

16. H. DeJager, "Musical Socialization and the Schools," **Music Educators Journal.** 53:6 (Feb, 1967), 32-42 and 108-111).

17. Irvan Doig. "Music Hope for the Ghetto," **Music Journal.** 23:8 (Nov, 1965), 43-44, 68.

18. Florence Foster. "The Song Within: Music and the Disadvantaged Preschool Child," **Young Children.** (September, 1965) 373-376.

19. Ibid.

20. Ibid.

21. Dorothy Maynor. "Arts in the Ghetto," **Music Educators Journal.** 54:7 (March, 1968), 39-40.

22. Ibid.

23. Ibid.

24. Eugene McCoy. "Music and the Disadvantaged Child," **Catholic School Journal.** 68 (December, 1968), 47-48.

25. Ibid.

26. Ibid.

27. David McAllister. "Curriculum Must Assume a Place at the Center of Music," **The Tanglewood Symposium**. R. Choate, ed., Washington, D.C., MENC, 1968.

28. Dolores Nicosia. "Music for the Disadvantaged Pupil," **Teaching the Culturally Disadvantaged Pupil**. J.M. Beck and R.W. Saxe, ed., Springfield, Illinois: Charles Thomas Publishing, 1965.

29. Ibid.

30. Ibid.

31. Ibid.

32. Bennett Reimer. "General Music for the Black Ghetto Child," **Music Educators Journal**. 56:5 (January, 1970), 94-97 and 145-152.

33. Ibid.

34. Ibid.

35. Ibid.

36. Judith Murphy, and Ronald Gross. **The Arts and the Poor: New Challenge for Educators**. Office of Education, U.S. Department of H.E.W., O.E.S. 7016 (June, 1968).

37. Ibid.

38. Ibid.

BIBLIOGRAPHY

Bachner, S. "Teaching Reading and Literature to the Disadvantaged," **Journal of** Reading, April 1974, pages 512-516.

Cady, Henry (ed.). **Music in the Inner-City Schools: A Symposium, Current Issues in Music Education.**

IV, Ohio State University School of Music, Columbus (June 21-22, 1968).

Chernow, F. B. and C. **Teaching the Culturally Disadvantaged Child.** Englewood Cliffs, New Jersey: Parker Publishing, Inc., 1973.

Conyers, James. "An Exploratory Studsy of Music Tastes and Interest of College Students," **Sociology Inquiry.** 33:1 (Winter, 1963), 58-66.

Dececco, John P. **The Psychology of Learning and Instruction: Education Psychology.** Englewood Cliffs, New Jersey, Prentice-Hall, 1968.

DeRoche, E. F. "Methods, Materials, and the Culturally Disadvantaged," **Clearing House,** March 1970, pages 420-424.

Eisman, Lawrence. "Teaching the Difficult General Music Class," **Music Educators Journal.** 55:3 (Nov, 1966), 51-53.

Fermont, Herbert. "Some Thoughts on Teaching Mathematics to Disadvantaged Groups," **Arithmetic Teacher.** (1964), 319-322.

Finkelsteen, Sydney. **Art and Society.** New York: The International Publishers Co., Inc. 1957.

Gardner, D. B., editor. "New Research Perspectives on the Young Disadvantaged Chile: symposium," **Merrill-Palmer Quarterly,** October 1973, pages 235-299.

Grant, C. A. "New Social Studies and the Inner-City Student," **Social Studies,** March 1974, pages 118-120.

Kaplan, Max. **Foundations and Frontiers of Music Education.** New York: Holt Rinehart and Winston, Inc., 1966.

Lesser, Gerald S.; Rosenthal, Kristine M.; Polkoff, Sally E.; and Pfankuch, Marjorie B. "Some Effects of Segregation in the Schools." **Intergated Education,** II (June-July 1964), 20-26.

Madison, Agnes. "Growth in Perception of Reading,

Writing and Spelling for the Educationally Disadvantaged." **Reading Teacher,** 22 (March 1969), 515.

Miller, Thomas W. "Musical Taste Influences Curriculum," **Music Journal.** 24:3 (March, 1966), 64-66.

Mintz, Natalie and Herbert Fermont. "Some Practical Ideas for Teaching Mathematics to Disadvantaged Children," **Arithmetic Teacher.** 12 (April, 1965), 258-260.

Olson, James and Richard Larson. "An Experimental Curriculum for Culturally Deprived Kindergarten Children," **Educational Leadership.** (May, 1965), 553-558.

Quie, A. H. "New Approach to the Education of the Disadvantaged," **American Association of Colleges for Teacher Education, Yearbook,** 1973, pages 38-47.

"The Big Tax Revolt," **Newsweek.** New York, (June 19, 1978-A) pp. 20-29.

"The Landmark Bakke Ruling," **Newsweek.** New York, (July 10, 1978-B) pp. 19-31.

Wilkerson, Doxey, "Programs and Practices in Compensatory Education for the Disadvantaged Children," **Review of Educational Research** (1965) pp. 426-440.

Chapter 3

THE EFFECT OF I.Q. TESTING ON THE ACHIEVEMENT

LEVELS OF CULTURALLY DIFFERENT STUDENTS

Charles E. Hicks

A few years ago the subject of intelligence
testing was broached on the popular television show,
"Good Times." In this episode, Michael, the youngest
child, was administered an IQ test on which he scored
poorly. His parents, upset because they were aware
that Michael was, in fact, very bright, went to see the
school's guidance counselor. In the course of their
conversation with him, they asked him several
vocabulary questions, none of which the counselor could
successfully answer, which had come from a "Black" IQ
test. The point made by the show's writers was that
there is no such thing as a "culture-free" IQ
inventory, and that the scales presently used in
American schools routinely discriminate against black
and other minority students and inaccurately measure
their aptitudes.

IQ and intelligence are not the same, although
many researchers use the two interchangeably. IQ is a
symbol which refers to a set of scores earned on a
test... nothing more. Williams asserts that IQ cannot
be inherited. Much of the research concerning the
intellectual differences between Blacks and Whites is
based on the differences in test scores. Since the
test are biased in favor of middle class Whites, all
previous research comparing Blacks and Whites should be
completely **REJECTED.** "If Black children score lower
on ability tests than White children, this difference
does not mean Black children are actually inferior in
intelligence; all it means is that Black children
perform differently on the tests than White."[2]

Jensen (1969) and Humphreys (1970), two
proponents of the deficit model, claim that in the
general population, Blacks are about 15 IQ points or
one standard deviation below whites. They claim that
Blacks are genetically inferior to Whites.

To say that a Black American is different from a
White American is not to say that the Black American is
inferior, deficient, or deprived. One can be unique
and different without being inferior. **The Cultural**

60

Difference Model recognizes the difference between **equality** and **sameness**. The deficit model is based on a "get like me" philosophy; The cultural difference model recognizes uniqueness and differences in individuals.

The chart in Table 3:1 shows the two schools of thought, while these are two points of view with respect to this controversy, it is germane to this book to present **only** the **Cultural Difference Model View.**

TABLE 3:1

BLACK INTELLIGENCE

TWO SCHOOLS OF THOUGHT

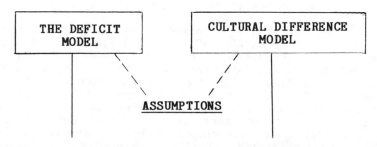

THE DEFICIT MODEL	CULTURAL DIFFERENCE MODEL

<u>ASSUMPTIONS</u>

BLACKS ARE DEFICIENT WHEN COMPARED TO WHITES IN SOME MEASURABLE TRAIT CALLED INTELLIGENCE, AND THIS DEFICIENCY IS DUE TO GENETIC, OR CULTURAL FACTORS, OR BOTH.

THIS SCHOOL OF THOUGHT ESPOUSES THE "GET LIKE ME" OR YOU ARE WRONG BELIEF.

THE DIFFERENCE NOTED IN INTELLIGENCE BY PSYCHOLOGISTS IN TESTING ARE THE RESULT OF PATHOLOGY, FAULTY LEARNING, OR GENETIC INFERIORITY.

BLACKS AND WHITES COME FROM DIFFERENT CULTURAL BACKGROUNDS WHICH EMPHASIZE DIFFERENT LEARNING EXPERIENCES NESCESSARY FOR SURVIVAL.

THIS SCHOOL OF THOUGHT RECOGNIZES THAT THIS SOCIETY IS PLURALISTIC IN NATURE WHERE CULTURAL DIFFERENCES ABOUND.

The **DEFICIT MODEL** therefore engages in faulty reasoning: if a child scores low on a test, he is classified as lacking the ability of those who scored higher. The model assumes that low scorers and high scorers had similar or equal opportunities to learn the knowledge required by the tests. **This assumption is false.**

Example:

> Two pieces of fruit... e.g., an **apple** and an **orange**... may be equal in weight, in quality of goodness, and in marketability, but they are not the same. An **apple** cannot become an **orange** and vice versa. Each must express its respective characteristics of "applesness" and "orangeness," yet both are fruit.[3]

These scales are supposed to serve as predictors of school achievement, of what individual students' learning abilities are. Guilford defines learning as change in behavior--"a movement from one behavioral status to another which does not necessarily reflect improvement".[4] He states, also, that "high scores on aptitude tests do not necessarily imply that a child is more intelligent than another who scores lower."[5] There is a correlation between aptitude and scores on IQ tests, but no cause-and-effect relationship between the two can be proven. Rather than assuming that a child is "advanced" because he is more intelligent, then, one might argue that high test scores simply indicate the student has learned more for any number of reasons.[6]

IQ testing is a complex myth, emanating from a common misconception that a number or a score can represent a human being's overall mental ability, when in reality, psychologists and educators cannot even agree on a verbal definition of intelligence. Intelligence is a hypothetical construct; that is, we develop a concept which we call intelligence in order to explain certain types of variations in observable behavior. Technically, the IQ is a measure of performance on specified tasks under standardized conditions. Although we use this measure of performance to make inferences about the hypothetical construct labeled intelligence, we must recognize that performance can be affected by a number of factors besides the basic intellective capacity of the person; such as his motivational level when the test is taken.

In short, the IQ can seldom be accepted as a "pure" reflection of intelligence alone.

Most people have believed that IQ is an accurate measure of innate intelligence of people. Many parents are now learning what many educators and psychologists have suspected for a long time: you are born with a potential for learning, reasoning, problem-solving and judgment. Heredity plays a role in how large that potential is, but how much that potential develops depends just as much on your experience and your environment.[7]

According to Guilford, "IQ and learning ability are neither the same trait, nor is either a universal one." . . . learning ability and intelligence involve many different components, depending upon the nature of the learning task and intelligence test. He also believes that the psychological factors in a given population may be determined by heredity, by environmental influences, or by a combination of both. Thus they are heavily determined by culture. "Striking differences" in aptitude factors may exist between populations which are accounted for by varying cultural circumstances.[8]

Research shows that teacher expectations of student potential have an adverse effect on the achievement levels of minority students (Rosenthal and Jacobson, 1968). Teachers' expectations are transmitted to students both formally, through grouping by academic ability, and informally, both of which may have a profound effect on the child's self-concept and his/her motivation to learn. On the basis of IQ tests, teachers give different academic assignments to students that they believe to be of high ability than they do students they believe to be of low ability. These actions are guided by the data they have received from the tests. Belief is a willingness to act, and since many teachers usually believe that the test results they receive are accurate, they tend to act on this information. . . . whether it is correct or incorrect. Smith further states, in many school systems the effectiveness of teachers is determined by the subjects that the test measure, hence the tests' contents determine the curriculum. For many students (especially minority students) this practice smacks at a basic denial of equal educational opportunity.[9]

Other investigators, e.g., Klineberg (1944), McQueen and Chum (1960), Price (1929), and Roen (1960), have taken the position that the observed differences in intelligence are due to differences in socioeconomic status. Researchers studying the test performances of black and white freshmen in black and white colleges, found that the difference in median scores was ten points in favor of the white students. Price found that twenty percent of the scores of the blacks exceeded the median of the whites. Any conclusions about the inferiority of Blacks, as a group, can only be considered superficial, because many blacks are apparently not inferior to their white counterparts.[10] Boone investigated the differences between black and white subjects on an "intelligence" test consisting of items indigenous to the black environment. Results from this study showed the broad cultural dichotomy found between black and white groups.[11]

In discussing the relationship between culture and the development of personality, Loree (1970) lists four cultural determinants: 1) Culture determines what parents teach their children and how. 2) Different cultures teach different lessons and train children in varying ways. 3) A child's early experiences will have a lasting effect upon his personality. 4) Similar experiences within a single culture tend to produce similar personalities.[12]

The significance of the home environment during the pre-school years, as well as throughout the childhood and adolescence of the student, cannot be overestimated with respect to its impact on the cognitive, emotional and social development of the child. If a child comes from a "deprived" home, whatever his race, he may suffer from an absence of "a variety of cognitive experiences and natural conditions" which could combine to handicap him educationally.[13]

Loree cautions educators to abandon the concept of a "fixed IQ" and that of "predetermined development of intelligence," however, citing the results of some researchers which indicate that however a child scores on intelligence tests initially, the nature of his follow-up educational experiences may be critical to the development of his learning abilities generally.[14]

While it is obviously a misnomer to term black children categorically as "deprived," the fact remains that because of cultural differences they may not test as well on IQ inventories reflective of the values of a dominant white culture. The question remains as to the significance of differences in IQ scores for the types of expectations educators have of black students and the type of educational experiences such students have.

Whether or not children from other cultures, specifically black children, succeed in school will depend on the interplay between the culture of the school and that of the community at large: the values, perceptions, and attitudes of school personnel and other students; the informal and formal relationships between parents and the school system; and the learning process within the classroom.[15]

There certainly does appear to be a relationship between one's intellectual abilities and learning. But many researchers have concluded that learning ability is not a single attribute, that there are a number of fairly independent abilities extant depending upon the cognitive task to be learned.

Since IQ testing generally begins quite early in a student's career, his performance on it is apt to influence others' expectations of him for the duration of his school experience.

In one study on the relationship of sources of institutional threat to elementary age children, it was revealed that below-average ability children were significantly more threatened by ability grouping than the above average ability students. The investigators concluded that schools needed to group students by different criteria, such as interest or specific need, rather than by ability.[16]

Expectations may also have a detrimental effect on a student's motivation to learn. It is a widely accepted tenet among educators that to facilitate learning a student must have goals set which are high enough that they are challenging, while at the same time realistic. The child must also feel that the goals set by the school are worthwhile for him and are consonant with values learned in the home.

If a black or other minority child tests poorly on an IQ test and his score is perceived by the school administration to be reflective of his scholastic aptitude, he may be grouped with other low-scoring children in classes which are not challenging enough, to face attitudes from teachers which are not supportive, to the detriment of his self-concept. Faced with such a situation, many students unfortunately either opt to accept an erroneous perception of their abilities as truth and integrate it into their self-concept, or actively reject the values of the school to protect their sense of self-esteem.

Further compounding this problem is the possibility that a real normative conflict may exist between the student's home and the school, and sensitive educators must be aware of this possibility. If the value of the need for education is not reinforced in the home, whatever the child's intelligence, he is apt to be caught in a normative cross-fire which might easily affect his willingness to strive toward the goal of academic achievement.

Much of the fault rests with the design of most standardized IQ tests. There have been four primary contributors to intelligence testing: Thorndike, Spearman, Thurstone, and Guilford. While each has developed his own theories of intelligence, at least three of the four share in common the fact that their scales reflect enormous cultural biases. For example, Thurstone postulated seven primary mental abilities: number, word fluency, verbal meaning, memory, reasoning, spatial perception, and perceptual speed. At least two of these--word fluency and verbal meaning--are clearly culturally-bound abilities, yet no provision has been made for differences in cultural experiences which might bias results.[17]

Guilford has cautioned that those educators who wish to ascertain intelligence quotients on a more comprehensive level than has traditionally been afforded, IQ scales must be modified. IQ tests are developed within the context of a particular race, and particular culture within that race, but subgroups within the culture may demonstrate significant differences in performance. It is impossible, he says, to infer anything about racial differences from present IQ tests, nor is it feasible to develop "culture-free" or totally "culture-fair" tests which will accurately measure IQ for all cultural groups.[18]

Many educators ascribe to the belief that one criterion of intelligence is the ability to adapt to

66

new learning situations, and the way in which an individual makes this adaptation is by transferring what he has learned on one task to another. Thus, "the reorganizations of Gestalt psychology are probably categorized as transformation," although the latter is a broader concept and is an information item which can be remembered and later used." The question, however, is whether or not IQ tests reflect this learning factor or if they instead concentrate on a small number of other abilities.[19]

In response to a Jensen article concerning IQ and intelligence, the Council of the Society for the Psychological Study of Social Issues stated:

> The evidence of four decades of research on this problem can be readily summarized. There are marked differences in intelligence test scores when one compares a random sample of whites and Negroes. What is equally clear is that little definitive evidence exists that leads to the conclusion that such differences are innate. The evidence points overwhelmingly to the fact that when one compares Negroes and Whites of comparable cultural and educational background, differences in intelligence test scores diminish markedly; the more comparable the background, the less the difference. There is no direct evidence that supports the view that there is an innate difference between members of different racial groups. We believe that a more accurate understanding of the contribution of heredity to intelligence will be possible only when social conditions for all races are equal and when this situation has existed for several generations. . . . We must also recognize the limitations of present-day intelligence tests. Largely developed and standardized on white middle class children, these tests tend to be biased against blacks (and other minority children) to an unknown degree.[20]

If it is true that Blacks derive meaning through a Gestalt perspective one might assume their tendency to learn better conceptually, rather than by rote. Traditionally, school systems have not taught conceptually but have concentrated, particularly at the elementary level, on teaching by memorization. IQ tests are used to predict school success and will thus reflect this type of teaching and learning approach. Consequently, it may be that although Black students generally perform more poorly on IQ tests, they will be more likely to retain what they have learned, precluding any type of significant relationship between IQ scores and achievement.

Studies of performance by black and white students on the Thematic Apperception Test have led Jerome Kagan to note that Blacks cannot be treated as a homogenous class. If anything, it would be more justifiable to ascribe the insignificant differences in scores on the (TAT) to socio-economic class differences. "Culture plays a role only in the interpretation of perceptions," according to the studies he cites.[21]

The Director of the Antioch Program for Interracial Education also disclaims the value of present IQ tests as indicators of learning ability, and states that certain behavior criteria have been found to be far more important in identifying gifted minority students. He includes "courage, realism, imagination, communication, success, stubbornness, tenacity, toughness, accessibility, judgment, humor, industry and complexity."[22] Clearly, none of these are qualities measured by standardized IQ tests.

He states, too, that while the disadvantaged student has traditionally been defined as a student who is unable to undertake the responsiblities of ongoing education, educators must take into account the fact that such students have a different lifestyle. "Their ways of believing, valuing, behaving, establishing goals, and working toward those goals are different from those experienced by the dominant elements of our society."[23]

Robert Hanson, past director of the Trenton Action Bound Program, states that all subject matter presented to the disadvantaged student will have to be on the basis of his interest and relevancies. This point of view is echoed by Leon Hymovitz, who charges the American school system with attempting to commit cultural genocide and alienating and isolating students from different cultures.[24]

RESEARCH: MUSICAL TALENT AND MINORITIES

There has long existed a popular belief that Blacks have an unusual natural talent for music. More specifically, African and the Negro's gift for rhythm was an innate talent unparalleled to individuals of other cultures. Are these statements true? Do they indeed rest on fact? Are there any empirical data to substantiate these claims? To provide some insights into these commonly held beliefs, we shall examine some research studies concerning minorities and musical talent.

Ethnic groups and musical aptitude has been of great interest to music psychologists. But within the last forty years, there has not been very much substantial research data available. Carl Seashore published the first standardized tests of musical aptitude in 1919 called the Seashore Measures of Musical Talent. The Seashore battery of tests reflected a philosophy that musical talent was "innate." Since that time however, many experimental researchers have continued to disprove Seashore's theory.

Lenoire (1925) conducted a study in which he found black children to be superior to white children in rhythm and tonal memory, but not inferior on other measures of aptitude. Peterson and Lanier (1929) found that whites scored higher on all parts of a music aptitude test except rhythm. Gray and Bingham (1929) in similar experiments, reported that Negroes equaled Whites only on the consonance test; while Johnson (1928) found no significant difference between the two groups. Peacock (1928) in research for his doctoral dissertation, compared Whites and Negroes on musical talent and intelligence; results from his investigation suggests that these tests favored Whites and was biased to Negroes in all of the categories.

Farnsworth (1931) using the Seashore-Kwalwasser Test Battery found that native-born whites were superior only in melody when compared with foreign-born Orientals. Using the Seashore Battery as a criteria. Garth and Candor (1937) and Isbell (1929) found Mexicans inferior in rhythm and pitch, while American Indians were superior in rhythm and time. Porter (1931) found that both Orientals and Whites that shared similar environmental backgrounds, scored below average on subtests within the test battery. Ross

(1936) conducted research using Indian and Japanese children, his study revealed that American Indians were found to be below average on all subtests except time, and Japanese children were superior in both consonance and time. Finally, Eells (1933) in research with native races of Alaska reported Eskimos scored below average on all of the six subtests.

Most recently much less research is being done concerning music aptitude and race for obvious reasons. Gordon (1967) reported supportive data obtained under more favorable experimental conditions, in which 658 students from two predominantly Negro junior high schools in the Midwest were tested. The data from these experiments were found to be very similar to those upon which his Musical Aptitude Profile norms were based.

It is believed by many researchers that social and economic factors related to disadvantaged environmental conditions probably exert more influence on musical attainment than do race, IQ, or nationality. According to Gordon, "the correlation between intelligence and musical aptitude test scores is positive but low. Academic achievement test scores correlate somewhat higher with musical aptitude test scores. . . . musical aptitude test scores predict success in musical achievement significantly better than either intelligence or academic achievement.".[25]

As suggested by Siegel, culturally defined musical experiences count more than the external stimulus in the perception of pitch. For musicians within a given cultural tradition, the perception of elementary auditory events in music is influenced as much by their knowledge and expectations as by the acoustic stimulus. The premise that the perception of music is more a matter of interpretation than that of hearing is a radical departure from the long held traditional psychoacoustic approach to music. As radical as this view might seem she contends that it is quite compatible with current information processing approaches to the psychology of perception. This view also has strong implications for cross-cultural assessment of minorities in music. If this model of human perception is correct, it would help us understand why all groups of students except those of the dominant white culture do poorly on IQ tests and other similar assessment instruments.[26]

If what we hear depends upon our musical environment, then it follows that musicians trained in different musical cultures will learn to focus on those variables that have musical significance for them. Siegel goes on to say that "there is some evidence that absolute pitch is a culturally based phenomenon."[27]

CONCLUSION

Minority children are pressured to change their beliefs, values and illusions about their culture, which in turn negatively affects their self-concept. Schools must mirror the diversity of their communities and offer each student multi-cultural experiences and activities.

"It is the child's cultural conditioning as an organized systematic structuring of values, beliefs, views, customs, and traditions which influence his every response to social stimuli. The different and non-different, therefore, have a different rate, pace, style, and quality of learning."[28]

Educators must both respect these differences and propagate them to fully reach all students. One of the first steps toward this goal would be the elimination of traditional IQ tests.

NOTES FOR CHAPTER 3

1. Robert L. Williams "Abuses and Misuses in Testing Black Children," In Reginald L. Jones (Ed.), **Black Psychology** (New York: Harper and Row Publishers, 1972), p. 78.

2. Ibid. pp. 81-82.

3. Ibid.

4. J.P. Guilford, **The Nature of Human Intelligence** (New York: McGraw-Hill, 1967), p. 268.

5. Ibid. p. 14.

6. Ibid.

7. Augusta Greenblatt, "The Truth about Your Child's IQ: What It Means... How You Can Raise It," **Family Circle**, (1975): 33-38.

8. Guilford, **The Nature of Human Intelligence,** p. 14.

9. William D. Smith, "Test Validity, Reliability: The Effect of Tests Results on the Black Self-Concept and the Educational Curriculum," **Black Psychology**, (1978): 84-94.

10. J. St. Clair Price, "Intelligence of Negro College Freshmen," **School and Society** 30:779 (November, 1929): 749:754.

11. James A. Boone and Vinvent J. Adesso, "Racial Differences on a Black Intelligence Test," **The Journal of Negro Education** 43:4 (Fall 1974): 429-436.

12. M. Ray Loree, **Psychology of Education** (New York: The Ronald Press, Inc. 1970.

13. Jules Henry, "Education of the Negro Child," cited in Murray L. Wax, Stanley Diamond and Fred O. Gearing, **Anthropological Perspectives on Education** (New York: Basic Books, 1971).

14. Ibid.

15. Ibid.

16. Robert L. Furman, "The Relationship of Three Sources of Institution Threat to the Self-Concept of Elementary Age Children," **Dissertation Abstracts International** 37 (September 1976): 1386.

17. M. Ray Loree, **Psychology of Education.**

18. J. P. Guilford. pp. 408-411.

19. Ibid.

20. E.E. Baughman, **Personality: The Psychological Study of the Individual** (Englewood Cliffs, New Jersey: Prentice-Hall, Inc., (1972) pp. 432-436.

21. Jerome Kagan and Gerald B. Lesser, **Contemporary Issues in Thematic Apperception Methods** (Illinois: Charles C. Thomas Publishers, 1961).

22. Peter J. Hampton, "Talent Among Disadvantaged Students," **Educational Forum** 38:3 (March 1974): 321-326.

23. Ibid.

24. Leon Hymovitz, **"Multicultural Education in American: Melting Pot Atonement or** at-one-ment?," **English Journal** 66 (March 1977): 23-28.

25. Edwin Gordon, **The Psychology of Music Teaching** (Englewood Cliffs, New Jersey: Prentice Hall, Inc., 1967), p. 36.

26. Jane A. Siegel, "Culturally Defined Learning Experience and Musical Perception," **Paper presented at the National Symposium on the Applications of Psychology to the Teaching and Learning of Music** (Ann Arbor: Michigan, July 30-August 2, 1979): 98-148.

27. Ibid.

28. Leon Hymovitz. pp. 23-28.

DISCUSSION QUESTION

1. What do the letters IQ represent? How is IQ determined?

2. Are current IQ test valid for Black Americans and other minorities?

3. Explain the differences between the "deficit" model and "cultural difference" model.

4. Can the theories of Arthur Jensen be proved or disproved in a scientific experiment?

5. How does IQ test scores affect a teacher's perception of student's abilities in general?

6. Aside from IQ testing, what other ways can cultural differences manifest itself?

7. Is there any positive correlation bewteen intelligence and musical aptitude? List some studies.

8. Compile a list of myths about IQ and be prepared to discuss in class.

9. Who are some of the contributors to IQ test and name the seven primary mental abilities they proport to measure.

10. If its true that minorities score lower than whites on IQ tests; discuss several reasons for this difference.

CLASS PROJECT

A. Obtain a copy of the Black Intelligence Test (developed by noted Black Pyschologist Robert Williams*, Washington University, St. Louis, Missouri) and administer it to a selected sample of Black and White students. Compile your results and make some generalizations about the data recieved.

B. Using appropiate sources, construct Black Music Test of fifty items and select a class of music majors to administer the test to. Discuss your results in class.

*The address for Dr. Robert Williams is, Department of Black Studies, Washington University, St. Louis, Missouri 63130.

BIBLIOGRAPHY OF FURTHER READINGS

Fitz-Gibbon, Carol T. "The Identification of Mentally Gifted 'Disadvantaged' Students at the Eight Grade Level," **Journal of Negro Education** 43:1 (1974): 53-66.

Green, Robert. "The Awesome Danger of Intelligence Tests," **Ebony** 29:10 (August, 1974): 68-72.

Hilliard, Asa G. "A Review of Leon Kamin's the Science and Nature of IQ," **The Journal of Black Psychology** 2:2 (1976): 64-74.

Jenkins, Martin D. "A Socio-Psychological study of Negro Children of Superior Intelligence," **Journal of Negro Education** 5 (1936): 175-190.

_____ "Case Studies of Negro Children of Binet IQ, 160 and above," **Journal of Negro Education** 12 (1943): 159-166.

Labov, William. **"Academic Ignorance and Black Intelligence,"** Atlantic Monthly 6 (1972) 59-67.

Newland, F. Ernest. "Assumptions Underlying Psychological Testing," **Journal of School Psychology** 11:4 (1973): 315-322.

Shapiro, D. **Neurotic Styles** (New York: Basic Books, 1965).

Sidran, Ben. **Black Talk** (New York: Holt, Rinehart, and Winston, 1971).

Snowden, Frank M. Jr. **Blacks in Antiquity: Ethiopia in the Greco-Roman Experience** (Cambridge: Belknap Press, Harvard University Press, 1970).

Tyler, Ralph W. and Wolfe, Richard M. **Crucial Issues in Testing** (Berkeley: McCutchen, 1974).

Williams, Robert L. "Abuses and Misuses in Testing Black Children," **Black Psychology** (New York: Harper and Row, 1972), pp. 77-91.

_____ "One Black Intelligence," **Journal of Black Studies** 4:1 (September, 1973): 29-39.

Whitehurst, "Comments on the Jensen Article on

Intelligence," **Congressional Record** 115:7:9426 (April, 17, 1969).

Wilson, Amos N. **The Developmental Psychology of The Black Child** (New York: Africana Research Publications, 1981).

BIBLIOGRAPHY

Baughman, E.E., **Personality: The Psychological Study of the Individual.** Englewood Cliffs, New Jersey: Prentice-Hall, Inc. (1972), pp. 268-273.

Bodmer, W.F., "Intelligence and Race," **Scientific American** (October, 1970), pp. 19-29.

Boone, James A., "Racial Differences on a Black Intelligence Test," **The Journal of Negroe Education** (1978), pp. 429-436.

Eells, Walter, "Musical Ability of the Native Races of Alaska," **Journal of Applied Psychology**, 17 (1933), pp.

Farnsworth, Paul, "An Historical, Critical, and Experimental Study of the Seashore-Kwalwasser Test Battery," **Genetic Psychology Monograph**, 9 (1931), pp. 291-393.

Garth, T.R., and E. Candor, "Musical Talent of Mexicans," **American Journal of Psychology**, 59 (1937), pp. 203-207.

Garth, T.R., and S.R. Isbell, "The Musical Talent of Indians," **Music Supervisors Journal**, 15 (1929), pp. 85-87.

Gordon, Edwin, "A Comparison of the Performance of Culturally Disadvantaged with that of Culturally Heterogeneous Students on the Musical Aptitude Profile," **Psychology in the Schools**, 15 (1967), pp. 260-268.

Gray, C.T., and C.W. Bingham, "A Comparison of Certain Phases of Musical Ability in Colored and White School Pupils," **Journal of Applied Psychology**, 20 (1929), pp. 429-436.

Hill, John, "The Musical Achievement of Culturally
Deprived and Advantaged Children: A Comparative
Study at the Elementary Level," **Journal of Musical
Therapy** (Sept., 1968), pp. 77-83.

Humphreys, L.G. "Theory of Intelligence," In R. Cancro
(Ed.), **Intelligence: Genetic and Environmental
Influences** (New York: Grune and Strstton, 1971).
pp. 31-55

Hunt, J.M. and G.E. Kirk, "Social Aspects of
Intelligence: Evidence and Issues," in
Intelligence: Genetic and Environment, ed. by R.
Cancro. New York: Grune and Stratton, Inc.
(1971), pp. 268-273.

Jenson, Arthur R. **Bias in Metal Testing** (New York: The
Free Press, 1980).

Porter, Raymond, **A Study of the Musical Talent of
Chinese Attending Public Schools in Chicago.**
Chicago: University of Chicago Press (1931).

Johnson, Guy B., "Musical Talent and the Negro," **Music
Supervisors Journal**, 81 (1928), 13, 86.

Lenoire, Z., "Measurement of Racial Differences in
Mental and Educational Abilities." **Unpublished
Ph.D. Dissertation**, University of Iowa, 1925.

Musgrove, W.J., "Comparisons of Low Socioeconomic
Black and White Kindergarten Children," **Academic
Therapy**, (Winter, 1970), pp. 163-167.

Peacock, W., "A Comparative Study of Musical Talent in
Whites and Negroes and Its Correlation with
Intelligence," Unpublished Ph.D. Dissertation,
Emory University, 1928.

Peterson, Joseph and Lyle Lanier, "Studies in the
Comparative Abilities of Whites and Negors,"
Mental Measurement Monographs, 5 (1929).

Robert Rosenthal and Lenore Jacobson, **Pygmalion in the
Classroom: Teacher Expectations and Pupils
Intellectual Development.** New York: Holt,
Rinehart and Winston, 1968.

Ross, Verne, "Musical Talents of Indian and Japanese
Children," **Journal of Juvenile Research**, 20

(1936), pp. 133-136.

Shuey, A.M., **The Testing of Negro Intelligence**, Second
     Edition. New York: Social Science Press, (1966).

Siegel, Jane A., "Culturally Defined Learning
     Experience and Musical Perception." **Paper
     presented at the National Symposium on the
     Applications of Psychology to the Teaching and
     Learning of Music.** Ann Arbor: Michigan, July 30-
     August 2, 1979, pp. 98-148.

Skeels, H.M., "Adult Status of Children with
     Contrasting Early Life Experiences," **Monographs
     of the Society for Research in Child Development,**
     Vol. 31, #3 (1966).

Smith, William David, "Test Validity, Reliability: The
     Effect of Test Results on the Black Self-Concept
     and the Educational Curriculum," **Black
     Psychology.** New York: Harper and Row, (1978),
     pp. 84-94.

Spears, David, et. al. editors, **Race and Intelligence:
     The Fallacies Behind the Race—I.Q. Controversy.**
     Baltimore: Penguin Books, (1972).

Stinchcombe, A.L., "Environment: The Cumulation of
     Effects Is Yet to be Understood," **Harvard
     Educational Review,** Vol. 39, #3 (1969), pp. 511-
     522.

Chapter 4

REFLECTIONS ON MUSIC BEHAVIORS OF BLACKS
IN AMERICAN SOCIETY[1]

James A. Standifer

At least two distinct musical traditions co-exist in America: that of the primarily White culture, based on Western tradition, and that of the Black culture, transplanted to the New World. To be sure, neither of these is unidimensional. In particular, unidimensionality should not be assumed for Blacks. All sorts of tastes in music exist among Blacks in America, as they do for other American groups. There are a range of music activities that Blacks enjoy, support, become actively involved with, or tolerate. Further, there is as much difference in taste between different socioeconomic and age groups in the total Black population as there are in the White population.

But while these two traditions co-exist, the White, Western tradition has tended to dominate, both in music education and in aesthetics in general. John B. Hightower, director of the New York Museum of Modern Art, reflects this view when he writes that "all of our major arts institutions are founded on a European tradition and approach to the arts. Their concerns are more reflective than immediate, more interpretative than creative. The works performed and the exhibitions displayed, more often than not, celebrate the creative talent of another century and another country."[2]

In spite of this, and in the face of widespread attempts to change or diminish the acceptability of such behavior, Blacks have held tenaciously to their way of creating and recreating art. An examination of the antecedents to current Black music behavior and an analysis of its underlying essence is presented herein as a means of motivating future scholarly study in this important and rich area of research.

Various communal gatherings and the church once provided the only organized outlet for Black music expression. All that is changed now, but for a long time in American history, the church in particular was the primary environment in which most of the unique music behaviors of Blacks were born and nurtured. Religious expression and Black music behavior were one and the same thing. Both were manifest in the singing of gospels, spirituals, hymns, and the like, and a resulting music behavior called variously "getting happy" or being "hit by the spirit." This highly individualistic but extremely infectious behavior includes shouting, dancing, arm-waving, screaming or hollering, swaying back and forth, moaning, singing, fainting, and the like.

As Blacks became converted into protestant religions such as Baptist and Methodist, these behaviors were generally integrated into the doctrines of the denomination and retained unchanged. In comparatively newer protestant sects consisting of large numbers of Blacks, such as Holiness, Pentacostal and Sanctified, we see forms of this behavior that are even less apt to have been diluted by the times and the influences of social mobility in America, than in the traditionally White religious groups. Tony Heilbut, describing the behavior of sanctified folk and/or other Blacks who "get happy" says of this behavior:

> Each saint has his own distinctive step. . .Some rock gently, lightly swinging their hips and shoulders in counterpoint to the music. Others contort violently, cutting steps in time to the music until their contortions knock them to the floor. Some wave their hands in the air, others hold one hand or arm erect. . .
> In a Sanctified church, the spirit can be called up by song and dance alone.[3]

It is safe, I think, to generalize that certain kinds of music behavior of Blacks in America are due, in large part, to the long historical consequence of the way slavery was practiced in this country and the ensuing consequence of the slaves' introduction into the enslaving society as a whole. The overt, seemingly uninhibited response to the dynamic processes of music often exemplified by Blacks also may be directly traceable to the mode of musical behavior of Africans: a highly active involvement in musical events which are non-differentiated among Africans from the realm of everyday life.

Black music behavior in America today--perhaps all Black music behavior--is to one extent or another a fusion of the African and American experience. Researchers generally agree that the particular hymns and the **a cappella** moaning style typical of these hymn arrangements (e.g., Amazing Grace, Must Jesus Bear the Cross Alone) provide graphic evidence of this fusion. Certainly these hymns were highly favored by the Black slaves in America and were probably the first hymns sung by them in the New World. But while adopting these rugged eighteenth century English hymns, early African-Americans greatly altered them and a typically Afro-American style of song emerged. In this style, called by a number of names, e.g., surge singing, lining out, long meter, or Dr. Watts, a leader recites a line of text, followed by the congregation or group singing the line of text in a slow, deliberate style. This manner of presentation permits intricate embellishments on the basic tune as well as much sliding within and among the basic tones. Such hymns almost always motivated the participants to "get happy." Thus, the style or manner of singing, the text, and the emerging sounds themselves combine to produce unique forms of music behavior typical of large numbers of Blacks then and now.

To be sure, Black musical behavior (in Africa and in America) is manifestly cultural in terms of its **movement "with" existence**, instead of the "ossification of existence that happens when an object of art is produced".[4] Ben Aning, Professor of Music at the University of Ghana, supports this thesis when he states that music education is first and foremost cultural education; and that music educators should rely increasingly on ethnomusicology for an understanding of this and related aspects of Black musical traditions. For example, in Africa, he says, music is made more in terms of the context of the society and culture. . .than in the West. It is seldom divorced from everyday life. Generally, performing groups are large and often sectionalized (a percussion section, a melodic instrumental and choral section, and dancers) with the audiences or onlookers comprising a significant and complementary section. However, unlike Western audiences, African music spectators are not passive receivers but are more often active participants, either as singers, hand-clappers or voluntary dancers. In short, African music behavior is an extension of the African's natural life activity. His attention, during aesthetic endeavors, is never diverted from life; he does not "stop living in his acts of daily life, or stop being directed toward their objects." Moreover, the act of listening (ostensibly a passive exercise for some cultures), still occurs but in a dimension that involves--not requires--the African's sense of being and behaving musically, **moving "with" existence.** If African music and music behavior teach a lesson it is this: such music and music behavior are about people--the way they move, the way they feel, the things they experience, the sounds they make. Thus, Aning's thesis emphasizes that the sounds and motions of African music and music making are analogous to conditions of African life and how African life feels. Lest he be misunderstood, however, Professor Aning adds:

> . . . . he (the African) is not unaware of the fine aesthetics of the art. It is this awareness that enables both musician and consumer to be discriminatory, selective, and critical of good and poor music or performances. It is not to all music that Africans dance. Nor is it all music that may have religious or ritual stimulation. Some, especially songs, are sung for the beauty of the melody or for their quality as a stimulant for action or movement.[5]

Movement "with existence, then, must be interpreted both in terms of aesthetic response and cultural affiliation. A brief discussion of its application to a completely different culture can help bring this notion into clearer focus. In Korean culture, dance is one of the most popular and expressive manifestations of **movement "with" existence,** yet the actual music behavior exemplified by Korean culture is totally [6] different from that exemplified by African culture. The ethics of Buddhism and Confucianism exert tremendous influence on the life and life dynamics of the people in this small country. Similarly, these philosophies serve to shape modes of expression typical of Korean folk music and dance. In notable examples of Korean dance, for instance, quiet and elegant shoulder movement is emphasized; the concept of time is irrelevant, or time in the Western or African sense is non-existent.[7] Spiritual exaltation achieved in quiescence is an overriding and guiding principle. The dancer may either move or stand still. In short, a religious ethic devotedly followed by a people, and strongly governing almost every aspect of their everyday life, makes up the essence of what is here called **movement "with" existence** in the experience of music. That is, in Korean music and dance, the austerities of Confucianism and Buddhism do little to afford freedom of movement because these religions have, as their very essence, prescribed movements and manners which are in and of themselves restrictive.

To return to the Black musical behavior which comprises the subject of this paper, it should be noted that it occurs primarily with music that may be classified as folk music: music that is a product of a race, music that reflects feelings and tastes that are communal, music and behaviors that are integrated with a surviving pattern of **community** life. It is music; no, it is behavior--the bond where the realm of ordinary experience fuses with the aesthetic.

Bringing the matter directly to our doorsteps, Hightower asserts that Black and ethnic sections of cities are where the arts are most immediate and full of life:

> For art to reach ethnic audiences, it must relate people to who and what they are--not to what someone else would like them to appreciate or hope they can become. The notion of the arts as something separate and apart from what happens to us everyday, as icons to be revered by well-rehearsed members of a club on special occasions, has no place and no meaning on the streets of Cleveland's Hough district, the Watts area of Los Angeles, or 119th Street in Harlem. The emphasis in such places is on the content of what is presented and the[8] involvement of those who experience it.

But, just as clearly, the dominant music behavior in other areas is the opposite. Indeed, the instances are regions where the tendency to divorce music and music behavior from life has resulted in sterile and alienating music education programs. Moreover, it is this tendency of art and aesthetic behavior to be removed from the worldly that has led some to assume that good aesthetic experiences of music are possible only for the elite, musically cultivated and mature individual. Fortunately, the trend today is largely away from this idea and toward the closer alignment of the aesthetic with "acts of daily life" and with the individual. Stewart's view of art as being a **movement "with" existence** is a reflection of this philosophy. The aesthetic experience of music **is** life. Moreover, if such an attitude regarding the aesthetic experience is adopted by school music teachers, they will have less difficulty providing significant, non-alienating musical experiences that are both aesthetically satisfying **and** intellectually stimulating.

That all music behavior is apt to be a form of true life experience is a very attractive assumption. It is life experience transformed by a total absorption of and immersion in the aesthetics experience of sounds and their myriad patterns. Teachers and researchers should consider the different effects on learning resulting from such absorption and immersion. Particular and consistent attention should be given to effects that result from 1) absorption deliberately planned for purposes of developing keener music perceptions and 2) absorption and immersion typical of social and spontaneous music involvement. Important music behaviors occur in both of these instances. It may be that equal weight, equal importance should be given to these two means of involvement with music. The idea is facinating enough to merit some serious study.

It has been emphasized in this paper that much Black musical experience is perhaps a facing of realities and, often, a relieving of the burdens of living. Black musical behavior often chronicles, interprets and even transforms reality. However, it never loses touch with life. That, after all, is the very essence of the behavior, what Stewart calls **movement "with" existence.**

The phenomenon may be due to the fact that Blacks in America have a legacy of music and music behavior from Africa that permeates their view of **art as life.** This legacy includes experiencing music in ways that give the individual insight into himself and reality. A musical response becomes a remaking of reality. While the individual may, in this sense, live on another plane of consciousness, the maze of activities necessary to deal with existence take on new and less formidable dimensions. To Blacks, a meaningful experience of music involves behavior that is in itself a facet of cherished reality. It is what John Dewey calls **an** experience. . . something highly valued, satisfying, even sometimes disturbing, but always sought out again and again. It is, at the same time, an escape from an involvement in the complexities of reality, a simplification, if you will, of reality into its most essential meanings.

Black musical behavior is, in this sense, inextricably tied to the belief that the concern of aesthetic being is to accompany reality, to "move with" and not "against it." Blacks often feel that musical behavior of the White culture "moves against life and thus against art." It follows that music and deeply felt responses to it, must be understood as the accomplishment and, more significantly, the **operation** of creating. The process, then, is immensely more important than the result. This is aptly pointed out by Stewart:

> What results therefrom (the operation of creating) is merely the momentary residue of that operation--a perishable object and nothing more, and anything else you might imbue it with (which White aesthetic purports to do) is nothing else but mummification. The point is--and this is the crux of our two opposing conceptions of being--that the imperishability of creation is not in what is created, is not in the art product, is not in the "thing" as it exists as an object, but in the procedure of it becoming what it is.[9]

The understanding of Black musical behavior--of the creative process--as **movement "with" existence** has pervaded and continues to shape, and influence the Black musical experience in America. Further, this concept of musical being and behaving makes clearly observable and understandable the resolute and infectious involvement that Blacks imbue in their experience of music. It may also acount for the fact that young and youth-oriented Americans and non-Americans continue to adopt, in overwhelming and ever-increasing numbers, this natural conception of being and musical behaving, in spite of other available and more dominant models. Briefly, this concept of behavior bespeaks of action, freedom, life, and how life actually feels and moves--a highly engaging concept in this time of seeking self-actualization.

Another point now presents itself: The question of whether the perceptual experience of different cultures are analogous or equivalent. It is erroneous to assume that because the Afro-American and the White cultures are so integrally related in experiences, and so easily interchange their use of, and response to, similar musical processes and structures, that similar and analogous connotations or associations are evoked and/or experienced in musical encounters. Leonard Meyer puts to rest one speculation in this area when he discusses E. von Hornbostel's observation that perceptual experience is one. Amplifying this thesis Meyer writes:

> Both music and life are experienced as dynamic processes--as motions differentiated both in shape and in quality. Such motions may be fast or slow, continuous or disjointed, precise or ambiguous, calm or violent, and so forth. Even experiences without literal, phenomenal motion are somehow polished stone, a jagged line--each depending partly upon our attitude toward it, is felt to exhibit some characteristic quality of motion and sound.
> ....
> The problem is not, as some have argued, whether music evokes connotations. . . . The question is whether similar musical processes and structures give rise to similar or analogous connotations in different cultures. A modest sampling of the evidence indicates these processes are cross-cultural.[10]

Meyer continues by emphasizing that similar concepts may be characterized differently in different cultures, or even within a single culture not because association is inconstant, but because the concept is viewed from different perspectives. One example illustrates this: the phenomenon of death and the myriad responses to it. Music behavior often

86

exemplified at funerals of Blacks in New Orleans is
highly objectionable to many Blacks not of that area.[11]

A study sponsored by the International Seminar on
Music Education for the purpose of their Fifth
Conference[12] showed that there are indeed many patterns
of music behaviors typical both of Americans in general
and of each of the several non-white groups in the
country. However, there was strong agreement on this
single idea: Afro-Americans' mode of behavior, when
involved in aesthetic encounters, is so pervasive in
current American society and has so strongly influenced
musical behaviors of others, as to be considered a
"norm." It is also suggested that this intercultural
mode of musical behavior permits a kind of flexibility
to be established in the mind and ear which in turn
makes possible more efficient moves to other and more
specific music styles and behavior. Using the tonal
memory of the ear has always been a critical musical
behavior among Blacks in that it has assisted them to
integrate and accommodate the diverse elements of the
two dominant American musical traditions.

It must be kept in mind that these elements are
not what remain constant from culture to culture. They
are simply tools--the musical vocabulary (scales,
modes, harmonic progressions and the like)--of the
culture. What does remain constant, however, is what
Leonard Meyer refers to as the psychology of human
mental processes: "the way in which the mind,
operating within the context of a culturally
established grammar, selects and organizes and
evaluates the musical materials presented to it. In
this context it is clear why Black musical behavior,
although bearing unique and easily identifiable
characteristics, is apt to differ widely within the
group and exist in very broad extremes. To paraphrase
Meyer, one may compare the diverse behavior styles of
the Black American with the diverse kinetic "behavior
styles of a piece of music. This unique behavior
stands out and influences our opinions of its character
as the musical behavior of a people is apt to shape our
opinions of their character.[13]

Numerous psychological studies support the
hypothesis that musical behavior is largely learned and
culturally determined. If we as educators accept this,
then we also must accept three important corollaries:
1) that music behavior is, first of all, an expression
of man's essential being; 2) that music behavior can

be shaped, modified and taught; and 3) music behavior is a reflection of culture and the feelings shared by individuals of that culture. These propositions are of extreme importance because they put the music educator in closer touch with how these behaviors function and come to be whatever they are. More than that, a commitment to these propositions should lead the music educator to understand, appreciate, and capitalize on the cultural pluralism that exists in schools today. Teachers, administrators, and citizens will see cultural differences as positive forces in the continuing development of a society which purports to possess a wholesome respect for the intrinsic worth of every individual. Thus, a primary aim in studying the music behavior of a group is to help children see the commonalities between various groups on the one hand, and to help them recognize, appreciate , and respect the differences on the other. This, in my opinion, is a highly accessible and realistic goal for music, indeed, for all of aesthetic education.

In one provocative and clearly written essay that gets directly at this problem, Bennett Reimer, educator and aesthetician, discusses seven major behavioral categories involved in aesthetic encounters. He shows that these categories contain within them any number of sub-categories and that all of these are at the level of generality where human beings actually function in their experience of the world. The seven behaviors he gives are: perceiving, reacting, producing, conceptualizing, analyzing, evaluating, and valuing. this paper in its narrow scope has focused primarily on three of these behaviors. **Reacting,** the total immersion of one's subjective being in perceived experiential qualities is "the payoff," as Reimer says, that accompanies the now-ness and "reality of sharing, being moved, being affected, being touched, being caught-up, sensing, empathizing." Obviously, aesthetic reaction as defined in these terms is inseparable from the behavior of aesthetic perception. **Producing** includes the acts of singing, playing, dancing, and the like. This behavior, in our sense, is an integral and necessary part of art/life encounters, which is to say that with Blacks, reacting deeply is highly contingent upon other behaviors, such as producing, that are a major means of **movement "with" existence** (perceiving and reacting) in aesthetic encounters. To state this in a different way is to say that to Blacks, the inner workings of their music making and consuming carry one along with the music

dynamics which are themselves analogous to--they are--
the experience of being and behaving. Finally, the
behavior of **valuing** includes admiring, approving,
liking, cherishing, respecting, treasuring, finding
satisfaction in, and identifying with. **Valuing** accrues
from the other behaviors and is short-circuited only
when there are obvious and/or subtle quests--on the
part of Blacks--for White approval.

Because Black musical behavior consists of, and is
so highly dependent upon, effective **Reacting,
Perceiving,** and **Producing** (all taking place
reciprocally, never in isolation of each other), the
highly important behavior of **Valuing** is a natural and
concomitant outcome. In this process of musical
behaving, feelings of acceptance occur through
effective **Reacting, Perceiving,** and **Producing** that
constitute the core of selfhood.

In closing, the following points discussed or
implied in this paper bear emphasizing. **First,** one
should avoid, at all cost, ethnocentricism in judging
music behavior of a culture. **Second,** despite broad and
obvious cultural differences among Black Americans,
they all share a common macro-culture due to their
African roots and their commonly shared experiences as
Blacks in America. **Third,** it is crucial for teachers
to understand and accept that Black students (indeed
others as well who share a good understanding of the
Black experience in America) will bring with them a
different view of citizenship in this republic.
Moreover, this view of citizenship is apt to strongly
influence their mode of appreciating, relating to, and
behaving with the experiences of music they encounter.
Fourth, the music behavior of any culture should be
viewed in terms of the culture from which it emerges.
Fifth, comparison of music behaviors of various
cultures or groups are often apt to fail in their basic
purpose. When such failures result, comparisons should
be avoided. **Sixth,** national and international
education and research organizations such as the Music
Educators National Conference, and the International
Seminar for Research in Music Education are currently
setting high priorities for the study of socio-music
behavior, defined as that behavior exhibited among and
within the variety of music cultures. It is notable
that research in music education today should be so
concerned with such behavior as to convene and gather
international thinkers agreeing on the fact that
research into socio-music behavior is the most basic

and most pressing task facing researchers and educators currently struggling with the problem of pluralism in music cultures. Such research and conferences already are contributing to the development of appropriate course content unique to particular cultures and, more specifically, are yielding highly exciting information regarding the ability of both the individual and groups to perceive and respond "appropriately" to the music of cultures other than their own. **Finally,** the study of Black Americans' music behavior is important not as an end in itself but as a means of understanding an important and fundamental truth: despite differences, no one culture or mode of behavior of a particular culture is ever intrinsically better than another. In a multicultural society such as America, there is an urgent need to learn and to understand **early** that cultural differences do not mean inferiority. Such differences merely involve alternative ways of feeling, looking at, and doing things. There is no one model music culture. Study of music behaviors is apt to provide us with insight not only into aspects of experience of which we were previously unaware, but may also help us to discover new and exciting human characteristics of individual, and most important, collective consciousness. One writer, Alexander Heard, noted for his writings on this problem, says the following: "The need for common goals and common ideals for the social glue that holds together people who are dependent upon each other has increased. Yet the sense of community has not. We are splintered--into geographic enclaves, subcultures variously defined. . . ."[15] The new discoveries of human characteristics of individual and collective consciousness then are even more necessary today, and such discoveries may be the most important humanistic lesson of our time!

NOTES FOR CHAPTER 4

1. This article is an adapted form of a paper presented by the author at the Fifth International Seminar on Research in Music Education (ISME) held in Mexico City, September 1975 (entitled "Music Behavior and Music Education in Different Cultural Settings"). Thirty (30) scholars representing twenty-three (23) countries

participated. Observer/Delegates from the various countries also attended.

2. John B. Hightower, "Who Are the Culturally Deprived?" **Saturday Review**, (July 16, 1790), p. 41.

3. Tony Heibut, **The Gospel Sound**. New York: Simon and Schuster, p. 17.

4. Jimmy Stewart, "Introduction to Black Aesthetics in Music," in **The Black Aesthetic**, ed., Addison Gayle, Jr., Garden City, New York: Doubleday and Company, Inc., 1971, pp. 81-96.

5. Ben Aning, Personal interview with Professor Aning during his professorship at the University of Michigan (Summer 1976). Content is also alluded to on page 4 of this chapter. "Musical Behavior and Music Education in African Countries," given by Aning at the **ISME conference** in 1975.

6. The article "Dance and Culture" by R.F. Thompson in **African Forum**, vol. 2#2 (Fall 1966) presents a precise and well-documented discussion of West African Dance and its relationship to music behavior of Blacks in the Americans.

7. Specific examples of such Korean dances are: the Choon-Aeng-Jun (Nightingale dance) and the Sal-Pu-Ri (to exercise the devil) dance. Descriptions of these dances are given in: Alan C. Heyman. **Dances of the Three-Thousand League Land**, Seoul, Korea: Dong-A Publishing Company, Ltd., 1966, pp. 20-21 & 39-40. Also during a research trip to South Dorea, I was able to observe, participate in, and document these and other dances. See: J. Standifer. **A Study of Korean Fold Songs and Related Music Acitivites of the Kyeongsang-Province..** A Rackham Research Project with Video-taped examples. Ann Arbor, Michigan: University of Michigan Graduate School, 1976 (Final Report).

8. Hightower, p. 41.

9. Stewart, pp. 81-96.

10. Leonard Meyer, "Universalism and Relativism in the Study of Ethnic Music." **Journal of**

Ethnomusicology, Vol. 4, NO. 2 (1960), pp. 51-52.

11. During such funerals, especially during the return march from the graveyard, jazz music is played to which the marchers and onlookers dance with the great and abandoned vigor. The famous tune, "Didn't He Ramble," is often associated with this ritual. The activity is well-documented in many sources (recorded and written) having to do with New Orleans jazz.

12. To acquaint Seminar participants with music behaviors and music education of the populations in the countries represented, a questionnaire seeking information on the Seminar topic was filled out by each participant. The participants(s) was urged to seek help in his task from a variety of carefully selected sources as a means of making resulting data representative of his country. Results, having been returned to the seminar chairman weeks prior to the conference, were tabulated and formed the basis for the semiar discussions.

13. Meyer, P. 52.

14. Bennet Reemer, "Aesthetic Behaviors in Music in **Toward Aesthetic Education.** Washington, D.C.: Music Educators National Conference, (1971) pp. 66-87.

15. Alexander Heard, "Priorities for Education in a Just Community," **The College Board Review,** n. 102 (Winter 1976-7), p. 6.

BIBLIOGRAPHY

Lee, Hey-ku, **A History of Korean Music.** Seoul. Korea: Ministry of Culture and Information, National Classical Institute, 1970, p. 33. Cited by Standifer in a Research Project on Korean Folk songs and Related Music Activities. Material in question resulted from a personal interview at Seoul National University with Professor Lee Hey-ku, 1976. Interview No. 2 on Korean dance, pp. 21-33.

Leonhard, Charles, "Human Potential and the Aesthetic Experience," **Music Educators Journal**, (April 1968), pp. 39-41; 109-111.

Standifer, James A. "Study of Korean Folk Songs and Related Music Activities of the Keongsang-Province." **Final Report of a Rackham Research Project.** Ann Arbor, Michigan: University of Michigan Graduate School, 1976. Videotaped examples accompany report.

Chapter 5

INTERFERENCE IN CROSS-CULTURAL COMMUNICATION

WITH HISPANIC STUDENTS: A SYMPTOM

Miguel Ruiz[*]

The following are some classic examples of cross-cultural communication misunderstanding between student and teacher, student and administrator, and student and student.

EXAMPLE I:

Actors: An Hispanic student (ranges anywhere from preschool age to death); A teacher (Anglo male or female).

Setting: Classroom

Action: The student has either by omission or commision warranted, from the perception of the teacher, a verbal reprimand.

Teacher: "Ralph didn't I tell the class to take out their books and open them up to page 10?" (Teacher is staring at Ralph.)

Ralph: (Lowers his vision and holds his posture.) Ralph is waiting for the teacher to focus away from him. If the teacher focuses away from him that will be the cultural cue that will permit him to respond in a corrective manner, in this case by taking out his book and opening it to page 10.

Dr. Ruiz is Coordinator of Latino Education at the Office of School and Community Relations, the Michigan Department of Education.

Reprinted with permission of the Progream for Educational Opportunity, School of Education, The University of Michigan from Charles D. Moody, ed., Cross-Cultural Communication in the Schools, Ann Arbor: Program for Educational Opportunity, The University of Michigan, 1978.

Teacher: (In an instructive tone) "I am talking to you Ralph. When someone talks to you, you should look at the person for eye-to-eye commununication." (In a commanding tone) "Now look at me when I talk to you." (There is no response from Ralph and the teacher perceives defiance, apathy, or Ralph's inability to understand English.)

Ralph: (With his vision lowered) He is still waiting for the teacher to focus away from his in order to initiate the demanded response. The teacher is still focused on Ralph. For Ralph to indulge in eye-to-eye communication when being "confronted" would mean defiance and disrespect which could only warrant more punishment. If the teacher persists in wanting a response from Ralph the teacher will either subdue him or force Ralph to defiance. This situation can only get worse in terms of class disruption unless the teacher focuses away from Ralph. However the situation couldn't get any worse for Ralph. The stigma that Ralph has "earned" (subdued, passive, withdrawn, dumb, etc) will remain with him in the eyes of his classmates and teacher.

EXAMPLE II:

Actors: A male Hispanic student: (ranges any-where from the point that the student "perceives" his self dignity to be at stake and is willing to risk consequences physical, expulsion, suspension, etc. in order to affirm his dignity). Risk-taking in defense of personal worth increases with a corres-ponding increase in physical size and/or in personal maturity, (this type of risk-taking behavior in general may be exhibited form about the age of twelve to death).

A school administrator: (Anglo male or female)

Setting: Junior high school

Action: The bell rings for 4th period; a group of three students, two Anglo and one Hispanic, are still conversing in a group in the hallway.

Administrator: Walks into the hallway right after the ringing of the 4th period bell. The administrator sees the group of students and approaches to say "You should be in class boys." The tone of the administrator is generally in consonance with how he or she views that particular group of boys. If the group is a "fine group" of boys then the tone is one of prompting. Conversely if the group is a "rowdy bunch" of boys then the tone is commanding. If a prompting tone is uttered by the administrator then chances are that the boys will respond to the prompting and will eventually go into into their class with that incident forgotten by the parties involved. If the tone of the administrator is commanding there is a greater possibility that the boys will feel they must respond in kind. There is a great possibility that in this instance there will be marked culutural differences in behavior on the part of the Hispanic student as compared to his two Anglo peers.

Boys: The two Anglo students will reluctuantly walk away, commenting "that Mr. So-and-So thinks he is big, but I'll get even with him, just wait and see." And sure enough Mr. So-and-So might have flat tires or an egg on his car at some later time.

On the other hand the Hispanic student is forced (win or lose) to defend his dignity "on site" because walking away is cowardly, deceitful, or a sign of weakness. Because of this invisible cultural code the Hispanic holds his ground to defend his challenged personal worth. Hopefully the administrator will de-emphasize the personal confrontation tone.

Administrator: Perceiving the marked difference in the behavior of the two Anglos as compared to the Hispanic, the Hispanic is viewed as defiant: "Didn't I tell you to go to class." This depersonalized command creates more confrontation which leads to the eventual demise of the Hispanic via expulsion, suspension, or discipline, since the administrator has the power of the system.

EXAMPLE III:

Actors: A male Hispanic student (age ranges from kindergarten to death); Anglo students (ages range from preschool to death.)

Setting: The playground.

Action: The Anglo students are playing, for example, football.

Hispanic: "Can I play with you?" The Hispanic wants to join in the "group activity."

Anglos: Their perception is that the Hispanic thinks he can "play football well."

Anglo assumptions: If the Hispanic cannot play the sport (football) well then he will be given low status within the group. The peer group rule of status is based on ability and upper class dominance. Peer group status based on football ability is accepted by everyone in the group except by the Hispanic. The Hispanic has a different cultural code relating to status in groups.

Hispanic assumption: Self-worth is not based on expertise in any area, including football; neither is it based on a specific activity. Self-worth for the Hispanic is internal and individualistic. It is normally not determined by external ability or compared to others in a group. Group members will more often than not be viewed as team members and not as rival competitors. The Hispanic will award everyone with personal worth unless they prove themselves unworthy.

Let's say that in the course of the game an upper classmate (Anglo) with good football abilities (high status) hits the Hispanic in the same casual way this Anglo student has been hitting other low-status peers. These low-status injured peers are tolerant (at least behaviorally) of the punishment because of the existence of the group's status code. When this upper-classmate hits or abuses the Hispanic, the Hispanic will feel his personal worth has been challenged. If the Hispanic defends his self-worth the rest of the group will castigate him at every opportunity for having defied "rules" which are invisible to the Hispanic. Without friends and with a lot of enemies, the Hispanic finds it difficult to stay in school.

It is not uncommon for a teacher or administrator to comment: He was a bright and model student **in the classroom"** (emphasis added).

Please note that in the three examples given not one had to do with the actual practice of teaching. In all these examples there was a spirit of **personalized confrontation** unknowingly initiated by those with the dominant cultural perception.

How can cross-cultural communication misunderstandings be prevented? By learning about the cultural values and perceptions of others. The Hispanics alone comprise a myriad of distinct cultures and subcultures which run a vast continuum. It would be difficult for any teacher to understand the subtle potential cultural communication difficulties which might arise in one classroom with only ten Hispanics. Given the practical impossibility of learning about all the potential cultural misunderstanding which might arise, then how do we minimize the potential for cross-cultural misunderstanding in our teaching and learning environments?

First let us recall the above examples and draw attention to the observation that of the examples given, none had to do with actual teaching/learning communication. In all the examples the teacher, the administrator, and the upperclassmate got side-tracked by indulging in personalized confrontation and expecting the Hispanic to be predictable by their own clutural expectations.

In attempting to respond to the above question of how to prevent cross-cultural misunderstanding I'll pose still another question: Has the presence of a dominant cultural climate interfered with learning and development in our schools? Let me address myself to this latter question first.

Since the inception of the American common school, teacher educators, teachers, and curriculum developers have been the "accidental" force behind the melting pot ideology. Please note that the emphasis is on teacher **educators, teacher,** and curriculum **developers.** As these actors played their educational roles they provided the fringe "benefit" of their Anglo-Saxon values and world-view, thereby perpetuating a pervasive Anglo-centric cultural dominance in the American common schools. While these teacher educators, teachers, and curriculum developers (the vast majority white and European) were, relatively speaking, prepared to teach and develop the curricula of the common schools, few, if any until very recently, received formal training about teaching and/or transmitting their culture.

Traditionally, the American common school has not been designed to provide for the scientific teaching and transmitting of culture; nonetheless the American common schools have done a remarkable job of being consistent in their daily **accident** of maintaining an Anglo-centric cultural domination over the school environment. This effect has been caused because administrative, faculty, and policy-making positions have been dominated by Anglo-centric personnnel.

It is important to understand that here lies the fault: a teaching-learning environment which is culturally biased. It is postulated that this cultural bias is common in our schools and will be difficult to alter by single attempts like revising the school curricula to reflect racial/ethnic representation. As an illustration, let's say a particular school district has been quite concerned about ensuring representation of Hispanics in their social studies textbooks, K-6. The district has now purchased the best text available and distributes it to the social studies teachers for class use.

Setting: The social studies classroom. The classroom has ten Hispanics, children of blue collar working-class parents. The rest of the students and the teacher are white. The other students have parents who are in the blue collar or the white collar working-class.

Action: The purchased textbooks are exceptionally sensitive to minorities; one particular page has a picture of a Hispanic wearing a business suit at work. The teacher interprets for the class the significance of the picture in question. "This picture proves that if you're ambitious enough you can have a good job no matter who you are (black, Hispanic, white)."

Neither the Hispanic students, the white students, nor the teacher have ever been in daily contact with a Hispanic white collar worker. They all know Jose, the janitor, but other than him there are no Hispanics employed by the school. All the white collar workers in the building are white.

Consequently the teacher and the school environment convey the real message to all the students in the class. Hispanics are not ambitious. Jose the janitor is not ambitious and Hispanics (as evidenced by their absence in the ranks of school staff and administration) have seldom been ambitious. The inference is that there are "some exceptions to the rule," like the Hispanic in the textbook.

It is not being suggested that review of curriculum content for racial-cultural biases or stereotypes is not an important educational objective. Any attempt to treat the symptom must be appreciated for what it can do. But one must understand that the existence of cross-cultural misunderstandings in our schools is only symptomatic of a deeper illness, and while the treatment of the symptom is important to the curing process, it is not treating the cause of the illness.

In the example above, the bias of the teacher had not been affected by the classroom use of the racial/ethnic-sensitive social studies textbooks. And the existence of this culturally biased school environment, as shown by the unbalanced racial composition of the school staff, has not been affected by the mere purchasing and use of new social studies textbooks. Review of textbook curricula in this case is only one of many education activities or concepts which are offered as panaceas to the racial illnesses in our educational environments both in suburbia and in the inner cities. It alone is not enough.

How then do we minimize the potential for cross-cultural communication difficulties in our teaching and learning environments? By affecting a cure of the cause of the symptom. I suggest that the cause of cross-cutural communication difficulties has been the continued existence of Anglo-centric cultural dominance in American common schools, American businesses, American politics, American industry, and American media. The American common school should not bear the weight of the whole cure; the American common school is only part of the illness.

How then do we begin the cure in the arena of the American common school? There are some factors which need serious consideration in light of our schools' inability to continue to support racial ethnic intolerance: We need to recognize that the victims of racial intolerance are all of us who have a stake in this world!

We need to take a serious and hard look at the effects of racial staffing in our schools, whether it be in the suburb or in the inner city. A school staff which does not reflect racial/ethnic diversity creates a fertile environment for cross-cultural misunderstanding. And the mono-racial staff which holds racial stereotypes and transmits them to students is isolated in its stereotypes from confronting the negation of those stereotypes through personal and daily contact with other racial group members. The environment which engenders cross-cultural misunderstanding is not altered. Our school staff should at least resist being host to our societal illness.

Our students are affected as well. The existence of mono-racial staffing in our schools delivers a powerful message to all students involved. For students who happen to be of the same race as the staff, a sense of superiority, genetic advantage, and a racially-exclusive sense of ownership is engendered. For the racially different student, the absence of staff role models with which they can identify creates a void in their sense of "wanting to be like...," "wanting to do like." For them only a lack of a sense of ownership of the school environment and school jobs in engendered.

Discussion Questions

1. What might administrators do that would prevent communication misunderstandings such as those listed in the chapter? Examples I, II and III.

2. Why is it important for teachers in a multicultural setting to be aware of minority cultural conventions?

3. How does the Hispanic student differ from the Anglo student in terms of adult authority? Explain in detail.

4. How does assumption about other cultures affect communication in the schools between the following groups?

CHAPTER 6

AN HISTORICAL RATIONAL FOR JAZZ IN MUSIC EDUCATION

Reginald T. Buckner

Jazz is an American phenomenon that came about as the result of a synthesis of two equally strong, dominant and potent cultures from the Old World. Although jazz is viewed as a twentieth century invention, it took a 200 year-long process of cross-fertilization between African and European elements to give maturity to this art form. With 80 years of history, this music has established a firm oral and written tradition in both cultures that is uniquely American; it has also survived and maintained at least three levels of visibility. Past styles such as New Orleans traditional jazz, swing and bebop still remain popular among many music lovers. Secondly, the present or current style in each period received enough recognition in order for many musicians to make a living. Thirdly, the future oriented or avante-garde styles in each period have always been spearheaded by creative-experimental jazz musicians who have turned continously to exploring new ways of expression. All in all, jazz, an American classic, has constantly transformed, either picking up new melodic structures, new harmonic systems, new rhythmic patterns, timbres and/or forms.

Unfortunately, the American music education establishment has historically made little use of jazz. With more and more attention given to this subject starting with the Yale Seminar in 1963, the concern reached a peak with the 1967 Tanglewood Symposium. The Tanglewood Declaration emphatically stated:

> Music of all periods, styles, forms and cultures belongs in the curriculum. The musical repertory should be expanded to involve music of our time in its rich variety, including currently popular teenage music and avant-garde music. American folk music, and the music of other cultures.[1]

Some music educators recognized that there were very serious problems in music education because of the lack of jazz and other non-Western music in the curriculum.

Allen Scott described the environment in 1968:

> Where were we 10 years ago with jazz educa-
> tion? We, the jazz educators, were around,
> here and there, keeping our heads down lest
> they get chopped off. We were at odds, in
> most cases, with the music education
> establishment in our schools, very much on
> the defensive over the concept that jazz had
> a place in music education.[2]

When four jazz bands performed at the MENC Seattle
Convention in 1968, the National Association of Jazz
Educators (NAJE) was created; thus, the largest jazz
education movement was officially launched. Since
then, music educators have increasingly been made aware
of this serious problem as it has affected both
teachers and students. Simmons, Standifer and other
music educators have kept issues before the profession.
Simmons said, "we can no longer send our middle-class,
lecture-oriented teachers unarmed educationally into
the inner cities."[3] Standifer, however, expounds that
the problem is greater than the inner city. In an
article, "Cultural Pluralism and the Education of Music
Teacher," he described a typical student who enters the
real world of music teaching and discovers it to be
multicultural. In knowing that some answers are in
students taking courses in blues, jazz, popular and
world music, he responded emphatically that "we need to
blast open teacher education programs and their rigid,
provincial, and often obsolete requirements to permit a
broader range or useful options for students...It is
obvious that major shifts in content and procedures
must take place if we in teacher education are simply
to stand still, let alone move with the rigid changes
in society and the world."[4] The MENC's **Teacher
Education in Music: Final Report** acknowledged the
recommendations of Tanglewood regarding curriculum
change and initiated first steps for this to happen.
The Report spoke to the needs of future music teachers
in their preparation to be able to improvise and
knowledgeable of other musics (including jazz).[5]
Unfortuately, ten years later, the Tanglewood
Symposium Revisited conveyed that the problems
identified at Tanglewood are still with us.

In spite of the poor progress report, non-Western
musics have made some gains in music education in the
last decade. There are more workshops and clinics
devoted to the subject in the **Music Educators Journal**

and the entire subject of jazz education in the NAJE **Educator**. In 1979, it was estimated that there were over 32,000 school jazz bands across the country.[6] Prominent and well respected musicians, such as David Baker, Jerry Coker, Gunther Schuller and Billy Taylor, have helped tremendously with their strong endorsements and support for jazz in colleges, major symphony orchestras and funding agencies. They have been most significant in leading the jazz education movement to the point that jazz is an important curricular item. However, with this recent surge, there is a danger if jazz is incorporated into the curriculum for the wrong reasons. There is a deep rooted past that should be explored before dealing with jazz as to why it should be and how it can be incorporated into the curriculum.

Historical Background: Americanisms versus Europeanisms

Throughout the history of the United States, this country has relied heavily on European culture. The arts, especially music, have looked to Europe for its wisdom, training, musical tastes and models. American musicians have traveled to the European continent for either conservatory or private study. In addition, the works of major European composers still dominate performances by major American symphonic orchestras and operatic companies as well as serve as the basis for American college and university music curriculum. Furthermore, Alan Rich points out in 1980," a career at home for an American-born conductor is still up against vestiges of old snobbery that attaches automatic cultural cachets to European manner and accent."[7] He cited that of the ten orchestras generally regarded as America's finest - or, at least, largest in terms of budget - none is currently being led by an American.

On the other hand, Europeans have gone on record for encouraging Americans to be themselves and to develop their own art. As early as 1892, some 116 years after the birth of this nation, Antonin Dvorak, said to his American colleagues to look to their own cultural heritage for inspiration, to value it, to explore it, and to cultivate it for new classical works. "Look homeward and cultivate your own garden."[8] Douglas Moore's Foreword in **American's Music** expressed similar sentiments:

We are ex-Europeans, to be sure, and as such
have responsibilities to the preservation
and continuance of European culture, but we
are also a race - and a vigorous one - and it
is increasingly evident that we are capable
of developing cultural traditions of our
own.[9]

Also, for the record, Europeans have maintained
consistent support for jazz.   Davis points out,
"Generally speaking, jazz has been more readily
accepted in foreign countries than in the United
States...European has made significant progress in
putting together a jazz community with enough political
and economic muscle to support jazz."[10]

America's music education system has been deemed
successful when assessing its growth and development.
From an early singing school orientation to the 1978-79
Ann   Arbor   Symposium,   where   music   educators
successfully interacted with noted psychologists in
the area of learning, music education has constantly
kept abreast in trends with other fields in education.
It   has   involved   millions   of   students   since   its
conception into the curriculum when Lowell Mason
introduced music education to the Boston Public Schools
in 1838. A brief assessment of Mason's contribution is
in order here to be able to adequately deal with the
subject of jazz as being part of today's music
education curriuclum.

Mason, a well-known musician and writer, received
national attention as an organizer and with his eight
editions of the Manual **of the Boston Academy of Music,
for Instruction in the Elements of Vocal Music on the
System of** Pestalozzi   This book became the major text
for many many early music education programs throughout
the country.   Birge acknowledged Mason as an early
pioneer in music education and what his influence has
meant.

When   in   1838   the   Boston   School   Board
authorized   the   introduction   of   music   by
public authority as a regular subject of
instruction, termed by the trustees of the
Boston Academy of Music the "Magna Charta of
Music Education in America," their action
was virtually a vote of confidence in the
musical possibilities inherent in children,

106

brought about largely through the activities of one man, Lowell Mason."[11]

By virtue of Mason's outstanding contributions, many consider him "the Father of American Music Education."

Where as Birge places Mason in a strategic position in music education history, recent research provides a different perspective. Howard Ellis carefully point out that Mason's system which he thought was based on Pestalozzian principles was not so in nature. Allen Britton accusses Mason as being the most important historical figure in music education who did not understand the principles of the Pestallozian method. Robert W. John points out Elam Ives, not Mason, had a clear understanding of both the principles and history of Pestalozzi. Gilbert Chase, who describes Mason's contributions in details, also states: "On American music tradition, as presented by our early New England music makers, into the background, while opening the gates for a flood of colorless imitations of the 'European master.' "[12] Britton adds "that the first teachers of music in the public schools who were singing-school teachers and the musical reformers brought into our schools the music of the reform -pretty, bland, unexciting - music of other nationalistic idioms, particularly English and German."[13]

Mason has been both praised and criticized. However, it would be unfair to think of him in isolation and that his decisions were made autocratically. He, like any other leader, was in tuned with the times and therefore knew the flow of the music education movement. His place in music education history must be considered in the same manner that leaders in other fields are normally perceived. Not to take anything away from him, Mason was the "tip of the iceberg" of the American music education value system of the mid-1800s. These preceding accusations pointing to Mason's negative contributions to American music education raise some controversial issues especially since Europeanisms still dominate American music education today: (1) is it possible that the system that evolved from Mason's so-called Pestalozzian adaption was a transplant European system and therefore was not based on the ideals and principles of which this country was founded? (2) is it possible that the sentiments expressed by Moore reflect the general attitude of this nation in that it is only ex-European in culture, and not ex-Africans, ex-Asians, and Native Americans, that can provide the ingredients for an American cultural tradition and that also includes music education? (3) is it possible that this country has never created an American music education system of the people, by the people and for the people? Furthermore, what were the Pestalozzian principles that Mason tried to adopt and what significance do they hold in today's music education in American?

Without any doubt, European music has and still holds a superior position in american culture, especially in music education. The American system is an European transplant. Britton points out the nonuse of American music in the early curriculum and that it has only been recently that a few examples of American music appeared in modern school textbooks. As for the general attitude of this nation, Moore's omissions imply that ex-Africans, ex-Asians and Native Americans have nothing to contribute to the development of American cultural traditions. Music from these ethnic groups have generally been overlooked and even when they are included, the music is not accepted for what it is worth and on its own terms. Moreover, music educators have consistently jumped on foreign methodological bandwagons in an effort to present a successful music education approach to American students.

During this century, foreign methods, namely the Orff Approach, the Kodaly System, the Dalcroze Eurythmics and the Suzuki Method, have received substantial support in American music education. The Orff Approach, developed by the German composer-educator Carl Orff, begins with simple rhythms. It is through the rhythm of the child's speech and movement that the child learns to explore music. Eventually the child learns to improvise, use bodily movements, play instruments and write their improvisations. The Kodaly Method, developed by the Hungarian composer-educator Zoltan Kodaly, essentially is a system of sight-reading which leads the child into the understanding of musical notation. Kodaly whose great knowledge and love for the music of the peasants of Hungary, chose this music as the vehicle through which to teach children. He felt that the child naturally learns his musical mother tongue - i.e. the folk music of his own country -before other music. Dalcroze Eurythmics, developed by Emil Jaques-Dalcroze, professes that unless the learner experiences aspects of music by bodily movement, the music performed by the individual later will be mechanical, without feeling and the expressive responsiveness essential to genuine musicianship may never develop. The approach consists of free bodily response to music that is improvised at the piano. Shinicki suzuki, who discovered that Japanese children could speak Japanese easily, felt that this training or this "perfect educational method: their mother tongue, "could be applied to other faculties. With emphasis on the "ear" instead of the "eye" pre-schoolers and/or young adolescents were able to perform very difficult compositions in a short time period.

The following observations are common denominators in the Orff, Kodaly, Dalcroze and Suzuki approaches to music education. First of all, each method was developed by foreigners and had origins in foreign countries: Orff, a German, Kodaly, a Hungarian, Dalcroze, a Swiss and Suzuki, A Japanese. Secondly, all are methods in music instruction even though the various labels, such as approach and system, are included in the titles. Thirdly, each method concentrates on developing and establishing basic musicianship. Fourthly, each method starts where the child is in both life and musical experiences in order to move the student successfully into the "world of music." Orff uses the child's speech and movement; Kodaly, the hand; Dalcroze, bodily movement; and Suzuki, the physical size matched with a string instrument. Finally, goals range from helping the child to be creative musicians through the reading and writing involvement of musical notation. In all methods, the step by step methodology provides a procedure that assists children to acquiring desired musical behaviors or basic and/or comprehensive musicianship.

In Mason's attempt to adopt Pestalozzian principles, it is evident that he was striving to present a program in comprehensive musicianship. Mason's Manual, which focused on correct singing and instruction in the elements of music, adopted little of the Pestalozzian philosophy, curricular content, and method:

1. to teach sounds before signs - to make the child sing before he learns the written notes or their names.

2. to lead the child to observe, by hearing and imitating sounds, their resem-

blences and differences, their agreeable and disagreeable effects, instead of explaining these things to him - in short, to make him active instead of passive in learning.

3. to teach but one thing at a time - rhythm, melody, expression are taught and practiced separately before the child is called to the difficult task of attending to all at once.

4. to make children practice each step of each of these divisions, until they are master of it, before passing to the next.

5. to give the principles and theory after practice, and as an induction from it;

6. to analyze and practice the elements of articulate sound in order to apply them to music. [14]

Instead, music education concentrated on "the eye" or on skills and de-emphasized "the ear" or the development of oral/aural skills. Birge pointed out, "how to teach music reading became the paramount question of the age and it was in fact the first problem which school-music set itself seriously to solve." [15] In an effort to correct this mistake, music educators in recent years have adopted foreign music methods for these reasons.

The success referred to earlier in music education has been attested to the large numbers of American children involved in both vocal and instrumental music. In most cases, instrumental and vocal music students have learned the basic principles of music reading that enabled them to reproduce the notes on the printed page. However, the acquistion of this skill is only one phase of musicianship. "Seeing" the notes has its limitations in that these students generally are ill-equipped in ear training, lacking in creativity, and unable to perform without the score. According to the "Musical Behaviors Chart" of **Instructional Objectives in Music** (See Table 6:1), the areas of concern are performance (improvisation and reproduction), reading and writing, listening and other cognitive behaviors. Collectively, both

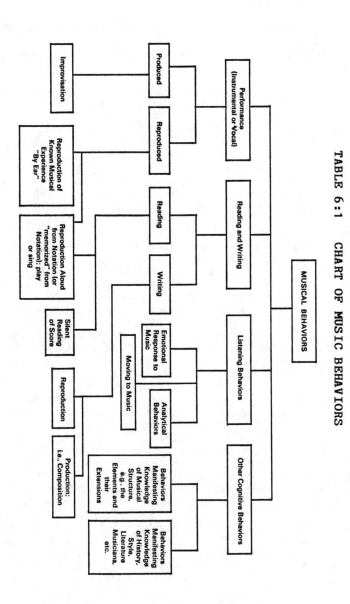

TABLE 6:1   CHART OF MUSIC BEHAVIORS

students groups have been short changed in comprehensive musicianship development. Because of a lack of encouragement in improvisation, creativity and American ethnic musics into the curriculum, american music education has been unable to produce a system that would foster and develop comprehensive musicianship in their students.

An American Method in Music Education Based on an American Music: Jazz

Jazz is America's only indigenous musical art form. After 200 years of the cross-fertilizing of European and African musics, the proper musical foundation was established firmly for a new musical creation: jazz. In this music, there is an oral/aural tradition as well as a newly developed written tradition. In the last 80 years, the jazz oral tradition, both instrumentally and vocally, has continued to expand from tonality to atonality in melody and in harmony; and the written tradition was introduced in the 1920's with relatively simple tunes and arrangements and also has continued to develop to the poin of complex, complicated arrangements and compositions. Jazz, a vocally oriented music and a highly skilled art has its roots in the American people. Therefore, a music that is created, listened to, enjoyed and experienced in many ways by Americans, should be the basis for an American music education methodology.

Largely through the efforts of the black musician, the art of improvisation in music was kept alive. After a 200 year period of musical cross-fertilization, a cadre of unique musicians made this musical synthesis of African and European musics which laid the foundation for jazz to develop. The next obvious step was for the next generation of twentieth century musicians to make application of these musical principles to their instruments in the form of improvisation. For 80 years, musical characteristics developed in jazz as can be witnessed in early New Orleans, Jazz, Chicago jazz, swing, Bob, Cool, Third Stream, Free Jazz, and the present jazz/rock or fusion jazz. Jazz musicians can spontaneously converse using melodies from major, minor, blues, chromatic and other synthetic scales; harmonies from the basic triads to seventh chords, ninth chords, eleventh chords, thirteenth chords, fourth, etc.; rhythms using whole, half, quarter, eighth, sixteenth, thirty-second and sixty-fourth notes in four-four, three-four, five-four, seven-four and multi-metered times, slowly, moderated or rapidly; forms or structures on the blues, rhythm changes, standard songs, and jazz compositions.

When the written arrangements were introduced into the jazz phenomenon in the early 20s, newer demands were then made on the jazz musician. Not only was it a mandate for the musician to use "the ear," it was now necessary for them to use "the eye" in order to read the charts that were written by the new school of jazz arrangers and composers. Literature now ranges from the early Jelly Roll Martin, Earl "Fatha" Hines and Fletcher Henderson charts to the present Stan Kenton, Maynard Ferguson, Thad Jones-Mel Lewis, Quincy Jones and Toshiko Akiyoshi-Lew Tabackin charts. These scores are notated and rooted in American sounds and bodily movements. Incorporated in this new American notated music are charts from the simple to the complex in melodic, rhythmic and harmonic elements. From the standpoint of musicology, this musical literature is a twentieth century phenomenon and therefore the next step in the history of musical notation.

It seems obvious that this new oral and written music should serve as a basis for American musican education. Jazz, an American phenomenon, is a music of the American soil. Its idioms are firmly based in Afro-American music and can be found in many forms of other American musics. It is the only folk music or indigenous music created in this country (i.e. America's ethnic groups still maintain their folk music from their mother countries and in those same traditions). Jazz in a complete development of comprehensive musicianship based on the oral tradition of African and European sounds and later to develop a written tradition based on the oral tradition.

How the traditional jazz musician learned "through the ear" and later "through the eye" to develop reading and writing skills can provide today's American music educator-researcher answers to current music education problems and also provide new territories and ground from which to unlock the mysteries of music learning. To solve this problem could provide the answers of how to successfully get music students - both band, orchestra, choir students and general music students - to develop comprehensive musicianship. In jazz, there are many built-in learing activities: bodily movement, singing, improvisation, composition listening, reading, and music history.

113

Finally, it is unique that many jazz musicians respect and have a deep appreciation for classical music. To think that jazz would replace classical music in the curriculum would not be the case. How jazz musicians develop, researchers need to deal with and find answers.

The statement was made earlier regarding jazz being placed into the curriculum for the wrong reasons. In recent years, jazz has made progress in being placed in the curriculum. In John Berry's article, "High School Jazz Bands: the State of the Art in the '70's," he cited that there were "around 16,000 high school jazz bands, and a good 600 college jazz bands in the country."[17] A later figure cited by John Kuzmich is over 32,000 jazz bands in junior high, senior high schools and colleges. Thomas Ferguson cited that there were at least 22 universities now granting degrees in jazz education or jazz performance; three offer Masters degrees.[18]

To the contrary, the last decade, Gunther Schuller calls school jazz a disaster area. He indictes school jazz is an illusion and rip off in the following points:

1.   Hundreds of mediocre musicians have found jobs as jazz educators.

2.   The bands play mostly arrangements by secondrate arrangers; and the most disturbing thing is that improvisation hardly is involved.

3.   The band creates an illusion that the kids are getting a jazz education. Jazz education has become an entrenched bureaucracy. And how should the kids know they're not realy playing jazz?[19]

Warwick L. Carter stated, "this writer does realize that mainly through the big bands are large numbers of students awarded the opportunity to participate in the jazz experiencing. However, there is doubt as to whether most of the big bands are actually engaged in performing jazz, in its truest form. Some critics argue that these bands are no more than concert bands with a rhythm section and/or very big and "loud" rock bands."[20]   Larry Ridley strongly indites the jazz

114

education community for the omission of black musicians in the movement. He states emphatically:

> Until we stop this subliminally racist attitude in the projection of jazz as some diluted homogenized "American music," we are adding fuel to the fires of cultural bias/"ripoff" and the abrasiveness of ethnic confrontation and communication. No musician/educator has difficulty in accepting European classical music as the diverse musical styles as defined by its leading proponents, i.e. Bach, Mozart, Beethoven, Brahms, Stravinsky, Bartok, Schoenberg, etc. Why then, the reluctance to accept Jazz as African-American classical music when its stylistic diversity has been innovated and defined by Joplin, Jelly Roll, Armstrong, Handy, James P. Waller, Ellington, Bassie, Hawkins, "Prez," Eldridge, Redman, Benny Carter, Fletcher Henderson, Lunceford, Christian, Monk, Powell, Gillespie, Roach, Miles, coltrane, Ornette, George Russell, etc. etc. etc.[21]

There is also a growing concern among noted black jazz musicians, namely; Ron Carter, Lou Donaldson, Rene McClean, and others, who raise similar questions. They question the lack of black professional jazz musicians as teachers at all levels where jazz is performed; the absence of large numbers of black high school and college students in jazz ensembles; the overabundance of disco and other popular music and not jazz pumped into America's black communities by black radio stations; and the recent and obvious support of jazz in attendance at clubs and concert halls by more white than black American. Why?

A cultural phenomenon is in the making. Before jazz was understood by white Americans, it was not considered music, and still to many, jazz has not reached the heights of European music. However, largely due to many scholars who have studied that music by listening to live and especially to recorded jazz, and analyzing it, **some** of its main features have been captured and identified. What these analysts have discovered is that jazz is melody, harmony, timbre, rhythm, dynamics and form. Other parts have been identified and labeled such as riffs, scales, chords, breaks, bridges, turnbacks, etc., etc. Thousands of solos have been transcribed; so students of jazz with excelent reading skills can play Parker, Coltrane, Armstrong, Tatum, Jelly Roll and others. In addition, today's music stores are flooded with new books on jazz improvisation. These method books have identified the improvisation content of melodic and harmonic elements and they instruct a student how to successfully use this information. If they "mix" these musical "ingredients" together at certain times as dictated by a jazz piece, they will be somewhat successful improvisors. The question can be raised: what has been created?

To the contrary, this is another form of a continuation of mis-education in music education. With the proper use of these improvisation books and transcriptions, musicians can move quickly in developing the art of improvisation. But to exclude the cultural experiences and most importantly, the creativity, as the giant of jazz experienced, will once again shortchange the new generation of students in jazz. Jazz is a mastery of many levels of musicianship in order to have a conversation among other players; but jazz is also an individual player's own expression. Gunter Schuller once again cites this as a problem:

> Still, I think that the danger people have been speaking about for decades, the danger of jazz becoming an endangered species once you try to codify it and put it in a curriculum, **it has come true.** There's no question but that danger is real, it's ever present, and it takes a very imaginative and open-minded director or faculty of such a program - or people sensitive to the very special qualities and special needs of jazz. But by now, music educators have become a big business in this country; there's security in it with very little concern about what's happening to the music and to the students. I'm very worried about it. I find the whole idea of stamping out these thousands of little Coltranes and McCoy Tyners and thises and thats just frightening. And I must say, its' a danger we never had before, not to this extent.[22]

A culture phenomenon that runs parellel to Mason's mis-reading or Pestalozzi is in the making with the acceptance of jazz in the curriculum. As Mason and his followers took what they wanted from the Pestalozzian based music education, they left the true essence or the heart of its content. Frederick Mayer explained Pestalozzi's emphasis on the importance of art in the curriculum:

> This was not only an outlet for the creative talents of children, but it also gave them a consciousness of their powers and it developed intellectual discipline. Children had to participate in art and not be mere bystanders. Instead of learning about melodies they should be encouraged to sing and play instruments. By necessity, their progress would be slow, and their ideas would differ from the ideas of adults, but the teacher should never exhibit an attitude of disapproval or condescension. Again, this meant a revolution in the curriculum. It implies an emphasis on the integrity of the student and a stress upon his creative abilities.[23]

American's music education system lacks its own creative approach and methodology. Mayer continues, "knowledge depends upon its motivational foundations; words are only secondary instruments."[24] Translated, the "words" in music are the elements of melody, harmony, rhythm, timbre and form. Americans, for the most part, are not formally motivated in music. There is a dire need for "the fine line" to be defined and developed in an American music educational approach, as the aforementioned foreign methods did for their cultures, in order for music education to be able to reach its own people. Jazz is American's music. The smaller parts in this music are present and are the real substance for which Americans can begin to absorb music aesthetically.

> According to my experience, success depends upon whether what is taught to children commends itself as true, through being closely connected with their own personal observation and experience. Without this foundation truth must seem to them to be little better than a plaything, which is beyond their comprehension, and therefore a burden.[25]

117

Rationale for Jazz in School Music Program

America has created its own music and it is jazz. On the other hand, America has not created its own music educational system. In the true essense of the methods by Pestalozzi, Orff, Kodaly, Dalcroze, and Suzuki, the American system must have its foundation in America's music. The music that could best serve as the springboard leading to the development of comprehensive musicianship is jazz. However, for music education to promote a "patchworking" approach to this important matter would be as detrimental to the profession as Mason's mistake. Therefore, those vital steps in how jazz musicians learned in both areas of the oral/aural and written traditions should be identified; and the only way this information can be obtained properly is through research. The fact that music education has been vulnerable in the last decade indicates the urgency of placing this research high on the list of priorities. The reason are obvious:

1. An American music methodology would bring about cohesiveness in the music teaching profession.

2. The American methodology would have its foundation in its own music.

3. The American methodology would establish a direct path of music learning (i.e. from the "sounds of music" to the "signs of music").

4. American music education would come closer to accomplishing "music for every child. . . every child for music".

5. With a music education that possible would increase the literacy rate, the main outcome, which is music appreciation, would produce positive kickbacks and thereby solidify the position of music in the curriculum.

Meanwhile, until the need for this research is realized, music education must attempt to recitfy the problem. To begin with, music education should enforce the recommendations in the **MENC Teacher Education in Music: Final Report** regarding music teachers being able to improvise and also to be knowledgeable of other musics including jazz. Since this report, several states have listed in their certification guidelines the requirement of acquiring improvisational skills. To move this forward, the profession would be putting first things first.

Many college and university music departments now offer courses in jazz improvisation. Leading jazz educators also offer workshops during the summer and through extension classes. Above all, almost every major metropolitan area and even some smaller cities have "qualified" jazz musicians who can teach improvisation. Music stores are stocked with jazz materials which can also assist the beginning, intermediate and advanced jazz learners. Music teachers can find Jamey Aebersold's 21 volumes on jazz improvisation very effective jazz aids. Of this 21 volume series, **A New Approach to Jazz Improvisation, Revised 5th Edition** (volume 1) (1979), **Jazz and Rock: Nothin' But Blues** (volume 2) (1976), **The II-V-I Progression** (volume 3) (1974), and **Gettin' It Together** (volume 21) are highly recommended. Each volume comes with a long playing record and an instructional book. The recording presents a rhythm section of piano, bass and drums in stereo. This allows the student to practice improvisation with the rhythm section.

Jerry Coker has published both textbooks and methods books. **Improvising Jazz** (1964), **The Jazz Idiom** (1975) and **Listening to Jazz** (1978) explaining the unique features and process in jazz. Coker's **Patterns for Jazz** (1970) also co-authored with Jimmy Casale, Gary Campbell, and Jerry Greene, provides the learner with many improvisational patterns to incorporate in jazz tunes. Another prolific writer is David N. Baker who has published **Jazz Improvisation** (1969) which is a comprehensive method of study for all players. Baker's most significant publication for teachers is his **Jazz Pedagogy** (1979). This book is a comprehensive method of jazz education for both teacher and student. Robert Klotman, writer of the foreword, states that **"Jazz Pedagogy** provides the music education profession with a comprehensive text book on every aspect of instruction as it affects the school jazz program."[28]

The jazz aids that have been listed are just a few. They can assist teachers tremendously, especially those who are just beginning. However, America has a need for its music educators "to rise to the occasion" of establishing its own American music methodology. In

Mason's situation, it could probably be said that the possibilities of truly adapting Pestalozzi's approach was impossible because American had not established its own music in the 1800s. On the other hand, today, America does have its own musical creation, jazz, which is a synthesis of African and European musics. This music is rich in both oral/aural and written traditions and must be utilized for its aesthetic worth in American music education, especially in secondary school music.

DISCUSSION QUESTIONS

1. What is a good working definition of jazz? Define jazz in terms of musical behaviors.

2. Why has the problem of jazz in mainstream music education been such a long lasting one? Is it likely that a solution is possible.

3. How would you describe the early jazz education movement? To what extent has mainstream music education accepted jazz?

4. Why have Europeans accepted jazz more readily than Americans?

5. What was Lowell Mason to music education? Identify his positive and negative contributions to the professions.

6. Do you agree that European music holds a superior position in American culture, especially in music education? If so, in what ways is this evident?

7. If jazz is to be incorporated into mainstream music education, should there be changes in the education of music educators? If so, what changes should be made?

8. Compare the six Pestalozzian principles to the area of jazz.

9. If you agree, how is jazz America's only indigenous music?

10. Why do you think improvisation fostered and developed in America's Black communities rather than in the White communities?

11. What is the main danger if jazz is incorporated into mainstream music education?

12. Do you agree that American lacks it's own music education system? Is it necessary to create one in order for music education to be effective in America?

13. Do you think research is necessary to establish an American system of music education?

NOTES FOR CHAPTER 6

1. Frederick Mayer. **A History of Educational Thought.** Columbus, Ohio: Charles E. Merrill Books, Inc., 1960.

2. Allen Scott. "The Past Ten Years in Retrospect," **National Association of Jazz Educators Educator,** 1978, 10 #3.

3. Otis D. Simmons. "Reach the Bedrock of Student Interest," **Music Educators Journal,** 1971, 58 #3.

4. James Standifer. "Cultural Pluralism and the Education of Music Teacher," **Music Power,** 1977, 5.

5. **Teacher Education in Music: Final Report.** Washington, D.C.: MENC, 1972.

6. John Kuzmich. "Jazz Education: An Assessment," **National Association of Jazz Educators Educator,** 1978-79, 9 #2.

7. Alan Rich. "Exoticism and the Conductor," **Minneapolis Tribune,** March 4, 1980, p. 6A.

8. Gilbert Chase. **American's Music.** New York: McGraw-Hill Book Co., Inc., 1955.

9. Douglas Moore, "Foward," **America's Music.** New York: McGraw-Hill Book Co., Inc., 1955.

10. Nathan T. Davis. **Writings in Jazz,** Second Edition, Dubuque, Iowa: Gorsuch Scarisbrich Publishers, 1978.

11. Edward Bailey Birge. **History of Public School Music in the United States (New & Augmented Edited).** Washington, D.C.: MENC 1966.

12. Howard Ellis. "Lowell Mason and the Manual of the Boston Academy of Music," **Journal of Research in Music Education,** 1955, III.

13. Allen P. Britton. "Music in Early American Public Education: A Historical Critique," in: Nelson B. Henry, editor, **Basic Concepts in Music Education,** Part one, The Fifty-seventh Yearbook of the National Society for the Study of Education. Chicago: University of Chicago Press, 1958.

14. Alice S. Beer & Mary E. Hoffman. **Teaching Music: What, How, Why.** Norristown, New Jersey: General Learning Press, 1973.

15. Shinichi Suzuki. **Nurtured by Love: A New Approach to Education,** translated by Waltrand Suzuki, New York: Exposition Press, 1969.

16. Robert W. John. "Elam Ives and the Pestalozzian Philosophy of Music Education," **Journal of Research in Music Education,** 1960, VIII #1.

17. David J. Boyle, (compiler). **Instructional Objectives in Music.** Vienna, Va.: MENC, 1974.

18. Jamey Aebersold. **A New Approach to Jazz Improvisation,** Revised 5th ed, Vol. 1, New Albany, Indiana: Jamey Aebersold, 1979.

19. Jerry Coker. **Improvising Jazz.** Englewood Cliffs, New Jersey: Prentice-Hall, Inc., 1964.

20. David N. Baker. **Jazz Improvisation: A Comprehensive Method of Study for All Players.** Chicago: Maker Publications, 1979.

21. Larry, Ridley. "An Assessment of Jazz Education, 1968-1978," **National Association of Jazz Educators Educator,** 1978, 10 #3. p. 53

BIBLIOGRAPHY

The Jazz Idiom. 1975

Casale, Jimmy, Gary Campbell, and Jerry Greene.
Patterns for Jazz. Lebanon, Indiana: Studio P/R,
Inc. 1970.

Getting it Together, Vol. 21, 1980.

Jazz and Rock: Nothing but Blues, Vol. 2, 1976.

The II-V-I Progression, Vol. 3, 1974.

**Jazz Pedagogy: A Comprehensive Method of Jazz
Education for Teacher and Student.** Chicago:
Maker Publications,. 1979.

Coker, Jerry. **Listening to Jazz.** Englewood Cliffs,
New Jersey: Prentice-Hall, Inc., 1978.

Coker, Jerry. **The Jazz Idom.** Englewood Cliffs, N.J.:
Prentice Hall, Inc. 1975.

Ewen, David. **All the Years of American Popular Music:
A Comprehensive History.** Englewood Cliffs, N.J.:
Prentice-Hall, Inc., 1977.

Gridley, Mark C. **Jazz Styles.** Englewood Cliffs, N.J.:
Prentice-Hall Inc., 1978.

Jones, LeRoi. **Blues People.** New York: Wm Morrow and
Co., 1963.

Leonhard, Charles & Robert W. House. **Foundations and
Principles of Music Education.** New York: McGraw-
Hill Book Co., 1972.

Nanry, Charles & Edward Burger. **The Jazz Text.** New
York: D. Van Nostrand Co., 1979.

Nettl, Bruno. **Folk Music in the United States: An
Introduction.** 3rd Ed. Detroit: Wayne State
University Press, 1976.

Phelps, Roger P. **A Guide to Research in Music
Education.** Englewood Cliffs, N.J.: Prentice-
Hall, Inc., 1970.

Reimer, Bennett. **A Philosophy of Music Education.**
     Englewood cliffs, N.J.:   Prentice-Hall, Inc.,
     1970.

Schuller, Gunther. **Early Jazz.** New York: Oxford
     University Press, 1968.

Southern, Eileen. **The Music of Black Americans: A
     History.** New York: W.W. Norton & Co., Inc.,
     1971.

Stearns, Marshall. **A Story of Jazz.** New York: Mentor
     Books, 1958.

Tanner, Pual O.W. & Maurice Gerow. **A Study of Jazz.**
     Duguque, Iowa: Wm. C. Brown Co., Pub., 1981.

PART II

Chapter 7

CONTEMPORARY PROBLEMS IN URBAN MUSIC EDUCATION

Donald J. Jones

Any discussion of contemporary problems in public school music education must first deal with the question of "survival." The issue of cutbacks in school music programs is presently one of the most perplexing dilemmas ever faced by music educators. It is a problem national in scope which affects school districts of all sizes in all parts of the country.

The problem stems from a taxpayer revolt coupled with the unwillingness of many state legislatures to adequately fund education. When these two conditions exist, something in the school curriculum has to go and it is usually the arts. The following represent some of the problems school districts have faced recently:

Detroit, Michigan - entire music program in the elementary and middle schools wiped out during the 1976-77 school year.

Seattle, Washington - supervisory staff reduced from six to one. Music teachers eliminated in most elementary schools.

New York City - music specialists eliminated, programs seriously curtailed in many schools.

San Francisco, California - elementary music program eliminated.

Columbus, Ohio - elementary music program eliminated.

Dayton, Ohio - music staff reduced.

St. Louis, Missouri - elementary music program axed; Vocal and Instrumental supervisors eliminated.

Philadelphia, Pennsylvania - elementary music cut.

In these examples and others, it is almost always the elementary program which is cut first. Realistically, how long can the high schools survive before the entire program crumbles?

Having gone through the experience personally, this writer has learned one important lesson: In the event of music cutbacks, it is almost a total waste of time to concentrate one's energies and efforts at the local level. Any changes must come from the state's official lawmaking body, the state legislature. Pleading for money for the arts at the local level is a waste of time.

Around many large cities parents simply put up "For Sale" signs and flee to nearby suburban districts or enroll their children in private schools. The real losers are poor minority students whose parents lack the mobility to simply pull up and leave. For many of these students, the public school offers the only hope for any formal musical training.

Rather than cuts being made in urban music programs, there is a much greater need for expansion of the present offerings to better meet the needs of an increasingly poor and minority school population. Art and music education is especially important for many of these students who are not exposed to the arts at home.

Much lip service has been given to the belief that the arts are an integral part of basic education. Yet, when the financial crunch comes, it is still the arts which get the axe first.

What to do in the Event of a Crisis

If your school district is facing a cutback, it is necessary to combine the efforts of school music personnel, parents, the music industry and other influential citizens in the community. It is extremely important to publicize the values of music education. The following are some suggestions for helping to keep music in the schools:

1. Effects of a curtailment--focus upon the number of people affected by curtailment of the music program. Included should be students, teachers and parents, many who have made large financial investments in instruments and lessons

2. Personnel cutbacks--if cuts have to be made emphasize an "across

the board" reduction rather than one entire department.

3. Inform the Public--supply the public with vital statistics relating to the program, including accomplishments of the music program.

4. Publicize the cost of the program per student. This formula is a way of doing this:

Cost of Staff + Cost of Materials and Supplies
$$\frac{\text{Cost of Staff + Cost of Materials and Supplies}}{\text{Number of Students Involved}} = \text{Cost Per Students}$$

Decide whether it would be more advantageous to do this for the entire program or for separate parts of the program, i.e., band, orchestra, etc.

5. Local Civic Organizations--seek the assistance of civic organizations such as churches, city, county and state governmental officials and service clubs. Seek the support of those groups which the school district has provided performing groups for. Also support should be sought from community art groups, the federation of musicians union, alumni of the school system, private music teachers and professional musicians across the musical spectrum.

6. Support school millage campaigns-- actively work for the passage of all school levies and bond issues. Parent organizations and music students can work in their communities through personal contact and the distribution of handbills.

7. Letters to the Editor--urge all those within the community to

write letters to the editors of
local newspapers expressing the
significance of music as a part of
basic education. In order to make
such comments effective, it is
important to provide factual, up-
to-date information regarding the
music program so that letters are
authentic in content.

8. Local Radio and Television--most
local radio and television
stations have guest viewpoints on
subjects of community interest.
Take advantage of this opportunity
if it exists as it serves as a
means of reaching a large
audience.

9. Other Districts as Resource
People--draw on the expertise of
other school districts which have
encountered similar crisis. Learn
what worked well and what did not,
then decide upon your own battle
plan.[1]

These are just a few suggestions which have been
used by school districts in coping with crisis. If
your school district has not been affected thus far,
then actively work to prevent a crisis from occurring.
Organize band parents clubs, keep the local news media
informed of the activities of school music groups and
communicate often with parents, administrators and
community groups. By working together with the entire
community you may very well prevent a crisis from
occurring.

Parental Support

One major problem facing the urban music educator
is the lack of parental support. Parent organizations
can provide valuable assistance to the school music
program by serving as a communication system between
the music program and parents, by encouraging attendance at concerts, assistance in fund raising and
serving as chaperones for outside performances.[2]

The lack of parental support is akin to the urban
school situation in general. Every effort should be

made by the school music director to solicit the support of parents. I believe that there is a direct correlation between parental involvement and success of the music program.

It is the director's responsiblity to articulate his/her plans, purposes and methods to parents if support is to be gained for the program. Parent groups may also include the parents of children who attend the school, but who are not members of musical organizations. The following are some recommendations for organizing a parents' club for school music groups:

> Form an executive committee to guide the group's program.
>
> Appoint committees to handle special or continuing responsibilities.
>
> Make one's self available for advice and consultation.
>
> Provide the club with some duties and responsibilities to perform.[3]

Parental responsibility in assuring their child's success in the study of music would include the following:

> Be sincerely interested and provide encouragement.
>
> Provide the best quality instrument possible.
>
> Provide lessons, if possible.
>
> Provide an adequate place for practice.
>
> Provide needed accessory equipment; reeds, oils, cleaning paraphenalia.
>
> Attend all musical events where your child performs.
>
> Be active in the school's parent organizations.

Parental interest has a profound influence upon the ultimate success of the music program. Studies have shown that the home has a much greater influence on learning than has the school. Every effort should be made by the music educator to actively communicate and seek the support of parents. Without parental involvement, a difficult task becomes almost impossible.

If the attitudes of parents are negative towards teachers, school, and the learning process, so will be those of the child. If they are positive, the child will mirror these in his/her behavior and attitude. Never has there been a greater need for parents to assume leadership roles in the pursuit of quality education, as the challenge we face today.

Scheduling

Of all the factors which affect teaching and learning, scheduling has perhaps the greatest day to day impact. The best efforts of enthusiastic students and highly competent instruction can easily be negated as a result of poor scheduling.

> The function of a schedule is twofold: first it represents an effort to organize someone's time, and second, it is a way of establishing priorities whether this be intentional or not. One usually plans a schedule, whether it be his personal one or for a student body, on the basis of what is most important.[5]

Because of the diversity of offerings in the secondary school, it is almost impossible to avoid some scheduling conflicts. However, if the music department is the only department within the school constantly involved in conflict, it does not imply a mechanical impossibility, but rather reflects the priorities of the local building administrator. The following are some of the major obstacles which impede the scheduling process:

Block scheduling

Tract scheduling (based upon reading and I.Q. scores, etc.)

Core programs

> Limited number of periods in the day
>
> Limited physical facilities
>
> Conflicting philosophies between teachers, administrators and community
>
> Philosophy of the counseling staff[6]

It is extremely important that all music classes be scheduled to meet during the school day. To do otherwise relegates the music program to a status of an extracurricular activity, less important than other school offerings. It is the responsibility of administration to devise a schedule which will insure that students have the opportunity to participate in music classes without conflict with required subjects throughout the student's school career.[7]

Music must be considered as important as any other subject in the curriculum and deserves an equal amount of time, money, and effort. It is a science and an art. It contains elements of mathematics, reading, writing, history, and physical education. It can provide both a vocation and avocation. What other subject in the school's curriculum contains all of these qualifications?

Facilities and Equipment

Another difficulty facing the urban music educator is that of inadequate equipment and physical facilities. Part of the reason for this is because urban schools tend to be much older that their suburban counterparts, with many buildings being built near or shortly after the turn of the century. Many urban school buildings are dilapidated, in need of replacement and never had the kind of facilities needed for a modern day, comprehensive music program.

The physical setting has a profound effect upon the quality of teaching in the school. Psychologically and acoustically, basements and other make-shift music facilities are a great deterrent to developing quality music programs. Many urban music facilities include no practice rooms, poor storage spaces, poor acoustics, no library or office space and limited classroom floor space.

Funds for new buildings or additions to old ones are allocated in the budgets of most boards of education under the heading of "Capital Outlay." Unfortunately, most of the recent court cases have not gone into the question of expenditures for school construction, or other capital outlays. However, in Rodriquez v. San Antonio School District, the court enjoined the defendants from giving any force and effect to sections of the Texas Constitution and Education Code related to the financing of education, including the minimum foundation program act. Since the education code included a provision for construction and capital outlay, the effect of the decision in that case was to rule on the discrimination in the method by which funds are raised for construction in capital outlay.[8]

For more specific information on facilities, see Music Buildings, Rooms and Equipment, Music Educators National Conference, 1902 Association Drive, Reston, Virginia 22091, (1955).

Equipment

Most school districts maintain a "table of allowance," which indicates the minimum number of instruments the school districts assure each school of having.[9] This is generally more than adequate if instruments and other equipment are actually allocated on an equitable basis.

In reality, however, they seldom are. Inner-city schools, in addition to being the oldest schools, also tend to be the most ill-equipped and most often ignored. In addition to the problems of equity, inner-city schools face the on-going problem of theft and vandalism. When instruments and other equipment are stolen, rarely are they replaced.

From experience, I have learned that any immediate solution must come from within. The urban music director must push for individual ownership of instruments from as many students as possible. It is totally unrealistic to expect any school district to provide an instrument for each student's use. From my observations, the best student performers are usually the ones who own, or rent, their own instruments.

132

The school district has the responsibility for providing background instruments such as tympani, tubas, marimbas, chimes, bass clarinets, etc. Instruments such as clarinets, flutes, saxophones, trombones, cornets and trumpets should be the student's responsibility.

Many would disagree with this philosophy by stating that we are dealing with economically deprived students. However, my experiences have been different. Students, no matter how deprived they appear to be on paper, seem to have funds for those things they value. It boils down to a simple matter of priorities.

The music program cannot be successful without a commitment from students. Ownership is the best method of acquiring student commitment. With the many excellent rental programs available today, it is economically feasible for almost every student to have an instrument for his/her personal use. There is a definite correlation between student ownership, instrumental progress and student drop-out rates.

School Finance

Any discussion of facilities and equipment or any aspect of the music program that requires funding would be incomplete without some mention of the source of funds. The lack of adequate financing is perhaps the greatest peril facing urban education today. Without a more equitable source of funds, the future of education in urban cities is in jeopardy.

The majority of operating revenues for most school districts derive from local property taxes and state aid. Another source comes from the federal government. The property tax, the primary source of local school revenue is simply an archaic, unequitable means of financing education.

Some school districts with high per capita incomes, great natural resource, industry or high value residential property can provide large amounts of money for schools. On the other side of the coin, a poor school district with a low tax base cannot provide the same amount of dollars even if they tax themselves at a much higher level.[10]

Urban cities additionally are required to provide high levels of non-educational services from their city

133

revenues, much higher than their suburban counterparts. This is called municipal overburden.[11] A
recent survey of forty-four of the nation's largest
urban cities confirmed that all had per capita
expenditures for non-educational services far above
their respective state-wide averages. The averages
were: fire protection, 91 percent; police protection,
53 percent; health services, 70 percent; and sewage
disposal, 66 percent. Further complicating the
situation is the large number of tax-exempt properties[12]
such as churches, state and federal office buildings.

This affects education in that as urban cities
attempt to regain these lost revenues, they must
increase taxes and/or reduce existing services, often
including education. The fact that many large Northeastern and Midwestern cities continue to lose
commercial and industrial properties to the suburbs
does not help matters. Drastic reforms are greatly
needed if urban schools are to even approach the goal
of "equality of educational opportunity."[13]

Possible Solutions

Money is not a panacea for all of the ills facing
urban education. But it can help solve many of the
educational needs which have surfaced recently. The
courts in recent years have determined that inequal-
ities in school financing based upon the wealth of
school districts are in direct violation of the "equal
protection clause" of the Fourteenth Amendment to the
Constitution.[14]

Any reform efforts must have two essential
purposes in mind: (1) To reduce the present dispar-
ities in resources among school districts, and (2) to
acknowledge and provide for the differing needs of
students.

I mentioned the differing needs of students
because urban education is more expansive than
education in rural areas. High construction costs,
salaries, more vocational programs, preschool programs, compensatory and remedial programs, and
programs for the handicapped add greatly to the cost of
education in urban cities.

What is needed to equalize funds is a cost-of-
education index similar to the cost-of-living index
maintained by the U.S. Department of Labor, which gives

comparative costs of consumer goods and services in various parts of the country. Such an index is greatly needed and is technically and administratively feasible.

The fund raising mechanism for public education must be transferred to the state level. Only the state legislatures have the power to reform school financing. I am convinced that any system approaching equity will have to be centered at the state level. Only by reforming the present methods of school finance will music education and other offerings presently being eliminated from the curriculum be able to stand on the firm financial foundation needed to develop quality, comprehensive programs.

Dropouts

Another dilemma facing the urban music educator is the ever increasing problem of drop-outs. While this is a problem of concern in school districts of all sizes, the problem in many urban areas is especially acute when as many as 50% of those students expected to return from year to year, drop out for varied reasons.

The following represent some of the reasons why students drop out of music programs in urban schools:

1. Lack of interest and commitment.

2. Poor articulation during the transition from junior to senior high school.

3. Lack of confidence.

4. Pregnancy.

5. Work to help support other family members (especially if the mother is the head of the household).

6. Poor scheduling (sometimes due to counselor apathy).

7. More interested in other school extra-curricular activities.

8. Personal conflict between student and director.

These are the most often cited reasons given this writer by students who drop out of music programs.

An important piece of research relating to high drop out rates in beginning instrumental music was initiated by the National Association of Band Instrument Manufacturers during the 1971-72 school year. The purpose of the research was to determine the effects of experimental recruiting procedures and individualized class instruction on beginning band enrollments, student dropout rates and musical achievement.[15]

Over 750 students enrolled in the public schools of West Allis, Verona and McFarland, Wisconsin were chosen to participate in the research. The results included a twofold increase in the number of students involved in instrumental music and experimental schools, a drastic reduction in student dropout rates from an average 48 percent to an average 15 percent, and significantly higher levels of musical achievement by students in experimental schools.[16]

Another study "Discovering Why Dropouts Drop Out at the Secondary Level" by Dr. Joseph Farruggia at California State University concluded that it was important that "students should be given a role in the evaluation process of the instrumental music program." He concludes that the "personality of the director" and "lack of junior-senior high articulation" are the major culprits.[17]

These studies are valuable and do contribute some significant insights to the problem, however, this writer feels that there is a great need for some current research done in the urban setting dealing with the problem of dropouts. Such a project would be an excellent topic for a thesis or dissertation.

Determining the real reasons for student dropouts is an extremely difficult task. Often the reasons stated are not necessarily the real ones. However, the following suggestions may be of some help in combating the dropout problem:

> 1. Keep open the channels of communication with all concerned: students, parents and counselors.

2. Be flexible in the type of music performed--all classics will not work, include some contemporary pop and rock numbers.

3. Involve students in all phases of the music program.

4. Make it a practice to contact students at the feeder schools. This can be done several ways. Take performing groups to the feeder schools, invite prospective students to concerts, or have a music day in which performing groups from the high school and feeder schools unite as a single unit and perform easy literature.

5. Be personable, let the students know you are human too; many students remain in the program because they like the director.

6. Combat apathy by attempting to develop a tradition in which it is considered prestigious to be a member of a music group. This sometimes entails the need to change the attitudes of all involved with the program. Administration, counselors, parents and students.

These suggestions are not intended as a panacea for the problem, however, they may aid in some way in slowing the growing number of student dropouts in urban music programs.

Minimum Competency Testing

In recent years there has been an increasing clamor for "accountability" in education. Scholastic Aptitude Test scores (SATs) and other major test scores of high-school seniors have gradually declined during the past decade. This continual retrogression in test scores, in addition to diminishing competencies in reading and mathematics, has resulted in a nation-wide "back to basics" movement.

One result of these concerns in many states has been the development of minimum competency tests. This represents the reaction of state legislatures and school boards, who also fear the threat of "educational malpractice" suits where parents and students have blamed educators for their own failures.

While the goals of the "back to basics" movement are exemplary and greatly needed, it serves to exacerbate the problems of instrumental music and all other electives in the school curriculum. In addition to the basic core of courses now required in most urban districts, (e.g. math, science, physical education, english, social studies) many big cities are now mandating new requirements such as consumer education; field practicums; basic law; sex education; vocational education and remedial reading and mathematics.

With so many requirements being mandated, many interested students find it virtually impossible to schedule music classes. The mistake too many school boards have made is to wait until late in a student's high-school career before testing for mastery of basic skills. A much better approach, I feel, is to concentrate remedial efforts in the lower grades, where it rightfully belongs.

To continue to expect high-schools to accept a remediation role for skills "assumed" to have been taught in the early grades is simply asking too much. It also leads to the demise of the entire high-school elective program, especially music.

No one can deny that "basic skills" are not essential to the development of the total student. But music is also an integral part of the finished product. Aesthetic and humanistic appreciations must be available to all students and should serve as a means for improving student achievement in other basic skill areas.

NOTES FOR CHAPTER 7

1. "What To Do When Your School's Music Program is Facing a Cutback," **Music Educators Digest,** September, 1976, pp. 1-8.

2. "Instrumental Music for Michigan Schools,"
   Pamphlet, **The Michigan School Band and Orchestra
   Association,** 1971.

3. Selmer, Magnavox Company, **How to Promote Your
   Band,** (Elkhart: 1966), p. 16-20.

4. "Your Child Deserves a Musical Education,"
   Pamphlet, King Musical Instruments.

5. Robert Klotman, **The School Music Administrator and
   Supervisor** (Englewood Cliffs, New Jersey:
   Prentice-Hall, Inc., 1973), p. 90.

6. Ibid., pp. 90-03.

7. "Instrumental Music for Michigan Schools,"
   **Pamphlet, The Michigan School Band and Orchestra
   Association,** 1971.

8. Clifford Dochterman, et. al., **Understanding
   Education's Financial Dilemma,** Report of the
   Education Commission of the States, Denver,
   Colorado, 1972, p. 18.

9. Klotman, op. cit., p. 112.

10. Dochterman, et. al., op. cit., p. 7.

11. John Oliver, Gerald Morris, "Cities' Schools
    Shortchanged," **American Teacher,** December, 1976,
    p. 9.

12. Ibid., p. 9.

13. Schools, People & Money, Report of the President's
    Commission, **School Finance,** (Final Report) p. 26.

14. Ibid., p. 34.

15. "How Self-Initiated and Self-Directed Study Can
    Help Reduce Dropout Rates in the Beginning
    Instrumental Music Program" **Conn Chord,** Vol. 17
    no. 3 (Fall, 1973), 3.

16. Ibid., p. 3.

17. Joseph Farruggia, "Discovering Why Dropouts Drop
    Out at the Secondary Level" **Conn Chord,** vol. 17,
    no. 3 (Fall, 1973), pp. 8-9.

Chapter 8

DISCIPLINE: AN ANALYSIS FOR CLASSROOM TEACHERS

Barbara A. Hicks and Charles E. Hicks

Discipline may be defined as the act of training or developing "by instruction and exercise," the disciple being the individual who "receives instruction from another." Discipline may originate from the self, or be imposed from without to encourage the individual to follow orderly conduct that is prescribed by society. Self-discipine is the regulation of the self for the sake of improvement and originates from the concept of the self or from the individual's respect for society's laws.

Discipline ought not to be confused with punishment. Whereas discipine is a part of the normal personality development in the home, school and society, punishment suggests retribution or penalty and implies pain or loss. In the relationship between parent and child or teacher and student, discipine is synonymous with teaching, correcting or molding the mental faculties or moral character.

From infancy to adulthood, the individual must learn to adapt to a complex society. Decisions have to be made as to what will be taught, when, and by whom. Respect for authority is an integral part of discipline. For example, in the parent-child relationship the child must learn to defer to his parents because of their superior knowledge and wisdom.

In relation to teaching in the classroom, discipline is one of the most difficult problems confronting new and experienced teachers. Albert Shanker, President of New York City's United Federation of Teachers comments that: "Many teachers must work in a state of fear and be subjected to continuing assaults, harassment, intimidation and insults."[1] The problem is not limited to New York. Lee Dolson, past president of the San Francisco Classroom Teacher Association,charges that: "Teachers are in a state of fear...many use their sick leave to stay away because they are too sick with fear to go to school and teach."[2] Throughout the country statistics on student violence bear out these fears, providing evidence of the failure to impose discipline in the classroom.

The concern over discipine is not confined within the school but has importance to the larger community. Discipline, whether or not it is satisfactory, has a direct effect on the teacher's instructional success and the student's academic achievement, but also affects the school's reputation and, in general, the entire educational process. Discipline has become the number one problem in the mind of the general public, as the Annual Gallup Polls of Public Attitudes Toward Education revealed.[3]

Because of the amount of time that has been spent on discipine in schools, instruction has become less of a priority. For instruction to be effective a realistic concept must exist regarding student control and the rules and regulations that establish order. In the 1960s and 1970s, certain disciplinary procedures have been challenged as the concern of students has grown about school questions and public issues.

Two different approaches to discipline may be presented. The first is the attitude of most people who, in speaking of discipline, "are thinking of a matter of obeying rules, respect the authority of teachers and school administrators and being considerate of fellow students."[4] Many of America's top thinkers and writers now consider a second kind of discipline, mental discipline, which consists of "acquiring the knowledge and skills needed in today's world even though such learning is often difficult and boring."[5] Educators also conceptualize discipline in two different ways. Either it refers primarily to coercive acts performed by the teacher to repress behavior or it involves all the techniques used in the classroom to control student behavior:

> Discipline is the sum total of those activities not given to the task of presenting subject matter to students. It is, in essence, the teacher's efforts to influence behavior other than that connected with learning facts. Discipline, as is instruction, is a means by which the basic goal of the educational institute can be attained. This goal is to prepare the

student   to   live   happily[6]   and
successfully within his society.

Classroom problems are primarily caused by either
the teachers, students, the schools or the parents, the
first   two   being   the   major   points   of   concern.
Environmental and administrative causes also play a
role.   For instance, there is a direct relationship
between discipline in the school and socioeconomic and
legal pressures that affect the student. In many large
cities disadvantaged students placed in schools with
traditional middle class values have problems of
adjustment with the result that when he returns to his
home environment and its value system he is further
confused. Before violence in schools became as common
as it now is, the majority of disruptive students came
from violent environments. Where parental relations
are poor, children show little respect in school
whereas in schools evidencing a mutual respect between
students and teachers, there is an acceptance of
disciplinary enforcement. Thus parental involvement
may be seen to be essential to the school, whether the
disciplinary   measures   used   are   physical   or
nonphysical. Schools cannot be considered in isolation
from the community, for there is an interaction between
the two that makes discipline a problem:

> Society accepts that education to be
> effective   must   be   conducted   in   a
> reasonably   ordered   situation
> and...schools cannot in this age
> operate in isolation; whatever happens
> and whatever is tolerated in the world
> has an effect in our schools.[7]

Within the school the problem of discipline ultimately
falls to the principal who is expected to provide a
quality education for students from all social,
economic, racial and religious backgrounds. He must
satisfy the needs of those who wish to go on to college
as well as those who would rather not be in school at
all.   The administrator's philosophy of discipline
affects both teachers and students "for it is within
this framework that they are all expected to function.
Here is where problems often develop."[8]

An authoritarian principal develops rules that students and teachers must follow but students tend to object to archaic, irrelevant or restrictive regulations, demanding to be consulted and given a say in determining policies that affect them.

Teachers cause discipline problems in several ways, and their reactions in certain situations often initiate trouble. Doubtless, authority is an essential concept in society and in the growing process all individuals must learn to cope with it. Without authority, anarchy and chaos could potentially result. In the school, the teacher must establish credibility with the students to make his authority felt. He must make himself understood, be factual, and present views that can be substantiated. Ideally, the teacher earns the respect and credibility of his students. However, some teachers take their authority too far and believe that anarchy will result if just one violation of the rules occurs. In such cases, student actions are given no validity at all. When strict observation of rules is demanded, there is a tendency to lose valuable instruction time by teachers who have lost sight of the priorities of education. It is possible that such teachers have a fear of dealing with students on a personal basis, hiding behind impersonal rules and regulations.

The good teacher voices enthusiasm about his subject to excite the students in their lessons. A bored-sounding teacher will only create boredom among his students. Some teachers cannot use a firm tone with their class even when such a tone is required and expected by students. Often, students who have passed the "limits of propriety" expect a firm reaction from the teacher.

Sarcasm is a tone and attitude developed by insecure teachers as a means of discipline. Its use negates the respect that is the student's right in the classroom, just as the teacher expects respect from his class. Needless offense to the student, even if offered unknowingly, potentially creates discipline problems. Chastisement ought to occur in private so that teacher-student confrontations will be eliminated.

A disturbing element in the classroom today is the lack of consistency shown by some teachers in terms of their everyday attitudes toward their students and the classroom situation. Consistent behavior and attitudes are important in the teaching environment for the student will be confused by changes that have no apparent cause. Consistency establishes a pattern in the classroom which enables the students to feel at home in the learning situation, so that discipline will not present a large problem. If the teacher jokes one day and is a tyrant the next, the students will not be able to ascertain what behaviors are acceptable in the classroom.

The teacher's view of himself determines whether or not he can maintain control in the classroom. Other factors are his confidence in his ability to deal objectively with a variety of situations and his ability to reveal a human image without fear of doubting his own ability. Teachers who expect students to accept all their utterances as profundities and who are afraid to narrow the gap between student and teacher by laughter, or who cannot bear to remove barriers that prohibit honest interchanges of ideas, will exaggerate the problems of control in the classroom.

A further mistake common among teachers is in criticizing the student rather than the act. Students must be told when they are wrong, but the good teacher will be sure to criticize not the student but his wrong answer. At stake is the healthy development of the individual's self-image. The student is affected by what the teacher thinks of him as a human being and is harmed by personal attacks in his self-esteem when he makes mistakes in the learning situation. The teacher must know the difference between declaring an action or answer unacceptable and declaring an individual unacceptable.

It can be seen, then, that the teacher can be a catalyst triggering unacceptable behavior in the classroom, and alienating the students. Each teacher should develop behavioral and academic requirements that he feels necessary for a good teaching-learning situation in his classroom. Further, the dignity of the student must not be infringed on, either by the careless use of his name, confiscating his possessions or using sarcasm to reduce the self-image of the student. The effective teacher will be consistent and open, and maintain flexible responses to disruption, realize the value of humor and retain a sense of proportion.

144

However, there is no hard and fast rule for all teachers, although "certain guidelines must be followed by all teachers if they are to effect positive discipline in the classroom."[9] Good discipline goes along with good teaching: "When the teacher offers instruction relevant to the learner few discipline problems will normally be encountered."[10] Preparation is useful to the teacher, involving creating assignments in a methodical and precise manner, but with a touch of personal creativity. Students recognize proficiency and competence in a teacher and when this occurs the problem of discipline is kept in proportion.

Nonetheless, it is recognized that achieving proper discipline is a complex and frustrating task, being the result of the teacher's self-image and his conception of his role. It is essential for the teacher to be in control of what occurs in his classes for teaching cannot be undertaken when students fail to pay attention. Control can be achieved through a number of devices, the primary one simply being that of "being in control:"

> He cannot be 'buddy' or 'pal' nor a member of the group, a contemporary or peer of the youngsters. He may be their friend and their confidante, and share experiences with them...if he does not feel he is the person in charge he can rarely, if ever, be an effective teacher. It is his task to structure the situation to see to it that he is.[11]

Disciplinary problems are less likely to occur in classes that have been well planned and effectively presented. Whatever system the efficient teacher uses to suit his personality, it must incorporate effective teaching as a foundation. Student-teacher interaction has an important bearing on the climate of the classroom, and a climate for learning where activities are carried out in an orderly manner is vital.

Turning to student-caused problems, it has to be remembered that young people are involved in the search for identity and self-worth that is a part of growing up. The school ought to assist in this process by providing a comfortable educational environment, but often this is not achieved. There may be too many complex rules that create rather than solve problems. Or students may be isolated from their peers as well as from adults, which teachers wrongly interpret as a lack of motivation, or label the student uneducable. The student is trapped in a system that he feels restricts his freedom and which he finds boring and irrelevant to his everyday life:

> Students are expected to learn what the faculty want them to learn in the way the faculty wants them to learn it,...freedom to explore, to test one's ideas as a means of finding out who one is and what one believes--these are luxuries a well run school cannot afford. The result at best, is to persuade students that knowledge has no relation to them, no relevance for the kinds of lives they will lead, it produces...alienation, the rejection of authority, the rejection of the whole notion of culture, of discipline and of learning.[12]

Students consistently receiving low grades feel lost and turn to defiance, disobedience, disorder, even psychotic withdrawal or "dropping out" to gain the status they lack. These so-called failures who are lonely and live in isolation challenge the world and break its rules, vandalizing the very institution that ought to have helped them, but instead rejected them.

Success is emphasized very early in the individual's school career, and can be achieved by following the rules, mastering the curricula and obtaining good grades. Apart from academic pressures, there are also peer pressures relating to drugs, alcohol and sex. It is demanded of the youngster that he form moral judgements that he may feel unable to deal with, so that he emerges immature and caught between equally compelling forces. Generally, more than one factor urges a child to disrupt the classroom situation:

> The child who wants the limelight may be one of ten in the family, often told,

> 'Children should be seen and not heard.'
> The hostile youngster, who fights at the
> drop of a hat or a word, may have had
> object lessons of brutality right in his
> own home, from a drunken father, or a
> sadistic brother. The little one who is
> unpleasant may be so because of hunger--
> physical hunger. The variety and number
> of problems which can involve children
> are unfortunately, unending. These
> problems may be physical or mental,
> social or economic.[13]

It requires experience to recognize that not all
interruptions in the class are caused by deviant
behavior. Bright or lonely students may seek attention
by constantly calling out answers, which the teacher
may find irritating so that disciplinary problems are
created. It also happens that the teacher labels
behavior deviant when it merely reflects the age of
dissent in which the student who challenges him or
disagrees with him, lives. Many teachers cannot
understand that the child is seeking to exercise
independent thought by offering alternative opinions.

Many teachers have a low tolerance for behavior
they regard as irritating. Some such behaviors--foot-
tapping, for example--may be eliminated by a look at
the student. Students who may be characterized as
"smart mouths" may be dealt with by neglect; in
ignoring the student the teacher denies him his
expected response. Otherwise, a firm tone to the
student and the class will make it clear that such
behavior is unacceptable.

The teacher may also be irritated when the student
fails to meet his responsiblities. Conflict is likely
when either the student or the teacher neglects his
obligations.

To understand disruption in the classroom it is
necessary to look at problems in the daily life of the
student that might affect his behavior, for many of
these have a direct relationship to their classroom
behavior. If the teacher can find the root cause of
the inability to adjust to the learning situation a
solution can be attempted.

There are several physical problems that ought to be examined, one of the most common of which is poor vision, which will affect the ability to read. A student unable to read may create disciplinary problems because of his frustrated understanding of what is occuring in the class. The visually disabled student is presented with enormous problems in a class geared towards reading comprehension.

Hearing problems also affect the ability to comprehend and the student becomes disinterested in the work, particularly if his imagination is lively. Made to feel an outsider, the hearing-impaired student may cause disruption in order to draw attention to himself. Other physical problems that affect classroom behavior in a similar manner include heart abnormalities, epilepsy, diabetic seizures, viral attacks, and hyper- and hypoactivity.

Mental illness often causes the most severe discipline problems; such illness may be hinted at by bizarre behavior or hallucinations. The latter may not always be revealed by the student but the teacher who wins his confidence may learn about them. Students with mental problems cannot remove them during the time they are in school, so that they may cause disruption as a result of a troubled state of mind, and are unable to concentrate on classroom assignments.

Psychological problems can be severe and dismaying to a child, whose hurt is increased if the teacher emphasizes his weakness or ridicules him. Worse, his psychological harm might become permanent.

The generation gap can also cause disciplinary problems and the teacher can help bridge the gap by "avoiding intellectual arrogance." By listening with respect the teacher can learn the student's values, leading to open and honest discussion in which both sides can present their points of view.

Home-oriented problems are experienced by many children, and these include quarreling parents, bullying elder siblings, broken homes, financial difficulties and so on. Any of these can contribute to misbehavior in the classroom. Whatever category of problem the child experiences the teacher will do well to try to determine the causes and empathize with the student.

Many approaches have been suggested for dealing with discipline problems, including authority or coercion, persuasion, situational contracting or relational contracting or manipulating the student. One study which examined these methods found that teacher coercion or authority invites unwilling student response; persuasion, situational contracting or relational contracting produces willing student response; and manipulation produces unwitting student response.[14] The authoritarian teacher uses his greater status or implicit threats of coercion; the coercive teacher uses force; persuasion is acceptable to the student as logically more desirable than their own judgement; in the situational contract situation the teacher bestows some benefit on the student in exchange for acceptable behavior; when relational contract is used results are attained by virtue of a longstanding, reciprocal arrangement where the teacher has bestowed benefit in advance of behavior; and in manipulative situations, there is an unwitting substitution by the student of the teacher's judgement for his own, which is accomplished when the student sees only the elements of the environment that the teacher wants him to see.

Discipline in the schools

Wide discrepancies exist between the number of disciplinary incidents reported by principals on the one hand and security personnel on the other; these include such serious offenses as assaults as well as incidents related to weapons and drugs. This information was reported by a U.S. District Monitoring Commission while monitoring the Detroit Public Schools.

The breakdown of discipline in many schools of the urban setting is a result of apathy and indifference on the part of urban administrators in dealing effectively with student disruptions in a uniform way. In two separate cases in 1975, the U.S. Supreme Court ruled that students are protected by the due process clause of the 14th Amendment. In the suspension case of Goss V. Lopez, the High Court stated that a student facing suspension must be given oral or written notice of the charges against him/her and an opportunity to present his/her side of the story. The majority opinion stated: "we do not believe we have imposed procedures on school disciplinarians which are inappropriate in classroom settings. Instead, we have imposed requirements which are less than a fairminded school principal would impose upon himself in order to avoid unfair suspensions......"

In another case, Wood v. Strickland, the Court stated further, that a student may sue school authorities for damages if his rights are violated. In this instance, the Court said: "while school officials are entitled to a qualified good faith immunity from liability of damages, they are not immune from such liability if they knew or reasonably should have known that the actions they took violated constitutional rights of students."

Many administrators believe the ruling would mean an erosion of local school control, a threat to discipline and generally a menace to both administrators and teachers. Shortly after the Supreme Court ruling, state departments of education begin printing brochures detailing students' rights along with their responsibilities. Also, local school boards were forced to publish policies relating to the issue of due process.

Those school districts that had a system wide discipline code in force before the 1975 court case have not been adversely affected by its verdict. On the other side of the coin, these court decisions have made unilateral and arbitrary proceeding against students ... a thing of the past.

Family Communication

Relationships in the average family has deteriorated to such a marked degree until many parents find themselves in confrontations with their children. These confrontations usually occur when parents ask the children to turn off the T.V./Hi-Fi Set, or do your chores. In order that families communicate better, games are being marketed to help unite the family. One such game that teaches people to communicate is the "ungame" entitles "Tell It Like It Is."

In Norman Wright's book **An Answer to Discipline,** he presents the PARENT-CHILD INVENTORY. This inventory consists of 12 items that was designed to help parents analyze the quality of their communication within the family.

It is suggested that each parent complete the inventory to show his or her communication with each child. After that, parents should get together and discuss the results, and plan ways to improve family communications. The parents can assist the teacher in solving his or her child's problems in shcool if home communication is good.

The ultimate goal of any strategy or procedure for discipline in schools or child rearing is SELF-DISCIPLINE. Wright suggests a "definite" procedure to follow to make this goal a reality. The numbers

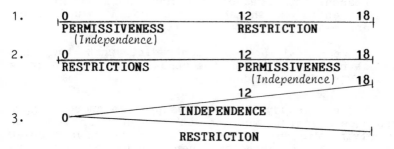

on the chart above refer to the ages of the child as he/she grows toward adolescence and adulthood. In the first example, during the first twelve years parents have used the permissive pattern of child rearing-letting the child do what he/she wants. At age twelve, they begin to impose restrictions, then problems begin to occur. For the first time they try to control the child, and meet with resistence, they experience conflict and even verbal abuse.[15] "The adolescent has already established his life style; why should he/she now respond to the new style his parents are seeking? This is foreign to the child." The second example is not as bad as the first, but it too has its problems. Some parents follow this second pattern too closely. Being totally restrictive during the first twelve years, then suddenly allow the child a lot of freedom that he/she is not able to handle causes problems for the child. The third pattern is the best alternative, it is a gradual blending process that includes restrictiveness as well as teaching the child how to be responsible. The child is allowed more and more freedom gradually coupled with independence as he/she

indicates that they are capable of handling it."[16] The
procedure is based upon the following assumptions:

1.   Teach a child to be responsible for what he/she
      does.

2.   A child should learn to accept the consequences of
      his/her actions.

3.   Children and teenagers should be allowed to make
      choices.

4.   Reasons for rules or standards should be given to
      the child when he/she is old enough to understand
      and reason.

5.   If parents' actions contradict what they are
      attempting to teach, the verbal instructions are a
      waste of time and energy.[17]

     The case study that follows provide some insights
into understanding, working with students, and a method
of solving discipline types. After you have studied
this case, try to approach other problems of discipline
in this same fashion.

A CASE STUDY[18]

by
Dr. Ezane Crumb

Dealing With Behavior Problems.

"THE CRUEL CHILD"

     Description: "The cruel child has been known to
fling animals into walls, set them afire, wring their
necks, etc. as well as being generally mean and hurtful
to peers and others. As opposed to pre-school age
children whose inquisitiveness leads them to sometimes
cruel acts, especially with animals, cruel elementary
school age children know what they are doing and
intentionally set out to hurt, injure, or even kill
with all the energy they have.

Reasons Why: The truly cruel child generally comes from a home steeped in violence. Adult models argue, accuse, scream, and fight with fists and weapons. The child is fought over and is severely beaten or punished in unusual and cruel ways by one or both parents. Little attention is paid to what he does or where he goes. His cruelty generally results from his imitation of other's actions and becomes increasingly violent as he gets frightened, lonely, or overwhelmed by anger. He generally, then, lacks self-discipline and control.

How To Control:

1. Care, understanding, regularity of living standards and consistent behavioral controls, ingredients missing from their lives, constitute an important part of the solution to the problem of the cruel child.
2. Attempt, with other professionals, to alter home conditions for the child.
3. Recommend professional assistance for the family through counselling or psychotherapy.
4. Be as consistent and positive an adult model as possible for the child.
5. Help him to find positive outlets for his anger and violence; i.e., punching bags, running, and other strenuous physical activities and sports.
6. Provide a "time-out" corner for him when things get overwhelming.
7. Don't allow cruel behavior to go unnoticed or not dealt with in some manner. Deal with the cruel behavior immediately and in a firm, positive, and consistent manner.
8. See to it that the child has at least one successful experience each day as success supports change.

Conclusion

Lack of respect for rules and regulations is currently a universal phenomenon, and schools will continue to be harmed unless corrective measures are enforced. Discipline must be considered not only a major concern of the classroom teacher but also of the school administrators, parents and the general public. Valuable instruction time is wasted in the classroom when disciplinary problems predominate. Good planning and teaching, and the setting of realistic goals for teachers and students will bring some improvement but

there is no universal panacea to eliminate all
disciplinary problems.

*CHILD BEHAVIOR PROBLEMS

1. Is disobedience normal in the growing child?

2. If a child constantly misbehaves, what can be done
    by the teacher?

3. What does it means when a child misbehaves to get
    attention?

4. What should the teacher do if a child is
    constantly disobedient?

5. What are the implications when a child always does
    the opposite of what the teacher ask him/her to
    do?

    a. Why does a child act this way?

6. What should be done to help a child who seriously
    misbehaves

    a. What should the teacher do if the situation
    gets worse?

7. What are some of the behavioral disturbances of
    children in trouble during the adolescence years?

8. What are some of the behavioral disturbances of
    children in trouble that are school related?

9. What are some other problems encountered by the
    child after adjustment to school?

10. What are some other problems encountered by
    students before and after adolescence?

*Note: Give the following questions to your local
school psychologist, guidance counselor or school
staff person who handles discipline problems on a daily
basis. Ask them to give general answers to the above
questions. Then, you study each question in terms of
your particular school and problem students that you
work with from day to day. This will equip you with
additional tools for handling a variety of discipline
types with a much better understanding for appropriate
corrective measures.

154

TV AFFECTS BEHAVIOR

According to a study at the UCLA neuropsychiatric Institute, dramatic television shows have a definite impact on the mood and behavior of individuals.

If a person is grouchy or belligerent, watching violent cops-and-robbers shows on television helps maintain belligerence. TV shows with warm, social interactions, on the other hand, help reduce agressive moods, it was found.

By the end of the week-long study, those who viewed violent programs exhibited significantly more "hurtful" behavior. Prosocial programs such as "The Waltons" and "Little House On the Prairie" appeared to reduce agressive or hurtful behavior.[19]

CLASS PROJECT

As a possible learning experience, use the results of the study above with one of your classes. Let the class have a hand in the planning and carrying out this experiment. A possible purpose of this study might be; what effect does that watching of violent T.V. programs have upon discipline in the classroom? Can T.V. aid in classroom discipline? How does T.V. affect student behavior in the classroom?

This type of activity could be a tool for students to find out about their own habits, relationships and related issues. This will also provide the teacher with information about each student and his/her home setting.

1. What effect does teacher expectations have on student/classroom discipline problems?

2. What effect does socio-economic factors, e.g. income, etc. have upon students within the school setting?

3. What effects do student peer pressure have upon classroom discipline?

4. Does self-esteem play a part in classroom discipline? If so, how? If not , why not?

5. How can a teacher's instructional procedure influence student discipline?

6. What effect does ability grouping have on student discipline?

7. What does discipline mean. Is it the same as punishment? Is discipline ever positive?

8. How can teachers help children internalize the rules and regulations of the classroom?

9. Children should be allowed to express any of the feelings they have, whether it be hatred, anger, jealous, etc.

10. It is better to teach a child to obey and then, when he/she is able to understand, share with him/her the reasons for what he/she is doing.

11. A misbehaving child is basically a discouraged child.

12. Is rewarding children for good behavior detrimental?

13. Since our society is based upon a system of rewards, it is desirable to reward a child with money for his good behavior.

14. Is Spanking detrimental?

BIBLIOGRAPHY of FURTHER READINGS

Dorothy Baruch, **New Ways in Discipline** (New York: McGraw Hill, 1949), chapter 4.

William Homan, **Child Sense** (New York: Basic Books, 1969),. chapter 2.

Rudolph Dreikurs, **Children: The Challenge** (New York: Duell, Sloan & Pearce, 1964), chapter 3.

Ibid., chapter 5.

Ibid., chapter 6.

James Dobson, **Dare to Discipline** (Wheaton, Illinois: Tyndale House, 1970), chapter 2.

Haim Ginott, **Between Parent and Child** (New York: Macmillan Co., 1965), chapter 2.

Ibid., chapter 5.

NOTES FOR CHAPTER 8

1. "Discipline Crisis in Schools: The Problem, Causes and Search for Solutions," **National School Public Relations Association** (1973), p. 1.

2. Ibid.

3. George H. Gallup, "Seventh Annual Gallup Poll of Public Attitudes Towards Education," **Phi Delta Kappan**, (December 1975), pp. 227-41.

4. Ibid.

5. Ibid.

6. Duane Brown, **Changing Student Behavior: A New Approach to Discipline** (Dubuque: William C. Brown, 1971), p. 23.

7. Ron Cocking, **Discipline in Schools** (Ward Locke Educational, 1973), p. 63.

8. Michael H. Jessup and Margaret A. Kiley, **Discipline: Positive Attitudes for Learning** (New Jersey: Prentice-Hall, 1971), pp. 26-30.

9. Jessup & Kiley, op. cit., p. 20.

10. Albert Stoutamire, "Preventitive Discipline--Ten Steps to Effective Classroom Control," **Music Educator's Journal** (November 1975), pp. 89-91.

11. Muriel Schoenbrun Karlin & Regina Berger, **Discipline and the Disruptive Child** (New York: Parker Publishing Co., Inc., 1972), p. 19.

12. Charles Silberman, **Crisis in the Classroom** (New York: Random House, 1971), pp. 75-8.

13. Karlin & Berger, op. cit., p. 39.

14. Ernest R. House and Stephen D. Lapan, **Survival in the Classroom** (1976).

15. Norman Wright. **An Answer to Discipline.** (California: Harvest House Publishers, 1976), p. 29.

16. Ibid.

17. Ibid.

18. Ezane Crumb. "Dealing with Behavior Problems-The Cruel Child." **The Learning and Behavior Bulletin** (September-October, 1977); p. 3.

19. Roderic Gourney, "TV Affects Behavior," **Report given to The American Psychiatric Association.**

BIBLIOGRAPHY

Auerbach, A.B. **Why and How of Discipline..** Revised edition. New York: Child Study Association of America, 1969.

Brown, Duage. **Changing Student Behavior: A New**

      Approach to Discipline. Dubuque: William C.
Brown, 1971.

Chamberlain, Leslie J. "Discipline and the Public
    School." **Education** (January 1967): 25-31.

Cocking, Ron. "School and Society." In **Discipline in
    Schools.** Ward Locke Educational, 1973.

"Discipline Crisis in Schools: The Problems, Causes
    and Search for Solutions." **National
    School Public Relations
    Associations,** 1973.

Dreikurs, R. and Grey, L. **Logical Consequences: A New
    Approach to Discipline.** New York: Meredith
    Press, 1968.

Gallup, George H. "Seventh Annual Gallup Poll of
    Public Attitudes Towards Education." **Phi Delta
    Kappan** (December 1975): 227-241.

Homan, William E. **Child Sense.** New York: Basic
Books, 1969.

Jessup, Michael H. & Margaret Kiley. **Discipline:
    Positive Attitudes for Learning.** New Jersey:
    Prentice-Hall, 1971.

Karlin, Muriel S. & Regina Berger. **Discipline and the
    Disruptive Child.** New York: Parker, 1972.

McConnell, A.P. "Classroom Discipline Works at Home."
    Parents' Magazine. (July 1968): 38-9.

Redl, F. & E. Kiester. "Psychologist's Guide to
    Disciplining Children." **Redbook** (November 1968):
    76-7.

Silberman, Charles. **Crisis in the Classroom.** New
    York: Random House, 1971.

Stoutamire, Albert. "Preventitive Discipline: Ten
    Steps to Effective Classroom Control." **Music
    Educator's Journal** (November 1975): 89-91.

Valentine, C.W. **Difficult Child and the Problem of
    Discipline.** 5th edition. New York: Barnes &
    Noble, 1965.

Chapter 9

THE URBAN SCHOOL MUSIC CURRICULUM

Warren C. Swindell

Introduction

By definition the term curriculum is broad and all encompassing. Some authorities believe that the curriculum includes all influences which the school brings to bear upon its students. Others believe that the curriculum only includes those outcomes that are directly related to classroom instruction. Leonhard and House emphasize at least two styles of music curriculum: (1) the activity curriculum, and (2) the core curriculum. The activity curriculum is an outgrowth of Dewey's pragmatic philosophy. "Activities are supposed to develop from the 'felt needs' of the students and classroom atmosphere is likely to be relatively improvised."[1] The core curriculum implies drawing upon subject matter from several disciplines. Allied arts, the humanities, and social studies approaches all may be used as examples of the core curriculum.

An acronym, PPPM, identifies Weyland's essentials of the music curriculum: (1) Personnel, (2) Program, (3) Place, and (4) Money. Personnel includes music supervisors, administrators, teachers, staff and committees which plan courses of study. Program refers to the projected music learning program. Place includes space such as buildings, rooms, stages, storage rooms, offices, studios, practice rooms, drill fields, and so forth, to carry out plans and ideas. Money, of course, is needed to purchase and pay for the three P's including materials to illustrate and facilitate plans.[2]

In his discussion of the music curriculum in American Elementary and Secondary Schools, Weyland Classifies two facets of the curriculum: (A) the general music program, and (B) the special music program. The general program is designed for all pupils and fulfills part of the general education requirements. The special program is intended for pupils who desire a pragmatic participatory experience such as performing music in a band, choir, or orchestra, or composing and arranging music. In brief, the paragmatic participatory experiences may be classified as those whose main purpose is to create or recreate actual music.

Traditionally, both the general music program and the special music program have been adopted by school districts throughout the United States. General music is ideally the core of the music curriculum and includes the balancing of singing activities, rhythm activities, listening activities, music reading activities, and performance on chordal (harmonic) and melodic instruments. Educators by and large acknowledge that general music belongs in the curricula of virtually all elementary schools. Elementary general music in some shape, form, or fashion reaches the total school population. The secondary general music program, in contrast, reaches only a small percentage of the total secondary school population. Highly specialized ensembles in some schools perform with an artistry which is unparalleled in both quantity and quality. Yet, secondary music programs, at best, reach only approximately 20 percent of the total school population.

Although most schools will follow some variation of the general music-special music programs, today there appears to be greater flexibility in the music curricula found in the various communities and regions of the country. Music educators, during the last decade or so, have begun to realize that there are several complex factors which influence the curriculum. Some of the complex factors or variables which influence the curriculum are identified by Chamberlain and Kindred: (1) custom and tradition, (2) textbooks, (3) pressure groups, (4) philanthropic foundations, (5) colleges and universities, (6) mass media, (7) public opinion, (8) government legal requirements, and (9) professional influences.[3] Other variables which heavily influence the music curriculum are the central administration of a school district, the administration of the particular school, and the position toward music taken by the state department of education and other accreditation agencies.

Because of the heterogeneous nature of the urban school any categorical urban curriculum recommendations ought to be quite broad. For example, customs and traditions will vary from one urban school to another; group pressure, and public opinion will also vary from school to school. The curriculum will serve

each school best when it is designed for that particular school.

Music Educators National Conference (MENC) is
committed to the development of comprehensive music
programs in all schools including urban schools. In
keeping with its commitment, MENC has recommended that
the music curriculum be expanded. The MENC National
Commission on Instruction (NCI) in conjunction with the
National Council of State Supervisors of Music has
outlined in a very broad manner the music curriculum
from early childhood through senior high school.[4] Their
curriculum is structured and grouped as follows:

(1) ages 3-5 (early childhood)
(2) ages 6-8 (grades 1-3; primary
    level)
(3) ages 9-11 (grades 4-6;
    preadolescence)
(4) ages 12-14 (grades 7-9; early
    adolescence)
(5) ages 15-17 (grades 10-12; high
    school level)

In the NCI outline, the instructional setting is
identified and objectives for each level are classified
under the headings of: (1) performing, (2) organizing,
and (3) describing. Students will perform, organize
the elements of music, and describe the music heard at
each level from age 3 through senior high school. For
example, during the early childhood period, the instructional setting includes only general music. At
the primary level, the instructional setting includes
general music and optional exploratory experiences on
instruments such as violin, piano, and recorder.
During preadolescence, grades 4-6, general music experiences are expanded and optional beginning and
intermediate instruction is included in strings, woodwinds, brass, percussion, and keyboard, as well as
other instruments such as guitar and recorder.
Activities are vastly expanded during the middle school
period. The instructional setting includes general music, folk instruments, music listening laboratory,
composition laboratory, electronic music, interdisciplinary studies, performing groups, keyboard classes,
instrumental classes and a non-select chorus class.

At the senior high school level, the curriculum is
quite comprehensive. The instructional setting in-

162

cludes basic musicianship (or equivalent), music literature, music history, music theory, composition, electronic music, non-western music (or other specialized music), interdisciplinary studies, orchestra or string orchestra, band or wind ensemble, choral groups, stage band, specialized ensembles (including, for example, Afro-American ensembles), exploratory instrumental classes, class instruction on keyboard instruments, voice, guitar, recorder, and other instruments as needed, and music theater.

Because of a current trend toward accountability in teaching, curriculum studies tend to be based on behavioral objectives. Behavioral objectives are designed to articulate what it is that students will be able to do after a given learning experience. Teachers desirous of referring to the NCI curriculum may wish to modify the given objectives and change them to the behavorial form by making minor modifications and furnishing additional information such as <u>when</u> the student will accomplish the specific objective; <u>how well</u> the student will accomplish the objective; <u>how will</u> one know that the specific objective is accom - plished ; and <u>what</u> minimal <u>conditions</u> are necessary to accomplish the specific objective. An example of such an objective might be stated as follows: given a one month preparation period, all students who complete the senior high school electronic music course with a grade of C or better will employ electronic music media as background material for a 15 minute radio documentary and receive critical approval by 75 percent of all other students who completed the course.

The NCI curriculum outline includes a variety of learning experiences encompassing the affective, cognitive, and psychomotor domains. Because the outline is stated in broad general terms, it could be of value to urban music teachers. The elements of music are constants.

Nature of Urban Schools

Urban music teachers are confronted with numerous problems that on the surface seem insoluble. In some urban schools, for example, there are as many as fifty nationalities represented in the student body. Unique problems exist today because pressures to integrate the schools have sometime brought together in the same school children of the poor and the wealthy, the illiterate and the highly educated. It must be borne in mind that the urban poor are anything but alike. Life styles of the urban poor are different. The Puerto Rican child, the Mexican-American child, the black child, the Appalachian white child, and the Indian all perceive and react differently to stimuli in the same environment.

Black youth in the various black belts of major urban areas are largely influenced and controlled by the norms and power of their peer groups. Appalachian white youths are influenced more by their families and the adult community. However, like their black counterparts, they are inclined to be resourceful and independent. The cultural milieu and family ties are so strong among Mexican-Americans that their youth are often more at variance with the norms of the school than either the Appalachian white or poor black. The Indian child has distinctly different outlooks and modes of behavior than his ethnic peers.

Generalizations about urban youth tend to under dramatize actual conditions. Silberman, in his text, **Crisis in the Classroom**, sheds more light on the personal backgrounds of some urban pupils. He explains that a group of students in the various classes involved in an educational project are from backgrounds which include:

> an orphan who lives with a blind grandmother, two children whose mothers are in mental hospitals, a child whose father was killed in Vietnam and whose mother is a prostitute, another orphan who had lived with his grandmother until she was incapactiated by a stroke, and who now lives with an aunt, a child who had watched her mother gradually destroyed by multiple sclerosis and who now lives with her grandmother, a child brought to New York from Jamaica and then abandoned, a child whose father had just been killed in an automobile accident, a child whose parents have been trying to abandon him for some time....[7]

Similar conditions have led Simmons to use the phrase social bankruptcy.[8] In spite of such dire circumstances Silberman mentions that the same children seemingly were able to express happiness as they danced to soul records.

Literature and Material

Music literature, type of music and music materials are variables--elements are constant. The use of ethnic musics and materials from cultures which populate urban schools is highly desirable. Urban music teachers who have received traditional training will probably experience ambivalent feelings when selecting music and materials for urban situations. Music educators with foresight, on the other hand, have long advocated the use of music materials which are atypical. Burmeister, for example, in a chapter of **Basic Concepts in Music Education** provides a very lucid argument for the use of innovative materials:

> The choice of musical materials should reflect an awareness of functional values. The quality of music should not be defined solely by authoritarian standards. Music which might not be acceptable in the concert hall can be used in a program of music education if it is eminently suitable for the purpose for which it is intended. On the other hand, this must not be construed as an endorsement of the practice of using cheap, shoddy materials even for functional purposes. The music educator who does so not only violates his integrity as a musician and debases his art but, what is probably more important, denies to learners their right to choose after having experienced the best that music can offer. Music education should attempt to reconcile 'music that is good for us' with 'music that is good by definition'.[9]

Burmeister confronts another controversial issue which is most germaine to urban instrumental teachers when he asks: "How can an insistence on standard instrumentation be balanced with the needs of children who want to play nonstandard or folk instruments?"[10] Whether or not the music is classified as soul, Latin, or Polish is determined by the manner in which the elements of music are manipulated. As David McAllester

165

explained in the Tanglewood Symposium Minority report: "when we have learned that any musical expression is 'music', we hope to be able to reduce the class barriers in our schools and concert halls."[11]

The history of American music education tells us that music teachers in the United States have not always acted accordingly. In a historical critique Britton presents evidence that leads him to conclude:

> It is particularly noteworthy that from the very beginning music education in the United States was conditioned by a deliberate desire on the part of cultural leaders to suppress indigenous music and to substitute something 'better' in its place. This was true of the Spanish Franciscans and French Jesuits in their work with the Indian. It is true in general of the modern music teacher playing a recording of Beethoven's Fifth Symphony for his general music class.[12]

Teaching Personnel for Urban Schools

Teaching urban students requires special skills that few colleges and universities are willing to develop among their graduates. For example, Bloom writes that it is well documented that teachers both black and white respond differently to white and black children as well as to children of different social classes. The lower class black child has all the learning problems of other poor children. Yet, in addition to these problems, he suffers from numerous other direct and indirect problems created by the prejudices and attitudes of others. Because of the economic blockade which has been maintained against blacks, many students feel that there is nothing to be gained by being educated.[13]

What type of training is desirable for those who teach in urban schools? Many ideas of the prophetic E. Thayer Gaston, although designed for the field of music therapy, probably could be adapted for urban music education. Gaston often suggested that music education ought to become more interdisciplinary. Some music educators agree with him. The Tanglewood Committee on Implications for the Music Curriculum, for example, recommends that colleges and universities prepare a type of music teacher who is a superb and sensitive musician and one who has concentrated intensely on music history and literature, music analysis, cultural anthropology, ethnomusicology, and aesthetics.[14] Gaston would probably add to the list the field of psychology.

If music therapists are in general agreement with the concepts espoused by Gaston in **Basic Concepts in Music Education**, Chapter XII, entitled "Functional Music", many of the cultural biases which influence the daily work of music educators are minimized among music therapists. Gaston shatters an old myth when he writes: that "there is no such phenomenon as a universal music. Musical taste is a folkway. A culture, therefore, determines its aesthetic ends and goals or adopts those previously maintained."[15] Each culture has its own musical values. The preceding statements raise a controversial issue--should transforming the music values of urban youth into mainstream values be a goal of urban music teachers?

Music therapists understand that music helps to provide freedom from the feeling of loneliness. Gaston believes that moods elicited by music are derived from what he calls the tender emotions. The tender emotions include love, love-making, family, love of parents, religion, patriotism, loyalty, and other similar relationships.[16] Just as music may effectively arouse that which is often at a low ebb in patients, it may do likewise for urban youngsters. More specifically, it may help to provide feelings of security. Security for the urban pupil is very important because secure persons are less anxiety ridden. According to Gaston, it is believed that anxiety is the basis for most emotional disturbances in the normal as well as in others. Without the establishment of a wholesome relationship with students, the urban teacher is doomed to become less successful. Given the proper training, urban music teachers could possibly adopt for use with their students the techniques used by music therapists to establish proper relationships with the handicapped child.

From the foregoing, one may conclude that music ought to be emphasized in urban schools to a much greater extent than it is currently stressed. Music will meet some student needs which would otherwise be ignored. Techniques adopted from the field of music therapy may raise the level of student educational receptability. Once the students rise above the need for therapist techniques, a higher level of musicianship may then be developed. Some of the nation's most gifted, and creative music giants have emanated from the ranks of the impoverished urban masses. The music curriculum must be structured so that such latent talent is discovered, nurtured and developed.

Application of Learning Sequence

Because of the innumerable obstacles which confront urban school personnel, it is imperative that urban music teachers prepare themselves by utilizing the best and most current information available on the teaching of music. One of the foremost recent proponents of music learning theory, Edwin Gordon has conducted seminal research on how one learns when one learns music. Gordon is a prolific researcher who develops theories based on his longitudinal inquiries . But while many theoreticians confine their work to the areas of research and postulations, Gordon develops his theories into pragamatic tools which are essential for elementary and secondary music teachers. He believes that learning has two functions: discrimination and inference. The following outline which includes the generic functions divided into hierarchical levels as well as subparts of the levels reflects the heirarchical structure of learning; the initial learning level is listed at the top:

DISCRIMINATION

AURAL/ORAL
Verbal AssociatioN
PARTIAL SYNTHESIS
SYMBOLIC ASSOCIATION
reading-writing
COMPOSITE SYNTHESIS

INFERENCE

GENERALIZATION
aural/oral - verbal symbolic
CREATIVITY/IMPROVISATION
aural/oral - symbolic
THEORETICAL UNDERSTANDING
aural/oral - verbal-symbolic"[17]

Music understanding, for example, is the key to all meaningful musical experiences.

Music literacy, music listening, music performance, and virtually all human interaction with music implies understanding. As the preceding outline implies, one must first of all understand some aspects of music before music literacy skills are developed. We refer to music literacy, because the reading and writing of music ought to be a major goal of the elementary and secondary music programs. The understanding of music implies a degree of familiarity with its aural elements. Two of the essential aural elements especially germane to the development of music literacy skills are those centered around tonality and meter.

Tonality is an essential aural element because a sense of tonality provides one with the ability to aurally discriminate or audiate (audiate is the hearing of sound psychologically, the actual sound not physically present), for example, between major and minor, or tonic and dominant. Meter is an essential aural element because a sense of meter provides one with the ability to audiate music, as being, for example, duple, triple, or mixed meter.

Knowledgeable teachers of music have historically advocated "sound before sign". Contemporary music psychologists also agree. Gordon, for instance, explains that to understand music in a functional manner audiation must precede the use not only of descriptive words but also of the definitions of musical symbols and structures. The ability to audiate musical sound in terms of tonality and meter constitutes the fundamental readiness on which any further study of music depends.

Readiness is a major factor in most all learning experiences. Without the proper readiness for music skills, verbal skills, or computational skills, results are doomed to be less than optimal. In order to read music, one must "hear" what is seen in music notation. When writing music, one must "hear" what is being notated. A majority of music teachers actually violates one of the most fundamental of all music learning theories when they teach musical symbols and definitions before developing readiness skills. Memorizing key signatures, clefs, and the names of lines and spaces are examples of busy work which does not provide readiness for music literacy. Neither does the ability to recite or identify the letter names and time values of notes constitute a readiness to read music. It is believed by music psychologists that one does not read the musical names of notes. Instead, one hears group of notes or tonal patterns as one reads. Only after an individual becomes capable of tonal and rhythm notational audiation can he or she make more relevant use of the names and definitions of musical symbols.

Although one may make relevant use of the names and time values of symbols, it must be repeated and stressed that we read groups of notes both tonally and rhythmically. We are able to give meaning to the musical patterns we read because we are able to audiate the notation. As a result of being familiar with the sound of the pattern, we are able to read the pattern.

An outstanding instrumental music conductor and teacher consistently chided his students by admonishing "if you can't sing it, you can't play it." Such a statement is in keeping with the dictum that one must be able to sing when audiating tonally because when one engages in tonal audiation, he/she is actually singing silently. In order to audiate rhythmically one must "feel" eurhythmically that which is seen in notation.

In his text, which includes specific information on curriculum development, Gordon includes both a tonal taxonomy and a rhythm taxonomy. Specific information on the sequential order of materials to be covered is available for those who are desirous of following learning theory constructs. Because it is beyond the purview of this chapter to provide a detailed explication of tometics, the reader is encouraged to refer to the sources written by Gordon included in the bibliography. Some music teachers are unfamiliar with tometics, or the application of learning theories to practical teaching situations. Yet, the knowledge and application of such theories might well be the best means of surviving as a new teacher in an urban environment.

Although the language and terminology used by Gordon differ from the jargon ordinarily found in most music education texts and journals, the information available is worth the effort which must be expended in order to understand the material. For example, over 400 comprehensive and specific sequential objectives are listed. An understanding of music learning sequence and the list of objectives will enable the urban music teacher to readily design a music curriculum to meet the needs of most urban schools, while simultaneously making allowances for meeting the individual needs of students within the group. Meeting the individual needs of students within the group is perhaps more important for urban music teachers than for typical music teachers because school attendance patterns of some urban students are erratic. Eash and Napolitan, for example, are quite specific on the need for more individualized instruction for urban pupils.[18] Learning sequences advanced by Gordon are in accordance with educators who feel that educational materials for urban youth ought to be programmed into several small steps. In a word, one of the main keys to success in the urban music curriculum is "structure".

Curriculum Changes

In order to accomplish new goals, most urban music curricula must be radically changed. Radical changes, however, ought to evolve slowly, over a long period of time. Klotman, in an excellent chapter entitled "Designing and Planning Curricula", from his text, **The School Music Administrator and Supervisor: Catalysts for Change in Music Education**, suggests that prior to arbitrarily introducing changes, a design might be structured based on the following five steps:

1. Determining the objectives of the new curriculum (based on student needs)
2. Developing a program of instruction
3. Implementing or developing instructional procedures and strategies for the new program
4. Preparing instructional materials
5. Evaluating both program and its instruction in keeping with its objectives[19]

After presenting a model design, he explains that when music administrators function in such a manner, they truly become architects for designing future programs for the curriculum.

171

Importance and Need for Urban Music

Prior to the decades which produced the urban slums that are so prevalent in the nation today, some ethnic groups which now populate the schools had rich musical experiences. Many persons although unable to perform on instruments or sing in accordance with the standards desired by American vocal teachers communicated their need for musical and aesthetic gratification in numerous ways. Shortly after slavery, for instance, when describing the lack of economic astuteness of former slaves, Booker T. Washington ironically illustrates the craving for aesthetic gratification by a black family when he wrote:

> I remember that on one occasion when I went into one of these cabins for dinner, when I sat down to the table for a meal with the four members of the family, I noticed that, while there were five of us at the table, there was but one fork for the five of us to use. Naturally there was an awkward pause on my part. In the opposite corner of that same cabin was an organ for which the people told me they were paying sixty dollars in monthly installments. One fork and a sixty dollar organ.[20]

In spite of the obvious absurdity in values, an overt statement was made regarding the musical needs of impoverished persons. Both Southern[21] and Roach[22] throughout their texts describe how music has been an integral part of black American life. Some of the most outstanding contributions to the world of music were made by the direct forebears and relatives of the very pupils who populate urban schools. But unless more government or philanthropic support of urban music programs becomes a reality, musical achievement by the vast majority of urban students will be past tense.

Regardless of seemingly insurmountable obstacles between 1865 and 1954 blacks made remarkable progress in music and education. Many blacks have migrated to urban centers from the southern United States. Educational opportunities in the south have come grudingly. Data collected by Redclay led him to conclude: "Even as late as 1930, more than 18,130 of the Negro teaching force in 15 Southern states had less than a high school education. Mississippi, alone, had

172

1,312 Negro elementary teachers who had only an elementary school background."[23] Washington, D.C., in contrast, had relatively excellent black schools during the same era.[24] Bond, in a more detailed study, generally paints a picture of remarkable progress in spite of conscious efforts to obliterate any educational opportunities whatsoever for the black minority.[25] This background contributes negatively to the present urban dilemma. Paradoxically, the south in numerous areas of education has, today, forged ahead of the north.

Why, then, is government or philanthropic support of urban music problems so critically needed now, when musical progress in the past was made in spite of obstacles? The answer is simply--economics. When the nation as a whole has experienced economic difficulties, the government usually has been able to alleviate the situation. John Maynard Keynes, for example, published his work entitled **The General Theory of Employment Interest and Money** in which he justified the need for a vigorous role by the federal government to stabilize and improve economic conditions.[26] The federal government, in fact, did adopt many of Keynes's recommendations. Still, large numbers of poor blacks were not among the beneficiaries of Keynesian economics. In 1962, for example, around 60 percent of all non-white families in the nation had incomes of under $4,000, while only 26 percent of white families were in this lowest income group. Many urban residents migrate from the deep south and at least 85 percent of such families have incomes which place them in the bottom economic group.[27] Children from these families experience extreme difficulty in meeting basic needs such as adequate housing, and clothing.

If a family faces difficulty in meeting basic needs, how will such a family afford musical instruments? Therein lies the reason why government or philanthropic support of urban music programs is absolutely essential. Before so called integration (1954), most urban schools, in which there were large percentages of poor persons, rented instruments to students who qualified. After integration, many teachers who taught in predominantly black schools were fired. They were replaced by persons who refused to rent instruments, largely on the basis that students who do not purchase instruments lack the commitment to discipline themselves and study the instrument in a

173

manner comparable to their peers who do purchase instruments.

Today, the cost of quality music instruments is beyond the economnic reach of most poor and low income persons. Yet, the children of these persons ought to be afforded opportunities to develop their innate music potential just as their more economically fortunate peers. Several years ago, urban schools were able to design their music curricula in a much more balanced manner than the urban school of today. Prior to 1949, Mississippi, for example, which had a despicable record for support of public school black education could boast of excellent music programs in the all black schools[28] of Jackson, the largest urban area in the state. Can we afford to retrogress?

In summary, the term "curriculum" refers to the activities planned by the school. The curriculum includes faculty, staff, school administrators, facilities, courses of study, learning acivities, and funding. Up until the past decade or so, the music curriculum had remained almost the same for approximately 50 years. Birge, in his interpretation of the early beginning of the modern music curriculum, documents that around 1920 the finest high schools included in their curricula mixed chorus, male and female glee clubs, classes in vocal techniques, first and second orchestras, bands, classes for instruction in all instruments, classes in harmony, counterpoint and composition, music appreciation and history, and a requirement for all students to take music appreciation. Symphonic orchestras and bands with idealistic instrumentation performed the finest music literature available.[29]

The emergence of instrumental music was impeded because of the puritanistic leanings of the nation. Only sacred music was widely accepted by the society. Instrumental music because of its secular connotations was looked upon with disfavor. Birge explains: "During the seventeenth century instrumental music was non-existent in the colonies. In the eighteenth century, pipe organs began to appear in the churches, and instrumental music began to have a place as a social diversion, but its serious cultivation was generally regarded as frivolous if not wicked.[30] Many curricula changes occurred during the first score of this century. Immediately following 1920, the music curriculum was relatively inert.

174

Music educators, in recent years, however, have combined efforts to design more flexible music curricula. Curricula changes, however, are more than mere chance undertakings. Careful planning and technical guidelines ought to be followed by educators who desire to revise or change their curricula. Urban schools pose special problems never faced before by American educators and because of their unique status, curricula patterns ought to be modified to meet the needs of each school. Although modifications are recommended, model curricula developed by learned, and professional societies ought to form the basic structure of urban music programs.

Music educators in the United States still look to foreigners for direction, often failing to realize that the cultures from which foreign methods and techniques have evolved are different from American culture, particularly urban American culture.

What path, then, may be tread by the urban music teacher? Once the teacher understands himself/herself well enough to transcend personal biases that would impede the learning processes of urban pupils, and once the teacher comprehends the social, psychological, and economic problems of urban youth, and once the teacher has fulfilled the requirements recommended by the Tanglewood Committee on Implications for the Music Curriculum mentioned above, it would be most advantageous for the teacher to apply music learning theories to actual urban teaching situations. When armed with ethnic music materials from the cultures which comprise the school population and a knowledge of how students learn when they learn music, urban music teachers will certainly become more effective.

Because of numerous complex problems which con-urban music teachers, it is recommended that a block of courses be taken in human behavior which parallels similar courses taken by music therapists. Music therapists have been highly successful in meeting the music needs of the handicapped. Special techniques, such as relating to atypical students, developed by music therapists could probably be used in urban schools until students advance to typical levels of achievement. Music curricula ought to be designed in such a manner that the transition from under-achievement levels to typical achievement levels can be made smoothly.

Urban student have many latent talents, and once pupils reach readiness levels that would enable them to achieve in a manner in keeping with regional and national norms, their teachers would probably become more successful by applying in their classes current music learning theories. The work of Edwin Gordon in the area of music learning sequence is especially noteworthy. By the utilization of the rhythm and tonal taxonomies that he has developed, teachers will be able to plan and structure objectives more effectively.

If the urban music curriculum is to be strengthened, additional sources of funding must be identified. Without government or philanthropic support of the urban music curriculum, this nation could well lose a generation of its most talented and creative future musicians. Along with additional funding, however, it is absolutely essential that curricula changes follow guidelines established by professional authorities and learned societies.

SUGGESTED CURRICULUM FOR URBAN MUSIC TEACHERS

The National Association of Schools of Music (NASM) has been designated by the Council on Postsecondary Accreditation as the organization responsible for the accreditation of all music curricula in higher education. In keeping with this responsibility, NASM has developed guidelines for model curricula in music education. For example, the recommended curricular struture will comprise between 120-132 semester hours or (180-198 quarter hours). Studies in music, including basic musicianship and performance, should comprise approximately 50 percent of the total curriculum. General studies should comprise around 30 pecent to 35 percent, and professional education, around 15 percent to 20 percent.

The model curriculum for urban teachers ought to be compatible with the general standards, essential competencies, desirable personal qualities, and recommended procedures articulated by NASM. Because of the trauma involved in making radical changes in music education curricula, the curricula could well retain most of the course titles traditionally found in college bulletins. But where traditional courses are structured around European art music, a structure which includes some art music along with jazz, blues, rock, country, and pop would be more beneficial to the

176

student. For example, in freshman theory classes, when developing a mastery of chord construction, scale construction, rhythm notation, and melodic notation, students should be afforded opportunities to use jazz, rock, and other more contemporary musics as didactic media. Students will become more highly motivated and they will be able to enthusiastically immerse themselves in the study of theory when they begin to understand the sounds which are heard daily on phonogrph recordings and radios.

Harmonic continuity, voice leading, and multiple part harmonization will also be taught under a traditional course title but the course content will include a bulk of pop, country, blues, jazz and rock idioms. Competencies, then, will include the ability to harmonize in a variety of styles.

Ear training courses should be revised to include intensive work in improvisation. A first course in ear training would include fundamentals or principles of improvisation. Pentatonic studies, modal studies, and improvisation on a given melody are absolute essentials for the music education curriculum. Work in improvisation must be pursued assiduously. Traditional approaches to ear-training which are structured around sight-singing, and dictation will reinforce one another. Advanced ear-training courses ought to include techniques of transcribing from phonograph recordings. The importance of transcribing cannot be over-emphasized. Transcribing is a critical skill.

Form and analysis classes ought to draw heavily from the contemporary musics mentioned earlier. That is form, including phrase structure, motivic development, repetition, and contrast can be studied by analyzing the music of Ray Charles, just as well as it can be by analyzing the music of Mozart. In fact, by including popular music earlier in the course, readiness for the study of Mozart will bring about higher levels of achievement.

Keyborad classes must include modern block harmonization, chord substitution, harmonization of improvised melodies, and modern chord progressions. At least 50 percent of keyboard classes for those students who major on instruments other than piano ought to be devoted to systems of accompanying based on the study of modern chord progressions, formulae based on the rules for block harmonization, and chord substitutions.

Music history and literature courses ought to be organized so that the history and literature of jazz, blues, rock, rhythm and blues, country, and pop are included in the required curriculum. This may be accomplished by synthesizing much of the history and literature content that the history and literature of jazz, blues, rock, rhythm and blues, country, and pop are included in the required curriculum. This may be accomplished by synthesizing much of the history and literature content that is normally covered in most music education curricula. Because more knowledge of western music has been accumulated in the immediate past few decades, music history teachers tend to cover many minute scholarly details that could be omitted in favor of a survey of contemporary popular culture when students are already immersed in the music too much already. The answer is that most students do not understand jazz, rhythm and blues, rock, nor pop any more than they understand the music of the baroque.

Orchestration-arranging classes, after covering the most essential principles of band and orchestra scoring, ought to include units on the practical as-aspects of audio recording, and music syntheses by electronic means. Students ought to be afforded opportunities to participate in multi-track recording, over-dubbing and mix down sessions. The music synthesis by electronic means unit ought to afford opportunities for the students to understand essential steps in the formation of musical sounds from conception and analysis through synthesis and final realization.

In those curricula where there is already a plethora of required courses, it might be desirable to eliminate four hours of major applied study and two semesters of major ensemble requirements so that students may take intensive courses in guitar, jazz/rock rhythm sections, and methods of teaching and rehearsing jazz/rock ensembles. Jazz and rock ensemble performance standards must be elevated and maintained at the height attained by the finest wind, string, percussion, and vocal ensembles. Guitar, bass guitar/double bass, and percussion set are essential aspects of modern American music. Students who lack even fundamental study of these instruments are placed at a decided disadvantage when placed in an urban music teaching situation.

A model, a suggested, or a recommended curriculum for urban music teachers should be structured in accordance with the guidelines established by NASM. Rather than radically restructure the present music education curriculum, it is recommended that traditional course titles be retained. However, the content of those courses ought to be broadened to include jazz, rock, gospel, and other present-day music. Improvization is a critically needed skill and should be added either as a new sequence of courses or incorporated in the current sight-singing and ear-training courses.

Theory classes should be restructured to include jazz, pop, gospel, rock, blues chords, modern chord progressions and the analysis of the music which permeates American popular culture. Keyboard classes ought to be correlated with theory classes so that students may apply the theory learned in a practical manner. For example, each music education graduate ought to be able to accompany at the keyboard by applying techniques learned when studying harmonic continuity, voice leading, and multiple part harmonization. Modal, pentatonic, and melodic improvisation ought to be included in keyboard classes along with the study of harmonization.

The history and literature of popular American musics should be included in the music education curriculum. The additional subject matter may be included by synthesizing some of the current content and by eliminating many small details which have crept into the courses during the past 30 years or so. The skill of transcribing recordings, selected practical aspects of audio recording, and music synthesis by electronic means are indispensable experiences that should be commonly shared by all urban music teachers.

Finally, guitar, bass guitar/double bass, and percussion set should be understood by anyone who plans to teach in the urban environment. Ability to teach and rehearse jazz/rock ensembles is essential for all urban music teachers, including vocal and general music teachers.

Any teacher who has developed the preceding competencies will certainly be better prepared to meet the needs of urban elementary and secondary music students.

Study Questions

1. What is meant by the term "music curriculum"?

2. Identify and describe two styles of music curriculum.

3. Before planning a music curriculum what factors are absolutely essential?

4. What is the purpose of the general music program?

5. Why is the special music program necessary?

6. What are the factors which cause variability among music curricula in the various communities and regions of the United States?

7. What official publication offers detailed information on the structure of the musical curriculum?

8. In accordance with this publication, describe the scope of objectives for each of the five levels of the curriculum.

9. What are behavioral objectives?

10. Describe the ethnic and racial groups which constitute urban schools.

11. Why is it difficult to teach in schools where the population consists of numerous ethnic and racial groups.?

12. Under what conditions do some urban students struggle?

13. What types of music literature and music materials ought to be used in an urban environment?

14. How do class, and race influence the music materials and literature selected for the urban curriculum?

15. What kinds of academic courses are recommended to prepare one to understand and teach urban students?

16. If each culture has its own musical values, what are the implications for urban music teachers?

17. How can music education help urban students?

18. Why is the application of music learning theories so important for urban music teachers?

19. How does the work of Edwin Gordon differ from that of some other learning theoreticians?

20. Define and describe the role of both inference and discrimination in learning.

21. Why is music literacy an important skill?

22. Why is an understanding of tonality and meter so necessary for students?

23. The fundamental readiness for all advanced studies of music is dependent on what ability?

24. Why is musical readiness so important?

25. Point out some errors made by most teachers of music?

26. What mental operations occur when we read music?

27. Why is it essential for urban music teachers to be familiar with tometics?

28. How should one proceed when attempting to change the urban music curriculum?

29. Blacks and the urban poor have never had control of their educational destinies in the United States. Explain why it can be said that in spite of efforts by the power structure to offer only the worst quality of education to blacks in the south, remarkable progress was made nevertheless.

30. What connection is there between rural southern blacks of the past and urban blacks of the present?

31. In general, how have economic policies in this nation affected blacks as a whole?

32. Why is government or philanthropic support of urban music programs essential?

33. How often was the music curriculum revised during the early years of music education in this country?

34. How do most urban school music curricula of today compare with the music curricula of the finest high schools around 1920?

35. Why can it be safely said that the historical past still casts a giant shadow over the urban music curriculum of today?

36. Why have music educators in the United States shown a predilection for foreign methods?

37. What must the urban music teacher do in order to be effective?

38. If college music departments which prepare their students to teach in urban schools are truly committed to graduating effective teachers, what courses of action would they follow?

BIBLIOGRAPHY

Birge, Edward Bailey. **History of Public School Music in the United States.** Washington, D.C.: MENC, Copyright assigned in 1966.

Bloom, Benjamin S.; Davis, Allison; and Hess, Robert. **Compensatory Education for Cultural Deprivation.** New York: Holt, Rinehart and Winston, Inc., 1965.

Bond, Horace Mann. **The Education of the Negro in the American Social Order.** New York: Prentice-Hall, Inc., 1934.

Chamberlain, Leo M. and Kindred, Leslie W. **The Teacher and School Organization.** 4th ed. Englewood Cliffs, N.J.: Prentice-Hall, Inc., 1966.

Choate, Robert A., ed. **Documentary Report of the Tanglewood Symposium.** Washington, D.C.: MENC, 1968.

Dabney, Lillian G. **The History of Schools for Negroes** in the District of Columbia, **1807-1947.** Washington, D.C.: Catholic University Press, 1949.

Gordon, Edwin E. **Learning Sequence and Patterns in Music.** rev. ed. Chicago: G.I.A. Publications, Inc., 1977.

Primary Measures of Music Audiation; A Music Aptitude Test for Kindergarten and Primary Grade Children. Chicago: G.I.A.

The Psychology of Music Teaching; Englewood Cliffs, NJ: Prentice Hall, 1971.

Henry, Nelson B., ed. **Basic Concepts in Music Education.** Part one, The Fifty-seventh Yearbook of the National Society for the Study of Education. Chicago: University of Chicago Press, 1958.

Klotman, Robert H. **The School Music Administrator and Supervisor; Catalysts for change in Music Education.** Englewood Cliffs, N.J.: Prentice-Hall, Inc., 1973.

Kovarsky, Irving and Albrecht, William. Black **Employment; The Impact of Religion, Economic Theory, Politics, and Law.** Ames, Iowa: The Iowa State University Press, 1970.

Leonhard, Charles and House, Robert W. **Foundations and Principals of Music Education.** 2nd ed. New York: McGraw-Hill Book Co., 1972.

MENC, National Commission on Instruction, **The School Music Program: Descriptions and Standards.** Vienna, Virginia: MENC, 1974.

Redclay, Edward E. **County Training Schools and Public Secondary Education for Negroes in the South.** Washington, D.C.: The John F. Slater Fund, 1935.

Roach, Hildred. **Black American Music; Past and Present.** Boston: Crescendo Pub. Co., 1973.

Silberman, Charles E. **Crisis in the Classroom.** New York: Random House, 1970.

Simmons, Otis D. **Teaching Music in Urban Schools.** Boston: Crescendo Pub. Co., 1975.

Smith, B. Othanel; Cohen, Saul B.; and Pearl, Arthur. **Teachers for the real world.** Washington, D.C.: The American Association of Colleges for Teacher Education, 1969.

Southern, Eileen. **The Music of Black Americans; A History.** New York: W.W. Norton & Co., Inc., 1971.

Walberg, Herbert J. and Kopan, Andrew T., eds. **Rethinking Urban Education.** San Francisco: Jossey-Bass, 1972.

Washington, Booker T. **Up From Slavery.** New York: Lancer Books, Inc., 1968.

Weyland, Rudolph H. **A Guide to Effective Music Supervision.** Dubuque, Iowa: Brown & Co., 1960.

Wilson, Charles H. **Education for Negroes in Mississippi Since 1910.** Boston: Meador Pub. Co., 1947.

NOTES FOR CHAPTER 9

1. Charles Leonhard and Robert W. House, **Foundations and Principles of Music Education,** second editon. (New York: McGraw-Hill Book Co. 1972), p. 220.

2. Rudolph H. Weyland, **A Guide to Effective Music Supervision.** (Dubuque, Iowa: Brown & Co., 1960), pp. 149-150.

3. Leo M. Chamberlain and Leslie W. Kindred, **The Teacher and School Organization,** 4th edition. (Englewood Cliffs: Prentice-Hall, Inc. 1966), pp. 287-293.

4. MENC, National Commission on Instruction, **The School Music Programs: Descriptions and Standards.** (Vienna, Virginia: MENC, 1974), pp. 7-10.

5. **Ibid.**

6. B. Othanel Smith, Saul B. Cohen and Arthur Pearl, **Teachers for the Real World.** (Washington, D.C.: The American Association of Colleges for Teacher Education, 1969), pp. 11-13.

7. Charles E. Silberman, **Crisis in the Classroom.** (New York: Random House, 1970), p. 304.

8. In a chapter entitled "The Social Bankruptcy of Urban Environments" Simmons offers more information on urban social problems. See: Otis D. Simmons, **Teaching Music in Urban Schools.** (Boston: Crescendo Pub. Co., 1975), pp. 22-38.

9. C.A. Burmeister, "The Role of Music in General Education" in Nelson B. Henry, editor, **Basic Concepts in Music Education**, Part one, The Fifty-seventh Yearbook of the National Society for the Study of Education. (Chicago: University of Chicago Press, 1958), p. 223.

10. **Ibid.**

11. David McAllester, "Curriculum Must Assume a Place at the Center of music" in Robert A. Choate, editor, **Documentary Report of the Tanglewood Symposium.** (Washington, D.C.: MENC, 1968), p. 138.

12. Allen P. Britton, "Music in Early American Public Education: A Historical Critique," in **Basic Concepts in Music Education,** p. 200.

13. Benjamin S. Bloom, Allison Davis, Robert Hess, **Compensatory Education for Cultural Deprivation.** (New York: Holt, Rinehart and Winston, Inc., 1965), pp. 29-31.

14. **Tanglewood Symposium,** p. 136.

15. E. Thayer Gaston, "Functional Music," in **Basic Concepts in Music Education,** pp. 292-309.

16. **Ibid.**

17. Edwin E. Gordon, **Learning Sequence and Patterns in Music**, revised edition. (Chicago: G.I.A. Publications, Inc., 1977), p. 8.

18. Maurice J. Esh and James T. Napolitan, "Insights and alternatives from a Black Street Academy" in: Herbert J. Walberg and Andrew T. Kopan, editors, **Rethinking Urban Education.** (San Francisco: Jossey-Bass, 1972), pp. 107-109.

10. Robert H. Klotman, **The School Music Administrator and Supervisor; Catalysts for Change in Music Education.** (Englewood Cliffs, N.J.: Prentice-Hall Inc., 1973), pp. 34-44.

20. Booker T. Washington, **Up From Slavery.** (New York: Lancer Books, Inc., 1968), p. 117.

21. Eileen Southern, **The Music of Black Americans; A History.** (New York: W.W. Norton & Co., Inc., 1971).

22. Hildred Roach, **Black American Music; Past and Present.** (Boston: Crescendo Pub. Co., 1973).

23. Edward E. Redclay, **County Training Schools and Public Secondary Education for Negroes in the South.** (Washington, D.C.: The John F. Slater Fund, 1935), p. 37.

24. Lillian G. Dabney, **The History of Schools for Negroes in the District of Columbia, 1807-1947.** (Washington, D.C: Catholic University Press, 1949), pp. 130-149.

25. Horace Mann Bond, **The Education of the Negro in the American Social Order.** (New York: Prentice-Hall, Inc., 1935).

26. Irving Kovarsky and William Albrecht, **Black Employment; The Impact of Religion, Economic Theory, Politics, and Law.** (Ames, Iowa: The Iowa State University Press, 1970), pp. 51-56.

27. **Compensatory Education,** pp. 29-31.

28. See: Charles H. Wilson, **Education for Negroes in Mississippi Since 1910.** (Boston: Meador Publishing Co., 1947), pp. 434-445.

29. Edward Bailey Birge, **History of Public School Music in the United States.** (Washington, D.C.: MENC, Copyright assigned in 1966), pp. 159-172.

30. **Ibid.**

Projects

1. Using the mongram published by MENC entitled The School Music Program: Descriptions and Standards as a general guide, and the tonal and rhythm taxonomies contained in Edwin Gordon's Learning Sequence and Patterns in Music as a content guide, structure three curriculums, one for below average students, one for average students, and one for above average students. Each curriculum is to be divided in 5 sections: (1) early childhood, (2) primary level, (3) preadolescence, (4) early adolescence, and (5) high school level. Depending upon a student's interest and preparation, a curriculum ought to be developed for general music - K-12, instrumental music and vocal music. Articulate the skills and musical competencies which are to be achieved at each level of each curriculum.

2. Determine which is most effective, traditional approaches to music teaching or the contemporary approach where one applies music learning theories in a teaching situation. The project will involve using two different music classes of similar socio-economic backgrounds, similar distributions of musical aptitude, and similar intelligence levels. The same goals and objectives will be established for both groups and after a given period of time, both groups will be appraised to determine the extent to which musical skills, musical initiatives have been developed.

Chapter 10

VIOLENCE AND VANDALISM IN URBAN SCHOOLS

Donald J. Jones

The alarming rise of violence and vandalism in public schools in recent years has gained the attention of educators, parents and politicians. Not only is violence on the rise in urban schools, but it reaches into suburban schools as well. The problem is so severe many teachers are forced to lock their classroom doors after classes begin. Students are afraid to leave books or coats in lockers for fear of their being stolen or burned. Many of those who own musical instruments are afraid to bring them to school for fear of them being stolen in transit.

Often this wave of violence is a spillover from the community. It takes many forms, ranging from actual physical attacks or threats of physical assault to harassments such as broken windows and slashed tires on teachers' cars. Obviously such an environment creates a climate of hostility and fear for many educators and students.[1]

The federal government, seeking ways to diminish violence, recently released the results of a three-year, $2.4 million study on violence in American public schools. The study, entitled "Violent Schools - Safe Schools," revealed that although the rate of violence nationwide is leveling off, it remains a serious problem, particularly in urban areas. The study also found that 2.4 million, or 11 percent of the nation's 21 million high school students have something stolen from them in a month's time and that 282,000, or 13 percent, report being attacked. Approximately 12 percent, or 120,000 teachers are victims of theft and 5,200 teachers are assaulted each month. During a time of dire economic crisis in public education, it has been estimated that over $600 million is wasted annually as a result of school violence--more than the total amount spent nationally on textbooks.

Another recent widely publicized study on school discipline was conducted by the United States Senate Subcommittee on Juvenile Delinquency. The committee's report, released by Senator Birch Bayh (Dem., Indiana), in April, 1975, revealed some startling statistics based upon a survey of more than 750 school districts nationwide. The study's preliminary findings revealed that between the years 1970-1973:

1. Homicides increased by 18.5 percent;
2. Rapes and attempted rapes increased by 40.1 percent;
3. (Robberies) increased by 36.7 percent;
4. Assaults on students increased by 77.4 percent;
5. Burglaries of school buildings increased by 11.8 percent;
6. Drug and alcohol offenses on school property increased by 37.5 percent;[2]
7. Dropouts increased by 11.7 percent.

Research conducted in 1975 by the National Committee for Citizens in Education indicates that no more than ten percent of the school population is responsible for the vandalism and violence in our nation's schools.[3]

The daily threats of abuse and physical and verbal assault heaped upon teachers have forced many to the breaking point. Many urban teachers now suffer what Los Angeles Psychologist Alfred Bloch refers to as "combat neurosis," a condition resulting from working constantly in an extremely stressful situation. Bloch, who has conducted research on teacher stress since 1971, recommends transfers to more tranquil schools for a period of "rest and recuperation" as a possible solution but added that most school systems have refused transfers for such reasons. He places most of the blame on vacillating school administrators who feel that the student can do no wrong.[4]

Often teachers and administrators are under great pressure not to report incidents of violence and vandalism. Administrators fear that to admit that there are problems somehow reflects on their ability to supervise. Teachers fear punitive evaluations and administrative charges that they have poor classroom management techniques. Adding to the problem are the courts which often dismiss many cases on technicalities.

The fallacy of ignoring the problem is that it never goes away. Rather the problem worsens, often creating a potentially explosive situation. The National Education Association, with a membership of

1.7 million teachers, believes that the number o
violent acts committed against teachers is much highe
than believed. The organization estimates that only 1
percent of the incidents of violence are ever actuall
reported.[5]

One school system at least acknowledges th
seriousness of the problem and has developed a progra
to aid battle-weary teachers. The Milwaukee, Wisconsi
Public Schools has set up a hospital program to trea
alcoholic teachers.[6]

Several factors have been identified as possibl
causes of the present violent wave in our schools: th
easy entry into many school buildings; increased use o
drugs and alcohol; overcrowded schools; violence o
television; and many parents who have lost all contro
over their own children.

The correlation between vandalism and th
survival of music programs is significant. Som
examples are:

1. Many students who own musical instruments ar
    afraid to bring them to school for fear of the
    being stolen in transit.

2. Often, stolen or severely damaged instruments ar
    never replaced in the inventory due either to
    shift in school district priorities (e.g.
    improvement of reading and math scores) o
    shrinking school budgets due to inflation an
    other causes.

3. Since most urban school districts provide a fa
    larger percentage of school-owned instruments fo
    student use than their suburban counterparts,
    reduced inventory often means fewer studen
    opportunities for instruction. This factor thu
    detracts   greatly from the overall quality an
    depth of the total instrumental music programs.

4. Violence and vandalism have almost eliminate
    night activities at many urban high schools
    Thus, football games and other events that migh
    produce more revenue for the schools have bee
    virtually eliminated.

Proposed solutions have included alternativ
education programs, increased supportive personne

(counselors, psychologists, social workers) and in-service training in crisis-prevention for teachers. To date, none of the proposed reforms have had any major impact. However, unless the problem is eliminated urban schools cannot survive as functioning institutions of learning.

Security guards, police and sophisticated alarm systems are stop-gap measures at best. Any permanent solution must be found in the home with parents. It is a problem with no teacher, principal or superintendent can solve alone. National Education Association Executive Director Terry Herndon states, "So much of society's responsiblity in raising children has shifted to the schools. For increasing numbers of youth, the church, the neighborhood and the extended family have ceased to play significant roles."[7]

The schools of today are not the same schools many of us remember from past decades. Unlike past generations, many parents of today's youth show little concern for their children's behavior in school. Parents must share the burdens and the glory of our schools. Without the full support of parents, the goal of "excellence in education" is a myth.

Prescription Programs

Many school districts in an effort to combat the rising wave of school vandalism have instituted innovative programs designed to eliminate or reduce the incidence of vandalism, theft and other crimes. Examples are:

> -At Northwestern Secondary High-School in Prince Georges County, Maryland, the school district instituted a student based security program. The plan involved 200 student volunteers in groups of six who take turns patrolling the parking lot, halls and locker areas. Student volunteers miss one class every two weeks, with schedules alternated so that no one has to miss the same class more than once a semester. Since the program's inception three years ago, vandalism has been reduced 98 percent. Also there has been a dramatic decrease in the number of false fire alarms.

191

-Until recently, San Francisco's Luther Burbank Junior High School had more than its share of vandalism related problems. In September, 1977, the San Francisco board of education gave the school's student council $12,127.00, the amount spent for damage during the previous semester. The agreement was that any new damages would be deducted from that amount. Whatever remained the students were free to spend as they pleased, so long as it was legal. In an effort to save money, the students organized antivandalism button and poster contests and openly publicized a running tally of the account's balance. After the first semester vandalism had been reduced drastically, school espirit de corps had risen and a total of $8,361.00 remained in the account. As a result of this drastic reduction in vandalism, the school board has decided to expand the program to other schools.

-Senator Birch Bayh, (D-Indiana) former chairman of the Sub-Committee to Investigate Juvenile Delinquency, in an effort to combat school violence and vandalism, released a sub-committee report, Challenge for America's Third Century: Education in a Safe Environment. The report focused upon and outlined the types of locally based programs thought to help reduce and prevent the rising tide of violence and vandalism. The report recommended not turning schools into armed camps, but instead programs designed to create the kind of atmosphere in which education should take place. The report's recommendations also included:

-Community education and alternative education programs

-Student codes of rights and responsiblities

-Curriculum reform

-Police, school, community liaison
 arrangements

-Inservice and preservice teacher
 preparation courses

-School security programs

-Improved counseling and guidance

-Improved school architectural and
 design techniques

-Increased parental and student
 involvement

-Alternatives to student suspension and
 expulsion.[8]

-The Detroit Public Schools have joined
 other county governmental and community
 organizations in a program coordinated
 by the Social Action Research Center, a
 non-profit research and educational
 organization, which has been funded
 through a grant from the U.S. Office of
 Juvenile Justice and Delinquency
 Prevention.

Agencies represented will form a task force which
hopefully will create programs which will have a
positive effect upon the lives of students. The first
project of the task force will be to involve students
in a program designed to reduce school vandalism.[9]

-The Sacramento, California Public
Schools, instituted a program in eight
schools in 1976, called "Conflict
Management" which has helped to reduce
violence in those schools. Under the
program, elementary and secondary students are trained to work with
potentially violent students in a "non-
punitive" attempt to ease and resolve
conflicts before they erupt into
violence.

Students are afforded the time and
privacy without peer, teacher or administrative interference to work out

their conflicts. This method provides students with an alternative to violence, which often is spurred on by an onlooking crowd.

The training for the program consists of lecture and open discussions on topics ranging from peer pressure to outsiders. The second half of the training is devoted to role-play facilitation. The role-playing consists of pairs of student teams; one team originates a conflict while another acts as a conflict management team. They listen to both sides of the conflict and then seek a solution acceptable to both sides.

The program thus far has avoided many potentially violent confrontations between students and is being expanded to include more schools. [10]

Environmental Design Crime Prevention

The Westinghouse Corporation has sponsored crime-prevention programs in four high schools in Broward County Florida, utilizing prevention through Environmental Design Techniques. Some of the ideas used are locker rooms being open only during the beginning and the end of the school day; windows located only in corridors and classroom doors and two-way radios used by the staff.

Vandal watch

The Elk Grove, California School District has reduced vandalism by twenty-five percent due to the presence of family "school-sitters" who live in mobile homes on school property. Under the program, the school district pays for utilities in exchange for families watching the school grounds. The resulting twenty-five percent decrease in vandalism saves the school district an estimated $20,000 per year.

-Dr. John T. Molloy, professor of management at Michigan State University strongly believes that teachers who dress in an authoritative and adult

> manner are less likely to be the target
> of attacks by students. Molloy
> believes that teachers who dress in
> ghetto styles and are dealing with
> students who come from backgrounds in
> which physical violence is the norm are
> saying "I am one of you and I settle
> things the same way you do."[11]

Although this is an almost totally new concept, it is an intriguing idea worthy of further study.

These examples represent a few of the programs instituted by various school districts in their attempts to grapple with the increasing problems of violence and vandalism. Also many states and local municipalities have formed task forces to investigate and make recommendations on ways to curb the rising tide of violence and vandalism which in 1977-78 cost school districts nationwide an estimated $600 million. Obviously a portion of this money could be put to better use in academic and elective programs within the schools.

The Scope of the Problem

- In 1981, an estimated 70,000 public school teachers will be assaulted in their classrooms.

- Eighty percent of the teachers in Los Angeles inner-city schools are on valium.

- For six consecutive years, discipline ranked as the top concern among the public schools. Secondary school teachers cited lack of it as the most important factor hindering their ability to deliver their best performances.

- Some urban high schools use metal detectors at the entrance to school.

- Seattle reported 1,886 crimes committed against students and school employees ranging from homicides to possession of firearms on school property.

- Schools nationwide spent more than $7 million on prevention and repair in 1974-75.

- The Chicago Public Schools spent $3.5 million on

property loss, $3.2 million for school security programs and $3 million for security guards--a total of $9.7 million.

- The Miami-Dade County schools reported 1,200 assaults.

- New York City reports an average of 2,500 attacks each school year--half against teachers.

Recent Research Studies

- Senate Subcommittee to investigate Juvenile Delinquency Senator Birch Boyh (D., Ind.)

Key Findings

1. Six thousand junior high and high school teachers are robbed at school in a month's time.

2. Over the same time period, over 5,000 teachers are physically attacked.

3. Juvenile crime has increased by 245 percent in a 13 year period, with approximately half committed by people under 21.

4. More students died in our schools between 1970-73 than the number of American soldiers killed in combat in the first three years of the Vietnam conflict.

Violence and Vandalism

5. Violence and vandalism is growing rapidly in suburban and rural areas.

- Safe School Study Report to Congress (1974). This 247 page study was completed by the National Institute of Education and represents a major analysis of school violence nationwide with a sampling of over 4,000 elementary and secondary schools.

Major Findings (In a typical month)

For the student:

1. a secondary school student has about one chance in nine of having something stolen.

2. one chance in 80 of being attacked.

3. one chance in 200 of being robbed.

For the Teacher:

4. one chance in eight of having something stolen.

5. one chance in 167 of being robbed.

6. one chance in 200 of being attacked.

7. Twenty-five percent of American schools, about 20,500 suffer from moderate to serious problems of vandalism.

- The National Association of School Security Directors Estimates that school vandalism diverts more than $590 million from education budgets. This sum exceeds the total amount spent on school textbooks in 1972.

- Recent statistics released by the National Center for Educational Statistics revealed that close to one fifth of the student body was absent in Boston and New York on an average day; in 18 other cities roughly one out of every 11 students missed school .

- Absenteeism was listed among the top ten "most serious issues" facing administrators today in a recent report of the American Association of School Administrators (AASA).

Discussion Questions

1. How can schools be made safe for its student?

2. Should all schools have a student code of conduct? If so, why?, If not, why not?

3. What role should the policies play in helping make schools safe for students?

4. What can administrators, teachers and parents do to provide a safe environment for learning?

5. How can the local school board assist in the fight against violence and vandalism in the schools?

6. What role can students play in solving the problem of crime and violence in schools?

7. How have recent court decisions restrained school personnel from exercising control over student conduct?

8. In terms of drugs and assualts on persons and property; should students be subject to the same laws as the rest of society?

9. Should rules in school in terms of lawful acts be the same as those outside of school, or should they be different?

Bibliography of Further Readings

Archerly, R.L. "Controlling Student Conduct," **Education Digest,** April 1970, pp. 12-15.

Brodbelt, S.S. "Problem of Growing Dissent in the High School," **High School Journal,** March 1970, pp. 365-366+

Highland, J.N. "Student Dress Codes: Fact of Fiction," **Illinois Education,** February 1971, pp. 114-116.

McCaffery, J.F. "Discipline in the Innovative School," **Clearing House,** April 1970, pp. 491-496.

"Revolt in the High Schools - The Way It's Going to Be," **The Saturday Review,** February 1969, pp. 83-84; 89; 101-102.

"Satisfied and Dissatisfied Students," **Personal Guidance**, March 1969, pp. 641-649.

Smith, E.W. and Others. "Students Codes," **Educator's Encyclopedia.** Englewood Cliffs, New Jersey, New Jersey: Prentice-Hall, Inc., 1961, pp. 508-509.

NOTES FOR CHAPTER 10

1. "Violence Stalks Detroit Schools," **The Detroit Teacher,** May 25, 1977, Vol. 36, No. 17, p. 1.

2. Our Nation's Schools, A Report Card: "A Study in School Violence and Vandalism," Preliminary Report of the Subcommittee on the Judiciary of the U.S. Senate (Washington, D.C.: U.S. **Government Printing Office,** April, 1975), p. 2.

3. Violence in our Schools: What To Do About It (Columbia, Md.: **National Committee for Citizens** in Education, 1975), p. 6.

4. **The Detroit Teacher,** op. cit., p. 1.

5. Marguerite Michaels, "Our Nation's Teachers are Taking a Beating," **Parade Magazine,** February 26, 1978, p. 7.

6. **Ibid.**

7. **Ibid.**

8. Birch Bayh, School Vilence and Vandalism, Problems and Solutions, **American Educator,** Summer, 1978, p. 6.

9. The Superintendent's Report, **The Detroit Public Schools Reporter,** November, 1978, p. 1.

10. Cas Piggot, "Classroom Corner," **American Educator,** Winter, 1978, p. 6.

11. John T. Molloy, "Button Up Your Overcoat--But First be Sure it Fits Your Business Image," **Detroit Free Press,** December 24, 1978, p. 100.

CHAPTER 11

THE MUSIC ADMINISTRATOR IN URBAN SCHOOLS

ROBERT A. KLOTMAN

In the Beginning: Attitude

Too often music administrators, regardless of race, have been patronizing in their approach to raising the level of music understanding within their constituency without even being aware of their own attitude.   This had been reflected by unnecessary concessions to mediocrity and is generally a result of confusion regarding differences in forms of expression as a misconception of what determines quality.   All music administrators should have as a fundamental goal that of achieving the highest quality of experience for the students in the community that they **serve**.   This aim of achieving quality should apply to every form of musical expression regardless of the idiom.   The confusion occurs when one tries to compare one form of cultural expression with another. Each is valid in its own right.   The only time educators should make any comparision among the versions of expression is to distinguish the differences that people utilize to express their experiences. Regardless of the idiom, one should seek the highest quality that exists in every cultural manifestation, for each is valid within its own context.

To succeed in an urban setting, administrators should possess a true conviction that their commitment in educating students is to impart the knowledge and understanding that will not only raise the quality of living in the area they serve, but will also enhance the cultural contributions that the people who reside in the area can offer.   A black administrator in Detroit, when discussing this problem, once stated that "we should not denigrate the beautiful heritage of black people while imparting music knowledge about Western traditions nor should we teach only Afro-American or Western music in our classes. **All** students need to learn about both musical genres." Furthermore, it is essential that students be exposed to experiences that will not only enhance their understanding of themselves and the contributions that their people have made to the American musical scene, but also help them become conversant with idioms that exist in other cultures.   They need to be exposed to the diversity

200

that exists in our society so that the knowledge acquired regarding artistic forms of expressions being utilized makes them aware of and more sensitive to the variety of cultural entities from which human experiences emanate.

Students whose origins are different from the primarily white society need to become conversant with idioms that govern that cultural milieu if they are to successfully compete in the same cultural arena. On the other hand, young people whose musical background is entirely based in the Western tradition of music need to be exposed to Black, Hispanic, and other cultural entities if they are not to be "culturally deprived." It is not a question of either, or. It is an issue that demands encompassing as much of **all** essential cultural forms as is possible.

If an administrator is to assist urban youth in becoming successful in functioning in a pluralistic society where many cultural forms should exist in mutual appreciation, he/she must comprehend and apply this broad concept of idioms education. As a matter of fact, it applies to administrating in any community!

Attitude -- that is where it begins. The music "leader" must recognize the musical values that reside in the culture from which urban youth emanate. They must see not only that it is given appropriate exposure, but also expand these experiences to include other forms of cultural expression as well. Herein is the essence of quality education in music.

THE SUPERVISOR MUST KNOW THE CITY SCORE[1]

Today the nation is involved in a social struggle in which public education is just one of the areas of conflict. The issues in the schools revolve around discrimination and prejudice and their effect on "quality education." Music is as much involved in this struggle as any other subject.

The major urban battlefield is the inner-city school. The residents of this area resent the fact that most of the teachers assigned to these schools are transients who enter the inner city in the morning and leave as quickly as possible in the afternoon. They are wary of the music administrator who represents the "downtown" authority, which has done little to ameliorate ghetto conditions over the past fifty years. Usually the resentment and antagonism are not directed against individuals, white or black, but against the Establishment, which has for generations ignored the needs of the residents in these depressed areas. Overcoming these attitudes and providing programs that will reflect "quality experiences" become the prime concerns for a responsible music administrator.

To indicate a change in attitude toward the inner city, administrators should visit classes frequently and appear at programs and functions that the residents of the community consider valuable. The mere appearance of the music director engenders such enthusiasm and support that he cannot afford to bypass any opportunity to be with the teachers, students, or parents. These visits should not be for superficial observation or politicking. They are an opportunity for real communication. People get to know each other better on a face-to-face basis, and the music administrator may use these meetings to solicit first-hand opinions from the residents and teachers about their needs. The administrator must be wary of dismissing these requests merely because they contradict his own values. If they have merit, efforts should be made to implement them.

Middle-class values are often alien and unacceptable to inner-city residents. They will request programs that are relevant to them but perhaps not to the Establishment. I recall one young man in the seventh grade asking me if I really liked Mozart. When I indicated that I did, he wanted to know what I knew about "soul" - a legitimate question. Some general music classes request soul music; others want to study guitar. In some schools, guitar classes have become a regular part of the curriculum. These classes are then used as a basis for organizing string programs. Instruction alternates between the traditional strings and the guitar.

Not every principal in the inner city is receptive to special programs being initiated in his school. Some have complained that they disturb the school day and interfere with "more important" instruction. Rather than take issue with their position, I usually suggest that the programs be moved to neighboring schools. Often, as the excitement and enthusiasm grows in schools having programs, parents and children from those schools that originally rejected these activities begin to question the reluctant principal as to why their schools are being "discriminated against." This tactic has been particularly effective with enrichment programs. Those programs that have been bypassed are soon added to reluctant schools - by request.

Because of the inner-city programs, many of the outer-city communities have cried inverse discrimination - a ridiculous accusation. How they could justify receiving the same equipment and materials when they are already better equipped than schools in deprived areas is inconceivable! This is not equal treatment. The inner-city schools, which for so long have been denied opportunities, need extra assistance to catch up so that they can at least enter the arena, let alone compete. Federal funds have helped revive deficient programs in many inner-city schools. Many of Detroit's inner-city schools that had not been in instrumental festivals in years are now regular participants.

It is not always possible for an administrator to deal with the psychological barriers that teachers build between themselves and their students. However, there are less subtle manifestations of prejudice that can be dealt with directly. For example, a teacher who professed no bias surrounded herself with chairs so that children who passed her could not come in physical contact with her. She was transferred. There was even a case of a teacher who purchased white gloves for all of the children in an interracial chorus because during a performance the children held hands. No one is fooled by these maneuvers, least of all the inner city.

Many textbooks, including music books, are blatantly prejudicial. One of the rationalizations made by publishers is that their concern is with the majority of the children. But our books should reflect our pluralistic society. Besides, in many urban schools, the majority of the students are Black or Hispanic: for example, at this writing Detroit, Michigan, has over sixty-percent of Black students in its school population. This represents **the majority** in that community.

The attitudes, behavior patterns, values, and concepts of beauty of Africans, Asians, South Americans, and many Eastern Europeans are completely different from Western attitudes, behavior patterns, values, and concepts of beauty. These people all fit into the matrix of what is referred to as "the American people." It is time we acknowledge that the musical discipline music Educators so assiduously pursue is only one of a multitude of musical disciplines - and even it is in a constant state of flux and change.

In 1967-1968, the music department in the Detroit schools conducted a study to select a new basal textbook for use in grades K-9. The committee making the selection was comprised of twelve people: blacks and whites, Christians and Jews, males and females, and representatives from all areas of the community. Rather than select a single series, the committee decided to select a book for each grade level that would best fit the Detroit curriculum. In spite of the committee's care and concern to eliminate prejudicial and offensive material, the human relations department still found objectionable material in virtually every book selected. For example, one excellent book had pictures of composers and performers in it, but in its section on blues and jazz, there was no picture of a Black. In fact, none could be found in the entire book. In one song, in German dialect, the second stanza referred to "poor people." So the illustrations were of Blacks! Outside of one or two ensemble pictures, there were no illustrations in most books of white and black children playing together, socially or in a band. When the editors of these series were given an opportunity to respond, they agreed with all of our objections. They also agreed to make the necessary changes that would make these books acceptable. Current songs such as "We Shall Overcome" were added to one series. Another, which had no songs in it with which Jewish children could identify, added two Israeli songs. Many changes were made in illustrative material as well.

A committee of supervisors and teachers have spent a year developing an Afro-American songbook which has been used to supplement the basic text. Through this text, Black children in the Detroit school system developed feelings of pride in the accomplishments and contributions that Blacks have made in music. In addition, white students have become more aware of black contributions to American musical culture.

Everyone - regardless of race - has some measure of prejudice. The individual who categorically denies that he does not have prejudice, is often the one who is the least sensitive and has the most difficulty in overcoming these feelings. It is not the job of the administrator to be a psychiatrist, but if music is to succeed in the inner city, the administration must help the teachers become aware of these feelings. What is most difficult is being certain that some of your decisions aren't affected by the prejudice surrounding you. This writer's device for working with this problem was to meet frequently with black teachers who held positions of responsibility seeking their advice and guidance. This proved indispensable as a tool for identifying the responsible leadership in the inner city. This approach is not only essential but would be appreciated by any superintendent of schools, who deals directly with conflict and confrontation. Any help given him by the music department in obviating conflict may increase the consideration he gives music in the schools.

If we are to plan valuable programs, we must have a better understanding of the inner-city child and his problems. To say that he is like any other child is to ignore the social factors that affect his life. He does not share the same values and cultural reference points as those living in the outer city. Of course, in terms of basic needs, this child is no different. Children's love, acceptance, and self-respect; possess an inner dignity that must be preserved and enhanced; and above all, they each have the ability to learn. However, when children are less-favored economically and educationally, they have a difficult time competing with those who have had a head start. They become victims of disillusionment and defeat. They become the alienated people. In this sense they are different.

Since all children are immensely interested in the arts, music teachers have a marvelous opportunity to break down much of the alienation that exists. In the arts, inner-city children can experience a feeling of accomplishment and achievement. The products of their work are their own creations, and their talent is a possession that cannot be denied them in the way material things are. The burden is on the individual teacher to improve the quality of instruction in the inner-city classroom. He must be a special kind of person - sensitive but firm, concerned but not panicked, flexible but organized.

Teachers fail in the inner city for many reasons: some because their attitudes are patronizing or condescending, others because they are so rigid they cannot adjust to the fluid situation that surrounds them. Some possess a type of prejudice that manifests itself in fear and anxiety. They have not learned to distinguish between cause for real concern and those fears that are only psychological.

In the classroom, the teacher must learn to be patient with a student's faltering efforts and his fear of failure. He must be careful not to interpret a student's hesitation as an inability to learn. He must find new ways to reach these students. Teachers of inner-city youth need an inner security to sustain them when they are threatened by failure or abuse. Their failure is often caused by the frustration and anxiety inherent in the situation and is not necessarily an indication of their own personal inability.

Many teachers prove daily that with energy, understanding, and conviction the problems of teaching in the inner city can be overcome.

To prepare teachers for the inner city, teacher education courses need to emphasize ethnic music - not just Black music but music of all of the ethnic groups that are a part of our nation. As a part of their training, teachers in inner-city schools should take special courses in social psychology, dealing specifically with the emotional patterns of the inner-city child. Teachers must learn the colorful language of the inner city - and I am not referring to obscenity.... In addition, teachers should be prepared to use music as a therapeutic device so that it becomes not merely a "skill" subject but also a means of developing positive self-concepts.

Students who profess interest in teaching in inner-city schools should spend considerable time observing classes in those areas under a variety of conditions. Special student-teaching assignments can be arranged for them in schools so that they may work with the most capable and successful teachers. Competency in music is not enough. To succeed, these

206

prospective teachers need a broad liberal arts orientation with special emphasis in the humanities to go along with the skills they acquire in music.

Music programs must catch the imagination of ghetto residents if school music is to survive. In one inner-city junior high school, where a concerted effort is being made to develop reading skills, electronic pianos replaced desks in the general music classes. Using the language of pilots - "maintaining radio silence," "post seven, over and out" -students are forced to apply reading skills through the use of the keyboards. Special units on jazz and African contributions to the American musical scene have been incorporated into regular classes.

Since discrimination and segregation are the major issues confronting urban communities today, any program designed to break down these barriers is welcome. Of particular significance in Detroit are programs and festivals involving "paired schools": having an inner-city school. Funds are provided for the schools to get together for rehearsals. They alternate rehearsal sites so that the children visit an area completely removed from the one where they pursue their daily activities. The staff works to develop cooperation and respect.

Residents of the inner city are just as eager to have unique, quality programs as people in advantaged areas. Parents in these areas have the same aspirations for their children as concerned parents have in any other part of the community. When vandalism and theft have threatened the extinction of instrumental programs, PTA's not only became involved in better security measures in schools, but also embarked on fund-raising programs to replace the losses. Further, they have appealed to the Board of Education for higher priority in allocating funds for instruments so that they could be proud of the musical achievements of their school organizations. . . .

The problem still facing these obsolete, economically starved areas is lack of resources. Without funds, one cannot secure the equipment or personnel necessary to provide the kinds of programs that will tear down the artificial walls that confine people intellectually and socially. Only a massive government effort can save these areas from utter chaos. The same kind of effort that can land men on the moon can eliminate ghettos. In music education, we need not wait for the millenium to reach people. One of the most significant contribution the Afro-American has made to American culture in his music. No one with any comprehension in this field can be patronizing about the impact that blacks have made in the field of music. Furthermore, music is an art form that involves people in a cooperative enterprise. It is for people.

PERFORMANCE - NOT PROMISES AND PLATITUDES

Residents in the inner city of our urban areas are disenchanted with the promises that have been made over the years but not fulfilled. It is incumbent upon a music administrator that he/she should not make any commitments merely to placate a concerned constituency. It is far more important to be direct and honest with parents who express concern. Every effort should be made to realize the aspirations of the community and all of the obstacles, as well as advantages, need to be identified. This is not to imply that one should be discouraged by obstacles, but rather that they should be identified and clarified so that the community can work with the music administrator to realize its goals and aspirations.

Commitments that will improve learning experiences and raise the level of performance of students need to be objectives. These objectives can be realized if they are selected on the basis of careful study and analysis. However, study should not be independent of those involved. It should include the constituency being served and should include them in the decision-making process. Only when those affected are included can one develop the appropriate support necessary to realize aims and goals that will enhance the musical experiences of the young people in the area.

Involvement includes everyone. Not just those who are overtly supportive, but also those who may seem to be unduly critical. In fact, much of the criticism that has been leveled at urban administration is that the people who want to work with and assist in building the program are usually excluded because they may not have the special expertise which the prevailing administration may seek or expect. On the other hand, those who are critical may have an expertise in an area which would support and enrich the knowledge of the existing administration. It is only when the various segments of the community that comprise all points of view are included that many of the obstacles, criticisms and resentments are overcome.

As indicated earlier, the aspirations of inner-city parents are, not significantly different from those of suburban parents -- the best possible education for their children. This is a mutual aim that permits everyone to meet on a common ground. Every music administrator should be fully committed to this objective, and when this occurs, the difficulties with parents who have the same concern is dissipated. Unfortunately, this pursuit of excellence has been used as a cliche, and too often it has not been pursued with the same dedication and energy that one devotes to just preserving "the job" or the status quo.

Change is inevitable. Music administrators and teachers cannot escape it. Change should be made to remedy educational ills and not to compound or preserve them. The music administrator can be a part of this catalyst, a revitalizing force acting to reslove and remedy the cultural abuses that have been perpetuated and frustrated urban youth. Music is a reflection of human experiences, and in an urban area it must reflect the humanity of its inhabitants.

All children bring their environment into the music classroom. The forms of expression may be different, but they are equally important and equally beautiful. Administrators must impart an attitude to teachers that they must value these cultural reflections for they reflect the human experience that enriches all of our lives.

Relevance, an important word, has been also an abused word. Much of the abuses occur because of our lack of understanding of its intent. Traditional music materials can be applied successfully in an urban area if they are presented in non-traditional ways. These children are not musically deprived. They are well acquainted with music in all of its forms. To the urban child, his music is relevant and very personal. It is music he understands. The difficulty occurs when the teacher is unable to relate the child's music to the traditional music that he/she has been taught. If there is a meeting of the minds, then the music can be

209

made meaningful and relevant in the life of the child. Only when this occurs will all music become a part of each child's life.

DISCUSSION QUESTIONS

1. Why should music teachers concern themselves with music other than that which is emanated from the great Western traditions?

2. Do you agree that it doesn't matter whether or not it is done well, just as long as you do it?

3. Why should children in the inner city be bothered with music other than their own?

4. Discuss similarities and differences among all children, regardless of race or creed.

5. What training should someone who expresses interest in teaching in the inner city receive?

BIBLIOGRAPHY

1. Klotman, Robert H. **The School Administrtor and Supervisor: Catalysts for Change in Music Education.** Englewood Cliffs, NJ: Prentice-Hall Inc.,

2. _____. **Music Educators Journal.** Washington DC: MENC, 1970.

BIBLIOGRAPHY OF FURTHER READINGS

Music Educators Journal. Washington, DC: March 1977.

Brand, Manny and Miller, Samuel D. "Career Counseling in Music Education." **Music Educators Journal.** Washington, DC: September 1980, p. 49

Reller, Theodore L. **Educational Administration in Metropolitan Areas.** Bloomington, IN: Phi Delta Kappa, Inc., 1974.

Simmons, Otis D. **Teaching Music in Urban Schools.** Boston MA: Crescendo Publishing Company, 1975

Chapter 12

TEACHERS FOR THE URBAN STUDENTS
Warrick L. Carter

The material presented in this chapter is concerned with two areas of preparation of teachers who work with urban children. The two areas are emotional and academic. Emotional preparation includes attitudes characteristics, traits, qualities and dispositions. Herein lies the aggregate of that learned, that experienced, that understood and that appreciated. Academic preparation is training at the college level via the bachelorate and advanced degrees. It also includes exposure to continuing education in the form of symposiums, workshops and in-service projects for ongoing preparedness.

Teacher Attitudes, Traits or Qualities

Joyce (1965) listed seven qualities and/or attitudes which he felt were necessary tools for the teacher of urban children: 1) the teacher must have a wide range of skills and teaching styles; 2) he/she should be discriminating regarding the children on terms other than those which show a reference to social class or race; 3) she/he should learn and use the forms of reference employed by the pupils to interpret their world; 4) she/he must be an experimenter with new methods and an educator of other prospective teachers of culturally different children; 5) she/he must be "willing to fail, to risk failure because she/he recognizes that her/his subject area which will enable him/her to use a variety of instructional approaches and "prepare additional material needed for the culturally disadvantaged."[1] In analyzing the "Operation Fair Chance Program" of Hyward, California, Olsen (1967) observed the importance of the teacher's cognizance of the urban student's milieu:

> If teachers ever are to work effectively with such children, they must first come to know through extensive personal, first-hand experience and rigorous conceptual analysis, the pattern of life, the value systems, and the motivational outlooks of these children as they live in their own daily environment. These teachers, then may be able to see education as the child views it, and plan their work in continuous relation to that perception.[2]

212

Gordon (1966) outlined eight factors of teacher attitudes which he felt were "appropriate to the educational characteristics and needs of children handicapped by social and economic disadvantage". Gordon described these attitudinal and behavioral factors in the ensuing manner:

1. Probably the overriding demand of teachers of disadvantaged children is for an attitudinal commitment to hope and expectation that these children can learn and that the teacher can create the necessary conditions to permit effective learning.

2. While we are dealing with attitudes, we must recognize that hope and expectation are necessary, but not sufficient, conditions for success. There must, in addition, exist the attitudinal capacity and the attitudinal readiness for controlled experimentation and innovation in directed learning.

3. Teachers of socially disadvantaged children will need to understand and appreciate the nature of the life conditions of their pupils--their homes and their communities--and the significance of these conditions for learning and development.

4. Since the school must emerge as a major consistently stabilizing influence in the lives of these children, the teacher must understand the sociology fo the school, the dynamics of its functions, and must be master of its appropriate utilization in the interest of these children.

5. For the foreseeable future, most of our teachers are not going to be the social peers of their disadvantaged pupils. Since we are beginning to appreciate the influence of the dynamics of intragroup interaction for behavioral change, the teacher's competence as a guide to an utilizer of intragroup interaction can be a crucial counterbalance to the social distance and discontinuity.

6. The challenge presented by the atypical learner requires that the teacher possess competence and skill in the educational

appraisal of each pupil. Such competence
cannot be limited to quantification and
classification of intelligence and
achievement but must include qualitative
evaluation and descriptive analysis of the
learning function and potential in the
child. Such appraisal should lead to
educational prescription.

7.   Children who are progressing at their
expected rate need good teachers. Children
who are not making it in the system--who are
handicapped by intrinsic or extrinsic
conditions--require exceptionally good
teachers with special competencies. The
skills to which I now refer are in the area
of psycho-educational processes.

a.   Mastery of content that enables
      them to be excellent teachers of
      their designated subject matter.
      The plea here is for excellence in
      basic preparation as a teacher,
      with the scope of knowledge and
      the quality of interpersonal
      skills that this implies.

b.   Skills in the utilization of
      knowledge and experience an
      infinite variety of ways to
      achieve maximal learning styles
      and learning strengths are known
      to vary extensively.

c.   Skill in relating knowledge of
      physical, mental, psychological,
      social, and educational status and
      of capacity for readiness for
      learning to the design of learning
      experiences and to the guidance of
      pupil development.

d.   Skill in the application of the
      laws of learning to academic,
      emotional, and social learning
      situations.

e.   Skill in the utilization and
      development of materials and
      procedures leading to the use of

214

appropriate aspects of the
environment and in the use of
oneself to influence and modify
individual and group learning.

f.   Skill in the conceptualization of
problems and in the use of logical
steps in problem solving as
prerequisites to continued growth
as a scholar and as a professional
worker.

8.   Integration of all the above-mentioned
types of understanding, knowledge, and skill
with personal attitudes and behaviors so as
to reflect respect for human life and
welfare, commitment to the search for truth,
maintenance of integrity, and the
achievement of social productivity for the
teacher as well as for the learner.[3]

Along lines similar to Rosenthal and Jacobson,
(1968) and Strom (1966) felt that teacher aspirations
serve as the primary criteria for success or failure in
the classroom, "govern academic and behavioral expectations and generally determine methods of instruction." Attitudes toward the various races or a
specific socioeconomic status also "affect the
motivation of both teachers and pupils, influence
objective observation of what is being learned, and
provide the base for rapport."[4]

Apart from the possible danger of adopting
attitudes which are unfair to the student, many
teachers face the hazard of developing an "emotional
logic," which Strom defined as "sorting people into
categories based on their income, color, or other
criteria," and selectively admitting "new evidence
about the persons in each category only if the
information confirms our previous beliefs."

Perceptions of Black-vs.-White Teachers

The concept of emotional logic is further
documented by the research of Gottlieb (1964) and
Torrance (1966). Gottlieb investigated the differences and similarities between the attitudes toward
their work and their students of 36 black and 53 white
elementary school teachers. Approximately 85 percent
of the students were black and from low-income families

attending six inner-city elementary schools. More than 80 percent of both teacher groups were female, with the black teachers tending to be somewhat younger, more likely to be married, with fewer divorcees or widows. Also, the black teachers tended to come from larger communities and were twice as likely to have attended public Colleges in urban centers. While the white teachers were generally raised in middleclass families, the black teachers come from lower class families with primarily manual occupations. To Gottlieb, the fact that the black teachers, more often than the white, came from a lower socio-economic stratum accounted for the differences in the attitudes and perceptions of the two groups.

When selecting from a list of thirty-three adjectives which most accurately described their pupils in the inner-city schools, black and white teachers differed significantly in their choices. In order of importance, white teachers most frequently selected **talkative, lazy, fun-loving, happy, cooperative, energetic,** and **ambitious.** The white teachers tended to omit those adjectives which are universal attributes of children and which are related to successful learning. Thus, white teachers were more likely than black teachers to list shortcomings and sterotypes which have generally been attributed to blacks; they also pointed to deficiencies in the system to explain their personal dissatisfactions.

After interviewing a large population of inner-city teachers, Torrance identified two types of negative teacher attitudes, which can impair the creative behavior of inner-city children. The first attitude is one where the teachers feel discipline is such a serious problem that fostering creative behavior would cause lose of control in the classroom and "that destructiveness and chaos would result." These teachers fear that the release of creativity would "unloose primitive impulses that would be overwhelming to them and their pupils."[5] The second negative attitude is that the teachers perceive their stuents as "apathetic" and "listless" and feel that it is impossible to foster creative behavior with these types of students. Torrance attributed these attitudes to the same kinds of emotional logic identified by Strom (1966). They (Strom and Torrance) both agreed that instructors reared in "more favorable environments" than the neighborhood to which a work assignment takes them, may respond by approaching their job with a sense of reluctance, a lack of desire, and/or a feeling of defeat. "For a teacher to so behave is to render academic expectation to economic or racial membership, and thus determine progress before instruction begins."[6]

The Successful Teacher

Goldberg (1967) constructed a "hypothetical model of the successful teacher" of urban students. His model reflects the type of attitude toward, the knowledge and understanding of, and familiarity with urban children. The successful teacher: 1) respects the children in her/his class and, therefore, receives respect in return; 2)observes the cultures of the students, not as a judge, but empathetically from the point of view of the students, understanding the backgrounds from which the students come, their values toward various achievements and the kind of life style to which they aspire; 3) is aware of her/his students' membership in the ethnic group, the history, traditions and social structure of that group, and how such membership shapes each student's image of her/himself and her/his world; 4) knows that the language of her/his students is closely tied to their life style and recognizes its functional qualities for the pupils; 5) has a sophisticated understanding of how a child's abilities are assessed and, therefore, a realistic perception of what these assessments of measurements describe and predict; 6) meets the children on a person-to-person basis; and 7) realizes the danger of the "self-fulfilling prophecy" of expecting, and consequently lets each student know that she/he expects more than the pupil thinks he can produce (the standards are never too high or remote, but are within the intellectual potential of the students). Goldberg characterized her hypothetical successful teacher in a single phrase: **"ordered flexibility."**[7]

Another hypothetical model of the successful teacher also emphasizes the teacher's knowledge of the children's background and the teacher's social relationship with the children. Webster's (1966) model was based on the difficulties middle class teachers find working in urban schools. These difficulities may be due to a conflict in attitudes, values, or desired social and academic behaviors. Webster offered several hypotheses to explain why some teachers remain and are successful, and why others leave. He believed that those teachers who remain possess many of the qualities and attitudes listed by Goldberg, i.e., respects the student, has understanding of the child's abilities, et al.

217

Additional studies have looked at desired teacher attitudes through social class (Becker, 1952; Charters, 1968; and Wolf and Wolf, 1962), subject matter areas (James, 1967; Trobowitz, 1968a; Andrews, 1967; K. R. Johnson, 1969; and Armstrong, 1968), or the use of meaningful or indigenous material (Trobowitz, 1968b; Carter, (1970, 75, 78 and Armstrong, 1968). In all of these studies, the authors stress the importance of the teacher's familiarity with the students' background and environment.

Recent studies have focused on qualities that contribute to effective teaching. These studies have covered teaching from all educational levels (primary to higher educational; and students from urban, suburban, and rural communities are presenting all Socio-Economic Status (SES) levels as part of their samples. The two projects which are of greatest concern here are those of Medley (1977), Soar and Soar (1973).

Medley's research was based on a review of 289 SES studies on children. From his investigation 14 studies dealt with questions pertaining to the differentiation of behavior(s) of effective teachers from those of ineffective teachers. These fourteen research projects were the theme of his work which focused on urban children from low socioeconomic status (SES) homes in primary grades one to three. Medley found that:

1. The teachers whose students attained high means gains in reading and math tests, devoted more class time to task related activities, thereby structuring activites so that the students spent the major part of the school day in organized learning experiences.

2. Effective teachers individualize assignments and spend more time actively working with small groups of students.

3. Teacher techniques proved successful with low SES urban students were ineffective with students from high SES homes. In fact, some successful methods used with children from high SES homes produced the reverse results with low SES children."[8]

218

The influence of students' SES levels on achievement was again supported by the work of Soar and Soar. The Soar and Soar project was conducted in Florida, and investigated the effect the classrooms' emotional climate and teacher instructional techniques had on learning. As expected they found that a negative learning climate, in which the teacher is severely critical of students' work and/or behavior, is destructive for all children. However, a negative classroom climate was found to be more destructive to the achievement gains of low SES students than to those of high SES.

The data also revealed that younger, low SES students, make fewer gains when the teacher employs a cognitive process. This last discovery supports the basis upon which the Head Start programs of the '60s were founded.

Music Teachers

The majority of the desirable attitudes and traits identified for music teachers, coincide with those previously discussed;however, there are a number of these attitudes and traits which deal specifically with the teaching of music to urban children. James (1967) believed that the music teacher best shows his/her trust and acceptance of the student's thinking by using "the popular music of the day alternating with other works to show comparisons." Further, "let your hair down, drive in and swallow your pride--don't be reluctant to play for your own enjoyment or express your likes and dislikes in music."

Several of the teachers' comments presented in the January, 1970, edition of the **Music Educators Journal** contain reference to appropriate teacher attitude or desirable teacher traits. A high school instrumental music teacher, from Los Angeles, suggested that the teacher must be flexible. "If you're working on a particular lesson plan and find it's not happening, you have to break away from it. . . .feel your class out and find where they are. . . . You have to use sensible rehearsal thought."

An Ohio elementary music teacher, stated that a good and effective teacher, of culturally different children, needs to develop the attitude that "there is essentially no right or wrong music, but varying degrees of excellence." Only after such an attitude is developed and communicated to the students, can the teacher help them find success and satisfaction in their accomplishments.

Carter's research supports and reinforces the suggestion made by these various teachers. It, additionally, has shown that specific knowledge and understanding of the music of the urban student is the "bottom line" of effectiveness for urban music teachers.

Teacher Education: Preparation for Urban Schools

Although a variety of systems, teaching styles and teacher education programs have been theorized, little research data is available to substantiate their effectiveness in the urban classroom situation. It is heartening to note, however, that educators in a number of colleges and public school systems have recognized the importance of preparing teachers more adequately for these responsibilities. According to a 1968 survey conducted by the American Association of Colleges for Teacher Education (AACTE), more than 200 institutions were either preparing teachers for urban schools or were planning to introduce such programs (Clifford, 1968). The discussion which follows includes a sampling of programs instituted between 1965 and 1980.

The program at California State College in Hayward is considered a "full-time program of experimental education." The program is operated for 32 weeks, divided into six stages of experiences and interrelations. The stages are:

1. Orientation (8 days)--includes a three hour test to measure attitudes, outlooks, values and culture orientation. The remainder of the time is spent in evaluations of the test and interaction with the various members of the class.

2. Community Study (2 weeks)--deals with an investigation of all conditions of the community: jobs, health, racial composition, and living conditions.

3. Job Corp Work (6 weeks)--an investigation of the Job Corp, and its

members to understand the attitude of the Job Corp members toward the school.

4. School and Community Work (4 weeks)--a variety of teaching and working situations in both schools and other community agencies, under very close supervision.

5. Supervised Student Teaching (18 weeks)--the activities are much like those in number four; however, during this period the prospective teachers are assigned to a particular subject area and school under a classroom teacher.

6. Summary Sharing (1 week)--a period of evaluation of the complete program to "take stock of all that has been done".[10]

The program at Michigan State University (MSU) is a joint venture with the Flint Junior College (FJC) Education Department. The objectives of the program are listed as:

1. getting any student interested in a teaching career to consider the challenge and rewards of teaching in inner-city schools and

2. give the prospective teachers an opportunity to learn about this challenge and reward of inner-city teaching.

These objectives are met through "five levels of activity" and interaction with urban students:

1. All MSU education majors visit and observe in inner-city schools.

2. Student involvement in tutorial and other volunteer programs for the urban school child. This volunteer work varies from a half day each week to two days a week.

3. Opportunity is provided for one hundred and fifty volunteer students from MSU

to participate in three months of study
and practice teaching in the Flint,
Michigan, inner-city schools.

4. In their junior year, 75 MSU students
are given the opportunity to
participate in a special six month
training program in the Detroit,
Michigan, inner-city schools.

5. Upon graduation, 25 MSU and FJC
students are given the opportunity to
work full-time for 28 months in the
Flint inner-city schools.

This program has an ample amount of flexibility. It
can accommodate any student who has an interest in or
desire to work with urban students, one who can give
only a few hours a week as well as those persons who
want to become inner-city teachers.

Pennsylvania State's Program

The program at Pennsylvania State University for prospective urban teachers is conducted on the University's Capitol Campus in Middletown. Any student
enrolled in the Bachelor's program of Elementary
Education is eligible, if she/he has completed a
minimum of 60 semester hours prior to admittance to the
Capitol Campus. Once admitted, students are enrolled
for six terms to complete 18 courses, three per term.
All courses are considered equal and the time allocated
for each course varies according to its objectives.
Many of the basic method courses are combined to
broaden the student's scope and concepts.

Ward Sinclair (1968), program director, states that the
program was established

. . . as an attempt to make professional
education courses more realistic to students
by incorporating laboratory experiences in
the public schools with each professional
course on campus. Not only would this
prepare the prospective teachers
academically, but also would provide them
with the necessary understanding and scope
to "cope" successfully with children from
the lower socioeconomic areas.[11]

222

The laboratory experiences are arranged through an agreement with the Harrisburg Public Schools. Through these arrangements, each students is given five different types of classroom experiences, ranging from one-half day per week to full-time student teaching. The student's classroom experiences are guided by both a university instructor and a classroom teacher. In their last term, the prospective teachers are enrolled in a class called "Social Philosophy of School." This class, using both educators and community lay persons, evaluates the previous five terms of classroom experiences and lectures. Such a class, is designed to acquaint the students with current educational questions and issues as presented by the professional educator. It also allows for expression of community and local concerns. At the end of the first two years of the program, an evaluation produced the following results:

1. A better relationship established between the college student and classroom teacher.

2. An outstanding development of school (college) and community relationship.

3. College students are better able to relate their lectures, readings and discussions in classroom to actual children and events with which they have had conact in public schools.

Programs at Other State and City Institutions

In an attempt to find common trends, Knapp (1965) investigated five programs which prepare teachers for urban schools. The programs were those of Hunter College, New York; California State College, Los Angeles; Mercy College, Detroit; City University of New York; and Project Mission, a cooperative venture of Coppin State College, Morgan State College, and the Baltimore Public Schools.

Knapp identified five common trends which were prevelant in each of the school programs:

1. Prospective teachers of the disadvantaged are receiving earlier and more extensive field experiences in selected lower socioeconomic areas

223

schools. . .

2. Field experiences are being expanded to include the community which the schools serve. . .

3. Participation in special programs proceeds upon a voluntary basis. Most of the students enrolled in the programs do teaching disadvantage schools. . . .

4. Special programs are resulting in changed perceptions of a "good" teaching situation.

5. There is closer contact between schools and college personnel than is normally true in conventional programs.[12]

Knapp also found problems which were common to all five programs. He posited that frequently the well-publicized breakthroughs, with the accompanying recognition, have caused teacher education to concentrate too heavily upon the urban student. Hence, a resulting neglect of suburban school needs and of the candidates who may best be suited for this setting. Finally, he discovered that too much of the program's planning was done by school administrators and college staff, with too few instances of involvement from classroom teachers.

Hunter College

Of all the programs he investigated, Passow concluded that "one of the more promising was that of Hunter College."[13] The Hunter program was unique in that it prepared teachers in the very school where they would eventually teach. The concepts being tested by this program were summarized thusly:

Student teaching can be both challenging and rewarding in a personal and professional sense; the apprehensions of prospective teachers are best alleviated and their perceptions modified by direct, wide contact with education and community workers and leaders; a team of professionals from the depressed-area school itself--such as subject matter specialists, curriculum experts, and social psychologists-is required for introducing the student teacher to the particular demands of these schools and for helping orient him to working with children in this special context; participation in a program for teaching in a depressed-area school should be voluntary on the student's part and must begin early in his college career."[14]

Governors State University Urban Teacher Education Program

The program at Governors State University (GSU) is especially designed to prepare elementary teachers for urban elementary shools. Based on the philosophy that in addition to the skills required of all elementary teachers; urban teachers must be "humanists, realists, and masters of their profession. . . .be especially knowledgeable about the social, political and economic forces and counter forces they can expect to encounter in the working environment. . . .skilled in the art and science of teaching, and responsive to those expressed an unexpressed needs of children in urban settings (1979).

These varied philosophical needs are met through two areas of preparation; (1) subject matter, and (2) professional. The former prepares the perspective teacher in areas "which represent success for children in the urban setting." They include: reading and language arts, mathematics, social and natural sciences, art and music, and health and physical education. The later includes training that will help the teacher develop an indepth understanding of child development as well as urban environmental factors which affect learning. These include: "knowledge of family structure, housing and income; the school plant, organization and staffing; history and current economic and social forces affecting educational policy and practices; and ideas that have influenced educational policy and practices."

The curriculum is designed to meet eight broad subject matter competencies and nine broad professional competencies, each of which have subcategories. A number of courses are assigned to each level of competencies; all geared toward bringing the student to the achievement of one or more of the broad and/or discrete competencies. Such required courses as "Edu-

225

cational Implications of Black History and Culture,"
"Urban Education" reflects the level of specificity in
urban related training required in this program.

As the University is located in close proximity to
Chicago, the student teaching experience is conducted
in the city of Chicago's providing the opportunity
opportunity for the "Urban Teacher Education" faculty
to actively engage in   urban education research and
other related activity.

Multi-Cultural Programs

A different approach for the training of urban
teachers is seen in the multicultural teaching
materials that have been developed over the past five
years (1975-1980). The idea underlining most of the
multi-cultural programs is the feeling that successful
teachers in a multi-cultural society must use
materials, methods, and approaches that reflect, in
illustration and content, the multi-cultural nature of
the society. Because urban areas are the most racially
diverse and at the same time the most racially
segregrated, the multicultural approach seems to be a
most logical one for urban educators. Of primary
importance to the supporters of the multi-cultural
educational approach is the use of materials that are
unbiased and free of racial and sexual sterotypes.

Racial and Sexual Biases in Text Books

In an attempt to identify the adequacy of teaching
materials with respect to race and or sex bias, Gloria
Grant (1975) examined six (6) widely used teacher
training text books. She offered the following instructions:

> If the teacher preparation materials ex-
> amined above represent the state of the art
> of material relative to ethnic and cultural
> biases and sex role stereotyping, it is
> clearly evident that teacher preparation
> materials are inadequate. All of the materi-
> als examined need to be "corrected" before
> they are used in teacher training institu-
> tions. It is disgraceful that we are pre-
> paring teachers to teach in a multi-cultural
> society using materials that are mostly
> unicultural.[15]

We cannot assume also that oblique references and discussions about children from different ethnic and cultural groups will enable teachers to develop the skills, attitudes, and behaviors to teach in a multicultural society. Futhermore, we cannot assume that professors of education will modify or supplement the existing bias in teacher preparaton materials with more relevant material, or that they will institute meaningful discussions in the area of ethnic, cultural, and sex biases. Teacher preparation materials must be unbiased from conception. I would like to recommend the following suggestions be used to help eliminate biases in teacher preparation materials:

1. Colleges and universities and publishers should establish criteria for selecting materials.

2. Illustrations, photographs, cartoons, etc., used in teacher training materials should reflect the multicultural nature of our society.

3. The content--where applicable--should include information about minority groups, male and females.

4. The content--where applicable--should discuss pupil-teacher interaction with children from various ethnic and cultural groups, and both boys and girls.

5. The content--where applicable--should discuss teacher attitudes and expectations toward both girls and boys of different cultural and ethnic backgrounds.

6. The content--where applicable--should explicitly explain how the curriculum and curriculum materials of the classroom can be made relevant and non-stereotypic.

7. Materials written by minority group

people and women in areas other than racial and sex bias should be sought and utilized.

Urban Music Teacher Education Program

A few music educators have also discovered that special preparation is needed for teachers of urban students. As with the general education and elementary education programs previously outlined, the musicians see a strong need for courses in urban sociology, cultural anthropology and psychology. Along with these course changes or additions, each music educator has recommended changes and/or additions within the specialized work in the field of music.

Andrews (1967) offers these specific suggestions for changes in the music courses:

1. A heavy emphasis on the properties of music as a common means of expression that has always existed in many cultures and at many levels.

2. A teacher commitment to the business of opening up understanding of music in the hearts and minds of children who are poorly cared for. . . .inadequately housed, clothed and fed.

3. An emphasis on learning by doing, by making much music. . . .The musical experience offered must be extremely rich in music itself, rather than talking about music or stressing the symbolic aspects of music. . . .The teacher should be prepared to make or join in and encourage pupils in the making of music that is indigenous to (them).

4. The training of the new breed of teacher in areas of applied, theoretical, and historical music must be both thorough and practical. . . .for it may well be that the teacher-violinist who can play a country fiddle tune as well as a Brahms "Hungarian Dance" will have more status in. . .the group with which he

works than will the teacher more
limited in his musical repertoire."[76]

Schwadron (1967) recommended interdisciplinary studies
in aesthetics, cultural anthropology, philosophy, and
the social sciences. Some of the purposes of these
studies would be:

1. To develop a broad understanding of the
   means and ends of music education in up-
   lifting socio-musical values.

2. To develop an understanding of the role
   of artistic conformity during periods
   of cultural crisis.

3. To develop an understanding of the
   relative social, political, and cultural development as these affect the
   functioning of music education in a
   free society.[77]

In regard to the cultural determinants and
differentiations of various musical styles
and expressions, Clayman (1961) offered the
suggestion:

> . . . .that the teacher-training insti-
> tution become a center for the
> transevaluation of cultural values, in
> order to extend to the teacher the
> opportunity to study his own values in
> relation to other cultures. In this way
> the teacher can gain invaluable insight
> into the "nature and nurture of man"
> who, strikingly diverse in his pattern
> of behavior, exhibit common values.[78]

Along with a number of socially oriented courses,
Klotman (1968) recommended that all music education
majors be required to take a series of courses in
ethnic music, including studies in African music, Asian
music, American Indian music, music of Appalachia and
Latin American music. In addition, all theory course
would include a unit on jazz, and a complete unit of
music history would be devoted to jazz. Finally,
(Klotman) pointed out that there should be sufficient
training in the use of music as a therapeutic tool "for
these children so that teachers may use music not

229

merely as a 'skill' subject but also as a means of developing positive self-concepts."[19]

State school systems and professional music organizations, working independently, have recognized the need for comprehensive effective teacher education programs. At the "Music in the Inner-city School Symposium" held by Ohio State University in June, 1968, teacher education was approached through ways in which this training could develop the appropriate attitudes needed for effectively teaching in inner-city schools. The members of the symposium placed considerable emphasis on the comprehensiveness of the teacher education program in developing, not only good teachers but also "good musicians," i.e., musicians comprehensively trained in "all kinds of music, and ...to have an open mind willing (enough) to use any kind of music" as instructional material.

Although the participants of the "Tanglewood Symposium" did not outline any specific teacher education programs for the prospective teachers of urban students, various committees offered several suggestions in relationship to the appropriate types of training needed by all prospecitve music educators. The committee on "Implication for Music in Higher Education and the Community" recommended that all teachers be "trained and retrained to understand the specifics of a multiplicity of music--avant-gard, art music, various mutations of jazz, and ethnic music." Further, the committee related that recent discoveries in musicology and theory as they relate to philosophy, sociology and learning psychology be communicated to the prospective teachers "without delay."

The committee on "Implications for the Music Curriculum" made the following recommendation for the inclusion of other types of music in both the teacher education and child education programs:

> We recommend that teachers be encouraged to experiment with an utilize many types of music in their instructional activities. In-service education programs instituted on a regional basis could equip teachers with the materials and techniques necessary to present a wider variety of music to children. The fulcrum of the repertoire should be shifted to include more of the many varieties

230

of contemporary popular and serious music as well as music of other cultures.

Historically, the instrumental program has developed entirely around the standard orchestral instruments. It is incumbent upon music educators to reevaluate this position and to consider the validity of adding other instruments, particularly those social instruments having a considerable effect upon American culture.

In the "Special Report on Music in Urban Education" in the January, 1970, issue of the **Music Educators Journal**, seven recommendations were made for teacher education programs in music. These recommendations were drawn from remarks and suggestions offered by a selected number of principals, school board members, parents, students, teachers, and music educators from various communities throughout the United States.

1. Teacher education courses that are preparing music teachers for positions in the cities should be directed by competent personnel who have first-hand knowledge of the situation and who maintain close articulation with music education programs in the city schools. . . .

2. Prospective music teachers should be provided with a thorough and realistic on-the-spot picture of urban teaching conditions, so that there is no danger of cultural shock when the teacher assumes his first teaching position. . .

3. Prospective music teachers who plan to teach in the city should be equipped with the most up-to-date information, understanding, materials, and techniques for teaching inner-city students successfuly. . . .

4. General music and general musicianship should be given special attention on the college level if they are to be taught effectively in the public

schools, particularly in the
city. . . .

5. Prospective music teachers should
    develop skill in communication and the
    ability to relate to others--students,
    parents, community administration and
    fellow teacher. . . .

6. Knowledge of the widest possible
    variety of musics--ethnic, rock, soul,
    jazz, electronic, aliatoric, serial, as
    wel as the historical literature--is
    essential if music teachers are to meet
    the demands of urban education. . . .

7. Music teachers who aspire to teach in
    the city should be required to develop
    in-depth cultural, sociological, and
    psychological understanding of the
    students they will be teaching.[20]

Innovative Preparation

During the past ten years (1970-1980) several colleges
and universities have developed specific courses
required for prospective urban music teachers. Typical
of many of these courses are those at Roosevelt
University in Chicago, University of Michigan and
Governors State University. In addition to the courses
required for regular music teachers certification, the
prospective urban music teacher takes courses in "Urban
Music Methods," "Seminar in Urban Music and Jazz, and
material for teacher education. Other institutions
(UCLA, California State and New York University) have
introduced classes in youth music method, gospel
related materials, Afro-American music history, Jazz
methods and materials, and Hispanic related music
classes.

As teachers trained in these type of programs were
being hired by urban districts, it was realized that
the district's tenured teachers were lacking in these
new skills and were frequently not as effective in
dealing with the new urban youth, as were the new
teachers. After the specific weaknesses were diag-
nosied, special in-service training was designed and
often required of all teachers who had not taken
specific urban related classes as a part of their
academic training.

232

Two important music in-service programs are those of the L.A. and Milwaukee school systems. The former required all of its general and elementary teachers (who are responsible for music instruction) to complete an eight (8) week in-service course in "Black Music and Culture." Developed by Betty Cox, Coordinator of the LAUSD program for the L.A. public schools, this course exposed the teachers to many forms of black music through performances, tapes, lectures, and/or demonstrations. The teachers were required to devise lesson plans for each of the styles presented. The L.A. experience was quite rare in that many of the legends (Eubie Blake, "Star Dust" green, Jester Harrison) of the various styles gave freely of their time to insure the success of the program. Through the work of Ella Washington, supervising music teachers for the Milwaukee public schools, the music division of the school system recently (January, 1981) hired an ethnomusicologist with a speciality in Afro-American music. It was felt that a specialist in Afro-American music could serve as a system-wide resource person able to help all music and general classroom teachers in developing lesson plans, specific modules, new teaching approaches, and related skills that are needed in Milwaukee because of its large population of Black students. This appointment reflects the Milwaukee school system's astuteness in recognizing that its school community is not culturally homogeneous but rather, multi-cultural. Hence, experts must be used to interpret what the various minority cultures identity as the significant artifacts, contributions, developments of their cultures to a multi-cultural society.

Chapter Highlights and Summary

In this chapter it should have become evident that no universally accepted program have been developed for the teachers of urban students. Where some writers have focused on the attitudes and behaviors of the teachers, others have emphasized the influence of teachers' aspirations. Available evidence suggests that black teachers tend to emphasize the shortcomings of the students. Hypothetical models have emphasized the teacher's knowledge of the children's background. However, within these varied emphases, all models suggest three desirable attitudes of qualities for urban teachers:

1. Through knowledge of the student, his background, his aspirations, his fears,

his habits, his talents, his
shortcomings and his life-style.

2. Knowledge of ways to direct and guide
the learning of the culturally
different child.

3. Skill in human relations, particularly
as they affect the attitudes and
behaviors of the students.

Many of these same teacher attitudes were also
identified for urban music music teachers. Added to
these were the need for teachers to understand and
accept the various types of popular music found in the
environment of the students.

The developments in teacher preparation programs for
urban teachers, have been earlier summarized by Passow.
These developments include:

1. Early and continuous contact with
children and adults in disadvantaged
areas in a variety of school and non-
school related activities. These range
from one-to-one tutoring of pupils to
supervising after school activities to
classroom observations and intensive
classroom teaching. These experience
are carefully supervised and often
analyzed in seminar or small group
sessions afterwards.

2. Intensive involvement of behavioral and
social scientists who apply research
and theory from their disciplines to
the specific needs and problems of the
disadvantaged area. These include cul
tural anthropologists, social psycholo
gists, architects, city planners,
historians and political scientists--
many of whom are actively involved in
field experience with students.

3. Intensive involvement of successful
school practitioners--classroom teach
ers, principals, counselors and others-
-in working with the teacher education
staff in planning, supervising, and
evaluating experiences. The two-way

234

flow of college and school staffs has been of considerable benefit to both. Rivilin has urged the use of affiliated schools as laboratories for urban teacher education drawing the analogy to the teaching hospital attached to the medical school.

4. Opportunities for pre-service teachers to work with non-school agencies, government and agency-sponsored, and to become actively involved in on-going projects for overcoming poverty, extending civil rights, and generally "reversing the spiral toward futility." Aside from the insights acquired into the life styles of the inner-city families, such experiences are apparently instrumental in more positive attitude formation to the problem faced in such areas.

5. Modification of college courses to develop those techniques and skills essential to teaching in depressed areas. These include help with diagnostic and remedial procedures, with methods and materials for individualization of instruction, with strategies for classroom control, and with personnel and material resources.

6. Opportunity to examine, discuss, and plan local program adaptations to known situations, current research, and experimentation being reported by other education centers.

7. Establishment of internships and other means of continuing relationships between the college and the teacher inservice so that the teacher has continuing supervisory aid as well as support.[27]

Along with the above-mentioned developments, music educators have emphasized courses dealing with ethnic music as well as music of the various cultures of American society. In addition, complete courses in jazz, both historical and theoretical; systematic instructions for use of musical instruments which are currently popular in urban centers and training in the use of music as a therapeutic tool, have also been included in the perspective teacher's education. Where teachers have been found to lack the necessary urban related training; school training; school systems have developed required in-service courses to remove dificiencies. Other systems have hired ethnic music specialist, to serve as "in-house" consultants for the development of special classes, materials, course outlines and the like for their teachers.

DISCUSSION QUESTIONS

1. What are the most desired qualities, attitudes, characteristics, dispositions, etc., for teachers of urban children? How do the attributes differ between the various authors discussed?

2. Are there differences between the expectation of black and white teachers who work with black children? If so, what are they? How did the expectation difference effect learning? What can be done to negate the effect of these expectation differences?

3. What is the most important attribute needed by teachers of culturally different students?

4. Discuss the six urban teacher education programs described in the chapter. How do they differ? How are they similiar?

5. How do the multi-cultural education programs differ from the urban teacher education programs?

6. How do the teacher training recommendations of Andrews, Clayman, and Klotman differ?

7. How can the recommendations of the "Inner City Symposium," "Tanglewood Symposium" and of the "Special Report ....." be made operational?

8. What additional materials, methods approaches can you suggest be required of urban music education students?

NOTES FOR CHAPTER 12

1. Bruce R. Joyce. "Teachers for the Culturally Disadvantaged," in **Teacher for the Culturally Disadvantaged Pupil**, ed. J.M. Beck and R.W. Saxe. Springfield, Illinois: Charles C. Thomas Publishers, 1965.

2. Edward G. Olsen. "Teacher Education for the Deprived: A New Pattern, **School and Society.** 95 No. 2291 (April 1, 1967), 232-234.

3. Edmond Gordon. "Desired Teacher Behavior in School for Socially Disadvantaged Children," in **Teachers for the Disadvantaged,** eds. M. Vsdon and F. Bertoloet Chicago: Follet Publishing Co., 1966.

4. Robert Rosenthal and Lenore Jacoblson. Pyqmalion in the Classroom: **Teacher Expectation and Pupil's Intellectual Development.** New York: Holt, Reinhart and Winston, 1968.

5. Paul E. Torrance. "Fostering Creative Behaviors," in **The Inner-City Classroom: Teacher Behavior's,** ed. R.D. Strom. Columbus, Ohio: Charles E. Merrill Books Inc., 1966.

6. Robert D. Strom. **Teaching in the Slum School,** Columbus, Ohio: Charles E. Merril Books, Inc. 1965.

7. Miriam Goldberg. "Adopting Teacher Style to Pupil Differences: Teachers for Disadvantaged Children," **Education of the Disadvantaged,** ed. A.H. Passow, M. Galdberg and A.J. Tannenbaon. New York: Holt, Reinhart and Winston, Inc. 1967.

8. Donald Medley. **Teacher Competence and Teacher Effectiveness: A Review of Process-Product Research.** Washington, DC: American Association of Colleges for Teacher Education, 1977. Available from the Publications Office, AACTE, One Dupont Circle, Suite 610, Washington, DC 20036.

9. Paul S. James. "Teaching the Underprivileged Child," **Music Journal,** 25 No. 8 (Nov. 1967), 29-58.

10. Edward G. Olsen. "Teacher Education for the Deprived: A New Pattern, **School and Society.** 95 No. 2291 (April 1, 1967), 232-234.

11. Ward Sinclair. "Teacher Preparation for Urban Schools," **School and Society** (1968), 339-345.

12. Dale L. Knapp. "Preparing Teacher of Disadvantaged Youth; Emergency trends", **Journal of Teacher Education,** 16; 2 (June 1965), 188-192.

13. Harry A. Passow. "Teachers for Depressed Areas". in **Education for Depressed Areas,** ed. Al H. Passow. New York: Teachers College Press. 1963.

14. Ibid.

15. Gloria Grant. "Are Today's Teacher Training Materials Preparing Teachers to Teach in a Multi-Cultural Society?" in **Shifting and Winnowing** Carl A. Granted University of Wisconsin, Madison (1975).

16. Frances Andrews. "The Preparation of Music Educators for the Culturally Disadvantaged," **Music Educators Journal,** 53 No. 6 (Feb. 1967).

17. Abraham A. Schwadron. Aesthetics: Dimension for Music Education. Washington, D.C., Menc. 1967.

18. Charles Clayman. "Value and the Teacher," **Journal of Education,** 143 (April, 1969), 23-27.

19. Robert Klotman. "Preparation for Teachers of Disadvantaged Youth: Emerging Trends," **The Journal of Teacher Education.** 16. No. 2 (June, 1965), 188-192.

20. **Music Educators Journal** 57:5 (January 1970) pp. 105-111.

21. Harry A. Passow

BIBLIOGRAPHY

Andrews, Frances. "The Preparation of Music Educators for the Culturally Disadvantaged," Music

Educators **Journal**, 53 No. 6 (Feb. 1967).

Armstrong, Naomis. "Music Education for Culturally
    Deprived High School Students,"
    The High School Journal (Now. 1968), 62-67.

Becker, Howard. "Social Class Variations in the
    Teacher Pupil Relationship," **Journal of
    Educational Sociology** 25 (1952), 451-456.

Carter, WL. "Teaching Around Ethnic Hang Ups," **Music
    Journal** 1974 Annual Vol 32 No. 6 (july 1974).

Carter, WL. "A Competency Based Music Program in
    Action," **NAJE Educator** Vol 9 No. 4 (April 1, May
    1975).

Clifford, Paul. "Education Professional Development
    for Urban and Depressed Areas," **The AACTE**

    Yearbook-- Teacher Education: Issues and
    Innovations, No. 18 (1968), 105-07.

Conart, James B. **The Education of American Teachers,**
    New York: McGraw Hill Book Company, 1963.

Daniel, Walter G. Teachers for American's
    disadvantaged with Special Reference to Race,"
    The Journal of Negro Educaion. 34, No. 4 (Fall,
    1965), 381-384.

Gottlieb, David. "Teaching and Students: The Views of
    Negro and White Teachers," **Sociology of
    Education,** 37 (1964), 345-353.

Haubirch, Vernon F. "Preparing Teachers for
    Disadvantaged Youth," in **Racial Crisis in
    American Education,** ed. R.L. Green. Chicago:
    Follett Educational Co., 1969.

Horrock, John E. "Culture Free Test of Intelligence,"
    in **Assessment of Behavior,** Columbus, Ohio:
    Charles E. Merrill Books, Inc., 1964.

James, Paul S. "Teaching the Underprivileged Child,"
    Music Journal, 25 No. 8 (Nov. 1967), 29-58.

Johnson, Kenneth R. "The Language of Black Children:
    Instruction Implication," in **Racial Crisis in**

American Education, ed. R.L. Green. Chicago Follett Educational Co., 1969.

Ornsteins, Allan C. "Preparing and Recruiting Teachers for Slum Schools," Journal of Secondary Education. 37 (1962), 386-372.

Rivillin, Harry N. "New Teachers for New Immigrants," Teacher College Record, 66, No. 8 (1965a), 707-717.

Soar, Robert, and Ruth Soar. "Classroom Behavior, Pupil Characteristics, and Pupil Growth for the School Year and for the Summer." University of Florida, 1973. In JSAS Catalog of Selected Documents in Psychology, Vol. 5, 1975, 200-MS No. 873.

Wolf, Elanor and Leo Wolf. "Sociological Perspectives on the Education of Culturally Deprived Children," School Review. 70 No. 6 (1962), 873-887.

Chapter 13

MAINSTREAMING MULTICULTURAL MUSIC

IN AMERICAN SCHOOLS

James A. Standifer

Increasing attention is being giving to federal law P.L. 94-124, the education of all handicapped children act of 1975. In brief, this law requires that large numbers of handicapped youngsters in the U.S. be mainstreamed from restricted residential centers or special class environments to the least restrictive environment, e.g., the "regular school class." For years, the handicapped child has received care in special centers which severely restricted his/her opportunity to become involved in the dynamic process of life as we know it outside of such centers or special instruction groups. Because of this, unfortunate attitudes and fears have developed regarding the handicapped that severely impede the successful functioning of individuals in the necessary and inevitable reciprocity basic to a democratic society. Race and culture conflicts in particular continue to threaten the well-being of Americans and, more than ever before, our nation's children are confused and frustrated by these conflicts. Today, our nation and communities have returned to practices and policies which intensify these conflicts in the minds of the young and old alike (e.g., the national return to tax breaks for segregated schools, the evolution versus creation science controversy, certain pronouncements of various interest groups in the country). The young teachers coming out of our colleges today are especially apprehensive and confused about their forth-coming involvement in today's schools. And, of course, all of this comes at a time when the nation is becoming more, rather than less, heterogeneous in its ethnic and cultural make up (e.g. the recent influx of Cubans, Haitians, Mexicans, and Asian boat people).

All of these events seem to cry out for our schools to increase the impetus for high quality curricula and instruction. It is, perhaps, not without some pre-design that P.L. 94-142 was preceded by the related and equally important P.L. 92-318 established by the 92nd Congress of the U.S. in June 1972. In a very clear and precise manner, this law not only promotes multicultural education, it also gives a solid rationale and legal basis for its practice. The Law does this in recognition of:

> the heterogeneous composition of the Nation and the fact that in a multiechnic society a greater understanding of the contributions of one's own heritage and those of one's fellow citizens can contribute to a more harmonious, patriotic and committed populace, and in recognition of the principle that all persons in the education institutions of the nation should have the opportunity to learn about the nature of their own cultural heritage, and to study the contributions of the cultural heritages of other ethnic groups of the nation.[1]

Indeed, P.L. 92-142 certainly emphasizes the uniqueness of each individual within the diverse and complex cultures that comprise American society. But more than that, like P.L. 92-138, its basis then is that because of this diversity and complexity, there is an overwhelming need in our society to have educational opportunities which are broad, humanitarian and unique for the individual, and groups of individuals. In short, the various means for meeting the needs of the different are as much in need of being pulled into the regular class or mainstream of teaching and learning as are the individuals towards whom these practices are directed. We know now, for example that "multicultural training can strongly influence perceptions of ethnic/cultural groups held by teachers in training...and that multicultural education for teachers is crucial if colleges and universities are to be effective institutions through which teachers can be prepared to teach in a culturally diverse nation."[2] Thus, the means (curriculum designs, intergroup involvement in preservice and inservice teacher training and so on) for implementing multicultural education and no longer tolerated as an appendage to this process. This, in my opinion, must be a major objective in institutionalizing multicultural practices and content into the usual process of education.

This chapter will argue that music practices of other cultures are excellent vehicles for achieving the above objective while emphasizing that such practices are also in dire need of being mainstreamed in American schools. Many of the negative attitudes, and fears regarding teaching and learning about other cultures have a genesis similar to that surrounding the handicapped and their movement into the mainstreamed system of education and life. Much of the growing ethnocentricity and prejudice toward things different in many U.S. communities and schools today could be greatly diminished if a systematic and well research approach to music world cultures were brought to and shared in our classrooms.

Fortunately, the field of ethnomusicology has long provided the necessary research on various music cultures which might now be mainstreamed in our school curricula. However, there continues to be too few materials and good methods of approach prepared specifically for use by school music teachers and their students. Further, too few teacher-training institutions are provided with programs and/or well prepared instructors that could systematically assist, in very practical and appropriate ways, pre-service and inservice teachers to become skillful multicultural music practitioners. Also, the few institutions that possess adequate programs of training in multicultural music and methods or, in the very least, have the potential for implementing such programs, tend to compartmentalize or place such services in "specialized areas (collections, museums, special studies and centers for example). Such compartmentalization often intimidates the very people that need the service most and is often so "specialized" as to admit only those individuals interested in a particular area as a career goal or for purposes related to a one time project. Seldom do such programs provide the kind of cross-cultural perspective and practical techniques needed by persons charged with planning and carrying out multicultural school music programs for youngsters and oldsters alike. It is reasonable to assume that the easy availability of carefully designed practical multicultural experiences would encourage schools and teacher training institutions to design, develop, disperse, and implement the appropriate kinds of learning experiences in multicultural education.

The lack of these well designed experiences and a myriad number of other factors contribute to the fear and resistance often encountered when attempts are made

243

at mainstreaming multicultural musics. This lack also accounts for the numerous haphazardly planned programs that currently exist and pass for music of other cultures courses in U.S. schools. It is probably still typically American, in fact, to respond to social problems by blaming and reforming various school programs. And, more often than not, such programs fall far short of the intended goal. Lawrence Cremins emphasized this in 1966 when he says the following:

> Eight years ago, when the Russians beat us into space, the public blamed the schools, not realizing that the only thing that had been proved, as the quip went at the time, was that their German scientists had gotten ahead of our German scientists. Today, almost a decade after Sputnik, the most rapidly growing area of the secondary school curriculum is not physics, not chemistry, not mathematics, but driver education. Hear the argument: 50,000 people a year are being killed on the highways, obviously, traditional forms of driving instruction are not working; some new institution must do it. It is a curious solution, requiring courses instead of seat belts, but typically American. On of my friends like to remark that in other countries, when there is a profound social problem there is an uprising; in the United States, we organize a course![3]

Fortunately, things are not quite this bad today. However, it is obvious to those specializing in the field that such superficial and foundationless attempts at passing on valid insights about music cultures are specious and, in the long run, irreparably damaging to those in whose hands rest the future of America.

As is true of mainstreaming the handicapped, systematically moving music of other cultures into the total school music curriculum must be viewed as a dynamic process, not as a products or onetime placement. The systematic and consistent inclusion of carefully prepared materials, and teaching and learning strategies into the school curriculum are certain to create new and highly challanging demands on

244

teachers. Moreover, the fear of change and the often detrimental personal biases held by many teachers in the arts will continue to be a strong force contributing to resistance to multicultural music education. Research indicates that teachers--far more than curricula--determine the degree of learning. In fact, according to a study carried out by the Educational Testing Service, "Educators make a major mistake when they develop a prepackaged curriculum that makes teachers less important." Teachers do make a difference and have far-reaching impact on youngsters' being and becoming, despite the acknowledged powerful influence of home and community. This position of the teacher in the school and the content of what is taught and how that content is taught. There is little question but what teachers can operationalize multicultural education and contribute significantly to the development of the content and process. However, the fear of change and the often detrimental personal biases held by many teachers in the arts will continue to be a strong force contributing to resistance to multicultural music education and the practices unique to this discipline.

As may be said of mainstreaming handicapped youngsters, the most pervasive contributor to resistance to mainstreaming music of other cultures is the factor that teachers feel terribly inadequate and unprepared to function effectively with this phenomenon. Happily, the pressure of the time and some highly creative thought and activity on the part of many scholars in this field are causing teacher-training institutions to make substantive changes in their curricula that should help in rectifying this problem. Certainly, the federal law 94-142 and 94-318 are two broad and national steps toward actualizing attempts to make changes in the area which are significant and out of which other and related attempts will emerge.

A Multicultural Music Education Model

The author initiated a multicultural music education project at the University of Michigan School of Music in 1974 which consisted of materials and approaches developed as a part of research grants received during the period of 1969-1972. During the period of 1973, the materials and approaches were tried in selected schools throughout the U.S. (primarily in the form of workshops in preservice and inservice techer training programs outside the State of Michigan, and in more systematic teaching experiences with preservice students taught in methods classes at the University of Michigan School of Music). After extensive re-evalution and reorganization of these materials, a more streamlined model was developed which could be tried at selected schools in the Detroit-Ann Arbor area. Some of these efforts consisted of specially designed summer courses for teachers in whose schools the multicultural model was undertaken.[4] During the past and current acadmic year, additional opportunities have been provided to share insights and practical experiences with pre- and inservice teachers enrolling in a Program for Educational Opportunity (U of M School of Education) lecture series in multicultural education. Several doctoral students also undertook school based research projects trying the materials and strategies outlined in the model. Finally, as a result of the foregoing efforts, a permanent course has been instituted in the U of M Music Education Department's curriculum and is entitled "Teaching Music in the Urban Environment." This course is one of a very few such courses in the Department which are required to contribute to the music education student's knowledge of cultural diversity.

In all of the above efforts, carefully selected music cultures (to include the "youth culture") are compared, contrasted and used as examples in developing the general theme: "Multicultural Music: Toward a Commitment to Cross-Cultural Education." Out of the activities used to meet the objectives of this theme emerged a theoretical and practical base for building multicultural music programs (K through College) having the potential for being mainstreamed in the school curricula. The musics and methods of approach proving to be most useful over the years demonstrated that music, in its broadest sense, is culture.

Some examples of the teaching strategies and materials of the model[5] in question are as follows:

Experiencing Cross-rhythms Using Two against Three

Much Latin American, Afroamerican and African music cultures make use of a rhythmic feeling of two against three. Students should be able to feel it almost automatically. The following activity and steps

can help in accomplishing this. Put the following
diagram on chalkboard or project on screen:

Left		Right
1	1	1
	2	
	3	3
	4	
	5	5
	6	

After they have practiced this combined exercise until
it is fluent, change the numbers as follows to
illustrate that they are performing two beats with the
left hand while performing three beats with the right
hand:

Left		Right
1	1	1
	2	
	3	
4	4	
	5	
	6	

Again have students tap the first pulse with both
hands, and 1 and 4 with their left hand. Repeat at a
reasonable but consistent speed until set.

Now have students combine the two, putting the
following on board or screen:

Left		Right
1	1	1
	2	
	3	
4	4	
	5	5
	6	

After they have practiced this combined exercise until
it is fluent, change the numbers as follows to
illustrate that they are performing two beats with the
left hand while performing three beats with the right
hand:

Left	Right
1	1
.	.
.	2
2	.
.	3
.	.

Have the students count aloud the beats played by the
right hand (1 - 2 - 3), then the left hand (1 - 2),
while keeping both hands going. Repeat this process
until students are able to keep both hand going while
they change counts from 1-2-3, 1-2-3, to 1-2, 1-2, and
so on.

Now start student on the left/right pattern without counting aloud. Have them lower their hands (open
palms) onto their desk tops or onto their thighs while

they are playing the pattern. Insist on precision in
the pattern, avoiding the tendency to rush. Students
who continually have difficulty accomplishing the
activity may profit from the use of words or syllables
chanted in the rhythm of two against three.

Example: <u>Not</u> - <u>dif-fi-cult</u>

LEFT	RIGHT
Not <u>i</u>	Not <u>1</u>
.	
.	dif <u>2</u>
fi 2	.
.	cult <u>3</u>

Students are encouraged
to snap fingers or tap
desk tops while
chanting the syllables:
<u>Not</u> <u>dif-fi-cult</u>

Finally, students are strongly encouraged to keep a
steady beat and a consistent tempo. Students in Western cultures often equate ability with speed. They
will be prone to rush the beats thus constantly
increasing the speed of the pattern. This should be
avoided and the phenomenon used to explain and/or
discuss yet another factor typical of one or another
particular music culture. The constant, repetitive,
almost unrelenting beat of some African rhythms may be
alluded to and contrasted with certain musics of
another culture having a different sense of time.

Help students to become more sensitive to the West
African's "sense of time" by having them learn the
following rhythmic patterns that are ubiquitous in this
culture:

Counting repeatedly from 1 to 12, clap on the
numbers given:

given: ‖ 1 . 3 . 5 6 . 8 . 10 . 12 ‖

        ‖ ⸖   ⸖ Repeat until set.

Clap: ‖ X . X . X X . X . X . X ‖

249

After the pattern has become set, use a low sound (L) on the first beat and a high sound (H) on beats 3, 5, 6, 8, 10, and 12. For example:

```
|| 1 . 3 . 5 6 . 8 .10 . 12 ||
|| L . H . H H . H   H    H ||
```

For the Low (L) sound strike top of thighs with open palms. For the high (H) sounds, clap hands. The African two-tone bell or gangoqui may also be used with this pattern. The large bell will produce a low pitch, while the small bell will produce the higher pitch. Below is given the same pattern, this time with notation (Western):

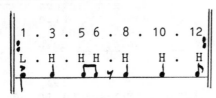

To obtain an even more authentic sound and achieve a finer sense of West African time and timbre, a rattle may be added to the pattern using the following rhythm:

Clap:	1 . 3 . 5 6 . 8 . 10 . 12
Two-tone bell:	L . H . H H . H . H . H
Rattle:	U . D U D D U D U D U D

When using the rattle, the "U" stands for an upward motion striking the open palm with the rattle. The "D" stands for a downward motion striking the top of the thigh with the rattle.

The students should repeat the patterns, counting softly all twelve beats of the pattern, until set. When set, students are encouraged to simply "feel" the natural flow of the pattern after which they may alter the pattern with appropriate improvisations.

As indicated earlier, two-against-three rhythms are frequently found in music of Latin America also. The example on page 252 is a listening experience which uses the two-against-three pattern in the beginning measures. The piece is called "Sanctus and Benedictus," from the folk mass, Misa Criolla by Ariel Ramirez*. A "blueprint for listening" or Call Chart is provided to direct the listener's attentions to specific musical events of the composition while they occur. In short, the listener is to read various descriptions of the occurring musical event during the listening lesson. The student's attention is directed to each line of descriptors by a voice calling out the numbers opposite the line in question. With repeated listening experiences using this technique, students find that they have little difficulty reading the descriptors, listening to what is described, and making relationships between what is heard and what is described. Moreover, not only will they become increasingly familiar with the given musical descriptors or characteristics, they will also begin to discover more subtle ones. To anticipate any reading problems among students, words in the descriptors should be as simple and closely illustrative of the musical event as possible. Words and/or sentences should always be descriptive, never interpretive. It would be more aesthetic to describe a sound of low strings as "thick and low pitched" than as "gloomy and foreboding." The goal in these experiences is the perception of musical expressive devices and their use in selected music cultures. Contrasts and comparisons between music cultures will take place more effectively when listening is directed to this end. (Indeed, it may be noted that all of the preceding activities are on the one hand highly varied but, on the other, unique to a specific culture(s). Such varied opportunities will enable individual students to become integrally involved in a cultural matrix while fulfilling their role as sensitive participants in the culture(s). Finally, teachers will find that students are able to concentrate at increasingly high levels using the Call Chart technique and associated activities. Students will soon be able to make their own "blueprint for listening" using familiar music from cultures of their choice.

---

*Note: A second Call Chart from the same mass and entitled "Agnus Dei" is also given following the "Sanctus" example. Translation of the Spanish is also provided.

The following listening experience from Misa Criolla is one sample from the Multicultural Model illustrating the Call Chart idea. While this example is useful in a variety of school music perception situations, it is an excellent opportunity for introducing "starter" experiences related to the Chicago movement in the U.S. which is receiving increasing attention as part of what is called La Raza. In connection with this listening experience, the Chicano student will of course prove to be an invalubale resource for other related activities.

NOTE:

Misa Criolla, a mass, was composed by Ariel Ramirez and is based strickly on music found in Argentine folklore. Each section is based on a particular rhythmical element indigeneous to Latin America. Students should be informed of this fact and use it as a basis for further study.

(Philips PCC 619)

MISA CRIOLLA
Call Chart   (Folk or Creole Mass for
     Soloists, for Soloists, Chorus & Orchestra)

by Ariel Ramirez

Sanctus (Santo)
(Side 1 Band 4)

Call
#

1.   Strings   Guitar
                    Bass   Strums
                    Guitar

2.   Persuccion   Claves
                    Sandpaper
                    Woodblocks
                    Drums

3.   Guitar - thicker strum

4.   Three (3) male soloitst - Chord outlined on:
        "Santo - Santo - Santo"
5.   Chorus   Text: Santo, Senor Dios del
                                      Universo!

6.	Soloists in octaves	Text:	Senor Dios del Universo!
7.	Repetitions of 4 - 6		
8.	Soloitst - two parts 　　　　　- unison 　　　　　- two parts	Text:	Llenos estan los 　　　cielos -Y la tierra de tu 　　　Gloria -　　Llenos estan 　　　los cielos -　　Y la tierra de 　　　tu Gloria
9.	Strings & Percussion interlude		
10.	Harpsichord -ascending arpeggio		
11.	Soloitst - two 　　　　parts (f)	Text:	Josana en las 　　altural!
12.	Chorus　- four 　　　　parts (p)	-	Bandito el que 　　viene En el nombre del 　　Senor
13.	Repeat of 11	Text:	Josana en las 　　altural!
14.	Repeat of 12	-	Josana en las 　　altural!

(Philips PPC 619)

MISA CRIOLLA

Call Chart　　　(Folk or Creole Mass
　　　for Soloists, Chorus & Orchestrs)

by Ariel Ramirez

Agnus Dei
Call　　　　　(Side 1, Band 5)

1. Harpsichord - interrupted
　　descending patterns

2. <u>Solo</u> (Chorus in -　　Text:　Cordero de Dios; Que
　　humming accom-　　　　　quita pecados del

253

	paniment) - acappella	mundo
3.	Soloists - two parts	Ten compasion de Nosotros
4.	<u>Chorus</u> - humming, <u>Harpichord</u> with embellishing accompaniment	
5.	(Repeat of 2): <u>Solo</u> - Chorus	Cordero de Dios; Que quita los pecados del mundo
6.	Voices: Unison to two part: harmony	Ten compasion de nosotros
7.	(Repeat of 4) - Chorus - Harpsichord	
8.	Repeat of 2 - 5 <u>Solo</u> - <u>Chorus</u>	Cordero de Dios; Que quitas los pecados del mundo
9.	Female voice alternating with male voices - acappela (echo effect)	Danos la paz; Danos la pas; Danos la paz; Danos la paz; Danos la paz.

Study Questions

1. What was the general but very prominent direction (movement) of the melodic and harmonic material of this piece?

2. What kind of harmonic material do we hear in call number 3 (soloists)?

3. Does the ending of the piece (its melodic, harmonic and rhythmic qualities as well as such things as dynamics, tone color, etc.) seem appropriate for the text? Discuss these qualities.

MISA CRIOLLA
(Folk of Creole Mass for Soloits, Chorus, and Orchestra)

Translation of Text

IV. Sanctus Carnaval
　　　cochabombino

IV. SANTO

Santo,	Holy,
Santo,	Holy,
Santo	Holy,
Santo	Holy,
Senor Dios del Universo!	Lord, God of the Universe!
Llenos estan los cielos	Heaven and earth
Y la tierra de tu Gloria	Are filled with Thy Glory.
Josana en las alturas!	Hosanna in the
Bendito el que viene	highest!
En el nombre del Senor	Blessed is he who
Josana en las alturas!	cometh
	In the name of the Lord
	Hosanna in the highest

V. Agnus Dei Estilo
　　　pampeano

V. Agnus Dei

Cordero de Dios	Lamb of God
Que quitas los pecados del mundo	Who takest away the sins of the world
Ten compasion de nosotros	Have mercy on us.
Cordero de Dios	Lamb of God
Que quitas los pecados del	Who takest away
Danios la paz.	the sins of the world
	Grant us peace.

　　The need to teach the musical content of a paticular example still remains a prime objective of any of the experiences in the process of multicultural music education. For example, one may use a class period or more to help students learn about the Black cultural experience, both contemporary and historical, of Blacks while focusing on the structure and musical and other expenssive devices unique to the 12-bar blues form developed by Blacks in America. Various nonmusical concerns may be addressed outside of class (assignments) or as introductory in-class material (e.g., make a list of contributions by American Blacks and compare these contributions with similar ones made by other American minorities; examine the ways Blacks have gained inclusion into the mainstream of todays society and compare these ways with that of other groups in America) and activities. The prime objective, however, for this lesson or unit might be simply that of having students increase their perception of the musical, textual, and structural content of the 12-bar blues form. In such a case, the lesson or unit may use content and activities similar to the following based on the tune "Mean Ole Bed Bug Blues" as sung by Bessie Smith. The recorded example of the music may be found on the album Columbia, number G 30818. The lesson is structured as follows:

Mean Old Bed Bug Blues, sung by Bessie Smith, has a four measure introduction played by the guitar. This is followed by four blues choruses, each of which has the same formal design and a different text, then an eight measure extra chorus. Listen to the blues here, and you will find that the beginnings and endings of the chorus on the record can be heard easily and followed (with the aid of the listening guide) with little difficulty. Below is a diagram for each of the four blues choruses:

Design for Listening

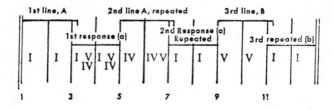

256

#A   Bed bug sho' is evil, they don't mean me no
       good.
A'   Bed bug sho' is evil, they don't mean me no
       good.
B   Thinks he's a woodpecker, and I'm a chunk of
       wood.

This pattern is a fine illustration of Call and Response frequently encountered in much Black and Black related musics. It is adopted here in the blues where the vocal phase, the call, is answered by the guitar phrase, the response. The use of the text and melody and the use of an accompanying instrument to play the responses are typical of the blues also: there are three vocal phrases, the first two with the same text phrase and melody and the last with a new text phrase and new melody. In the two measure intervals between vocal phrases, the accompanying instruments play a phrase, usually improvised commenting on the vocal phrase. That means that each chorus, in effect, contains three call and response units. For additional material on this and related music, the reader may wish to consult the World of Popular Music: Afro-American, by Sidney Fox, James A. Standifer, and Barbara Reeder Lundquist. (See bibliography in this Unit for more complete data on this source).

The teacher may wish to play other examples of the 12-bar blues and reinforce the fact that the form in the harmony is also very similar, i.e., primarily a I IV V I pattern is used (as shown in the diagram on the preceeding page. After listing to several blues examples -- here are two different but similar (in form and harmony structure) blues examples that might be used. Have students sing the harmony patterns as well and identify the basic form of the text and music. Discuss the difference and similarities they might discover between Mean Old Beg Bug Blues and the examples suggested:

Little Red Rooster, Side 1, Band 6. Feliciano 10-23 RCA Stero LSP -4185.

The Man Ain't Nothing But a Woman Cryin' for Her Man. Side 1, Band 1. Roulette Record, Inc. SR-25189-A

Compare the above readings with:

Mean Old Bed Bug Blues, Side 4, Band 1 and 2. Follett Publishing Company's World of Popular Music: Afro-American, Record Album, SL-11; P-12193. See also Columbia records, G30818. A Teaching Guide accompanies this record album from Follett. 1010 Washinging Street. Chicago, Illinois. (Album located in the Ann Arbor IMC, Board of Education)

Notice that the chorus itself -- the twelve measure blues harmonic pattern -- is played four times, that the last response in each chorus is the same, that the voice sings only two different phrases, A and B, but repeats A immediately, and that the guitar's first two responses in the second chorus are repeated in the fourth chorus. Note that the fifth chorus, the one that isn't blues chorus, is like the previous four choruses except that the middle four-measure unit is omitted.

Below is notated a basic version of the voice's A and B phrases. The listener is encouraged to observe the small variations made during the course of the performance.

MEAN OLD BED BUG BLUES   by Bessie Smith
Album: Columbia
        G 30818

DIRECTED LISTENING CHART

1. Introcution ---- |✓ — — —|✓ — — —|✓ — —|✓ — —|Guitar alone
                       1 2 3 4 1 2 3 4 1 2 3 4 1 2 3 4

2. Voice Two measure phase; 1st line of text. (A)

3. Instruments - Two measure phrase; commenting on vocal phrase 1st response (a)

4. Voice - Two measure phrase; 2nd line of text. (A)

5. Instruments - Two measure phrase; commenting on 2nd response - (a) repeated

6. Voice - Two measure phrase; 3rd line of text (B)

7. Instruments - Two measure phrase; commenting 3rd response - new melodic idea (closing)

*This listening chart may be used as an aide to understanding and perceiving the elements use in the 12-bar listening experience. The teacher may choose to call each number prior to the material entrance (or she may have a student volunteer to do this. In any case, direct the student's attention to the various elements use in the song as the event occurs.

Begin at 2 for four more repetitions of the given material - new verses.

[6]The recording for this lesson is found in The World of Popular Music: Afro-American by Fox, Standifer and Reeder, Follett Publishers, 1974. The album is available through the Instructional Media Center, Ann Arbor Schools.

Directions (Listening Grid: Student Involvement)

Listen to the recordng of "Mean Old Bed Bug Blues" while using the above grid to assist in counting beats and identifying the harmonic motion. By counting and listening to the harmonis patterns, you will be kept in place by the grid. To further assist you in the identification of the beats and harmony, you might check (✔) the first beat of each measure.

LISTENING GRID: STUDENT INVOLVEMENT

Beats and Harmonic Patterns

The listening grid (a table with VERSES 1–5 across the top, labeled columns for VOCAL and GUITAR, measure counts "Counts on beat per measure / 1234", and a harmony row):

			VOCAL	GUITAR	VOCAL	GUITAR	VOCAL	GUITAR		
measures #:			1	3	5	7	9	11		
harmony:			I	I	I IV / IV I / V IV	I VI / IV I (omitted in final chorus)	I	V	V	I

note: Guitar class should play along with record using given chords.

After feeling reasonably comfortable with this activity, use the Grid with other 12-bar blues examples and you may discover the similarities and differences that may exist. Finally, return to the Call Chart given on page 258. This Call Chart will help you immeasurably in perceiving the material of the blues under study. It can be used with any 12-bar blues. Any perceived changes can, of course, be indicated in the Chart as the need arises. This change or changes, in turn might be a subject for class discussion.

The teacher may want to extend this lesson by having students explore the poetic form of the Blues. The following and similar blues text may be used as a starter:

THE BLUES

Verse Structure: AAB

"Good Lookin Woman"[7]

A Good Lookin' woman make a bull dog break his chain

B Good lookin' woman make a bull dog break his chain

C Good lookin' woman make a snail catch a passenger train

As indicated in the Listening Grid provided previously, the three line pattern given above was interwoven into the 12-bar of each blues verse resulting in the typical Vocal -A Instrumental; Vocal - -A, Instrumental Vocal -B, Instrumental form.

Poetically, the form may be explained as follows:

MELODY	POETRY
A Statement	Situation introduced;
A Re-statement emphasizes builds up tension.	Re-statement stresses importance of phrase the situation; possible consequences implied or given.
B Resolution of the tension built up in restatement.	Phrase contrast; new material resolves problem

Excellent examples for use in the study of the poetry of the blues are John W. Work's American Negro Song, Philadelphia; Theodore Press, Co. 1948, and Samuel Charters' The Poetry of the Blues. New York: Oak Publications, 1967.

The teacher might move the lesson further by comparing and contrasting the blues text example with that of other poetic forms, for example Japanese Haiku. The following offers brief ideas upon which the teacher may build:

HAIKU

1. Give a brief history or background information on Haiku.

2. Point out that the Haiku verse form consists of three lines totalling 17 syllables and always is written in a specific form:

	Structure	Example
First line	5 syllables	A river leaping
Second line	7 syllables	tumbling over rocks
		roars on as the
Third line	5 syllables	mountain smiles.

3. The traditional subject matter of Haiku is nature and the impact of nature on one's senses. Use words, phrases, sounds and rhythms to evoke images that closely approximate what you feel about your subject and how to respond to it.

4. Have students avoid the temptation to end lines in rhyme when writing their own Haiku.

5. Ask students to read Haiku verses aloud, and listen intently to judge whether the verse meets with class expectations.

6. After a class evaluation of Haiku written by class members, ask students to adjust their Haiku as needed to achieve the effect they are seeking.

In the instance of this lesson, the primary focus may be the instrinsic poetic content and how that content compares or contrasts with the poetic content of blues. As with the blues, additional study will be done relating the Haiku more closely with the culture out which it emerged. An excellent example for additional study on Haiku is: Modern Japenese Haiku: An Anthology. Toronto: University of Toronto Press, 1976, by Ueda Makoto (compiler and translator). This example gives Haiku examples in a format that carries the original Japanese wording, with a word-by-word

English translation.

Some Advantages of the Multicultural Model

Many unexplored advantages of teaching a course or courses which use in a systematic way, various music cultures and associated approaches as means of sharpening perception and increasing sensitiveness to the essence of all music soon become apparent. The techniques of Call Charts, movement, and personalized instruction so effective in well developed multicultural courses all have little value if the teacher does not bring a well developed and comprehensive and open-minded attitude to the class coupled with a high degree of scholarship and competence in music. The teacher must understand that multicultural education is the process of incorporating into a teaching/learning environment activities that involve individuals in experiencing a variety of cultural perspectives and techniques. While a strong philosophy of multiculultral education is crucial to the success of programs in any discipline, it is especially critical in the arts and humanities, since these discipines in particular seek to document and influence the individual's affective attitudes as well as the social interaction of groups. They must know that multicultural education involves individuals in experiences that are typical of selected culture (s) on the one hand and experiences that are common among cultures on the other. They must be committed to the idea that it is a process that recognizes cultural diversity and similarities as a fact of life, and that it requires teaching strategies that both intellectualize and humanize.

Finally, most of us tend more to emphasize difference in things and people than commonalities, and to evaluate those difference in terms of ourselves and our own cultures. This may be inevitable. However, a strong and internalized philosophy of multicultural education can diminish the effects of such ethno-centricity and assist individuals to evaluate people, things, and behaviors in terms of the cultures and experiences that produced them. Further, this philosophy helps us discover ways in which we and other cultures are alike and to appreciate and respect the ways in which we may be different.

If we, as teachers, can accomplish these aims, we have more than a reasonable chance of helping our students deepen their appreciation for their own cultures. That is, the learner can begin to see things which may have been labelled distasteful in one culture that are perfectly acceptable in others. This knowledge can lead to a better perspective from which to view and understand the behavior in question. Further, the learner may truly begin to see other cultures as complementary rather than contradictory ways of organizing and dealing with the social world.

This global view is particularly necessary in a pluralistic society such as America where, perhaps more than ever before, we need to know that cultural differences may be assets that simply involve alternative ways of looking at and doing things; and that these differences are not absolute or mutually exclusive. This view is the very essence of operationalizing multicultural education.

We have a long way to go to actualize the vast number of definitions, pronouncements, and the like on multicultural education. We will continually need updated guidelines and practical examples. More than that, we will need experience in putting the guidelines and practices to work. Teachers and administrators and parents must somehow capitalize on culturally relevant past experience and combine forces to develop appropriate frames of reference for constructing and putting into action approaches to multicultural education in their particular school and community.

What I believe is one of the most important statements on multicultural education issued during the past decade. In part, it says:

>...Multicultural education recognizes cultural diversity as a fact of life in American society, and it affirms that this cultural diversity is a valuable resource that should strive to preserve and enhance cultural pluralism.

>To endorse cultural pluralism is to understand and appreciate the differences that exist among the nation's citizens. It is to see these differences as a positive force in the continuing development of a society which professes a wholesome respect for

the instrinsic worth of every individual[9] American Association of Colleges for Teacher Education, 1972).

At this point, it might be prudent to point out that besides the necessity for the teacher to have a strong philosophy of multicultural education, it is also important that this teacher provides the necessary "mix" of experiences needed to give the student more than a reasonable chance to internalize such experiences. In this curriculum, for example, it is crucial that careful coordination and use of visual, aural, and psychomotor activities in any one experience are given great emphasis to increasingly bring the learner to the center of the teaching/learnig experience. Such careful coordination insures and enhances student involvement in the life of music cultures explored. It is one very effective way to insure that students have more than a reasonable opportunity to explore these music from the "inside out," and to have direct and meaningful experiences with meaningful "processes" of the culture studied.

The material of the Call Charts may of course be put on chalkboard, projected on a screen or copies may be made so that each student may follow and study the material in a more individualized manner. A self-administered evaluation sheet should also be provided with each Call Chart to check students' progress. (In the Multicultural Model described here, all the material associated with a particular learning experience is provided in a programmed format to include cassette tape of all of the music, exercises and directions for listening.)

Building on the experience of two against three and the reinforcement provided by the listening examples, comparisons and contrasts between another music culture may be provided. For example, the Oriental culture uses instruments in its folk music that are similar to that of Africa and Afroamerica. Also, the cross-rhythms and the custom of using improvised techniques is a striking and common feature among these cultures.

In Korea, one rhythmic pattern of nine beats and called "Saemach'i" is highly popular and provides a fine sense of time typical of Korean folk music culture. The "Saemach'i" rhythm (pronounced "Say' machae") is made very prominent in various musical examples by being played on the changgo--one of the most popular musical instruments of the country. It is a two-headed drum which looks much like an oversized hourglass on it side. (Similar hourglass shaped drums are used in both eastern and western Africa.) Each head of the drum is covered with animalskin. The skin of the left side is thick and has a low-pitched sound. It is struck with the palm, sounding soft and low-pitched. The skin of the rightside is thin and is struck with a stick held in the right hand. The sound is hard and high-pitched. Both sides, of course, may be struck simultaneously when desired. A similar instrument is a pair of bongo drums. Students may be encouraged to tap out the following rhythm pattern of Samach-i. In Western notation, the pattern looks like this.

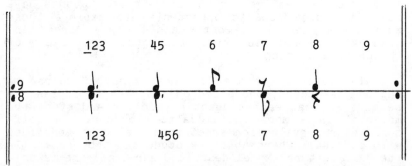

To assist students in learning this pattern, put the following numbered exercise on chalkboard or project on screen so that they might practice it:

Count:	1	2	3	4	5	6	7	8	9
Strike desk top (with both hands):	X			X		X	X	X	

The "X" symbols indicate when to strike the desk or table top - open palms. Students should count the numbers above each X so they will know how long to keep the hands on the desk top. The dot (.) means to rest, making no sound. Start the pattern very slowly so that students are not frustrated. As they gain skill, increase the tempo repeating the pattern again and

again without stopping. After the rhythm is set,
students are asked to clap the pattern using a
consistent tempo and beat. Have them listen to the
resultant sound.

Now try the pattern below using both hands,
striking the desk or table top at different times:

	Counts:	1	2	3	4	5	6	7	8	9
Strike Desk	Right Hand:	X				●	X	●	X	
top with	Left Hand:	X			X			X		

After the rhythmic pattern is set, try again, this time
keeping half of hand (back portion of palm) on the desk
or table top, raising only the fingers and striking
them on the desk top. Keep trying the pattern again
and again until students can perform in a relatively
fast but consistent tempo. Listen to the resultant
sound.

The teacher may play a variety of Korean folk
music, (especially folk songs such as: "Nodul
Kangbyon," "Miryang Arirang," "Toraji," "Yangsando,"
"Ulsan Agasi," or "Yong'byonga,") which use or are
based on the saemach'i pattern. Students should be
encouraged to play the pattern in accompaniment to the
example chosen.

In spite of the many advantages of the multicultural curriculum, there are still many troublesome
and unanswered questions related to building curricula
mainstreamed with music of other cultures. For
example, how does one deal effectively with the
persistent stereotypes and misconceptions held by
educators, parents, and students? How do we develop
efficient and immediate means of determining the extent
to which students' attitudes have been changed or
significantly influenced by involvement in multicultural course . Can teacher-training institu-tions
realistically and adequately prepare teachers to cope
effectively with the problems intrinsic to
multicultural education at the grass roots? The
following quote from Bennett Reimer, noted educator and
aesthetician, provides a partial answer:

Until the education of music teachers become as broadly based both musically and generally as we are suggesting here, the result of music teaching in the schools can not be expected to be any wider or more valuable than they are at present. We are not asserting that present practices in music education are totally invalid and ineffective. They are certainly not. But our theory of the nature of aesthetic experience allows us to evaluate the field in a new light. Our point of view cuts to the heart of music's significance in individual and cultural life, throwing open for question everything presently being done in the teaching and learning of music.[10]

The questions posed earlier and many others warrant careful considerations to insure optimum use of teaching and learning strategies thus far developed for use in multicultural education. The answers to these questions are critical to emerging programs which are attempting to avoid the superficialities and "add ons" so often treated by ethnic studies. They can also be decisive and fundamental steps toward multiculturalism in all of American education.

Finally, multicultural education as aptly pointed out by one writer on the topic is not starry-eyed or so idealistic in teaching children to respect each other or so intent on teaching cross-cultural content that it lacks the practicality of monocultural education. It is practical; but in a sense that emphasizes the quality of our lives. In fact, the wonder of main-streaming music of other cultures--of multicultural education--is that the process presents a variety of life styles, and a variety of ways of responding to experiences of life among peoples of all the world. These experiences,--in music, the sounds and their logic--must be met however on their own terms. The inevitable question asked in any course which studies musics of other cultures is this: Is it good music? The question itself suggests that the student has not yet reached the crucial stage where he is inclined to evaluate a music culture in terms of those means employed by its practitioners. An important stage in the multicultural music course is when the learner is able to grasp and accept the fact that the "value" of any music must be seen in a cultural context. On this important point, William Malm, ethnomusicologist, says the following:

> ...an answer to such a question as "Is it good music?" can only be made after a reply is given to yet a further question--"Good for what?" An instrumental variation piece played by a professional musician on the Korean kayakeum zither or on a Burmese harp and a song about water buffalo herds sung by a blind street musician playing a monochord in a Thailand village market are, in this sense, incomparable. They can really be evaluated best by members of the society that inspired them. They are of potentially equal value for a foreign listener only to the degree that he can understand their original cultural context, or, perhaps, relate them to some aspect of his own cultural or personal aesthetics.[11]

This idea is at once a challenge and a warning. The inventiveness and sensitiveness of a people cut across broad areas of experience. Our schools must be able to help our students become knowledgeable about such experience. More than that, they must assist them in recognizing the value of the variety of experience reflected in the many systems of music available in today's world.

CONCLUSION

One's perception of any culture's expression seems to be in direct proportion to the extent of personal and active involvement with it. Such direct and active experience serves as a catalyst for intellectual understanding and sensitivity. Conversely, when sufficient direct experience is lacking, various culturally determined characteristics of music, for example, may be a force of irritation and disorientation for individuals not of the stimulus music culture. In fact, the experience may be so unpalatable as to alienate in some cases, and thus be a prime source of isolation and exclusion of one culture from another.

The question arises as to whether the study of music of other cultures involves and/or requires skills or behaviors that are different from the study of music in general. One answer may be that the study of music of X culture, especially in a curriculum having a multicultural emphasis, is important not as an end in itself, but as a means of grasping and understanding an essential and fundamental truth: despite differences, no one culture or mode of behavior of a particular culture is intrinsically better than another. Rather, cultural differences involve alternative ways of feeling, looking at, responding to, and/or doing things. The differences are hardly absolute or mutually exclusive. In fact, the differences pinpointed about a culture's (or generation's) contribution will often lead to the discovery of common bonds existing between all cultures and generations. One may discover, also, that irrespective of time or distance, there are surprising similarities that suggest that there are primordial elements that exist among the world's cultures that neither time nor distance can alter.

In schools using a variety of means to personalize instruction, considerable benefits can accrue from mainstreaming multicultural musics. Parents, teachers, and students alike will begin to discover and cherish the fact that the process of learning to look apropriately at one's own culture and at that of other cultures will sharpen cognitive and affective skills in dealing with all kinds of life experiences. In the arts, this sharpening of the cognitive and affective powers is the development of aesthetic sensitivity and a feeling for what it is like to live in a different time, place or culture. It is also the ability to (1) perceive the aesthetic content of various products of a culture, and (2) respond meaningfully to the content. It is also an open-mindedness regarding the functional aspects of the music culture and a respect for values that may be drastically different from one's own. All of these are prerequisite for opening the minds and hearts of students to knowledge, insights and to various ways of feeling typical of peoples of other times and places. In essence, a music culture documents and symbolizes in sound experiences of life among all mankind. To perceive and react to the aesthetic products of a culture, then, is to learn to appreciate and respect that culture. "Liking that culture may or may not result. This kind of education makes it possible for the learner to have and use alternatives, and choices fundamental to the development of sensitivity to a variety of technical and expressive aspects typical of a music culture. This kind of education is multicultural in its truest sense.

Two important implications have been drawn from attempts at using this model to mainstream music of other cultures: First, cultural and cross-cultural enrichment can indeed result from appropriate and well researched materials and teaching procedures. Second, as Alan Lomax, America's major collector of folksongs and author of note, has said: "The touchstone is style. Every human being is drawing his fingers across the string of his life experience. Whether as a listener, a participant, or a creator, he reinforces the patterns by which his culture lives. In this sense, the artist is the heart and soul of every culture, but without the sensitive and sustaining allegiance of his audience, the artist would be nothing. In simpler societies artist and audiences are the same."

Mainstreaming music of other cultures is not a panacea. However, it seems reasonable to assume that it could form a useful springboard toward a significant advance in understanding and harnessing the mysterious power of the arts to help men understnad and respect other men.

NOTES FOR CHAPTER 13

1. Congressional State of Policy Pertaining to the Ethnic Heritage Program. See 20, United States Code Annotated, Section. 900.

2. Gwendolyn C. Baker. "Multicultural Education: Two Perservice Training Approaches.: Journal of Teacher Education 28:3, (May-June 1977) p. 32

3. Lawrence A. Cremin. The Genuis of American Education. New York: Alfred A. Knopf and Random House, 1966, p. 11.

4. James A. Standifer and Comp., A Guide for Multicultural Music Education in Todays Schools.

Ann Arbor: The University of Michigan School of
Education, Program for Educational Opportunity,
1981.

5.   James A. Standifer and Barbara Reeder Lunquist.
     Source of African and Afro-American Materials for
     the Music Educator. CMP₇. Washington, D.C. Music
     Educators National Conference, 1972, pp. 32-33.

6.   James A. Standifer, (ed. and Comp.) A Guide For
     Multicultural Music Education in Todays Schools.
     Ann Arbor: The University of Michigan School of
     Education, Program for Educational Opportunity,
     1981, pp. 69-73.

7.   John W. Work. American Negro Songs.
     Philadelphia: Theodore Presser Company, 1967. p.
     30.

8.   Prentice H. Baptise Jr., and Mira Baptiste.
     "Multiculturizing Classroom Instruction.
     Approaches for Achieving a Multicultural
     Curriculum. Ann Arbor,: The University of
     Michigan School of Education, Program for
     Education Opportunity, 1980, p. 11.

9.   American Association of Colleges for Teacher
     Education. "No One Model American," Principle
     Statement on Multicultural Education. 1972. See
     also, Journal of Teacher Education No. 4, Special
     Issue on Multicultural Education, (Winter 1973).

10. Bennett Reimer. The Common Dimensions of
     Aesthetic and Religious Experience. Ph.D.
     dissertation, Ann Arbor: University Microfilm,
     1963, p. 282.

11. William Malm. Music Cultures of the Pacific, the
     Neast, And Asia. 2nd ed. Englewood Cliffs, New
     Jersey: Prentice-Hall, 1977, p. 215.

Bibliography of Supplementary Readings

Cardenas, R. and L. W. Filmore. "Toward a
    Multicultural Society, Today's Education (Sept.-
    Oct. 1973)

272

Citron, Abraham R. "Multiculturalism: An Education for Americans," Multicultural Education: Instruction and Curriculum. Ann Arbor: Program for Educational Opportunity, School of Education, The University of Michigan, 1977.

Hunter, William (ed.) Multicultural Education Through Competency-based Teacher Education. Washington, D.C.: American Association for Colleges of Teacher Education, 1974.

Reimer, Bennett. A Philosophy of Music Education. Englewood Cliffs, New Jersey: Prentice-Hall, 1970.

Kaplan, Leonard. "Survival Talk for Educators: Multicultural Education." Journal of Teacher Education Vol, XXVIII, No. 3 (May-June 1977), p. pp. 55-56.

Gollnick, Donna M. Multicultural Education: The Challenge for Teacher Education." Ibid., pp. 57-59.

Moody, Charles D., and Charles B. Vergon. Multicultural Education: Instruction and Curriculum, Ann Arbor: Program for Educational Opportunity, The University of Michigan, The School of Education, 1977.

Moody, Charles D., and Karen Lind. Cross-Cultural Communication in the Schools. Ann Arbor: Program for Educational Opportunity, The University of Michigan, The School of Education, 1978.

Moody, Charles D., and Charles B. Vergon. Approaches for Achieving a Multicultural Curriculum. Ann Arbor: Program for Education Opportunity, School of Education, The University of Michigan, 1979.

Frostig, Marianne. Education for Dignity. New York: Grune & Stratton, 1976. (See, especially Chapter 11, "The Role of the School in Moral Education.)

Hamilton, Andrew. "Education and La Raza." American Education (July-1973), p. 5+

Research News. "Ethnomusicology: The World of Music Cultures." Special Issue written by James E.

Haney (consultant: William P. Malm.) Research News (August 1970) Office of Research Administration, The University of Michigan.

Levine, Toby et al. Jumpstreet Humanities Project (Learning Package) Washington, D.C. Greater Washington Educational Telecommunications Association, Inc., 1981.

Music Educator Journal. Special Report. The Music Educators National Conference, 56: 5. (January 1970).

CHAPTER 14

A GUIDE FOR NEW TEACHERS

Effie T. Gardner

Recently, I received an urgent phone call from a former student in music education who had graduated at the end of the last school year. She had been an excellent student, interested and enthusiastic about her future as a teacher and had done a fine job in her student teaching experience (Which was far from the so-called "ideal" situation). Now she found herself in a Southern county school teaching elementary music without benefit of a room, a piano or other instruments, textbooks, not to mention a phonograph or recordings, tape recorder, film projector and films, and all of the other essentials for an adequate music program. Her only materials were a set of teachers manuals for a current music series. In addition, her administrator gave no hope of filling any part of the rather ambitious order for supplies which she had been requested to submit. It would be an understatement to say that she was frustrated and disallusioned after only a few weeks of work.

While this may be an extreme case in teaching circumstances, I had only to think back to my first public school day in a large urban situation. Luckily I had a room, but that was all - no chairs, books, or piano, only a room. While a few supplies did eventually arrive, I remember being faced with a similar feeling of despair in trying to find materials with which to work. It occurred to me while trying to help this new teacher deal with her problem that her dilemma is not an uncommon one. Unfortunately, undergraduate methods classes seldom deal with these very real situations but rather assume that at least a minimum of equipment and supplies are provided. Even student teaching experiences are usually manned by teachers of some experience who have already developed materials and equipment. What does a new teacher do? What are his or her sources of assistance?

The following suggestions may be helpful in getting past those first weeks of that first job.

1. After meeting the immediate administrator, the next important person to know is the local music supervisor or consultant. This resource person

275

usually knows where material and equipment is located which may not be in use. In addition to giving helpful ideas and lots of encouragement, supervisors many times can influence principals to upgrade your music program.

If your local situation has no specialist in music, locate the supervisor of instruction under whom all educational programs will fall. Try to get a copy of the school system's curriculum guide for your area.

2. Contact experienced teachers in the area. In many cases, they were challenged with a similar set of circumstances and have developed materials and ideas which they may be willing to share.

3. Who are your state and regional MENC officers? There should be in their possession a list of music persons in your area, one of whom may be of assistance. The information on MENC personnel is usually published in the September issue of the Music Educators Journal and lists addresses as well as terms of office.

4. Determine whether there is a book depository in your town. Books found there may be dated, but with a little ingenuity and creativity, they can be used. These books are usually available at no cost.

5. Go to your principal and document your needs with those standards as set up by the MENC publication, The School Music Program: Description and Stand-Standards. While all that you require may not be received whatever comes out of this meeting(s) will certainly be beneficial to your program.

6. Locate and visit local music stores, teachers' stores, college book stores, and art supply stores. Begin to develop your own stock pile of bulletin board necessities and other visual aids for your teaching.

7. Once employed, obtain school stationery and write to publishing companies and ask to be placed on mailing lists. Also ask for desk copies of books which you may be interested in using in your classes or for your personal reference.

8. Check professional magazines for publishing
    company advertisements and take advantage of
    their offers of free books and recordings. Other
    materials which may be obtained in this manner are
    packets of octavo and band arrangements,
    catalogs, biographical sketches, some tests,
    posters, brochures, and even instruments.

    This is a good strategy for junior and senior
music education students. It is very helpful to have
during those first weeks, current catologs of materials
just in case you are given funds for ordering.

9. Begin a file of references and catalogs. This
    file can also be started during your student days
    and can include the following categories:
    a. Elementary series
    b. Special education
    c. Dictionaries and references
    d. Elementary text books
    e. Secondary text books
    f. Band methods
    g. String methods
    h. Aptitude and achieveent tests
    i. Uniform and equipment catalogs
    j. Fund raising projects brochures
    k. Theory text books
    l. General music/appreciation texts
    m. Choral technique books
    n. Ethnic music

Annotated entries make the file much more valuable in
later years.

10. During the school year, try to attend as many one
    day and weekend workshops as possible. Meet
    people and get ideas. Someone is or has been in
    your situation.

11. Attend your state and national MENC meetings and
    other professional conventions related to your
    interests. By all means, take advantage of the
    exhibits. Discuss your situation with the sales
    representatives and ask for their suggestions
    with regard to materials and equipment that can be
    used. Take a few minutes at the beginning of the
    convention to plan each day so that you can attend
    all the sessions in your interest area and have
    time for exhibits. Both are so important.

12. Don't forget to take methods text books with you on your new job. Most have valuable appendices which list records, for various uses, music series, addresses of publishing companies, choral and band arrangements suitable for various grade levels, information on codes of ethics, and copyright laws. Each chapter will, in most cases, give materials and references pertaining to the information covered.

13. Contact the music consultants who service with various publishers of music texts. Their expertise is invaluable and they may be at liberty to loan materials for your classes. Some publishing companies will give sets of teacher's manuals to graduating seniors. It is certainly worth the effort to inquire.

The most important thing to remember is to search out people who can help you. Be assertive and sell your program. If you encounter an insensitive administration, approach the problem by demonstrating to parents the type of activities that your music classes are doing. An activity which works effectively is a quarter party: A program is prepared that features demonstration classes and performing groups -in short, your music program. Each parent brings a dish which, after the program, is sold at a quarter a sample (a healthy spoonful). Parents are usually willing to support those school programs that are doing constructive activities with their children. These parents have influence over principals.

Music, in many places, still has an uphill fight as a subject of worth. For new teachers, getting an effective start is a great part of that fight. However, as accomplishments begin to be achieved and gains are made, that sense of accomplishment will make the struggle well worth the effort.

CHAPTER 14

A GUIDE FOR NEW TEACHERS

Suggested Class Project

1. Determine whether your school system has a book

despository. Visit it and discover the kinds of music materials which have been discarded. List at least three books which may be useful in a classroom.

2. Interview an experienced teacher. What were his/her encounters during the erly years of teaching? List solutions to some problems in this teacher's experience.

3. Place your name of the mailing list of ten publishers and/or manufacturers of music materials.

4. Discuss and formulate other innovative ways of presenting a music program before parents and administrators.

BIBLIOGRAPHY WITH HELPFUL APPENDICES

Hoffer, Charles R. Teaching Music In The Secondary Schools, 2nd ed., Belmont, Cal.: Wadsworth Publishing Co., 1973.

Leeder, Joseph and William Haynie, Music Education In The High School Music, Englewood Cliffs, N.J.: Prentice-Hall, Inc., 1960.

Nye, Robert and Vernice Nye, Essentials of Teaching Elementary School Music, Englewood Cliffs, N.J.: Prentice-Hall, Inc., 1974.

Nye, Robert and Vernice Nye, Music In The Elementary School, 4th ed., Englewood Cliffs, N.J.: Prentice-Hall, Inc., 1977.

Regelski, Thomas A, Teaching General Music, Action Learning for Middle and Secondary Schools, New York: Schirmer Books, 1981.

Swanson, Bessie, Music In The Education of Children, 4th ed., Belmont Cal.: Wadsworth Publishing Co., 1981.

Chapter 15

JAZZ EDUCATION IN THE COLLEGE CURRICULUM

William Theodore McDaniel, Jr.

In recent years, the significant changes in music department curricula on both the secondary and collegiate levels have occurred with the addition of courses dealing with some aspect of jazz. The seventies has seen a resurgence in jazz throughout the nation, and the campus has been a major focal point for this music. It is safe to say now that almost every high school and college in America which has an instrumental music program has some sort of big band, dance band, stage band, or jazz ensemble, or whatever nomenclature one chooses to use. Too, academic courses in jazz have seen a tremendous proliferation. In short, there very definitely is a new, alive phenomenon on the campus called jazz.

The strength of jazz is now in American schools and colleges where it has been given a new lease on life. Many colleges have teacher training programs that emphasize jazz, an increasingly large number of stage and jazz lab bands are coming into existence, and jazz festivals are held on campuses in all parts of the country. Jazz has been included in the curriculum as a subject of serious study because of its aesthetic sociological, and historical importance, and it is now a highly respected performance medium.

Suber's "A Guide To College Jazz Studies"[1] provides an excellent account of the history of the jazz education movement. The first signs of interest in formal college level jazz instruction came after World War II as the dance band musician faced a shrinking market for his services. Out of economic necessity, he followed the lead of his World War II counterpart, the concert bandsman; he sought employment as a school music teacher. If he was certificated, he probably went right into secondary school teaching, but more likely he used his G.I. Bill education benefits to finish his degree.

Professional training schools, such as Westlake (Los Angeles) and Berklee (formerly Schillinger House, Boston) came into prominence in the years 1945-50. A "Dance Band Major" was begun at North Texas State

University (Denton) in 1948 by Gene Hall and other ex-dance band players. Bob McDonald began a "commercial music major" program in 1946 at Los Angeles City College, a two-year community school. By 1950, stage (jazz) band programs for credit were inaugurated at Northern Arizona University (Flagstaff); Sam Houston State University (Huntsville, Texas); California State Polytechnic University (Pomona); and Lamar University (Beaumont, Texas). In spite of these precedents, by 1954 there were only a half dozen colleges offering jazz related courses or ensembles for credit; about a dozen more had resident stage bands but not as part of the music curriculum.[2]

If the colleges were slow in adapting their curricula to an examination of 20th century American Music, the high schools were not. A rapid expansion of high school stage bands ("Stage" was a handy euphemism in those areas where "dancing" and "jazzing" were non rigeur) accompanied the post-World War II population boom. The ex-dance band players and the graduates of North Texas, Sam Houston, etc., were entering junior and senior high schools in steadily increasing numbers. They knew from personal experience that playing jazz would not cause debauchery, cause madness, or ruin an embouchure. They also knew the positive attributes of jazz performance--increased motivation and interest, heightened creativity, wider appreciation of different idioms, etc. The availability of jazz-oriented music educators plus the natural attraction of young players to their own music resulted in some 5,000 high school stage bands in full swing at the beginning of the 1960s.

It was further noted in Downbeat Magazine's invaluable "A Guide To College Jazz Studies" that the years 1965-69 recorded a quantum increase in both the number of colleges offering any type of jazz course or ensemble for either academic credit or non-credit. In those years, 94 schools inaugurated non-credit offerings and cumulatively, there were 165 such offerings in contrast to the previous 5-year period in which only 29 such programs were listed. To that point, the cumulative total was a mere 71.

On the academic credit side of the ledger, Scott[3] reports that there is a similar figure; 94 schools giving credit for either an ensemble or course in the jazz field. The cumulative total in this area for 1965-69 also was encouraging with the 5-year figure showing 135 such credit offerings while in the previous years (1960-64), only 41 schools reported such offerings. As modest as these figures may seem, it behooves us to look at where we were 20 years ago when only 21 schools were offering any type of jazz credits and only 42 reported any type of supervised jazz activity.

In spite of the rather slow start, the development and rapid expansion of the jazz education program in the late sixties and early seventies were really astounding. In 1965 there were approximately 8,000 jazz bands in the schools.[4] By 1971 there were an estimated 16,000 jazz bands in America in just the junior high and high schools.[5] The results of a survey taken in 1973 by the American Music Conference, in cooperation with the Music Educators National Conference, led to an estimate of 19,000 stage/jazz bands in the junior high and high school. Also in 1973, an additional 800 college jazz bands were in existence and many colleges had as many as two or three jazz bands with an average membership of twenty in each band.[6]

Further proof of the tremendous attention given to jazz has been the addition of academic courses to the curriculum. The two most popular courses are concerned with a history of the jazz tradition and improvisation. Provided below are examples of two course outlines by the writer and David Baker.

THE HISTORY OF JAZZ
(as taught by W.T. McDaniel)

Course Description

This course is designed for anyone interested in Afro-American studies, thus, no formal knowledge of music theory and history or previous background in music is required. Music majors, however, may be encouraged to take the course as well. The course will provide a general survey of the history of jazz from its beginnings to the present, with major emphasis placed on the stylistic and evolutionary development of the music and the significant contributors to jazz styles. Although primarily a lecture

course, films, slides, demonstrations,
live performances, and phonograph
recordings will be used too.

Objectives

1. To develop a deeper and more
   meaningful appreciation and
   understanding of the black
   man's contribution to Western
   music and culture.

2. To present historical facts
   about jazz and the sociology
   from which it developed.

3. To create an awareness of
   styles and forms which
   characterize major periods in
   jazz music.

4. To develop an understanding
   of how the music was and is
   performed through a study of
   the various composers and
   performers.

Outline

I. Precursors of Jazz

A. The Blues

1. Classical, Rural, and Urban
2. Biographical studies: Ma
   Rainey, Bessie Smith, Lead
   belly, Big Bill Broonzy, et.
   al.
3. The literature of folk
   expression; communicating
   about personal and social
   conditions
4. Music development; the 12-bar
   blues structure
5. Influence on jazz

B. Ragtime

1. Definition; origin of its

form and rhythm; use in
written piano compositions

2. Styles in Sedalia, St.
Louis, New Orleans, and New
York

3. Dances inspired by ragtime;
the cakewalk, the Charleston,
etc.

4. Scott Joplin, Eubie Blake,
and other exponents

5. Performance of Treemonisha in
Atlanta, Ga., 1972

C. Boogie-Woogie

1. Boogie-Woogie as an aspect of
the blues (fast blues)

2. The musical concept of the
boogie-woogie

3. Socio-economic use in rural
and urban areas (i.e. rent
parties, rail camps, etc.)

4. Jimmy Yancey, Meade Lux
Lewis, Pinetop Smith, and
other exponents.

5. The Harlem School of Stride
Piano: James P. Johnson,
Willie "The Lion" Smith,
Luckey Roberts and others.

II. Schools and Idioms of Jazz

A. New Orleans

1. Focal point, melting pot

2. Free Negro and the creole of
color

3. Marching bands, brass bands

4. Instrumentation of the
typical New Orleans Jazz Band

5. Self-taught techniques:
collective improvisation

6. Buddy Bolden, Jelly Roll
Morton, Joe "King" Oliver,
Louis Armstrong, et.al.

B. Chicago

1. The exodus from Storyville in
1917

2. Black and White Chicago
3. a. Musical and social
      influences of South Side
      Negroes on North Side
      Whites
   b. North Side Jazz developments
         (Nork, Bix Biderb
      ecke, Austin High Gang)
   c. South Side jazz men (Joe
      Oliver, Louis Armstrong,
      etc.)
4. Vice and corruption in the
   city; its influence on jazz
5. Crystallization of the New
   Orleans style; Hot music

C. The Big Bands and Swing

   1. Instrumentation and role of
      the big band
   2. Commercialization: impact of
      live, recorded and broadcast
      performances
   3. Kansas City and the Southwest
      a. The Pendergast political
         machine from 1927 to 1938
      b. Kansas City formula of the
         riff; approach to the
         blues
      c. The influence of Kansas
         City sideman ("Pres,"
         "Hawk," Mary Lou, et.
         al.)
      d. Jay McShann, Bennie Moten,
         Count Basie, et. al.
      e. Territory Bands
   4. The jam session
      a. Definition
      b. Spontaneous improvisation
         as a vital source for jazz
      c. The jam session as a
         proving ground for new
         expressive forms and
         talent
      d. Live and recorded jam ses
         sions, including the JATP
         and Commodore series.
   5. New York (The Big Apple):
      Focal point of sheet music,

radio, recording, and booking
business (Mighty Whitey)
6. Fletcher Henderson and the
evolution of the big band
a. The major white bands of
the late 20's and 30's
b. The major black bands of
the late 20's and 30's
7. Lester Young and Coleman
Hawkins
8. Mr. Edward Kennedy Elling-
ton--The Duke

D. Bebop (1940's)

1. The combo
2. Culture and socio-economic
status in the U.S. before ,
during, and after World War
II
3. Jam session: Scats and Runs
4. The effect of the sessions at
Minton's Playhouse and the
result of these new concepts
5. Jargon, dress, and other fads
6. Evolution of Bop: Charlie
Parker, Dizzy Gillespie,
Thelonius Monk, Kenny Clarke,
Fats Navarro, Charlie
Christian, Bud Powell, Art
Tatum, et. al.

E. The Fifties

1. Cool jazz
a. Reaction to bebop style
b. The intellectuals and the
appeal of cool jazz
c. The emergence of
technically skilled
composers and musicians.
d. Miles Davis, Lennie
Tristano, Gerry Mulligan,
et. al.
e. The "West Coast" School
2. Sonny Rollins and the hard-
boppers
3. Soul, Funky jazz
a. The Negro in the 50's and
his search for identity

b. The translation of this identity with the return to the blues

4. Third Stream Jazz
   a. The academic approach to jazz in the schools
   b. The merger of jazz elements with those of the "classical" idiom
   c. John Lewis and the Modern Jazz Quartet
   d. An appraisal of the works of John Lewis, Gunther Schuller, and Jimmy Guiffre
   e. The effect of the concert image in jazz

III. The Avant-garde

A. Definition

B. The Civil Rights movement of the 60's

C. Black power, ethnicity, race riots, segregation-integration, black nationalism, atonality, polytonality, modality, Pan-Africanism, Mysticism, African instruments and drums, etc.

D. Energy Music, Space Music, New Music.

E. The emergence of the new Negro

F. The new method of Free expression

G. Music as a political statement and form

H. The influence from literature of James Baldwin, LeRoi Jones, Nat Hentoff, Claude Brown, Frank Kofsky

I. Evolution of the New Music: Thelonious Monk, Ornette Coleman, Charlie Mingus, Cecil Taylor, John Coltrane, et. al.

J. My main man, John Coltrane--Sheets of Sound

K. Then Archie Shepp, Pharoah Sanders, Sun Ra, Don Cherry, The Art Ensemble of Chicago, et. al.

L. Where to?????

IV. The Eclectic Electrics of the Seventies

A. The 1969 recording of "Bitches Brew" of Miles Davis

B. Emphasis on electronic gadgetry

C. Age of synthesized and simulated music and sounds

D. The best of the lot: Weather Report, Mahavishnu Orchestra, Herbie Hancock, Donald Byrd, Return to Forever, Billy Cobham, George Duke, et. al.

CONTEMPORARY JAZZ AND SOUL MUSIC
(as taught by David Baker)

Objectives

1. Identify and place in perspective seminal figures, representative works, major styles and style periods, etc.

2. Show how this music reflects and is reflective of black life styles.

Outline

I.   Jazz
     A.   Mainstream

          1. Swing
          2. Dixieland
          3. The big bands
          4. Post-bebop

     B.   Soul Jazz

     C.   Influences on jazz from other
          ethnic music

          1. Spanish
          2. Eastern
          3. Indian
          4. Caribbean
          5. Gypsy
          6. Others

     D.   Liturgical Music

          1. Reasons for origin
          2. Cultural, moral and
             religious implications

     E.   Experimental jazz (Third
          Stream and Symphonic Jazz)

          1. Forms
          2. Media
          3. New Instruments
          4. New   Uses   of   Old
             Instruments

     F.   Avant Garde

     1.   Cerebral
          a. Extensive ordering of
             music
          b. Restrictive forms; extreme
             scale techniques
     2.   Intuitive
          a. Return to the organic
          b. Re-introduction of
             simplicity (Primivitism)
          c. Major-minor triadic
             harmony

                    d. Emphasis on melody and
                       harmony
             3.   Unique relationships of this
                   music to the black culture
             4.   Nationalism and jazz
             5.   Avant garde jazz in
                   relationship to the "Academy"
                    a. Birth of theoretical
                       systems
                    b. Teaching methods

 II.   Soul Music

 A.   General definition

 B.   Origin and debt to gospel music

 C.   Relationships to the black commu-
       nity

 D.   Influences on American music

 E.   Rhythm and blues since the twen-
       ties

 F.   Representative figures

             1.   Performers
             2.   Writers
             3.   "A&R" men
             4.   Recording co-owners (includ-
                   ing Motown, Atlantic) and
                   their influence

 G.   Influences on the current popular
       scene

 H.   Economics

             1.   Black music exploited by
                   whites
             2.   Economic advantages to the
                   imitators
             3.   Constant revitalization by
                   the innovators

     The above outlines exemplify courses that deal
with the historical tradition of jazz. In many
instances, Tanner' learned in his study that many
instructors teach this material with a chronological

290

approach, since jazz is a music of evolution and each style is closely related to what was played before. Almost all the instructors went back as far as pre-jazz African music, showing (but generally without great emphasis) the rhythmic roots of jazz. It was not unusual to find teachers who, in the other direction, carried the historical study of jazz all the way up to today's rock, free form, and electronic musics.

It is common to find that most improvisation courses include players who can form a rhythm section, thereby making immediate laboratory situations possible. With a rhythm section composed of students in the class, students do not feel the pressure while improvising that they would feel in a performance. Consequently, even players who have never improvised before begin to progress and students also learn from each other a great deal.

The real advancements in jazz education have occurred in the colleges in the area of curriculum improvements. Perhaps this is best evidenced by the broad spectrum of jazz or jazz-related courses for credit in the jazz education program of many colleges and universities which include the following: Improvisation I-IV (2 years); Arranging and Orchestration; composition; Afro-American Music; Theory-Harmony I-IV (2 years); Copying/Notation; Combo or Small Groups; Various Size Jazz Ensembles; Keyboard Harmony & Ear Training; Electronic Music/Technology; Film Scoring; Commercial Music Writing; History, Evolution, and Development; Jazz Styles and Analysis; Legal Aspects (copyrights, etc.); Materials and Literature; Pedagogy, Recording Techniques; Vocal (Swing Choir, etc.); African Music; Guitar Workshops; Business of Music (Marketing, etc.); Multiple Percussion; Instrumental Instruction such as jazz piano, bass, etc; and others. These courses and others now make it possible for many universities to offer majors in jazz. The jazz major is no longer an idea but a reality on many campuses throughout the nation.

The colleges have not been alone in the area of curriculum development in jazz education however. Much of the success which colleges have had in the seventies with jazz education has been a direct result of the increased attention given to jazz offerings at the secondary level. Many junior high and high schools do offer jazz related courses which count toward credit for graduation. Of significance is the Texas State

Board of Education[8] on September 13, 1975, approved the
addition of "Stage Band" and "Vocal Ensembles" to the
Texas Education Agency List of Approved Courses.
Approval was the final step in a process requiring more
than two years for completion. The new courses are now
available for addition to the local music curriculum,
subject to district approval, without application to
the Texas Education Agency. A description of the
"Stage Band" course follows:

STAGE BAND, GRADES 7-12

Prerequisite:
> Concurrent membership in band or
> orchestra; exceptions permitted
> for piano or organ, guitar, bass,
> vocalist(s). Student assignment
> determined by the director.

Time: Grades 7-8
> Semester Plan, 130 clock
> hours, minimum
> Quarter Plan, 135 clock
> hours, minimum

Credit: Grades 9-12
> Semester Plan, 1/2 - 4 units
> Quarter Plan, 1, 2, 3, quar-
> ters per year, up to 12
> quarters

Course Description:
> The stage band is a musical
> organization serving as a
> laboratory for students of
> instrumental music. Instru-
> mentation is flexible, but
> organizations maintain suffi-
> cient size and balance of
> instrumentation to perform
> good literature authentically
> and artistically. The stage
> band provides students with
> an opportunity to explore
> alternative styles and ins-
> trumental techniques utilized
> in American jazz and jazz-
> derived musical idioms,
> fosters creativity through
> improvisation, and serves as
> a basis for music vocations
> and avocations. The stage

band may serve as a vehicle
for performance of student
compositions, as well as commissioned and published materials. The stage band is
under the direction of a
certified teacher.

The following is a description of the "Vocal
Ensembles" course in the State of Texas:

VOCAL ENSEMBLES, GRADES 9-12

Prerequisite:
> Concurrent membership in a choral
> music organization. Student as-
> signment determined by the direc-
> tion.

Credit: Grades 9-12
> Semester Plan, 1/2 - 4 units
> Quarter Plan, 1, 2, 3,
> quarters per year, up to 12
> quarters

Course Description:
> Vocal ensembles meet the
> needs of students with a
> special interest in singing
> and in performing choral
> literature other than that
> studied in the parent choral
> program. Size and composi
> tion of each group is
> designed to meet requirements
> of the music to be studied.
> Vocal ensembles are
> encouraged to perform student
> works in addition to the
> study of published materials.
> Three groups are under the
> direction of a certified
> music teacher.

Many states have followed the lead of Texas in
giving credit for jazz related courses at the secondary
school level.

Without question, one has to admit that the number
and diversity of courses that deal with jazz and the
presence of so many jazz ensembles lend credence to the

293

fact that jazz education does exist in some form in most schools and colleges. As well, we must admit too that the "jazz education movement" really came to fruition in the late sixties and early seventies (and is still growing) although the seeds of the movement were planted back in the forties as has already been mentioned here.

Perhaps it would be certainly worth considering why jazz has taken so long to gain acceptance by academe. David Baker, brilliant composer, performer, author, and teacher who heads the Department of Jazz Studies at Indiana University and one of the real champions of the jazz cause in academe, has some very pointed remarks about this:

> Jazz is a Black music. The Black man gave this music--the language, the vocabulary, the essence--to the world, and every advancement and major innovation of this music has come from him. It is perhaps this fact of the music's Black origins that has hindered its unbiased acceptance into academia. Because jazz had its origins in a tradition outside the perimeters of Western art music, its lack of acceptance was virtually assured. Myth is predicated on the belief in the superiority of Western musical traditions over all others. Couple this with some association with Black culture and we can easily see how this music was not accepted in academe.[9]

Kofsky[10] advances a similar argument along racial lines to explain the difficulties with the acceptance of jazz. He believes that white Americans who are in the jazz world proper tend to deny that jazz is first and foremost a black art--an art created and nurtured by black people in America out of the wealth of their historical experience. On the other hand, if they are not a part of the jazz community, white Americans will automatically assume that jazz is indeed black--though not an art--and therefore, though this may go unstated, worthy of no serious treatment or respect.

There seems to be little question that the racial dilemma in America has had a tremendous effect on the slow acceptance of jazz in the academic arena. Too, there is little doubt that the public (and certainly including "educated" persons) has been led to believe that jazz is anything but a music that is worthy of serious, scholarly pursuits. Many leaders of the music establishment in America, until recently, vigorously fought against jazz receiving any kind of musical seriousness and respectability.   Leopold Stokowski said:

> Jazz has come to stay because it is an expression of the times, of the breathless, energetic, superactives times in which we are living, it is useless to fight against it. Already its new vigor, its new vitality is beginning to manifest itself... America's contribution to the music of the past will have the same revivifying effect as the injection of new, and in the larger sense, vulgar blood into dying aristocracy. Music will then be vulgarized in the best sense of the word, and enter more and more into the daily lives of people... The Negro musicians of America are playing a great part in this change. They have an open mind and unbiased outlook. They are not hampered by conventions or traditions, and with their new ideas, their constant experiment, they are causing new blood to flow in the veins of music. The jazz players make their instruments do entirely new things, things finished musicians are taught to avoid. They are pathfinders into new realms.[11]

Hentoff's[12] argument as to the slow acceptance of jazz in academic circles hinges upon the widespread ignorance which administrators (including musicians as well) have about the nature of the music. He further suggests that there is a real need "to educate" administrators and the powers-that-be that run the academic establishment. If jazz is to become part of the culture in the schools, if jazz interests are to become part of the criteria for identifying the gifted and talented, there is going to have to be a great deal of what used to be called "woodshedding" concerning jazz among teachers and administrators because for all the occasional   very brief, glorification of jazz as our most valuable indigenous art form, most teachers

295

and administrators are denotatively ignorant about the music, its history, and its socio-cultural-psychological roots. If anybody is really serious about affective education, and that's what culture is all about, it is long past time for jazz to be taken seriously by those who try to determine what "high culture" is, especially for kids.

Like any new kid on the block, jazz education programs, despite the phenomenal growth during the last 15 years, have not been without internal problems. Baker[13] suggests that a major problem lies with the teachers of jazz. Jazz education, particularly at the university level, needs jazz professionals, not clasisically-trained musicians with little or no jazz experience--however much they might like jazz. Expertise in the jazz tradition is what is needed in the classrooms of jazz courses. The administrator must realize that if the teacher is to fulfill his function, which is not only to teach techniques but also to shape taste and give the student direction, he must be an expert. These administrators would not hire a vocal coach to teach orchestration or composition.

Perhaps the most valuable jazz teachers would be the jazz musicians who excel as players, writers and arrangers for they could teach others certain musical principles indigenous to jazz performance such as: How to create endlessly varying melodies and rhythms in a particular idiom, using a given set of chords; how to fashion continuous harmonic variations for a given melodic line in one or a multitude of forms; and how to design combinations of melodic, harmonic, and rhythmic variations for this spontaneous improvisational form we call jazz.[14] This idea would certainly provide for the needed expertise alluded to in the previous paragraph and it would allow the jazz musician to be the ideal jazz teacher.

Carter[15] believes strongly that the jazz teacher does not have to be apologetic, nor must he qualify his reason for teaching jazz. Jazz educators must stop trying to establish credibility by references to their classical training. It appears that we all must be legitimatized by such statements as "in addition to his jazz experiences, Mr._____ has done extended orchestral and band work, or Mr. _____ is also a fine symphonic musician." As long as we use outside standards of training and performance skills as our standards, we will continue to be treated as 2nd class musicians.

In spite of the progress that has been made in Jazz education, Gunther Schuller believes that it should be looked upon very cautiously. Speaking to a group of classical music critics who were studying jazz at the Smithsonian Institute, Schuller became impassioned over what he called "an illusion" and "a ripoff." He commented:

> What has happened to jazz in the schools is the typical thing in American society. Jazz is still looked on as an aberrational activity in schools, but someone learned how to bottle and sell it... Stan Kenton and a few others took hold of jazz and sold it to the National Association of Jazz Educators. Most of these jazz educators aren't musicians. They own a sax and played 'Body and Soul'--without swing--in the local bistro... Hundreds of mediocre musicians have found jobs as 'jazz educators.' It takes a very talented kid to circumvent that kind of instruction. The bands play mostly arrangements by second-rate arrangers. They get the chart and its the same stupid hack writing that's been going on for 30 years. They don't play the repertoire they should--Ellington, Basie, Woody Herman. And the most disturbing thing is that improvisation hardly is involved... But--everybody has a grand time. The band creates an illusion that the kids are getting a jazz education. Jazz education has become an entrenched bureaucracy. And how should the kids know they're not really playing jazz?... It's the same old goddamn ripoff of black music by whites... The point of my life has been to see that jazz and classical music were looked on as equal. I want people to see that maybe an improvisation by Jelly Roll Morton, Charlie Parker or Charles Mingus is as great as a so-called masterpiece...[16]

In conclusion, music education could benefit greatly from Schuller's remarks. In spite of the expected growth pains during the last two decades, jazz education has made many very meaningful strides. Jazz educators must continue to push for better qualified teachers and continue to make advancements in the way of curriculum development. One must not overlook the point that the recognition of the National Association of Jazz Educators (even with its myriad of problems) by the Music Educators National Conference at the 1968 convention in Seattle has given NAJE a kind of legitimacy in education circles. A cursory glance at dissertations by Carter, Hall, Noice, Chickanzeff, Parman, Weitz, Barr, Branch, Ferriano, McDaniel, and others would seem to indicate that some educators are beginning to deal seriously with jazz. Recognition of jazz education programs by the National Association of Schools of Music would seem to put an official stamp of approval by academia for academia.

At the college level, at least 22 universities now grant degrees in jazz education or jazz performance and three universities offer a master's degree. At the high school level, over 20 State MENC-NAJE organizations have established All-State High School Jazz Bands alongside the All-State Orchestra and Bands. Thousands of high school instrumental and vocal jazz ensembles are feeding potential majors into colleges, or at least[17] promoting a new enlightened audience of ex-players. More attention is given to jazz by television and radio stations. The big White House jazz concert summer of 1980 has not hurt the cause one bit. It appears that jazz and jazz education are indeed alive and well and on the move.

DISCUSSION QUESTION

1. In what year was the first jazz degree offered? What schools were the first to offer a jazz major?

2. Name some of the music educators who were instrumental in getting jazz into the college curriculum.

3. Name at least five schools today that offer a major in jazz education? Select two that you feel

are tops and discuss the reasons for your decision.

4. Why do you thing music schools (colleges and universities) have been so slow in instituting jazz degree programs?

PROJECTS

A. Develop a comprehensive annotated bibliography of jazz and related materials that would be useful for students studying for a jazz degree.

B. Compile your own list of "jazz authorities" (performers, composers, educators, etc.) active today in jazz education. Give a short rationale for your selection.

C. Develop a list of competencies that are necessary in any teacher preparation program in jazz.

D. Evaluate one jazz degree curriculum in terms of course content, quality of the offerings, balance between areas (history, theory, edcuation, performance) and appropriateness for teaching and the world of work.

Bibliography Further Readings

Banks, James A. Teaching Strategies for Ethnic Studies, 2nd ed. Boston: Allyn and Bacon, Inc., 1979.

Barr, Walter L. "The Jazz Studies Curriculum," (Doctoral dissertation, Arizona State University, 1974).

Ostransky, Leroy, "Early Jazz," Music Educators Journal, 64:6 (February 1978), pp. 34-39.

Southern, Eileen. The Music of Black Americans: A History. New York: W.W. Norton, Inc., 1971.

NOTES FOR CHAPTER 15

1. Charles Suber, "A Guide To College Jazz Studies,"
    Music Handbook '74. Chicago: Maher
    Publications, 1974.

2. Ibid.

3. Allen Scott, "The Past 10 Years In Retrospect,"
    NAJE Educator, 10 (February-March, 1978), 8-9.

4. Paul O. Tanner, "The Musical Values of the Stage
    Band," Music Educators Journal, 51 (April-May,
    1965), 83.

5. Paul O. Tanner, The Study of Jazz (Dubuque: Wm.
    C. Brown Co.., 1973), 117.

6. Charles Suber, "The First Chorus," Downbeat, 40
    (December 6, 1973), 6.

7. Paul O. Tanner, "Jazz Goes to College, Part I,"
    Music Educators Journal, 57 (March, 1971), 58.

8. "Texas Board Approves Jazz Offerings," NAJE
    Educator, 10 (February-March, 1978), 15.

9. David Baker, "The Battle for Legitimacy: Jazz
    Versus Academia," Black World, 23 (November,
    1973), 20-21.

10. Frank Kofsky, Black Nationalism and the
    Revolution in Music. New York: Pathfinder Press,
    1970.

11. J.A. Rogers, "Jazz At Home," The Black Aesthetic,
    ed. Addison Gayle. Garden City: Doubleday & Co.,
    1972, 104-111.

12. Nat Hentoff, "Jazz and the Schools," from the
    Proceedings of the National Conference on Arts
    and Humanities/Gifted and Talented, ed. Richard
    Grove. Washington, D.C.: National Institute of
    Education, 1975.

13. Sister M.T. Keating, "A Tanglewood Convention,"
    Music Educators Journal, 57 (March, 1971), 55-56.

14. Cannonball Adderly, "Jazz in the Curriculum,"
    Reflections on Afro-American Music, ed. Robert

Klotman. Kent: Kent State University Press, 1973.

15. Warrick Carter, "An Assessment of Jazz Education 1968-1978," NAJE Educator, 10 (February-March, 1978), 12.

16. Arlyn Nelhaus, Ibid.

17. Thomas Ferguson, "An Assessment of Jazz Education 1968-1978," NAJE Educator, 10 (February-March, 1978), 16.

BIBLIOGRAPHY

Walter L. Barr, "The Jazz Studies Curriculum" (Doctoral dissertation, Arizona State University, 1974).

London G. Branch, "Jazz Education in Predominantly Black Colleges" (Doctoral dissertation, Southern Illinois University, 1975).

Warrick L. Carter, "Ethnic Music As A Source for the Musical Development and Enrichment of Culturally different Students in General Music Classes" (Doctoral dissertation, Michigan State University, 1970).

John L. Chickanzeff, "Popular Dance Music in High School Instrumental Teaching" (Master's thesis, Eastman School, 1938).

Frank Ferriano, "A Study of the School Jazz Ensemble in American Music Education" (Doctoral dissertation, Columbia University, 1974).

Morris E. Hall, "The Development of Curriculum for the Teaching of Dance Music At A College Level" (Master's thesis, North Texas State University, 1944).

William T. McDaniel, "Difference in Music Achievement, Musical Experience, and Background Between Jazz-Improvising Musicians and Non-Improvising Musicians at the Freshman and Sophomore College Levels" (Doctoral dissertation, University of Iowa, 1974).

Albert H. Noice, "A Survey and Analysis of Teacher Training and Experience in Relation to the Stage Band Movement in the Public Secondary Schools of Minnesota with Implications for Teacher Education" (Doctoral dissertation, Colorado State College, 1965).

Milton C. Parman, "The Place of the Dance Band in the School Music Program" (Master's thesis, Ohio State University, 1942).

Lowell E. Weitz, "The Stage Band as Part of the High School Music Program" (Doctoral dissertation, University of Southern California, 1964).

Chapter 16

GOSPEL MUSIC: POPULAR ALTERNATIVES

FOR THE URBAN SCHOOLS

Barbara W. Baker

Introduction

Black gospel music is a distinct musical genre as well as a cultural phenomenon that touches the musical life of millions of Americans. Black gospel has been performed at such national sites as the Smithsonian Institution, the John F. Kennedy Center in Washington, D.C., and the White House. Gospel type commercials for McDonald's hamburgers and gospel style theme songs for television shows like The Jeffersons and Good Times can be heard on television sets throughout the nation. Despite this exposure to black gospel music's stylistic harmonies, melodies and rhythms, black gospel music still remains an enigma to many music educators. Few music educators, however, are acquainted enough with this genre's history, its styles or its educational and pedagogical uses to incorporate this music into their vocal and general music programs. Despite recent efforts to include the music of all Americans in the school music curriculum, black gospel music is probably one of the least studied and performed genres in American school music programs.

This chapter focuses on the need to include black gospel music in the total music program with specific emphasis on the secondary school level. Included in this discussion are a brief historical and stylistic overview, educational rationales for including this genre in the music curriculum, and possible teaching approaches for the novice. While the primary focus of this chapter is the urban school music program, the rationales and teaching approaches can be adapted for use in any setting.

Historical Overview

Black gospel music is an amalgam of various elements of its precursors, Negro spirituals, jubilees, blues and white gospel music, as well as elements of its contemporaries, rock and roll, rhythm and blues and popular music. Yet, gospel has its own distinct history and styles. Black gospel music, as opposed to

303

gospel music that is performed, composed or arranged by non-black musicians, is a comparatively modern idiom in relation to traditional Catholic and Protestant church music. Although its roots reach back into slavery, black gospel evolved as a separate musical genre from all other types of black religious music around the turn of the twentieth century. As with various artistic expressions, the exact date this music was first sung is unknown and probably can never be determined with certainty since there are no written accounts of its precise beginnings. Perhaps a significant watershed associated with this genre's evolutions was the schism between the black Baptist Church and a group from its fold. This splinter group eventually evolved into the Church of God in Christ.

The early history of black gospel music was entwined with the development of this fundamentalist church. In 1895, Charles Henry Mason broke away from the Baptist Church in disputes over the literal interpretation of the Bible and the desire to sing more "spirited" songs than the orthodox church allowed.[1] As this new denomination spread to large urban centers, so too did the body of music sung by its members. One eye-witness described the music sung in the Church of God in Christ during those early years as "rhythmic singing accompanied by piano, tambourines or sometimes just hand clapping."[2] These church songs were probably what can be characterized as black gospel music sung in a "folk style."[3]

This music did not appear spontaneously as an isolated style sung by these church members without antecedents or roots linking it to other types of black vocal music. The precursors of black gospel were the Negro spiritual, the jubilee, the blues and white gospel music. Each of these styles contributed elements to the black gospel song.

In the last quarter of the nineteenth-century, the Negro spiritual emerged as one of the predominant musical styles of black vocal music. These spirituals were brought to the nation's attention by the successful European-American tours of the Fisk University Jubilee Singers during 1871 through 1878. These spirituals have been classified into three basic types: (1) the call and response chant, (2) the slow, sustained, long-phrased melody, and (3) the fast, syncopated, segmented melody.[4] Spirituals were sung without accompaniment or vocal improvisation.

The jubilee, unlike many of the spirituals, was a happy song that became popular in the early 1900's. This song type was usually performed by a small group of men singers (four to eight), sometimes with a female singer added to the group.[5] The jubilee was generally performed without accompaniment, but on occasion, the singers used a guitar or a small organ for accompaniment.

Another precursor of the black gospel song was the white revival hymn, sometimes referred to as a camp-meeting spiritual or gospel song. The term "gospel song" was used as early as 1873 to describe the music sung at religious crusades conducted by evangelist Dwight Lyman Moody (1837-1899) and his music director, Ira David Sankey (1840-1908), predecessors of contemporary evangelists like Billy Graham and his music director, George Baverly Shea. These white revival hymns used lively rhythmic patterns and varying responsorial and antiphonal patterns.

Each of these three sacred precursors contributed elements to the black gospel song. The Negro spiritual gave the black gospel song a variety of song forms. The jubilee contributed its jubilant mood with lively syncopated rhythms. In addition to its name, the white "gospel song" contributed responsorial and antiphonal practices that were added to the hymn or strophic form. This fusion of the responsorial and antiphonal practices from the white gospel song with the black gospel music material may well have been one of the most significant structural features of black gospel music according to one author.[6]

Early black hymn writers, exposed to Negro spirit-uals, jubilees, and white revival hymns, developed a repertoire of religious folk hymns. These folk hymns existed primarily in the oral tradition and were spread by itinerant black evangelists as they traveled to fundamentalist churches in the South and to urban centers of the North. Significantly, it was a black Methodist minister, Rev. Charles Albert Tindley, who is credited with having published the first gospel hymn. Tindley, originally from the South but living in Philadelphia around 1900, copyrighted "What Are They Doing In Heaven?" in 1901.[7] Ironically, Tindley's role has only recently been acknowledged. His songs, however, were used as models by various "holiness" groups, including the Church of God in Christ, who began "developing a style of religious song characte rized by free expression and rhythmic instrumental accompaniment."[8]

Thomas Andrew Dorsey (b. 1899), the often acknowledged "Father of Black Gospel Music," was exposed to these early black gospel hymns, to Negro spirituals and to white revival hymns as a child growing up in rural Georgia and later in Atlanta. Dorsey was to mold these sacred styles and one important secular style, the blues, into what we presently characterize as black gospel music. Dorsey blended simple, tuneful melodies with blues progressions, added "blue" notes (flatted thirds, fifths, and sevenths) syncopated the percussive piano accompaniment with heavily accented rhythms and recoined the term "gospel song." Dorsey, a prolific composer, wrote lyrics, melodies and/or harmonies for over 400 gospel songs. His name was to become synonymous with black gospel music. Even songs written by other composers were called "Dorsey's."[9] His mature compositions, written after the early 1930's, became the prototype for black gospel music which followed. His songs emerged as the standard by which all others were judged.

Until the 1960's, black gospel remained primarily "church music" despite the sporadic television appearances, commercial recordings and concerts, and international tours by famous performers such as Mahalia Jackson, Sister Rosetta Thorpe, the Ward Singers (with Gertrude and her daughter Clara), and the Roberta Martin Singers. In 1968 at the funeral of Dr. Martin Luther King, Jr., Mahalia Jackson sang what was probably the most famous Dorsey gospel song ever written, "Take My Hand, Precious Lord."[10] As she sang, the medium of television introduced large multi-racial/multi-cultural audiences of all ages—all who watched and listened—to black gospel music. This occasion, and one other event, have been turning points for black gospel music. From being purely black church music, gospel became more secularized.

A group originally called the Northern California Youth Choir, and later renamed the Edwin Hawkins Singers, released a recording of "Oh Happy Day," a new arrangement of an old hymn that became a tremendous national success. This group, and this one recording, placed gospel music before the national community in a way perhaps unparalleled in all of black gospel music's brief history. The Edwin Hawkins Singers achieved national recognition as a result of this recording and this particular record focused attention of an emerging new style of black gospel. This style was harmonically more complex than the traditional I, IV, V_7, I chords used in the folk style. The Hawkins Singers' harmony reflected a more modern sound incorporating large, chromatically altered chords, unusual chord movement, and modulations.[11] Judging from this record's ascent to the top of many popular music charts during 1969, gospel had perhaps become an integral part of the music listened to by millions of Americans.

These two events highlighted black gospel music as a major artistic expression that has since become a part of American popular culture as well as music for serious study. Black gospel music is now used in television theme songs and commercials, performed in nightclubs and prestigious concert halls and at jazz festivals. This genre continues to gain wide acceptance and to grow in popularity.

As gospel choirs spring up in high schools and colleges throughout the country, music educators are increasingly being called upon to work with groups of students who want to sing gospel music. The undertaking of directing a gospel choir may be somewhat unsettling for someone who has had little or no training in gospel music and who may have had no direct experience with the music. Moreover, the music educator may be asked to justify the inclusion of such a musical genre as a legitimate addition to the music program. Here are a few basic educational rationales for the inclusion of gospel music in the school music curriculum.

Educational Rationales

A. Secondary Vocal Music

There are at least four compelling reasons for including black gospel music in a comprehensive vocal music program. First, gospel music performance can be a vehicle for raising the level of musical literacy of the students who perform and study it. Musical literacy encompasses all aspects of music reading and includes such basic components as understanding symbols used in the score, as well as the broader concepts of form and style. Just as reading English prose is more than word calling, music literacy is more than simply note reading. For those students who cannot read music and might otherwise be excluded from

307

a choral experience, a gospel choir offers an opportunity to develop basic music reading skills. Once this entry level is gained, the conductor has the opportunity to teach music reading and all the collateral music skills as well as good vocal technique.

Although much of gospel music can be learned through an aural/oral approach, there are simple arrangements of gospel songs available that can and should be used for developing music learning and reading skills. Some of the compositions of Andrae Crouch, Walter and Edwin Hawkins, and Thomas Dorsey are prime examples of the type of musical literature available in print. Once these arrangements have been mastered, the student[12] is taught to add specific stylized vocal devices that enhance the quality of the performance. Specific teaching approaches and materials for developing musical literacy are included below.

A second rationale for using gospel music in the music curriculum is that gospel music can be used to raise the overall level of musicianship of the students through the development of skills such as ear training, vocal and keyboard improvisation, ensemble and solo singing. Gospel music provides an opportunity to aid in the development of the students' capacity to hear inner voices in close harmony, to execute intricate melismatic passages, and to blend with other voices in ensemble singing. The gospel song also lends itself to helping the singer master various musical forms such as call-and-response patterns (whether between soloist and chorus, soloist and accompaniment, or soloist and audience), and strophic verse. Black gospel music uses these two forms extensively.

In addition to these skills, there are other benefits directly related to raising the level of musicianship of the gospel music listener. One author, describing the artistic and aesthetic standards of a particular gospel music performance, observed that:

> The audience's musical sophistication is remarkable; it's nothing rare to see thousands of people roaring their approval for the subtlest change in tune, time, or harmony.[13]

This author seems to suggest that somehow, listening to

gospel music can have a positive effect on recognizing subtle changes in the music. If positive exposure to gospel music results in a type of intuitive learning, surely students who have sequentially structured learning experiences can reach and surpass the level of musical sophistication described in this instance.

A third reason for including gospel music in the music curriculum is that gospel music can be used to broaden and enrich the musical experience of those students currently in the vocal music program. American music--music that is uniquely American--has historically been excluded, for the most[14] part, from the music taught in the public schools. According to Allen P. Britton,

> from the very beginning music
> education in the United States was
> conditioned by a deliberate de-
> sire...to suppress stylistically
> indigenous music and to substitute
> something "better" in its place.[15]

Black gospel music, as well as other genres of black music (the blues, rhythm and blues, soul, rock-and-roll, and popular music) has traditionally been considered undesirable for school use. The growing popularity of swing choirs and stage bands, jazz and dixie-land ensembles, however, tends to signal a new willingness to expand the scope of school music from the narrow, classical Western-European musical tradition, to include indigenous American music. Black gospel music is a uniquely American art form that can enhance and enrich the musical diet of secondary school music students of all cultural and ethnic backgrounds.

The fourth reason for including black gospel music is that it can be a positive alternative to traditional, European oriented choral groups which may be perceived as too remote from the experience of many urban school students. In general, the addition of a gospel choir provides another ensemble that meets the needs of a large segment of urban school populations, as well as increasing the overall participation in the vocal music offerings. Black gospel music is a genre that students who live in urban centers have probably been exposed to either in their homes, at church, on the radio or television, or in some instances from simply living in the black community. A teacher might choose to start with the familiar and move to the less familiar by using gospel music as a point of departure for historical study or simply for teaching other styles, concepts and understandings. Again, students who otherwise might not participate in a traditional choral group, might be more inclined to join a gospel choir. Thus, the establishment of a gospel choir could provide an opportunity for students to have a positive and fulfilling musical experience.

B.   Secondary General Music

Several of the rationales listed above apply equally to the choral music class and to the general music and special elective classes as well. General music is required in most states in the seventh grade, less often required in the eighth grade, and is generally an elective in grades nine through twelve. The curriculum of the general music class must appeal to a wide range of students from various cultural and ethnic backgrounds, and various skill levels. Black gospel music offers musical material that can be used to teach a variety of skills, understandings and attitudes in specialized electives like a piano class.

Piano classes are fast becoming a popular elective in many secondary schools. Black gospel music uses the piano as a primary instrument for accompaniment. Gospel music could be incorporated into the piano class curriculum with relative ease since the basic chord progressions in black gospel parallel those progressions already being taught in many classes throughout the country. With the addition of a few standard patterns, syncopated rhythms and blue notes, the beginning piano student can accompany a large number of gospel songs.

Students also have the opportunity to master such musical instruments as drums (congos and bongos), guitars and tambourines. Students who play these instruments in the gospel song performance also gain valuable ensembles skills as well as performance opportunities. In a unit on instruments, gospel music provides music material and a performance opportunity that can be instantly successful.

The general music teacher may also gain valuable experience in organizing and conducting instrumental and vocal ensembles. Some gospel arrangements use saxophones, trumpets, triangles, strings and woodwinds. The conductor's skill as a choral and instrumental musician, arranger, and sometimes accompanist, are sure to be challenged.

In addition, students can gain an understanding of the importance of musical design, historical perspective, integration of knowledge,[16] and relationships between music and human endeavors. Black gospel songs were written in a variety of forms as style periods changed. A knowledge of these various forms and the ability to transfer this knowledge to other types of musical styles would be a signficant educational achievement for any student. Moreover, students can develop positive attitudes towards music while developing critical faculties and high musical standards, which should be the minimal outcome of every high school student's musical education.[17] Gospel music is simply another genre that can be used to attain these outcomes. Specific approaches for using black gospel music are included below.

Possible Teaching Approaches

Very little has been written about the ways (i.e., methods approaches, systems, ideas and techniques) available for teachers to teach black gospel music in the vocal and[18] general music class at the secondary school level. In a choral class, an understanding of gospel styles can be acquired through study and performance of the music. It is not unrealistic to assume that a teacher with no prior training in gospel music can hope to train students to perform gospel music. Admittedly, the task requires an expenditure of time and effort, and most certainly a trip to the local gospel music store or popular record dealer.

The teacher should imerse himself/herself in listening to the recording of the song in conjunction with looking at the sheet music. Where only the sheet music is available, the teacher must have a firm idea of the harmonic progressions used in the song and ideally, the skill to play the progressions at the keyboard. Before panicking at the thought of attempting to play gospel music, remember that a little practice at the keyboard makes teaching the piece a great deal easier. You might even consider recording one hand at a time and build your own layers of accompaniment. Remember too that the better you can play and sing the part(s) to be taught, the better and more at ease you will be while teaching it.

If no sheet music is available, the teacher should write out each part as close to the recording as possible. Having this sketch of the vocal parts can prevent wasted time during the rehearsal of the song. The teacher should give the student an overall idea of the song and how it should be performed. Then, allow the creative process to be your guide. Gospel music performance relies heavily on the vocal improvisation of the melodic line and no two gospel music performances are ever the same.

If the teacher has no keyboard skills, perhaps a student could be found to assist in teaching the song. In desperation, if no accompanist can be found, the recording is your best friend when attempting to teach gospel music.

Simple is best when beginning to work with gospel music. The novice should begin with gospel pieces that have a repetitive solo and refrain or chorus. If the teacher can secure a recording, allow the soloist to first learn the solo (aurally) then add improvisational flourishes to the recorded version. The refrain can be taught to the group phrase by phrase, adding one, then two parts to the melody. In the gospel song, the tenor line is often sung by the soprano voice an octave higher than written (like a second inversion chord). This type of three-voiced harmony is frequently used in many gospel songs even where there could conceivably be SATB voicing. On the other hand, the novice teacher of gospel music might be more successful at teaching three vocal lines, especially if the group is not equally balanced with men and women.

In the secondary general music class, various activities involving singing, playing instruments, composing, music reading, listening, conducting, drama and media have been integrated into the music curriculum using various teaching methods. These methods, for lack of a generic term, need not be discussed at this time. There is, however, a rather significant lack of black gospel music being taught using any method. How then can teachers begin to use gospel music as musical materials for teaching?

In addition to the most well known approaches to teaching general music, there are three specific approaches developed by this author that enable the teacher to include black gospel music in the general music class. The first approach is called the Additive

Approach. Black gospel is used as a means of illustrating the musical concept to be studied. This approach is probably the easiest means of integrating gospel into the music class. Black gospel has melody, harmony, rhythm, form, style, text, and extra-musical elements.[19] When these elements are taught in the general music class, gospel music should be used as musical material. Gospel provides a rich store of material that can be added to the music lesson for illustration. For example, a lesson designed to explore one aspect of rhythm--syncopation--would use examples selected specifically to illustrate various syncopated patterns. Musical selections could be drawn from the classical or popular repertoire, and may include examples as remote from each other as the Beethoven Pastoral Symphony to a Scott Joplin rag. Gospel music examples that could be used to illustrate syncopation could include: (1) Walter Hawkins and the Love Center Choir, "I Won't Be Satisfied;" (2) James Cleveland and the Charles Fold Singers, "Jesus is the Best Thing That Ever Happened to Me;" or (3) Andrae Crouch and the Disciples, "Soon and Very Soon." Each of these pieces demonstrates some aspect of syncopation either in the piano accompaniment, in the voices or in the instrumental parts. These examples could be a point of departure for individual or class activities.

The Activities Approach is another way of using gospel music in the classroom. As stated above, members of the class could devise their own projects for illustrating a musical concept, idea, or theme using a gospel song or a group of gospel songs. The Activities Approach relies upon the inventiveness and creativity of the teacher and students. Some areas for projects might include the following:

1. Movement: learning intricate rhythmic hand clapping, thigh and foot patting, rocking or other appropriate movement.

2. Photography: making a pictorial history of gospel music from magazine photographs, making a slide-tape presentation of a gospel performance.

3. Instruments: accompanying a gospel song with bongos, congos, drums, piano, organ, guitar, tambourine or other instruments.

4. Literature: explication of lyrics, writing gospel lyrics, poetic meter, imagery in lyrics.

313

5. Composition: composing gospel songs in different styles, supplying alternative harmonic progressions, writing obligatos, arranging for various voicings.

6. Conducting: conducting a gospel song in class or at a school performance.

This list is not intended to be complete nor are these the only areas for activities. In using this approach, the teacher must prepare the students for the project selection so that this activity is part of a larger musical unit.

The third approach for including gospel music is perhaps the most sophisticated in that it requires specific skills and knowledge on the teacher's part before it can be presented. This method is called the Historical Approach, and is probably best used in a large unit or in a number of mini-units--each with music and activities designed to accomplish definite goals. As a part of an American Music Unit, black gospel styles could be included as a separate mini-unit, or as a part of another mini-unit of black religious or popular music. The black religious unit might include the Negro spiritual, gospel and the jubilee. This kind of approach demands that the teacher be able to guide the students to discover musical history, repertoire and styles. The general music class should already have had a strong foundation in the elements of style (form, harmony, melody, rhythm, etc.) found in other types of music.

These are only a few of the many possibilities for including gospel music in the urban secondary school general music class. There is no "one and only way" to utilize gospel music, hence, many methods of teaching music can be adapted to the use of gospel music.

This author has designed a tool for working with gospel music for use by secondary school music teachers and students. *The Baker Black Gospel Analysis Model was designed to include those concepts and to require those skills that should be, and could be taught in the general music, choral or theory class. This model is to be used for analysis of black gospel music. Each term is defined in the glossary. Using this model, the

*Refer to Appendix A for Baker's Black Gospel Analysis Model and Glossay.

314

teacher will be able to draw a blueprint or guide for each gospel song performed and/or studied. Working with the recording of the gospel song, the teacher can focus upon any particular style trait contained in the model and can build a lesson around that trait using various teaching approaches.

Finally, the teacher who attempts to use gospel music in the classroom, whether choral or general music, must be prepared to answer some unfounded criticisms about this genre. One of the major criticisms of using gospel music in the choral class is that poor vocal technique could lead to the general abuse of the student's voice. It should be remembered that a primary responsibility of the choral director is to teach the student "good" singing skills and habits, no matter what music material is used. It is possible to achieve an authentic gospel sound without doing harm to the voice.

A reason often cited by people who are unwilling to teach gospel music is that a particular cultural background is required in order to teach black gospel. On the contrary, no special heritage is required to teach gospel, any more than a particular ethnic background is needed to teach a Palestrina Motet or a German Lied. What is required to teach gospel music is a general knowledge of style and performance practices, skill in teaching methods, an understanding of the students to be taught, and of course, students who are willing to learn. The watchwords for teachers who teach black gospel music should be---listen, sing, study, and enjoy.

SEQUENCE
LESSON PLAN OUTLINE

General Objectives: Mastering the musical elements

Specific Lesson Objectives: Students should be able to:

1. identify events in a song using a call chart
2. recognize and identify instruments in an ensemble
3. recognize and identify voices in an ensemble

4. focus listening to identify layers of sound
5. identify changes in dynamics
6. distinguish staccato and legato singing and playing
7. identify call and response patterns
8. tap a steady beat
9. tap a syncopated rhythm while other students tap steady beats

Notes: Each of the above objectives could be expanded to fill an entire lesson, depending on the musical experience of the students and other factors such as time per class meeting. The following procedures are intended only as guideposts for the use of Black gospel music in the general music class room.

Learning Experiences/Activities:
1. guided listening with call charts
2. Singing
3. Creating examples of elements using Black gospel as a model
4. Moving to beat
5. Conducting
6. Arranging

In this series of lessons, various activities should be planned. Samples of teacher-oriented call charts and evaluative, student-oriented charts have been included. Singing a gospel song is perhaps one of the easier activities for the teacher to include. Creating examples of elements could range from something as simple as composing an ostinato to fit a gospel song, to something as involved as doing an entire rhythm score for a gospel song. Students should be encouraged to move to the music, as well as to conduct and arrange it.

Evaluation: Were the students able to demonstrate understanding and mastery of the basic musical elements? Can the students transfer this mastery to other types of music?

TEACHING A BLACK GOSPEL SONG

1. Chosing a song
    -Find a song that has a recording and/or printed music.
    -Select a song that is in the verse-chorus form, where the soloist sings the verse and the choir sings only the melody.
    -Student input can be helpful in selecting an appealing and popular gospel song.

2. Learning the song
    -Listen to the recording until you know the chord changes, melody and harmony throughly.
    -Write out your own sketch of the harmony and voicing.
    -Sing through each voice to anticipate problems.

3. Getting the appropriate sound
    -Know what sound you want and be able to demonstrate tone quality and stylistic traits.
    -Be able to isolate on the recording or illustrate vocally such devices as bends, portamentos, fill-in notes and vocables.

4. Teaching the song
    -Introduce the song with a recording or tape.
    -Provide the words and any music available. Your own sketch may prove helpful.
    -Work with the chorus, without stopping to include the soloist.
    -Work with the soloist either before or after class, so that valuable class rehearsal time will not be wasted.

5. Putting the accompaniment together
    -Add appropriate instrumental accompaniment. Allow the record to be your guide. Basic instrumental accompaniments include: piano, drums, bass and lead guitars.
    -Give players a chart of harmonic progressions or play the recording for the ensemble.
    -Help melodic instruments with improvising in gospel style.
    -Work on blues scales, syncopation, rhytmic drive, fill-in notes and chords.

6. Putting the song together
    -Combine instrumental and vocal ensemble with the soloist.

-Practice until you are satisfied with the results.

CALL CHART

"PREPARE TO MEET HIM"

James Cleveland and the   Savoy SGL 7035
Southern Cal. Comm. Choir   Side 2, Band 1

Call Number   Circle the letter of the
                                     correct response

1.   Which instruments play this rhythm?
            a. trumpet and sax b. bass and piano

2.   Entrance of solist with a: a. moan b. growl
            c. shout

3.   Staccato figure played by: a. piano
            b. trumpet c. sings melody

4.   Chorus sings melody while soloist: a. stops
            b. improvises c. sings velody

5.   At the words "though you think your work is
            done," chorus sings: a. legato
            b. staccato

6.   Which voices sing "prepare to meet the Lord?"
            a. sopranos b. altos c. tenors

7.   What is the soloist doing while the group sings
            b. "prepare to meet him? a. improvising
            singing melody c. singing harmony

8.   Which voice enters next? a. tenors b. altos
            c. sopranos

9.   Which voice enters after #8? a. tenors b. altos
            c. sopranos

10. On repeat of "though you think your work is done,
            what do the instruments do? a. continue
            to play b. stop

11. What instrument is improvising? a. bass guitar

318

b. trumpet c. organ

12. The meter is: a. triple b. asymetric
    c. quadruple

13. The dynamics were consistently: a. soft b. loud
    c. neither

CALL CHART

"HE SAID HE WOULD AND HE DID"
21st Century Singers

3 min., 19 seconds
Creed 5224

Call No.

1. Introduction, trumpet, tombone, guitar, piano, organ, drums.

2. Full chorus (3 parts, syncopated verse.) Short, staccato melody gradually gets louder, then softer.

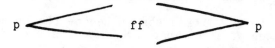

p   ff   p

3. Solo voice and ensemble
   Trumpet has counter melody.

4. Verse II by chorus, harmony filled in using chord tones.
   Bass has quick notes.

5. Solo voice repeats No. 3.
   Trumpet has counter melody.

6. Responsorial solo and chorus
   Full ensemble
   Interjection of vocables (yeh, yeh, etc.)

7. Repeat of solo and chorus, vocables, counter melody in trumpet: do, re, mi, fa, so, la, do

319

DISCUSSION QUESTIONS FOR THE MUSIC EDUCATOR:

1. What rationales can the educator give for the inclusion of black gospel music in the music education curriculum?

2. Define and give one example of the Additive Approach to teaching black gospel music.

3. Define and give one example of the Activities Approach to teaching black gospel music.

4. Define and give one example of the Historical Approach to teaching black gospel music.

DISCUSSION QUESTIONS FOR THE MUSIC STUDENT:

1. What were the precursors of black gospel music?

2. When and how did gospel music evolve as a musical genre?

3. What significant elements did the Negro spiritual, the jubilee and the white rivival hymn contribute to the evolution of black gospel music?

4. Explain how Thomas Dorsey became the acknowledged "Father of Black Gospel Music" instead of Charles Albert Tindley.

5. Two events propelled gospel music from the black church into popular American music. Can you explain what these events were and why you think they had such an effect on gospel music?

NOTES FOR CHAPTER 16

1. Horace Clarence Boyer, "Gospel Music Comes of Age: An Overview," Black World, November 1973, p. 46.

2. Mrs. Gertrude Roberts Cooper, daughter of one of the founding bishops of the church, and organist and professional accompanist for many gospel sin

gers including Sister Rosetta Tharpe. Interviewed in Chicago, Illinois, March 23, 1975.

3. This term refers to music sung primarily in churches by untrained singers.

4. John W. Work, American Negro Songs and Spirituals (New York: Bonanza Books, 1940), p. 19. There are some excellent sources for more elaborate history of the Negro spiritual. See for example: John Lovell, Jr., Black Song: The Forge and the Flame (New York: The MacMillan Company, 1972); George R. Ricks, "Some Aspects of the Religious Music of the United States Negro: An Ethnomusicological Study With Special Emphasis on the Gospel Tradition," (Ph.D. dissertation, Northwestern University, 1960); Eileen Southern, Readings in Black American Music (New York: W.W. Norton & Company, 1971); Southern, The Music of Black Americans: A History (New York: W.W. Norton & Company, 1971); and John Wesley Work, Sr., Folk Songs of the American Negro (Nashville, Tenn.: Fisk University Press, 1915).

5. Ricks, "Some Aspects," p. 133.

6. William H. Tallmadge, "The Responsorial and Antiphonal Practice in Gospel Song," Ethnomusicology 12 (May 1968): 235.

7. See Sunday School Publishing Board, Gospel Pearls (Nashville, Tenn.: National Baptist Convention, 1921), p. 69.

8. Ricks, "Some Aspects," p. 133.

9. Marshal Stearns, "If You Want to Go to Heaven, Shout," High Fidelity, August 1959, p. 92.

10. For a more detailed account of the history of this particular song, see Thomas A. Dorsey, "Precious Lord," Decision, December 1974, p. 4.

11. Boyer, "Gospel Music Comes of Age," p. 84.

12. See Baker Black Gospel Analysis Model and accompanying glossary for definition and usage.

13. Tony Heilbut, The Gospel Sound (New York: Simon & Schuster, 1971), p. xi.

14. Britton, "Music in Early American Public Educat-
    ion: A Historical Critique," in Basic Concepts
    in Music Education, National Society for the
    Study of Education (Chicago: University of
    Chicago Press, 1958), p. 200.

15. Ibid.

16. Karl D. Ernst and Charles L. Gary, eds., Music in
    General Education (Washington, D.C.: Music
    Educators National Conference, 1965), pp. 4-8.

17. Ibid., p. 4.

18. A chapter on teaching gospel music was included in
    Luvenia A. George's, Teaching the Music of Six
    Different Cultures in the Modern Secondary School
    (West Nyack, N.Y.: Parker Publishing Co., 1976),
    pp. 105-109.

19. Elements that are non-musical but are a part of
    the gospel music performance. See for examples
    "Vocables" and "Textual Interpolations" in the
    glossary.

20. Definitions in this glossary are in part from the
    following sources: Jan LaRue, Guidelines for
    Style Analysis (New York: W.W. Norton & Company,
    Inc., 1970); Horace Clarence Boyer, "The Gospel
    Song: A Historical and Analytical Study," (M.A.
    thesis, University of Rochester, 1964); Jack
    Sacher, ed., Music A to Z (New York: Grosset &
    Dunlap, Inc., 1963); and James Standifer, "Table
    of Expressive Musical Elements," in Black Music
    in Our Culture, Dominique-Rene deLerma, ed.,
    (Kent, Ohio: Kent State University Press, 1970),
    pp. 224-226.

21. Bert Konowitz, "Jazz," in Music A to Z, ed. Jack
    Sacher (New York: Grosset & Dunlap, Inc., 1963),
    p. 119.

SELECTED RESOURCE MATERIALS

A. Music Collections.

1. Andrae Crouch and the Disciples, "Keep on Sing-

322

ing," Lexicon Music, Inc.

2.   Walter Hawkings, "Jesus Christ is the Way," Lexicon Music 37814, 1977.

3.   _____, "Love Alive," Lexicon Music 37760, 1976.

4.   Mahalia Jackson, "Favorites of Mahalia Jackson," Hill and Range Songs, Inc., B3-2779, 1955.

B.   Choral and Solo Arrangements

1.   Doris Akers (Simon arr.,) Lead Me Guide Me, SATB, Hill and Range Songs, Inc.

2.   James Cleveland (Morris arr.,) I'll Do His Will, SATB, Savoy Music Co.

3.   Thomas Dorsey, "Standing Here Wondering Which Way to Go," SATB, Dorsey Pub.

4.   _____, "Peace In the Valley for Me," S or T solo, Big 3.

5.   Edwin Hawkins (Sanford arr.,) "Jesus Lever of My Soul," SATB, 913, Big 3s.

6.   _____, (Metis arr.,) "Oh Happy Day," SATB, 494, Big 3.

7.   Kenneth Morris, arr., "I Can't Help But Serve the Lord," SATB, Excellorec Mus.

8.   Myrna Summers, "God Gave Me A Song," SATB, Elma & Carl's Music Pub.

9.   J.B.F. Wright, "Precious Memories," S or T solo, Big 3.

C.   Recordings

1.   James Cleveland and the Angelic Choir, Vol. III, Savoy MG 14076.

2.   James Cleveland and the Charles Fold Singers, "Jesus Is the Best Thing that Ever Happened to Me," Savoy DBL 7005.

3. James Cleveland and the Southern California Community Choir, "Give Me A Clean Heart," Savoy 14270.

4. Andrae Crouch, "I'll Be Thinking of You," Light LS 5763.

5. Andrae Crouch and the Disciples, "The Best of Andrae Crouch," Light LS5678.

6. _____, "Live at Carnegie Hall," Light LS5602-LP.

7. _____, "This Is Another Day," Light LS-5683.

8. "Fisk Jubilee Singers," Folkways FA 2372.

9. Aretha Franklin, "Amazing Grace," Atlantic SD 2906.

10. "Gospel Songs of Thomas Dorsey," Columbia KG32157.

11. "Gospel Sound," Columbia G31086.

12. Edwin Hawkins, "Oh Happy Day," Buddah 5086.

13. Walter Hawkins and the Love Center Choir, "Love Alive," Light LS5686LP.

14. _____, "Jesus Christ Is the Way," Light LS5705.

15. Don Shirley, "The Gospel According to Don Shirley," Columbia CS 9723.

16. Myrna Summers and the Refreshing Spring C.O.G.I.C., "I Found Jesus," Savoy 14407.

17. Twenty-First Century Singers, "The Storm is Passing Over," Creed 3060.

Chapter 17

BLACK ETHNIC MATERIALS AND TEACHING STRAGEGIES
TO IMPLEMENT THEIR EFFECTIVE USE IN THE
INNER CITY CLASSROOM

Tilford Brooks

Introduction

While the music of Black Americans is a unique facet of American culture, this uniqueness is not peculiar only to the United States. Having common roots in the music of West Africa, American Black music bears strong resemblance in many ways to the music of other Black people of the New World, including South America and the Caribbean. When American Black music is examined, the evidence points overwhelmingly to African musical survivals as having contributed to its uniqueness.

It was extremely difficult for any African musical characteristics to remain in the music of the American Black man. Black Americans were not encouraged to retain African elements in their music due to the attitude of White society towards Blacks. Since the slaves were regarded as being inferior, their music was ignored.

In Africa, music has no abstract function. It functions in the social, political, economic, and religious structures of African society; thus, music and other aspects of this culture are interrelated. For example, music is used by the tribal farmer to accompany his work in the field.

Although the African slaves in the United States were not encouraged to retain their African musical style, they still were able to preserve certain characteristics in their music, no matter how difficult. From the beginning of slavery, the music of the slaves, like African music in many ways, was used to accompany specific human activities such as work, religious worship and dance. This constant use probably helped to preserve some African characteristics in American Black music.

Musical Characteristics

Those musical characteristics which are indigenous to American Black music include its rhythmic character, syncopation, improvisation, call and response patterns, blue notes, and the predominance of the human voice. Sources for appropriate materials as well as teaching strategies which will aid in conveying an understanding of the above concepts to students will be suggested. Neither the kinds of materials or the teaching strategies suggested are meant to be all-inclusive. They are to be used merely as a guide in an effort to communicate these concepts to students of all ages.

Its Rhythmic Character

In most regions of the United States, the African drums were outlawed.[1] Plantation owners were afraid that their slaves would use drumming to communicate from plantation to plantation and organize revolts. While African drums were outlawed, the practice of drumming survived. Pots and pans, the floor, and even their own bodies were used by the slaves as substitutes for drums all through the period of slavery.[2]

In West Africa, the so-called "talking drums" are capable of producing a variety of pitches. After the outlawing of drums in this country, slaves attempted to imitate the various pitches of these drums by using various parts of the body to produce a variety of sounds. Should one slap the thigh and then the back of the hand, the second slap is higher in pitch than the first. If one taps the foot and slaps the thigh, the slap is higher in pitch than the tap.

*[6]Some of the strategies presented in the following section are based on concepts developed by Standifer and Reeder in their very important book, Source Book of African and Afro-American Materials for Music Educators. These specific strategies are identified by a footnote indication at the beginning of the strategy.

Teaching Strategy One

Objective: To explore the variety of timbre employed in American Black music.

1. Play the recording of "Hambone"[3] for the students. Point out to them that various parts of the body are used to pat rhythms over and over. Ask the students to observe the variety of timbre produced.

2. Have the students tap their feet and pat their thighs in the following manner:

Pat Thigh

Tap Foot

3. If individual students have difficulty in tapping their feet and patting their thighs to both rhythms at the same time, divide the class into two groups. Have one group tap their feet and the other group pat their thighs as indicated.

4. Have the students listen to the differences in tonal color between the foot tapping and thigh patting.

During slavery, many slaves danced the Juba. They used patting as one means of providing the music by which they danced. In its simplest form, music is ordered (arranged) sound and silence. Since performed rhythm contains both of these characteristics, "pattin' a juba" can be said to be music.

Teaching Strategy Two 6

Objective: To explore the rhythmic quality of American Black music.

1. Have the students tap and pat the following rhythm pattern which is "pattin' a juba."

327

Pat Thigh

Tap Foot

2.   Play a recording of <u>Juba Dance</u>[4] by
the Black composer, <u>Nathaniel</u> Dett
(1882-1943), and use the Listening
Guide to make the students aware
of certain musical events including its rhythmic character, as
they occur in the music.

Listening Guide

Juba Dance

from In the Bottoms Suite by Nathaniel Dett

Events

    a. The A section; "pattin' a juba"
rhythm in the bass line; fast,
agitated sixteenth-note passage
in the right hand.

    b. Change of key; the B section.
Stepwise, agitated passages in
the bass that are punctuated by
chords in the following rhythm:

    c. Repeat of the A section; return
to original key.

    d. The C section; change of key;
moderately soft. New melody -
change in character of composition; rhythmic sequences
between the left hand and the
right hand; section is more
horizontal in structure.

    e. There is a return of the A
section but is not an exact
repeat; change of key to minor.

> > f. A repeat of the A section in the
> >   original key.
> >
> > g. Closing section chordal in
> >   structure; based on "pattin' a
> >   juba" rhythm; gradual increase
> >   in volume
>
> 3. Play the recording again, this
>   time having the students tap and
>   pat the juba rhythm with the
>   recording. Determine if they can
>   recognize the various melodies
>   used in this composition.

Rhythm of the Jube

> 4. Play this recording for a third
>   time and have your students raise
>   their hands each time a new
>   section is heard. Have them try to
>   determine the form for this
>   music.[5] Point out to the students
>   how the composer achieves some
>   degree of dynamic constrast be-
>   tween sections and within sections
>   through the use of loud and soft.

Cross-rhythms are common to the rhythm patterns of American Black music. However, they do not persist consistently throughout the length of each musical entity as they do in African music.

Syncopation

One of the most characteristic qualities of Black music is its syncopated rhythms. this can be done by accenting a beat that is normally not accented, or by removing an accent from a beat when it is normally expected.

Teaching Strategy Three 6

Objective: To convey to the students an understanding of the concept, syncopation.

1. Have the students clap each of the following rhythms [6] several times, making sure they count aloud and tap their feet on each rhythmic pulse. Instruct the class to clap louder on those beats that have the accent mark (>).

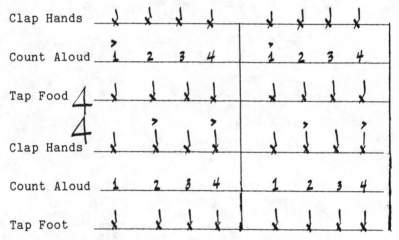

2. Make the students aware that the heaviest accent normally occurs on the first beat of the measure of a rhythm pattern as was done in the first exercise.

3. In the second exercise, the accents were shifted to the second

and fourth beats of each rhythmic
grouping. Ask the class if it felt
awkward when they initially clapped the second rhythm.

4.   Have the students clap the following rhythm pattern, making sure
that they count aloud and pat
their feet on each pulse as they
did before.   They are to repeat
this   exercise   several   times.
There   are   no   written   accents
(>).

Clap Hands

Count Aloud

Tap Feet

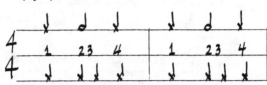

5.   Inquire of the students if it felt
natural to place an accent on the
first beat of each measure or did
they want to place the accent
elsewhere? If so, on what beats?
According to the definition of
syncopation given above, is this
exercise syncopated?

6.   Ask the students to clap the
following rhythm pattern.   They
should clap it several times,
counting aloud and patting their
feet on each pulse so that they may
get the "feel" of this rhythm.

Clap Hands

Tap Foot

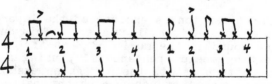

7.   As an additional activity, divide
the class into two groups. Assign
the syncopated rhythm to one group
and the basic pulse to the other.
Have the class substitute syllabl-
bles or words which can be chanted
to the combined rhythms.   As an

331

example, substitute the word "re-spon-si-bil-i-ty" for the clap and the phrase "got-to-go-now" for the tap. Let the students continue to play these rhythms as they chant softly. They may become more a-ware of the syncopation against the basic pulse.

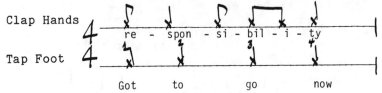

Clap Hands

re - spon - si - bil - i - ty

Tap Foot

Got   to   go   now

8. The students are now ready to create their own syncopated rhythms. Have the class continue patting their feet to the basic pulse while each individual attempts to create syncopated rhythms. The class should tap their feet for eight beats before each individual student starts clapping the original rhythm pattern. The class should continue to tap their feet after each student begins.

Tap Foot

1 2 3 4 1 2 3 4

Improvisation

Improvisation is another of the important characteristics of American Black music. This quality, which is also found in the music of West Africa, is the act of creating music spontaneously, using a melody or a rhythm pattern as its basis. As an example, when the students created syncopated rhythm patterns earlier, they were improvising on the rhythmic pulse which was tapped by their classmates.

In the performance of American Black folk songs, improvisation is used widely. The singer may create a new melody from the original melody, or he may change the words with each performance. New, complex rhythms may be created from the old patterns. Each kind of improvisation may be used by itself or in any combination with the others.

The drummer in jazz, an American Black music form, often improvises on the basic rhythm pattern. Besides using a snare drum and a bass drum, the jazz drummer also uses tuned tom-toms, cymbals, woodblocks, and cowbells.

Teaching Strategy Four

Objective: To communicate to the students an understanding of the concept of rhythmic improvisation.

1. Have your students listen carefully to a recording of rhythmic improvisation by a jazz drummer.[7] Point out that the basic pulse is played on the drum sounding lowest in pitch, the bass drum. Against this basic rhythmic pattern, the jazz drummer improvises all kinds of syncopated rhythms against it. The basic rhythm pattern is:

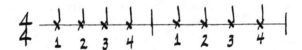

Bass Drum

Teaching Strategy Five

Objective: There are many ways in which improvisation in music may be achieved. One manner in conveying an understanding of this concept[8] is through the use of the human voice.

1. Initially, have each student say his/her name aloud over and over. They should then respond with their voice in the manner suggested by the teacher. The following suggestions should be given: Say your name as if you are "happy." Say it as if you are "bored." Say it as if you are

"running." Now say it as if you are "tired." Say your name as if you were at the "bottom of a deep pit."

2. Finally, have the students improvise on their name by varying the tempo (speed), dynamics (volume - loud or soft), and pitch (high and low). The students have just created vocal improvi sation by changing these three elements of sound while saying their name.

3. As an additional activity in using the voice in creating improvisation, divide the class into two groups. Place two lists of moods and dynamics on the chalkboard. The list should include terms such as "happy," "sad," "bored," "tired," "loud," "soft," "crescendo," and "descrescendo." Have each group alternate reciting a given name in the manner suggested by each term. The groups should alternate using terms. This is also improvisation.

Teaching Strategy Six

Objective: In an effort to give the students a greater understanding of the concept of improvisation, the teacher may utilize a basic rhythm pattern while exploring the use of dynamics, accents, and tempo to achieve another kind of improvisation.

1. The teacher should clap a basic rhythm pattern of no more than two measures in length and ask individual students to respond with an identical pattern. As an example:

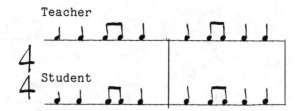

2. Now the teacher should clap the same rhythm as before, but include a new element, such as accents. Have the students listen carefully and include the new element in identical manner in their response.

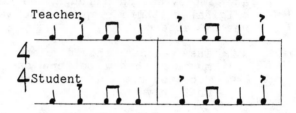

3. Next, instruct the student to respond with a contrasting answer, changing only the element being stressed but <u>not</u> the rhythm.

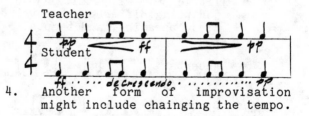

4. Another form of improvisation might include chainging the tempo.

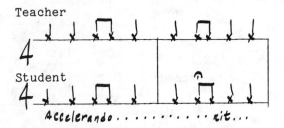

5. The teacher may also suggest combinations of varying the dynamics, accents, or tempo.

Teaching Strategy Seven

Objective: To have the student initiate improvisation through the use of original rhythmic responses to various rhythm patterns.

1. The teacher should clap a two-measure rhythm pattern and instruct the class toclap back exactly what they hear.

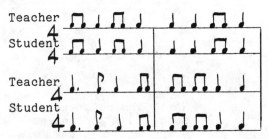

2. The teacher should clap a few more patterns making each one just a little more rhythmically complex and using different accents, dynamics, phrasing, and tempos.

336

Tempos

Phrasing

The class should repeat each example exactly as heard.

3. The teacher should now select individual students to clap their own rhythm pattern using a variety of musical concepts. The class is asked to give an exact response.

4. The teacher should clap a rhythm pattern using the above concepts and ask individual students to give their own original contrasting response, two measures in length, varying the rhythm, accents, phrasing, tempo, dynamics, etc. The teacher's rhythm pattern should be placed on the chalkboard.

5. Each student is then asked to clap a long contrasting response to a rhythm pattern clapped by the tacher. Students are now actually performing an "improvisation," due to the fact that the original musical idea has been modified in several ways.

Call and Response Pattern

The call and response pattern is one of the easily recognized characteristics of some American Black music. In this music, there seems to be a natural tendency for two-part singing. The first part is that of the leader and the second is that of the group. In a typical call and response form, the leader makes a statement of one or more phrases. Then the group completes the statement of the leader or adds to his statement with a response. In teaching strategies six and seven, in which the primary focus was conveying a concept of improvisation, the call and response concept was also being utilized. The responses given to the various rhythm patterns, whether they were exact or in contrast to the original statements, were a kind of call and response.

Teaching Strategy Eight

Objective: To give the students an understanding of the concept of call and response.

1. The teacher should teach the class the Black children's ring game song, I'm Goin' Up North, whose structure utilizes the call and response pattern.

2. Initially, the teacher should sing the lead part with the class singing the response. After the class has had an opportunity to learn the lead part, individual students should be given the opportunity to perform as leader.

I'm goin' up north
Satisfied!
And I would tell you
Satisfied!
Lord I am
Satisfied!
Some peoples up there
Satisfied!
Goin' to bring you back
Satisfied!
Ain't nothin' up there
Satisfied!
What you can do
Satisfied!
Mamma cooked a bull
Satisfied!
Have to get all the boys
Satisfied!

Their bellies full
Satisfied!
I'm goin' up north
Satisfied!
And I would tell you
Satisfied!
Lord I am
Satisfied!
Some people up there
Satisfied!
Goin' bring you back
Satisfied!
Mamma cooked a chicken
Satisfied!
Have to get all the girls
Satisfied!
Their bellies full
Satisfied!

3. A second children's ring game song, I Must See, is also based on the call and response pattern. Teach this song to your class, allowing individual students to perform the leader's part. After this experience, the class should be able to recognize the call and response pattern whenever it is encountered.

I Must See[10]

Take your partner down the line,
    I must see, I must see.
Take your partner down the line,
    I must see, I must see.
Take your partner down the line,
    I must see, I must see.
Swing your partner, swing again,
    I must see, I must see.
Take your partner down the line,
    I must see, I must see.
Take your partner down the line,
    I must see, I must see.
Swing your partner, swing again,
    I must see, I must see.
Swing your partner, swing again,
    I must see, I must see.
Swing your partner, swing again,
    I must see, I must see.
Take your partner down the line,
    I must see, I must see.
Take your partner down the line,
    I must see, I must see.
Take your partner down the line,
    I must see, I must see.

340

Use of Blue Notes

American Black music, whether it be work songs, religious songs, jazz, and others, often contain partially lowered third and seventh tones of the scale while at other times these tones are used at the natural pitch level. (In the key of C, the partially lowered tones are E and B).

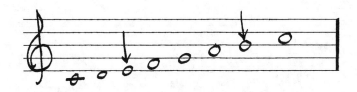

The aberration of these tones may be microtonal in nature and thus do not necessarily coincide with any scale or mode. These lowered tones, which are commonly called "blue notes," are believed to be of African origin. They give American Black music a distinctive sound.

Teaching Strategy Nine

Objective: To teach the students to recognize blue notes aurally when they are performed as a part of American Black music.

1. The teacher should now demonstrate the use of blue notes by playing a recording of the Black spiritual, "Row, Michael, Row." If the students listen carefully, they should be able to distinguish the partially lowered tones from the natural tones. (Since it is impossible to notate the exact pitch of a blue note with our present notational system, arrows are used to indicate those tones which should be sung as blue notes.)

Row, Michael, Row[11]

Row, Michael, row,
    Hallelujah,
Row, Michael, row,
    Hallelujah.

Oh, row the boat ashore
    Hallelujah,
Row the boat ashore,
    Hallelujah.

Oh, see how we do row
    ..(etc)
Oh, row the boat ashore...

Can't you row, Michael,
    row...
Jump in the jolly boat...

Oh row the boatashore...

Row, Michael, row...

Row the boat ashore...

Row, Michael, row,
    Hallelujah,
Row, Michael, row,
    Hallelujah.

2. Without permitting the students to see the music, ask them to determine where the blue notes occur in the melody.

3. Once the students are able to identify where the blue notes occur in the Black spiritual, "Row, Michael, Row," they should be taught this song with the blue notes being sung in the appropriate places.

4. Relate to the students that a call and response pattern is utilized.

5. The students should now be taught other songs containing blue notes so that this concept is fully understood.

Rhythm.... Improvisation.... Call and Response.... Blue Notes.... these important characteristics of American Black music are directly related to the traditional music of West Africa. These are the traits that have made American Black music so unique and have influenced American music in general.

The Black Vocal Sound

The human voice is the most frequently used means for carrying the melody in folk musics. It dominates Black folk music just as it does the music of West Africa. In addition, the voice occupies a position of such traditional importance that it influences the Black instrumental sound which will be discussed later.

A great variety of timbre pervades all of American Black music, whether it be vocal or instrumental. In pure vocal musical can be found differences in the qualities of sound of different voices. Various singing conventions are employed in American Black music to produce a wide variety of sound. While some of these effects are not peculiar only to American Black music, they are generally not found in other American music outside of the Black idiom.

In American Black music, it is not the so-called "good" voice that is most often used, but the voice that has a pleasing personality which seems to appeal to Blacks.

343

Raucous Voice

A voice quality used in the singing tradition of both Africans and Black Americans is the foggy, rough voice. Often, there is no effort made by the singer to sing in a "smooth" and "sweet" manner. In American Black music as in West African music, it is the personality of the voice that is important.

Teaching Strategy Ten

Objective: To acquaint the class with the quality of voice that is raucous in nature.

1. Many of your students have probably heard this quality of voice on recordings by Black American singers. Since it could be quite difficult to produce this quality of sound, the students should not be encouraged to do so.

2. The class should be directed to listen to recordings which demonstrate this quality of sound. Any recordings by Ray Charles or James Brown are excellent examples of the raucous voice quality [12] to common to American Black music.

Falsetto

Often, Black American singers use falsetto tones. Falsetto tones are artificially produced tones sung above the normal range of the voice. This singing technique is used quite extensively in African singing.

Teaching Strategy Eleven

Objective: Impart to the students an understanding of this quality of singing through listening to recordings and through experiencing this singing style by actually trying to imitate it.

1. Direct the students to listen to a recording of falsetto singing. [13]

344

2. The teacher should have the students produce this quality of tone by placing the tone high in the head. The class should be asked to try singing in a falsetto voice by using a song familiar to each of them. Of course the teacher should check the quality of tone to make sure it is falsetto.

3. While the idea is to permit the students to sing in a falsetto voice to make sure that they understand this characteristic quality of American Black singing and how it is produced, care must be exercised to insure the the student does not cause any permanent damage to the vocal mechanism by singing for too long a period of time in this manner.

Portamento

Portamento, an effect obtained by sliding or gliding from one tone to the next, is extensively used in American Black music, whether it be vocal or instrumental. Singers of American Black music often attack and release notes in a variety of ways. They include the use of swoops, slurs, smears, and glides, all of which are forms of portamento.

Teaching Strategy Twelve

Objective: To give the students an understanding of the technique of singing portamento.

1. Since the technique of singing portamento is not easily mastered, an understanding of this concept would be facilitated through the use of recordings.

2. Have the class listen to a recording of "Porgy," by the late Billie Holliday.[14]

3.   Point out to the class the manner
      in which the singer slides,
      glides, slurs, and swoops from one
      tone to the next.

Scat Singing

While scat singing is more identifiable with the
Black instrumental sound, it is a vocal technique. For
that reason, it will be discussed here. In essence,
the Black instrumental sound is an imitation of the
Black vocal sound. However, in scat singing, the sound
emitted is an imitation of the Black instrumental
sound.   Through the use of nonsense words and
syllables, the singer improvises on the melody just as
an instrumentalist would do.

It is generally accepted that scat singing was
introduced to jazz in the late 1920's by the great
Black trumpet player, Louis Armstrong. [15]

One of the foremost scat singers today is Ella
Fitzgerald. Her concept of this style of singing is
very similar to that of an instrumental improviser in
jazz.   In addition, for many years she has been a
favorite singer of popular songs in her own Black vocal
style.

Teaching Strategy Thirteen

Objective: To impart to the students an
understanding   of   the   techniques
involved in scat singing.

1.   Have   the   class   listen   to   the
      recording by Louis Armstrong in
      which   he   performs   the   first
      recorded version of scat singing.

2.   Listen to a recording of a modern
      version of this art form by Ella
      Fitzgerald. [16]

3.   Have the students compare the two
      recorded versions of scat singing.
      Hopefully, the students will gain
      some   appreciation   and   unders-
      tanding of this vocal technique.

346

Blue Notes

Although blue notes are a most important component of the Black vocal sound, this vocal technique was discussed earlier. However, when vocal techniques are being discussed, it would be appropriate to review the teaching strategy associated with blue notes.

Religious Singing Styles

The American Black religious singing styles have their roots in two bodies of religious music. . . the spiritual song and the gospel song.

While the singing styles eminating from these two bodies of religious music are quite distinct, they also possess certain qualities which are common to both. At the risk of over-simplification, an effort will be made to define each of the singing styles associated with the spiritual song and the gospel song respectively, while comparing and contrasting these two kinds of Black religious music.

Black Spiritual Song

From the beginning of slavery in this country there were present many different musical elements which may have contributed to the development of the American Black spiritual. Among these were the folk songs of western Europe, the hymn songs of the Protestant Church, and the songs and rhythms of western Africa. It was the American slaves who created the spiritual from these musical elements.

A large number of the spirituals probably came from two sources. One source consisted of the African melodies that occurred in Africa. Some of the African melodies brought to these shores by slaves did survive the change in culture and were used as patterns for Black spirituals. The second source involved the on-the-spot creation by talented individuals. They may have used as song material some sentence from a preacher's sermon. They were perhaps joined by other members of the congregation. The Black preacher, using a "reciting-tone" (half-sung, half-spoken) delivery, often established a call and response pattern between himself and the congregation. In many instances, the preacher would repeat one line over a period of time. At the end of the sermon, this material may have been used as the basis for song. If this song was repeated at a later date, it possibly became a part of the worship service of the American Black church.

While the melodies of some spirituals contain all of the tones of the major scale, many other spiritual melodies use only the five tones of the pentatonic scale. (The fourth and seventh tones are not used.)

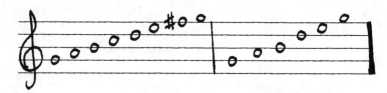

Major Scale   Pentatonic Scale

Teaching Strategy Fourteen

Objective: Through teaching the class a spiritual, enable the students to discern what tones are utilized in a spiritual melody.

1. It would now be appropriate at this point to teach the class a spiritual such as, "Swing Low, Sweet Chariot," in unison.

2. The class should now be asked to follow the music as it is sung and decide how many different tones there are in the melody.

3. The teacher should help the students to determine if the melody contains all of the tones of the major scale or only the tones of the pentatonic scale.

As was discussed earlier, rhythm is one of the most important features of the American Black music. Many of the spiritual melodies contain syncopated rhythms.

Teaching Strategy Fifteen

Objective: To teach the students to determine if and when syncopation occurs in the American Black spiritual.

1. The teacher should review the definition of syncopation with the class (refer to the earlier section on rhythm).

2. The class should now be asked to determine if there is syncopation in any of the measures of the spiritual, "Swing Low, Sweet Chariot."

3. If syncopation does occur, the class should determine in which measure or measures it occurs.

4. In addition to rhythm, this spiritual should be sung using another outstanding characteristic of American Black music, the call and response pattern.

Swing Low, Sweet Chariot

Black Gospel Song

Although many religious groups were involved in the development of gospel music, the Church of God in Christ of the Holiness group is considered to have exerted the greatest influence on the gospel tradition. While the first published American Black gospel songs which included words and music on a single sheet of paper were those written by Reverend C. Albert Tindley between 1901 and 1906, the person who has exerted more influence on the gospel music style than any one other individual is Thomas A. Dorsey. Dorsey has been involved with this musical style since 1921.

Gospel music includes the use of jazz rhythms and blues singing in religious music. The "soul-singing" style has a great similarity to the singing style found in the blues. Of course, a strong beat is important. However, there are occasions when gospel music is very free and flexible.

The gospel song is often accompanied by one or more musical instruments. Those most commonly used are the piano and organ, either together or separately. Other instruments which are sometimes used include the tambourine, saxophone, trombone, and drums.

Teaching Strategy Sixteen

Objective: The teacher should identify for the class, rhythmic, harmonic, and vocal qualities which are indigenous to gospel music.

1. The teacher should play a recording of gospel music.

2. Complex, syncopated rhythms should be pointed out when and where they occur.

3. Jazz harmonies used in gospel music should be isolated and played on the piano so that the class can become familiar with their function in this context.

4. Finally, the characteristic vocal sound associated with gospel music should be identified including the

350

use of blue notes when they occur, the use of improvisation (the singer has a great degree of freedom to apply his interpretation to the music as he so desire; the melody line is used only as a guide), and the use of melisma (many notes sung to each syllable).

Teaching Strategy Seventeen

Objective: To teach the class the similarities and differences between the spiritual song and the gospel song.

1. The teacher should place the chart below on the chalkboard.

2. Have the class sing the spiritual, "Swing Low, Sweet Chariot," and play a recording of a gospel song.

3. Ask the class to identify as many characteristics found in the chart as they can. Perhaps the students can add some characterstics that are not included here.

AMERICAN BLACK SPIRITUALS	MODERN GOSPEL SONGS
Folk songs handed down by oral tradition from slavery time	Composed songs
Performed unaccompanied by musical instruments	Usually accompanied by musical instruments such as piano, organ, drums, and electric bass
Words are often based on stories from the Bible	Words are often a personal expression of faith and hope in salvation
Usually the melodies are simple with never more than a few notes sung	Often the melody is embellished with many notes sung to

351

to each syllable	one syllable (melisma)
Sung in unison or simple harmony	Usually contain modern harmonies often associat ed with jazz
Syncopation is used, but not in complex patterns	Several synocopated rhythms are used simlata- neously (polyrhythms)

BOTH CONTAIN

Call and response patterns
Syncopation
Rhythmic emphasis
Vocal improvisation
Emotionally inspired

Blues Singing style

No one knows exactly when the blues came into being. The blues grew from mournful songs, from sorrow songs, and from field calls and hollers of the slaves. Singing the blues was an emotional release from misery, loneliness, and despair--a personal statement of the singer's own suffering. It was not religious music.

From the singing of the blues has evolved a singing style which is peculiar to Black music. It must be remembered, however, that the blues singing style may be utilized to sing not only the blues but any other song material. Therefore, it is appropriate that your class be given some understanding of the evolution of this style and all that it encompasses.

Field Hollers, Calls, and Cries

Field hollers, calls, and cries are unusual styles of singing that originated in West Africa. It is quite difficult to determine one from the other since their meanings are so similar. They were as useful in this country as they were in Africa.

Some hollers and calls were used to communicate all kinds of messages were used for a variety of purposes. Some were intended to bring workers in from the fields. Others were used to summon them to work. They might be used to attract the attention of a girl in the dis tance, to signal hunting dogs, or simply to make one's presence known.

Other sounds, sometimes described as cries, were often used as a release from the hard work in the field. The cry might be one of joy or sadness. Sometimes it was nothing more than a single line or phrase. On other occasions, it might take the shape of a simple song.

Teaching Strategy Eighteen

Objective: To acquaint the class with the blues-like quality of the singing associated with field hollers, calls, and cries.

1. Have your class listen to the field holler, "Arwhoolie."[18] Stress the fact that like most hollers, the singing style has a blues-like quality (including blue notes).

2. It should also be pointed out that the melody moves downward just as many American Black melodies (including the blues) and most West African melodies.

3. Since at times, it is difficult to distinguish the field holler from the country blues, direct your class to listen to "Cornfield Holler."[19]

4. Direct their attention to the use of blue notes and the downward shape of the melody.

The Blues

The blues is one of the most distinctive song forms that was created out of the social and cultural environment of the United States. This American Black song style is not only a musical expression, it is also a social expression.

While it is not known exactly when the blues came into being, it is believed that this music form

353

developed sometime between 1865 and 1875. However, its development was gradual and over a long period of time. The field holler, which was just discussed, is believed to be the major predecessor of this music form.

Prior to the twentieth century, the blues structure was very flexible. Each blues singer felt free to use the number of measures necessary to state his story. There was no set number. Consequently, the early blues were done in such a free style as to fall into no clear-cut pattern at all.

In the early 1900's, the blues developed into a music that had a definite form, was notated, and usually had an accompaniment. The distinctive blues singing style is recognized by various vocal sounds such as moans, shouts, groans, growls, swoops, and slides from one tone to another.

Of course, the blues make use of "blues notes." These blue notes emphasize the mournful qualities of the song.

Teaching Strategy Nineteen

Objective: To make students aware of the blues singing style by making them more familiar with the blues song.

1. Have the class listen to the recording of "Poor Man's Blues"[20] as sung by Bessie Smith, one of the greatest of all blues singers.

2. Direct the class' attention to certain tones that are slightly lowered (usually the third).

3. Point out where slides, swoops, and moans are used.

4. Also point out the fact that the melody of each phrase tends to move downward just as it did in the field holler.

5. Have the students compare what they hear with the musical score.

354

Poor Man's Blues

Rhythm and Blues

Rhythm and blues is a catch-all term that has been
applied to most American Black popular music. It must
be emphasized that to be called rhythm and blues a song
does not have to be blues. Quite often the lyrics
simply serve to make the song a novelty because of the
humor they contain and the music is more rhythmic than
blues. However, it is important to realize that the
blues singing style predominates.

Teaching Strategy Twenty

Objective: To familiarize students
with the blues singing style found in
rhythm and blues.

1. Have the class listen to the
    recording "Bloodshot Eyes,"[21] by
    Wynonie Harris.

2. Direct their attention to the
    humorous quality of the lyrics and
    the heavy, forceful, driving beat
    of the music.

355

3. Emphasize that the shouting vocal style heard on this recording is very closely related to the blues singing style associated with modern blues singing. Point out, however, that this particular song is not a blues.

Soul

As Black Americans began to search to determine their cultural roots during the 1960's, a new term came upon the horizon--<u>soul</u>. While initially the term had no musical implications, but was used to imply a kind or quality of lifestyle, more and more it was used to designate a style of American Black music.

Soul, however, is a quality rather than a style. It has its roots in Africa. Soul was simply a new term for an old feeling that is common to all American Black music.

Teaching Strategy Twenty-One

Objective: To become aware of the blues singing style heard in so-called soul music.

1. Have the class listen to a recording by Areatha Franklin entitled, "Soulville."[22]

2. Direct the attention of the class to the vocal inflections of the solo singer. Point out that she uses swoops, slurs, slides, and glides in her singing which are characteristic of the blues singing style.

3. Discuss with the class the fact that the voice quality of the solo singer is not what would be termed a "good" voice by European standards, but a lively voice with a great amount of personality.

4. Indicate that this song has a strong, heavy beat which makes this music highly rhythmic.

356

Contemporary Black Music

Contemporary American black music may be called blues, rhythm and blues, rock n' roll, or soul. Regardless of the terminology applied, this kind of music is characterized by the use of the blues singing style.

Teaching Strategy Twenty-Two

Objective: To familiarize the class with the blues singing style found in contemporary American Black music.

1. The class should listen to the recording, "Walkin' in the Sun,"[23] by the group Rufus.

2. This recording is a contemporary example of the blues singing style. Note the blue notes utilized, the use of slides, glides, etc.

The Black Instrumental Sound

A considerable body of American Black music came into being near or soon after the beginning of the twentieth century. Interestingly enough, all of this music, with the exception of jazz of the New Orleans variety, is notated. This was the first step among many, in which this music was affected by European music. However, American Black music maintained enough African influences to retain its special character. This music is still a unique expression and has continued to remain so because of the social environment in which it took place.

The Black instrumental sound is a mixture of a strong rhythmic beat, the accents of syncopation, and in some instances, the improvising of new melodies with and around a basic melody. In all instances, the Black instrumental sound is an imitation of the Black vocal sound. Ragtime attempts to imitate the syncopated rhythms of Black singing while jazz performers use the slides, swoops, and slurs of the blues singing style.

Ragtime

Ragtime is essentially a piano music which flourished for about twenty years, from 1896 to 1917. It is not jazz or is it just an older name for jazz. However, it is one of the influencing musics on jazz. Both were developed about the same time and ran parallel to each other until ragtime virtually died out after the end of the First World War.

As distinct from jazz, which is an art of improvisation, ragtime was essentially a composed music with many printed and published examples. Piano ragtime consisted of regular melodic lines syncopated in a highly complex manner over a march-style bass.

In style, ragtime was an extension of the cakewalk and the syncopated Black vocal style associated with minstrel tunes. In form, it developed from the march played by brass bands of the era. It is significant that ragtime developed in the midwest where marches were popular.

Ragtime piano music is notated and derived from European instrumental and Black vocal influences. The classic ragtime form consists of four different 16-bar parts: AA BB A CC DD.

It was Scott Joplin (1868-1917) who produced rags which contained certain characteristics that controlled the ragtime style throughout its history. Among these characteristics were a structure containing several equally important melodies, a change of key at some point in the composition, and the two-beat regular rhythm of the left hand against syncopation in the right hand.

As mentioned above, in ragtime, the right hand plays uneven rhythms with the accents occuring where they are not expected. In the left hand, the accents sound on the beat.

Teaching Strategy Twenty-Three

Objective: To convey to the class the syncopated feeling of ragtime music.

1. Divide the class into two groups. Using the exercise below, have one-half of the class tap several

measures of four beats each--left
foot, right foot, etc.

2. Then have the other half of class
    add the hand-clapping as indicat-
    ed. Be sure to accent the notes
    marked.

3. Now have both groups begin
    together and tap and clap their
    respective rhythms simultaneously.

4. Once this is accomplished with
    some success, have each member of
    the class attempt to perform both
    rhythms individually, clapping and
    tapping simultaneously.

Teaching Strategy Twenty-Four 6

Objective: To familiarize the class
with various rhythms that occur in a
specific rag, "The Easy Winners."[24]

1. "The Easy Winners" is a popular
    rag that was composed by Scott
    Joplin in 1901. The march-like
    bass consists of three patterns
    which occur throughout this compo-
    sition. Have the class perform
    each of these patterns several
    times.

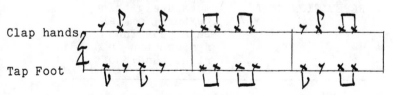

The students should perform each
of these patterns until they feel
comfortable doing them.

2.	In the right hand, several synco-
pated rhythms are used. Have the
class clap each of these rhythms
until they experience no difficulty in performing them.

Clap hands

3.	Ask the class to listen to a
recording of Joplin's rag, "The
Easy Winner." The students are to
observe the musical events taking
place by comparing what they hear
with what is indicated in the
listening guide. (Sections: Introduction, AA BB A and (Interlude). After several hearings of
this recording, ask the class to
complete the listening guide. Do
not expose sections C and D to
class. The students should
determine the musical events of
these sections.

Section	Events
INTRODUCTION	The melody moves by steps; both hands play in unison.
A REPETITION OF A	This section contains harmony; moderately thin texture; om-pah bass; continuous syncopation in right hand; soft.
B REPETITION OF B 360	Melody moves by steps; texture is thin; om-pah bass;

	continuous syncopation in right hand; melody moves by leaps; broken chords (arpeggio) in both hands.
REPETITION OF A	Same as above.
INTERLUDE	Change of key; broken chords (arpeggio) in both hands; texture is thin; harmony; two measures in length.
C REPETITION OF C	Melody moves by wide leaps; moderately soft; texture is thin; accented chords.
D REPETITION OF D	Harmony; texture is thicker; another melody in left hand; texture is thinner; melody moves by leaps; repeat of this section very loud; melody in bass emphasized; soft.

4. After the class has heard "Easy
   Winners" several times, ask the
   students to choose the rhythm
   pattern that is heard most often
   in each major section---A, B, C,
   and D.

1   𝅘𝅥 𝅘𝅥 𝅘𝅥   𝅘𝅥𝅘𝅥𝅘𝅥   (C)

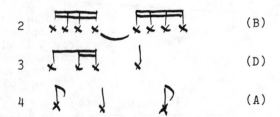

Jazz

Blues and ragtime fused with the music of the brass band and syncopated dance music. The resultant product was a music called jazz with its own characteristics.

The most outstanding characteristics of jazz were perhaps derived directly from the blues. It must be remembered that jazz is a vocally oriented music. While the performers of this art form replace the voice with their instruments, they try to recreate the Black singing style and blue notes by using scoops, slides, growls, whines, and falsetto effects. Since improvisation is such a vital part of jazz, the players themselves have a great influence on the style. In essence, the performer is the composer.

New Orleans Jazz

One of the most important and influential jazz performers was trumpeter Louis Armstrong (1900-1971). He changed jazz from a style based on collective improvisation (several performers improvising simultaneously) to a style based on solo improvisation (one performer improvising at any one time). Armstrong has been credited with being the most important single influence in all of jazz.

From 1925 to 1929, Armstrong recorded with the Hot Five and the Hot Seven. The recording, "Struttin' With Some Barbecue,"[25] was recorded by the Louis Armstrong Hot Five. The instrumentation included cornet, clarinet, trombone, piano, and banjo.

Teaching Strategy Twenty-Five

Objective: To familiarize the students with the principle of collective improvisation, the cornerstone of New Orleans style jazz, and solo improvisation the basic principle underlying swing and subsequent jazz styles.

1. Use the listening chart as a guide and observe when and where collective improvisation takes place. Contrast this technique with solo improvisation and the manner in which it is used.

2. Observe the solo "break" and the ensemble "break." Compare the two.

3. Have students become aware of the effective manner the background instruments support soloist.

LISTENING CHART

Section	Events
INTRODUCTION	Twelve-bar introduction; collective improvisation.
FIRST CHORUS	Collective improvisation; cornet, clarinet, and trombone improvise at same time; two bar banjo break.
SECOND CHORUS (First Half)	Clarinet improvises; (solo); the background consists of piano and banjo on each beat of measure;

363

	two-bar clarinet break.
SECOND CHORUS (Second Half)	Trombone improvises (solo); the background consists of the banjo on each beat of the measure and the piano on the 2nd and 4th beats of each measure; trombone break.
THIRD CHORUS	Cornet improvises (solo); two-bar cornet break; the background consists of piano and guitar on the 2nd and 4th beats; four-bar ensemble break.
FOURTH CHORUS	Collective improvisation; cornet, clarinet, and trombone improvising at the same time; two-bar banjo break; tag on end; ensemble break.

Contemporary Jazz

Through the years, the style of playing jazz has undergone many changes. Combinations of instruments and the number of performers vary as much as the styles employed. One of today's important jazz players is Herbie Hancock. While Hancock was trained as a pianist, he now uses not only the conventional piano in his music, but also the electric piano and two different synthesizers.

One of Hancock's initial successes as a composer was "Watermelon Man."[26] The theme of this composition consists of a short melody that imitates the cry of a street vendor calling out "Hey, Watermelon man."

Many Afric rhythms are being utilized in contemporary jazz. In "Watermelon Man," layers of rhythm are stacked one on the other. Each of these patterns contain different syncopations. When these patterns are performed simultaneously, cross-rhythms are set up.

Some of the instruments used in this recording are: hindewhu whistle, pipes, log drum, electric bass, drums, cymbal, marimbula (a kind of thumb piano), electric piano, saxophone, and vocal sounds.

Teaching Strategy Twenty-Six

Objective: To familiarize the students with the sounds of contemporary jazz, including the use of complex rhythms, African instruments, and artificial sound sources (electronic instruments).

1. Have the class listen to the recording "Watermelon Man" while following the listening chart.

LISTENING CHART

Events

1) Rhythm started on Hindewhu Whistle:

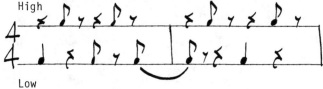

2) Voice added; new rhythm started on Hindewhu:

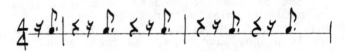

3) New rhythm started on pipes:

4) New rhythm played on log drum:

5) Rhythmic melodic line played on electric bass:

6) Drums and cymbals added

7) Short melodies played on the marimbula:

8) Electric piano and saxophone in call and response pattern

9) Marimbula and saxophone perform together

10) Electric paino and saxophone in call and response pattern

11) Electric piano and saxophone together

12) Marimbula and saxophone perform together

13) Electric piano and saxophone together

14) Electric piano and saxophone continue

15) Marimbula pattern returns

16) Hindewhu whistle enters; vocal sounds; other rhythms as at the beginning; fades out.

2. Using the chart below, compare "Watermelon Man" with "Struttin' With Some Barbecue." Play both recordings again for the class.

Watermelon Man	Struttin' With Some Barbecue
Moderately fast tempo	Fast tempo
Strong beat	Strong beat
Little improvisation	Much improvisation (both solo and collective)
Few instruments	Fewer instruments (five)
Many cross-rhythms	Fewer rhythmic overlaps
Rhythm very important; melody less important	Melody very important; rhythm less important

Summary

American Black music is that great body of music which is rooted in the African musical tradition on one hand, but is not without European influences on the other. Because of circumstances--social, economic, and religious--this music could have happened only in America.

This music is one of the most important forces in the music world today. When one hears music that

367

contains syncopated rhythms, music that uses blue notes, music that is improvised, music that has call and response structures, and music that uses instruments like voices and voices like instruments, more than likely it has its roots in American Black music.

The influence of American Black music has been far-reaching. Not only has it shaped the popular music of this country, but it has also had an effect on the classical idiom as well.

The materials and strategies suggested here are given merely as guides as to how an understanding of the concepts presented may be conveyed to the students of your class. Hopefully,this is merely a beginning.

NOTES FOR CHAPTER 17

1. For listening experiences in African drumming, hear the recording, African Music, Side 2, Band 6, Folkways Records, FW 8852.

2. Although the instruments were destroyed, the activity itself was not. American Black music still contains a percussive quality.

3. "Hambone," The Music of New Orleans, Vol. 1, Samuel Charters, ed., Side 1, Band 8, Folkways Records, FA 2461.

4. The music is available from Summy-Birchard. Available on recording: Natalie Hinderas Play Music by Black Composers, Desto

5. The form of this composition is: A(aa), B(bb), A, C(cc), A(a'a²a), Coda.

6. See James Standifer and Barbara Reeder, pp. 103-114 for additional exeercises which may be used to communicate to the students the concept of syncopation.

7. "Jazz Drumming," African and Afro-American Drums, Harold Courlander, ed., Side IV, Band 23, Ethnic Folkways Library, FE 4502.

8.   See Bert Konowitz, Music Improvisation as a Classroom Method, New York: Alfred Publishing Company, Inc., 1973, for many suggestions for teaching the concept of improvisation.

9.   "I'm Goin' Up North," Negro Folk Music of Alabama-Secular, Vol. 1, Harold Courlander, ed., Band 6, Side 1, Ethnic Folkways Library, FE 4417.

10. "I Must See," Negro Folk Music of Alabama-Ring Game Songs and Others, Vol. VI, Harold Courlander, ed., Side 1, Band 8, Ethnic Folkways Library, FE 4417

11. "Row, Michael, Row," Been In the Storm So Long, Guy Carawan, ed., Side B, Band 3, Folkways Records, FS 3842.

12. As an example of the raucous voice quality, listen to: Ray Charles in Person, Atlantic 8039.

13. An example of falsetto singing can be heard on the recording, The Dramatics, by The Dramatics, ABC Records, ABCD-916.

14. Listen to recording, "Porgy," The Billie Holliday Story, Side 4, Band 3, Decca Records, DL 78930.

15. "Heebie Jeebies," Louis Armstrong Story, Side 1, Band 2, Columbia, CL 851.

16. "Lemon Drop," Ella Fitzgerald: Newport Jazz Festival Live At Carnegie Hall, 1973,   Columbia Records, KG 32557.

17. An excellent record for listening to gospel music as sung by a solo singer and choir is Areatha Franklin's Amazing Grace, Atlantic Records, SD2-906.   Other outstanding performers in the modern gospel song style are: Reverend James Cleveland, Reverend Cleophus Robinson, Andre Crouch, The Beverly Glenn Singers, and the Edwin Hawkins Singers.

18. "Arwhoolie," Negro Work Songs and Calls, B.A. Botkin, ed., Side A, Band 6, Library of Congress, AAFS-L8.

19. "Cornfield   Holler,"   Negro Blues and Hollers, Marshall Stearns, ed., Side A, Band 2, Library of

Congress, AFS-L59.

20. "Poor Man's Blues," The Bessie Smith Story, Side 2, Band 4, Columbia Records, CL 856, Vol. 2.

21. "Bloodshot Eyes," Wynonie Harris, Anthology of Rhythm and Blues, Vol. 1, Side 2, Band 5, Columbia Records, CS 9802.

22. "Soulville," Areatha Franklin, Unforgettable: A Tribute to Dinah Washington, Side 2, Band 5, Columbia, CS 8963.

23. "Walkin' in the Sun," Rags to Rufus, Rufus, Side A, Band 3, ABC Records, ABCX-809.

24. "The Easy Winners," Heliotrope Bouquet, 1900-1970, William Bolcom, piano, Side 1, Band 2, Nonesuch Records, H-71257.

25. "Struttin' With Some Barbecue," The Louis Armstrong Story, Vol. 1, Side 2, Band 1, Columbia Records, CL 851.

26. "Watermelon Man," Headhunters, Herbie Hancock, Side 1, Band 2, Columbia, KC 32731.

Bibliography

Blesh, Rudi and Harriet Janis. They All Played Ragtime. New York: Alfred A. Knopf, 1950.

Courlander, Harold. Negro Folk Music, U.S.A. New York: Columbia University Press, 1963.

Helibut, Toney. The Gospel sound. New York: Simon and Schuster, 1971.

Jones, Leroi. Black Music. New York: William Morrow and Co., 1967.

_____. Blues People. New York: William Morrow and Co., 1963.

Konowitz, Bert. Music Improvisation as a Classroom Method. New York: Alfred Publishing Co., Inc., 1973.

Oliver, Paul. The Story of the Blues. Philadelphia: Chilton Book Co., 1969.

Roberts, John Storm. Black Music of Two Worlds. New York: Praeger Publishers, 197 .

Schuller, Gunther. Early Jazz: Its Roots and Musical Development. New York: Oxford University Press, 1968.

Southern, Eileen. The Music of Black Americans: A History. New York: W.W. Norton and Co., 1971.

Standifer, James A., and Barbara Reeder. Source Book of African and Afro-American Materials for Music Educators. Washington, D.C.: Music Educators National Conference, 1972.

Walton, Ortiz. Black, White & Blue. New York: William Morrow and Company, 197 .

Discography

African Music, Folkways Records, FW 8852.

Anthology of Rhythm and Blues, Vol. 1, Columbia Records, CS 9802.

Armstrong, Louis. The Louis Armstrong Story, Columbia, CL 851, Vol. 1.

Bolcom, William. Helitrope Boquet. Nonesuch Records, H-71257.

Botkin, B.A. (ed.). Negro Work Songs and Calls. Library of Congress, AAFS-L8.

Carawan, Guy. Been In the Storm So Long, Folkways Records, FS 3842.

Charles, Ray. Ray Charles in Person. Atlantic 8039.

Charters, Samuel (ed.).   The Music of New Orleans, Vol. 1, Folkways, FA2461.

Courlander, Harold (ed.).   African and Afro-American Drums. Ethnic Folkways Library, FE 4502.

Courlander, Harold. Negro Folk Music of Alabama.
Secular. Vol. 1. Ethnic Folkways Library FE 4417.

_____. Negro Folk Music of Alabama. Ring
Game songs and Others, Vol. VI, Ethnic Folkways
Library FE 4474.

Dramatics, The Dramatics, ABC Records, ABCD-916.

Fitzgerald, Ella. Newport Jazz Festival, 1973,
Columbia Records, KG32557.

Franklin, Areatha. Amazing Grace. Atlantic Records
SO2-906.

Hancock, Herbie. Headhunters. Columbia KC 32731.

Hinderas, Natalie. Natalie Hinderas Plays Music by
Black Composers. Desto Records, DC-7102/3.

Holliday, Billie. The Billie Holliday Story, Decca
Records, DL 78930.

Rufus. Rags to Rufus. ABC Records, ABC8-809.

Smith, Bessie. Bessie Smith Story. Columbia Records,
CL 856, Vol. 2.

Stearns, Marshall. Negro Blues and Hollers. Library
of Congress, AFS-L59.

Chapter 18

FOSTERING MUSICAL CREATIVITY: IMPLICATIONS

FOR THE URBAN CLASSROOM

Lawrence McClellan, Jr.

INTRODUCTION

Since the beginning of this century, music educators have discussed the importance of creative experiences in the music classroom. In 1903, Calvin Cady[1] claimed the educational value in creative music. His book of compositions by piano students represented over fourteen years of experimentation. Later, Stewart MacPherson[2] suggested that educators give children the opportunity to create their own melodies.

In 1915 Satis Coleman[3] recognized the value of music composition for children. Throughout a number of experiments she taught children music by having them create their own music and construct their own instruments. In 1929 the Music Supervisors National Conference emphasized the place[4] in the curriculum of creative experiences with music. Three decades later, pilot projects conducted in Baltimore, Maryland; San Diego, California; and Farmingdale, New York suggest that Music study through creating provides interest and motivation for children.[5]

Recently, Aston and Paynter designed 36 creative projects in music growing from experiments involving children in primary and secondary schools, as well as students at the university level. Results from the experiments indicate that musical creativity stimulates student interest and involvement in music learning.[6]

Musical creativity is a unique learning activity which involves music listening and performance during the creative act. Creating forces one to learn through self-discovery and free inquiry. Moreover, the learner is able to study and manipulate music materials largely through trial and error. Traditionally, musical creativity refers to improvisation and composition; in addition, these acts are thought to reinforce a

373

learner's understanding of musical structure and notation. The musical creator works with "sound" ideas,
rather than the verbal ideas, and during the
improvisational or compositional process, he synthe-
sizes musical elements in a unique way.

Some psychologists have considered creating as a
simple and natural process with built-in motivating
power.[7]   Creative ways of learning satisfy "human
motives" as the creative process unfolds. Satisfaction
gained from a specific set of responses stimulates
production of additional similar responses.   Such
responses act as reinforcers.[8] Thus, creativity as a
reinforcer supports the notion that it is a motivating
learning experience.

If creating is, in fact, a way of learning that
occurs through self-discovery and free inquiry, it
could be an experience that is rewarding and satisfying
for most students. Alice Miel states that creativity
is present if "the individual has made something new to
himself that is satisfying and in that sense useful to
him, and if the product is 'surprising' (that is, new)
to him."[9] The discovery of an unsuspected ability might
help to produce positive attitudes toward learning and
motivate students to high levels of achievement.

This chapter will focus on some suggested creative
music learning activities and experiences that may be
used in public school music classes and college-level
music courses.

CREATIVE EXPERIENCES

When initiating creative experiences in the music
classroom, the teacher should act only as a guide. It
is important that learners have freedom to create and
perform their own rhythms and melodies. For example,
if students are expected to learn the Dorian mode,
experience in singing, listening to, and even improvising or writing a melody in this mode facilitates their
understanding of its structure.   Similarly, all
important aural concepts need realization through
various experiences such as writing a song using the C
major scale to learn the notes in that scale.

Next, the teacher should provide an environment
for students that is conducive to creativity. Such an
environment is considered as a "responsive environment" by some experts interested in research on

creativity. A "responsive environment" allows students to study, manipulate, and experiment with musical elements individually and in groups. For example, if a group of learners are asked to compose an eight-measure rhythmic composition, they need freedom to arrange different rhythmic patterns without relying solely on the teacher. Here, a teacher can point out the need for phrases, etc., but the final product should represent the student's ideas.

Although a "responsive environment" might help learners develop their innate creative abilities, this type of environment must not be confused with a "laissez-faire environment." A responsive or free environment should be structured for maximum learning. Students can function conscientiously in a "responsive environment" when it is planned and structured with behavioral objectives as shown in Example 8 on Page 384. In the following unit, learners know the kinds of activities they will experience and what they should know at the end of these activities.

Creative musical experiences should begin with the study of simple rhythmic concepts e.g., pulse or time. A device similar to the time line in Example 9 on page 385 may be used to demonstrate the alternation of sounds and silences in time.

Rhythmic concepts might include the ostinato using nonmusical notation. This kind of unit or experience located in Example 10 (page 386) can serve as an introduction to musical notation for beginning music students.

In addition to the ostinato, other compositional devices e.g., augmentation, diminution, and retrograde can be studied through rhythm. For instance, a learner could write an original four-measure rhythmic composition and study retrograde by performing it backwards. In addition, devices e.g., motives, motivic development, or musical phrases may be studied through rhythm. Students can perform rhythmic pieces either by clapping their hands, tapping on desks, or playing simple rhythm instruments normally used in the general music classroom.

The teacher might consider spending plenty of time on rhythm. Knowledge of basic rhythmic concepts is essential before one can engage in a meaningful study of tonality. Melody or pitch usually follows rhythmic

375

study after students have learned musical notation and acquired some basic music reading skills. Likewise, creative musical experiences should follow the same order.

As the teacher explains tonal materials, e.g., scales and intervals theoretically, creative experiences can serve as supplementary class work. Students can learn to improvise and compose melodies using different scales as well as musical form and other compositional devices.

In Examples on the following pages, a number of activities are outlined to supplement study of the pentatonic scale. These activities include improvisation, composition, use of canonic devices, musical form, singing, and use of the ostinato. It is interesting to note that assignments in the following unit consist of two musical compositions based on the pentatonic scale. These compositions require two-voice writing (melody and ostinato) along with the specified instrumentation. Learners can perform the music with simple mallet instruments, rhythm instruments, and/or the piano.

Improvisation

The popularity of rock, soul, country music, jazz, and reggae is increasing and today's youngsters are becoming interested in performing these musical styles. General music teachers especially can help students learn popular music styles by allowing creativity to take place in the classroom. Moreover, teachers can encourage youngsters to develop basic improvisational and compositional skills through the study of music fundamentals.

Music learners can improvise and compose easily at the beginning of their music training. For example, basic rhythmic concepts like the sound (♩) and silence (✗) may be used as a basis for improvisation. Learners can improvise patterns and musical phrases over a simple ostinato as shown below:

Example 1:

Ostinato

Improvisation
Sample

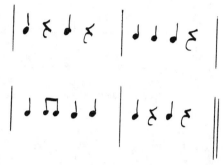

Musical games may be guided by placing students in a circle and teaching them a simple ostinato to play as a group. Afterwards, the instructor can start the improvising with two 8-beat rhythmic phrases (16 beats) and then let each student around the circle take a turn at improvising similar rhythmic phrases.

Tonal improvisation may supplement studies in pitch and notation. Again, the ostinato can be a very effective device to use when guiding activities in improvisation. The simple two-note ostinato located below is usable for improvising on both the pentatonic and major scales.

Example 2:

Learners can begin with improvisations consisting of 2 two-measure phrases similar to those in Example 7 and continue with longer melodies.

Example 3:

Improvisation may take place in a group situation as discussed earlier. Students can play the ostinato as a group with each individual improvising one after another.

Composition

Short rhythmic compositions may follow in the same manner as rhythmic improvisation. The teacher can initiate music composition with non-musical notation as follows: sound (X); silence (O). Learners should be required to write short pieces at the beginning. Four and/or eight-measure compositions are long enough for beginners. Later, most students will be able to write sixteen and thirty-two measure pieces with proper guidance.

A short rhythmic composition written with non-musical notation might consist of two contrasting sections and serve as a study of binary (A-B) form. Example 4 shows a composition in two-part form.

Example 4:

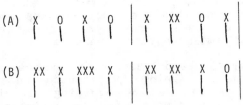

Ostinato:

In the example above, the first measure is used as the ostinato for the entire piece. This same procedure is applicable to compositions written with musical notation as shown in Example 5.

378

Example 6:

Melody:

Ostinato:

Melody:

Ostinato:

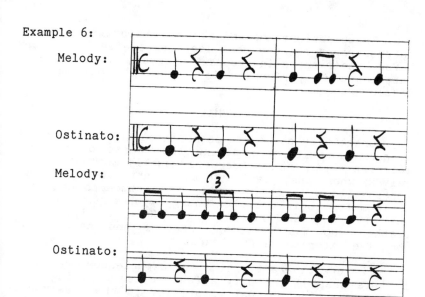

The instructor will discover that numerous musical concepts and compositional devices are teachable through rhythmic composition. As one guides experimentation with melodic writing, many ideas previously covered with rhythmic writing will come to learners quickly as they write melodies. Tonal composition is guided in the same manner as that illustrated with rhythm in Example. For example, students can learn to write single-line melodies and a melody line over an ostinato (See Example 7 on the following page).

Later, students will be able to write longer pieces as they experiment with phrase structure, canonic devices, or musical form. Also, learners should be asked to write their music on blackboards, if available, so that the entire class can read the melody or full score as the composition is being performed.

Example 7:

Melody:

Ostinato:

Group performances of student compositions should be encouraged because most learners prefer to perform before their peers in groups. However, those students interested in performing individually should not be discouraged.

SUMMARY

Creativity can serve as an invaluable aid to both teachers and learners during the course of a music learning experience. Learners usually motivate themselves when they can inject a part of their own personalities in their work. Many students can find outlets for their creative energy with experiences in music writing and improvising. However, it is the teacher who must develop original and challenging creative experiences for learners.

The creative activities and experiences presented in this chapter are only a few samples of things one can do to guide musical creativity in the classroom. Each individual teacher should decide what he or she wants a particular class to experience with music learning. Also, it is suggested that learning experiences be identified, sequenced properly, and cast in the form of behavioral objectives. Most learners tend to excel when they know in advance what is expected of them during and after a learning experience.

IMPLICATIONS

Most students who attend inner-city schools, have natural talent for improvising and performing popular music. This abundance of raw talent deserves to be nurtured and developed in the urban music classroom. Moreover, inner-city youngsters come in contact with improvised and popular music almost daily.

Teachers in the urban music classroom owe their students a chance to develop whatever creative musical talents they may have. Elementary and junior high school general music classes can be the breeding grounds for young improvisers and composers. The foundation must be laid at the elementary and junior high levels. Education in musical creativity should continue at the high school level in music theory and other classes. Compositions and improvisation can be an integral part of weekly lessons in music fundamentals and theory class.

Although the college-level music fundamentals course is not designed for potentially professional musicians, it can serve as a means of stimulating the music lover's appreciation of improvised music and music composition. Therefore, musical creativity should be taught at the college level. The general college student is a potential consumer of music and part of the music educator's job is that of teaching the general public to appreciate music.

The fundamentals of improvisation and composition can be taught at any level (elementary school through college) and the urban music educator should seriously consider teaching musical creativity to inner-city students. Improvised music developed in Urban America and it would indeed be a tragedy in the year 2000 to see the music performed and appreciated more by people from everywhere else except the inner-city.

Example 8:   Text Translation

OBJECTIVES:

At the end of this unit, you should be able to:

1.   Chant word phrases and tap the rhythmic patterns to the syllables of the words.

2.   Aurally identify and notate rhythmic patterns derived from the syllables of the words.

3.   Aurally and visually identify a rhythmic cadence.

A.   Text Translation:

John - ny went to town and came back with a frown

B.   Experiences:

1.   The instructor and class will chant and translates word phrases into rhythmic patterns.

2.   The class will work in groups to translate short texts and perform.

3.   The class will experience, identify, and understand the function of rhythmic cadences through performance.

C.   Assignments:

1.   Take a short text from a metrical poem and translate into rhythmic notation noting rhythmic cadences.

Example 9: Time Line

OBJECTIVES:

At the end of this unit, you should be able to:

1.   Tap a steady beat.

2.   Aurally differentiate between sound and silence within a steady flow of pulse.

3.   Aurally differentiate between steady pulse and variable pulse.

A.   Time Line:

1. Tap a time line with a steady pulse and count the correct number of beats.

2. As the instructor points to each vertical line, recite your name with class in a steady flow of time.

Example 10:   The Ostinato

OBJECTIVES:

At the end of this unit, you should be able to:

1. Write an eight-beat ostinato using sound and silence symbols.

2. Aurally and visually recognize ostinato patterns.

A. The Ostinato (example):

```
X     X    XX    X    '    X    O    XX    X

|     |    [     ]         ]    [    [     [
```

B. Experiences:

1. The class will perform time lines created in Unit II adding Ostinato patterns.

C. Assignments:

1. Write a four-beat ostinato to the sixteen-beat time line composed in UNIT TWO.

2. Write an eight-beat ostinato to the twenty-four beat time composed in UNIT TWO.

Example 11: Pentatonic Scale

OBJECTIVES:

At the end of this unit, you should be able to:

1.   Write a pentatonic scale beginning on any note.

2.   Sing a pentatonic scale using letter names and numbers starting on C, F, G, D and B^b.

3.   Improvise a melody consisting of two similar phrases beginning on any note.

4.   Compose an eight-measure melody using the pentatonic scale. Employ any or all of the following compositional devices: (a) augmentation, diminution, and retrograde.

5.   Aurally/visually identify a short pentatonic melody.

6.   Aurally/visually identify two-part form (e.g., ABAB or AB).

A.   Pentatonic Scale:

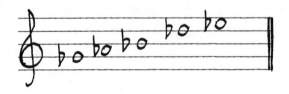

B.   Experiences:

1.   Lay the scale out on the black notes of the piano keyboard (starting on G^b) and study the distance between each note in terms of half and whole steps.

Example: 1   (1)   2   (1)   3   (1 1/2)   4   (1)   5.

2. Construct/write the scale beginning on C, F, G, B♭, and D.

3. Sing the above using letter names and numbers.

4. Play on the piano.

5. Given an ostinato consisting of two scale tones, improvise an eight-measure melody using repetition and contrast.

   a. Improvisaton (Individuals)

   b. Ostinato (Other class members)

C. Assignments:

1. Compose a one or two-measure ostinato, using only two tones from the scale. Organize rhythmic units into a logical configuration.

   a. Write the composed ostinato on the lower staff of a double staff. Repeat it three times for a total of eight measures.

   b. Compose an eight-measure melody over the ostinato:

      1. Givens:

        Meter

        Sound/Silence Symbols

        Pitch - Pentatonic Scale (1 2 3 5 6)

2. Compose a sixteen-measure composition. Use repetition and contrast to create unity and interest:

   a. Givens:

      Meter

    Any Sound Silence Symbols

    Pitch - Pentatonic Scale (1 2 3 5 6)

b. Parameters - according to the above, create a two-part two-voice composition as follows:

Section A - 2 similar phrases (8 bars)
Section B - A contrasting set of 2 similar phrases (8 bars)

Texture

 Voice I composed melody

 Voice II Ostinato (2 scale-tones)

c. Media

 Voice I Voice or Instrument

 Voice II Piano/Mallet Instrument

d. Mode or preparation - written in two treble staves.

DISCUSSION QUESTION

1. Who are some of the music educators responsible for stressing the importance of musical creativity in the music classroom.

2. Why is a "responsive environment" necessary for fostering musical creativity in the classroom?

3. Why is it necessary to develop creative musical experiences with behavioral objectives?

4. When introducting creative musical experiences to learners, what concepts should be stressed initially?

5. What are some of the compositional devices that teachers can introduce to learners through creative musical experiences?

Bibliography of Further Readings

Marksberry, Mary L. Foundation of Creativity. New York: Harper and Row Publishers, 1963.

Reed, H. Owen, and Sidnell, Robert G. The Materials of
Music Composition.   Reading, Mass.:   Addison-Wesley
Publishing Co., 1977.

Torrance, E. Paul.   Encouraging Creativity in the
Classroom. Dubuque, Iowa: William C. Brown Co., 1970.

Torrance, E. Paul. Guiding Creative Talent. Englewood
Cliffs, NJ: Prentice-Hall, Inc, 1963.

Torrance, E. Paul, and Myers, R.E.   Creative Learning
and Teaching. New York: Dodd, Mead and Co., 1970.

NOTES FOR CHAPTER 18

1.   Calvin Cady, Music Education (Chicago: Clayton F.
     Summy Co., 1903).

2.   Stewart   MacPherson,   The Music Education of the
     Child (Boston: The Boston Music Co., 1916), p.
     63.

3.   Satis   N.   Coleman,   Creative Music for Children
     (New York: G.P. Putnam's Sons, 1922).

4.   Journal of Proceedings (Washington, D.C.:   Music
     Supervisors National Conference, 1929), pp. 99,
     271.

5.   Experiments in Musical Creativity (CMP_3) (Wash-
     ington, D.C.: Music Educators National
     Conference, 1968).

6.   John Paynter and Peter Aston, Sounds and Silence
     (Cambridge: The University Press, 1970), p. 9.

7.   E.   Paul   Torrance   and   R.E.   Myers,   Creative
     Creative Learning and Teaching (New York: Dodd),
     Mead and Co., 1970), p. 49.

8.   Henry   C.   Ellis,   Fundamentals of Human Learning
     and Cognition (Dubuque, Iowa: Wm.   C. Brown Co.,
     1961) p. 6.

9.　　Alice Meil, Creativity in Teaching (Belmont, California:　Wadsworth Publishing Co., 1961), p. 6.

BIBLIOGRAPHY

Cady, Calvin B.　Music Education.　Chicago:　Clayton F. Summy Co., 1903.

Coleman, Satis N.　Creative Music for Children.　New York:　G.P. Putnam's Sons, 1922.

Ellis, Henry C.　Fundamentals of Human Learning and Cognition.　Dubuque, Iowa:　Wm. C.　Brown Co., 1972.

Experiments in Musical Creativity (CMP_3).　Washington, D.C.:　Music Educators National Conference, 1966.

Journal of Proceedings.　Washington, D.C.:　Music Supervisors National Conference, 1929.

MacPherson, STewart.　The Music Education of the Child.　Boston:　The Boston Music Co., 1916.

McClellan, Jr., Lawrence.　"The Effect of Creative Experiences on Musical Growth."　Ph.D. dissertation, Michigan State University, 1977.

Meil, Alice.　Creativity in Teaching.　Belmont, California:　Wadsworth Publishing Co., 1961.

Paynter, John, and Aston, Peter.　Sound and Silence. Cambridge, Mass.:　The University Press, 1970.

Torrance, E. Paul, and Myers, R.E.　Creative Learning and Teaching.　New York:　Dodd, Mead and Co., 1970.

Chapter 19

A COMPREHENSIVE APPROACH TO INSTRUMENTAL MUSIC
IN THE
HIGH SCHOOL BAND -- SELECTED STRATEGIES

E. O'HARA SPEARMAN

The concept of comprehensive musicianship is not a term that refers exclusively to the education of student performer-musicians, but also to the receptive uninformed listener, who may or may not be interested in developing his innate musical capabilities. In a society in which young people seem to be looking to the arts for self-expression and in which they are surrounded by multi-media influences, the effect and knowledge of music can be a potent force in their life-styles, leisure activities, and cultural development. The Young Composers Project was one of the most influential and effective catalyst to bring about change in the educative forces of the Music Educators National Conference (MENC).[1] The result of this project led to the formation of the Contemporary Music Project (CMP) of the MENC in 1963. Since its inception, CMP has exerted a tremendous influence on music curricula and music pedagogy in an attempt to meet the needs of a changing society and to improve and broaden the concept of music education. The impact of CMP has permeated various levels of music pedagogy, and the effectiveness of its psychological and philosophical implications did result in the development of comprehensive music curricula such as the Hawaii Comprehensive Music Series.

The comprehensive approach makes an attempt to synthesize and correlate diverse facets of music history, music literature, theory, and performance pedagogy into a unified whole. It is an attempt on the part of curriculum planners and music teachers to pursue and explore the ultimate range of music in its complex dimensions and interrelationships, rather than the memorization of historical events. Those who view CMP as serving only the needs and interests of twentieth century practices should be made aware of the fact that CMP's commitment is toward the total develop

ment of music comprehension and includes the above as
well as music of various ethnic groups and periods. By
analyzing music through its common elements, students
can gain awareness and comprehension of the elements
that are present in the music of any culture, tradition, period, or style.

The following outline of the nature of music can
be used in organizing a sequence of comprehensive
musicianship:

1.   Music is sound.

2.   Sound exists in time and space,
and its elements are:
      Frequency (Pitch)
      Intensity (Loudness)
      Duration
      Timbre

3.   The organization and interaction
      of these elements produce music.

      Horizontal Organization
      Movement through time--a separa-
      tion on into units or the genera-
      tion of a sense of continuous
      time.
      Rhythm
      The division of duration of sound
      and silence into long or short,
      regular or irregular groupings.
      Melody
      The interaction of rhythms and
      frequencies.   Frequencies are
      heard as white sounds; registral
      sounds (sounds   of   indefinite
      pitches); single pitches. A range
      of frequencies can be used in a
      continuous manner (sweeps) or be
      divided into units (scales).
      Vertical Organization
      How many simultaneous sounds.
      Texture
      Qualities of the density of simul-
      taneous sounds or the accumulation
      of individual lines.
      Expressive Qualities
      Intensity   (volume,   dynamics)--
      energy that gives sound   its
      qualities of loudness, from very

390

soft to very loud. Intensity can
involve both abrupt and continuous
changes and can be used for such
aesthetic effects as climaxes or
surprises.
Timbre
The color or tone qualities of
music derived from such sources as
voices, band and orchestral instruments, synthesizers, non-western instruments, and "non-musical" sources.

4. Form or structure is the shape
    that results from the organization
    of these elements.

5. Context in the consideration of
    music.
    Historically
    Socially
    Aesthetically[3]

At present, some music educators feel that the
comprehensive approach to the study and teaching of
music pedagogy is probably the most effective and
efficient concept to emerge in the field of music
education during the twentieth century.

A review of comprehensive curricula indicates
that various psychological and philosophical concepts
are inherent in structural sequences of various musical
strategies and serve as the foundation of such curricula as the Manhattanville and Hawaii Comprehensive
Music Curriculums.

David Willoughby, former Administrative Chairman
of CMP (1970-1973), clarified in a concise and
informative manner the present and future objectives of
CMP in the following outline. Willoughby stated:

1. Comprehensive musicianship empha-
    sizes the concept of humaneness in
    teaching. The purpose and respon
    sibility of music educators is to
    be sensitive to the human
    condition and to develop in
    students an aesthetic awareness,
    creativity, and skill which can
    serve him in contemporary society.

2. Comprehensive musicianship emphasizes long term objectives and an approach to learning which emphasizes conceptualization of structural principles inherently part of each discipline.

3. Comprehensive musicianship is an approach to music teaching and learning which draws from many learning theories. Gestalt psychology as applied to music learning approaches music as a totality through a process of discovering relationships of constitutent elements which contribute to an understanding of the whole.

4. The behaviorist/associationist theory of learning emphasizing memorization of facts, rote learning, drill for attainment of musical skills, and programmed instruction are recognized as valid strategies only if they are employed within the broader framework of contributing to musical understanding.

5. The essence of comprehensive musicianship is based on the belief that music is a discipline and an art form founded on essential issues, concepts, and principles which remain unchanged at all levels of maturity. From the CMP perspective, all musics, regardless of cultural, ethnic, or style period backgrounds have commonalities (and differences) which can be perceived and conceptualized at a level of understanding. The common elements approach, then, is a framework of fundamental principles though which a developmental curriculum can be built to provide sequential learning experiences which can lead to music under standing and music sensitivity.

392

6. Comprehensive musicianship
   suggests that the content of the
   music curriculum should include
   the study of all musics represent
   ing many cultures, style period,
   and ethnic origins.[4]

A DESCRIPTIVE ANALYSIS OF SELECTED INSTRUMENTAL
MUSIC WORKS AND TEACHING STRATEGIES

In this chapter, the author will discuss two in
strumental works. The selections were chosen for their
historical, structural, and stylistic features; and
the dimensions of these works are used to develop
strategies through which musical knowledge can be
attained. This knowledge involves general information
about the composers, the musical forms, and the structural elements which appear to be most evident in
each selection.

The material affords a wide range of musical
experiences for high school students in instrumental
music programs to explore as their musical perception
broadens. Simply stated, the musical examples were
chosen because of their inherent musical qualities,
potential student interest and availability, and
because the content lends itself to the teaching of
musical dimensions used in music(s) of certain styles
and periods.

The strategies following the analytical descriptions do not exhaust the numerous possiblities which
can be contrived to develop a more in-depth knowledge
of music on the secondary level, but this method is one
approach that can be used in the development of comprehensive musicianship. It should be made explicit that
the commitment on the part of teachers, students, and
school administrators is essential for the implementation and success of an innovative curriculum which
attempts to revise traditional expectations by means of
an untraditional curriculum. The strategies in this
study will allow students to further their music
education in a manner commensurate with their
individual capabilities, and as their readiness levels
develop hopefully their ability to perceive concepts of
a more complex nature will emerge. It is for these
reasons that the departure from tradition has been
made.

Some of the dimensions will be discussed within the content of the analysis and others will be discussed under the section "Dimensions As They Relate" to a selected piece. It should become apparent why different approaches are necessary in describing different musical works. The diversity of the selections is such that the teacher can assign different instrumental groups, i.e., large ensembles, brass, woodwind, and percussion ensembles, different sections to work on simultaneously or separately.

Somersault, A Twelve Tone Composition for Concert Band

By Hale Smith.   Published by Frank Music Corporation, New York, N.Y. 1974.

Somersault, composed for concert band in 1964 by Hale Smith, an American Black composer, is one of several band compositions employing the principles of twelve tone techniques. Smith was born in Cleveland, Ohio, on June 29, 1925, and his formative training in piano was with Margaret Heller. In January 1946, Smith enrolled at the Cleveland Institute of Music where he studied theory with Ward Lewis and music composition with Marcel Dick. After completing his B.M. degree in 1950 and the M.M. degree in music composition in 1952, Smith moved to New York City to further his music career as a composer and where he became an advisor to several renowned musicians and instrumental groups. Also, Smith became editor for the Frank Music Corporation. In addition to Somersault, Smith composed Expansions, which was commissioned for the concert band at Southern Illinois University in Edwardsville in 1967 and published by E.B. Marks Music Corporation. Trinal Dance, an elementary band selection, was published by Duchess Music (M C A) in 1968. The two works commissioned by Frank Music Corporation are Somersault (1964) and Take a Chance (1965), an aleatory composition (aleatory refers to chance music and is based on the Latin word alea which means dice).

General Information about the Twelve Tone Method

The twelve tone method is credited to Arnold Schoenberg (1874-1951), who, perhaps most than any other twentieth century composer, devised a system of compositional techniques which rejected the traditional principles of tonal organization. The purpose is described to be that of:

> . . . liberating the twelve tones of
> the chromatic scale from the diatonic
> functional association they still re-
> tain in chromatic music--to dissociate,
> so to speak, the chromatic scale from
> chromaticism.[5]

The method became the modus operandi for a succession
of musical works by composers such as Alban Berg (1885-
1935), Anton Webern (1883-1945), Roger Sessions
(1896), Luigi Dallapiccola (1904), and in a highly
modified version in the latter stages of his music
career, Igor Stravinsky (1882-1971). These composers
and others devised techniques and methods which made a
tremendous impact on the future course of twentieth
century music, both tonally and aesthetically.[6]

Although classical twelve tone music implies the
use of all twelve tones of the chromatic scale in some
manner, some composers have departed from this rather
rigid practice. One example is an eight-note series
found in Full Fathom Five, in Three Songs from William
Shakespeare, By Igor Stravinsky. Other composers used
various combinations of tones from the possible twelve
which in one sense is a departure from the strict order
of the early twelve tone method. In addition, the rule
concerning the repetition of tones before the original
row is expressed was often ignored, e.g., Wallingford
Riegger and Luigi Dallapiccola.

A few of the rules that governed the classical use
of the twelve tone method are as follows:

1. The set comprises all twelve tones
   of the semitonal scale, arranged
   in a specific linear order.

2. No note appears more than once
   within a set.

3. The set is statable in any of its
   linear aspects: prime, inversion,
   retrograde, and retrograde
   inversion.

4. The set in each of its transformations (that is, linear
   aspects) is statable upon any
   degree of the semitonal scale.[7]

395

A Descriptive Analysis of Somersault

Somersault, composed for concert band in 1964 by Hale Smith, is one of several band compositions employing the principles of twelve tone techniques. The original tone row and its transformations total forty-eight transpositions, twelve in each of its four versions as follows:

1.   Original twelve tone row (0)
       G, Ab, C, Bb, F, D, C#, A, B, F#, E.

2.   Inversion of the original tone row (I)
       G, F#, D, E, B, A, C, C#, F, Eb, Ab, Bb.

3.   Retrograde of the original tone row (R)
       E, F#, B, A, C#, D, F, Eb, Bb, C, Ab, G.

4.   Retrograde inversion of the original tone
       row (R.I.) Bb, Ab, Eb, F, C#, C, A, B, E, D, F#, G.

The numbers which appear vertically and horizontally represent the number of half steps between each interval. It is also possible to simply number each member of the row consecutively from 0 to 11 or from 1 to 12. In the pitch matrix the intervals are numbered from 0 to 11.

Figure 1

Casey: Pitch Matrix--Hale Smith: Somersault

(O)---------------   ---------------(R)

	0	1	5	3	8	10	7	6	2	4	11	9
0	G	Ab	C	Bb	Eb	F	D	C#	A	B	F#	E
11	F#	G	B	A	D	E	C#	C	Ab	Bb	F	Eb
7	D	Eb	G	F	Bb	C	A	Ab	E	F#	C#	B
9	E	F	A	G	C	D	B	Bb	F#	Ab	Eb	C#
4	B	C	E	D	G	A	F#	F	C#	Eb	Bb	Ab
2	A	Bb	D	C	F	G	E	Eb	B	C#	Ab	F#
5	C	C#	F	Eb	Ab	Bb	G	F#	D	E	B	A
6	C#	D	F#	E	A	B	Ab	G	Eb	F	C	Bb
10	F	F#	Bb	Ab	C#	Eb	C	B	G	A	E	D
8	Eb	E	Ab	F#	B	C#	Bb	A	F	G	D	C
1	Ab	A	C#	B	E	F#	Eb	D	Bb	C	G	F
3	Bb	B	Eb	C#	F#	Ab	F	E	C	D	A	G

[14]

(R.I.)

Somersault is divided into four sections. The first section is in $\frac{4}{4}$ and $\frac{3}{4}$ meters with a metronome marking of ♩ = 92-96 (allegro moderator), measures one to fifteen.

In section two, the meters employed are $\frac{6}{8}$ and $\frac{4}{4}$ with a rhythmic instruction that the dotted quarter should equal the quarter note in section one (measures sixteen through fifty-two).

Section three of Somersault in in $\frac{4}{4}$ meter with a metronome marking of ♩ = ca. 84 (poco meno mosso), and includes measures fifty-three to eighty-four. Between the third and fourth sections of Somersault, there is a brief six-measure transitional section (measures eighty-five to ninety) which leads to the coda or fourth section. The concluding section is in $\frac{6}{8}$ meter with a metronome marking of ♩ = 92-96.

Section 1 (bars 1-15). Somersault is scored for full concert band and opens with the melody utilizing the original row stated by the flutes and clarinets in unison. The row stated by the flutes and clarinets in unison. The row is divided into two segments with the second segment having the same order of pitch intervals as the first segment in inversion.

Example 1

Smith: Somersault

INVERSION

The intervallic arrangement of the original row appears to favor the use of major and minor seconds, thirds, fourths, and fifths, but in measure four, third beat, the second hexachord (last six tones of the row) of the prime set or row is stated by the flutes, oboes, and clarinets in unison beginning on concert D, a fifth above⁻ the first note of the row, and ending on E, a minor seventh below. Smith does not employ the full instrumentation of the band in the beginning section, but tends to augment the instrumentation as the music evolves. Below the melody in measure three, the trombones and French horns state a dissonant triad which consists of Eb, G, and Ab.

Although the original row is treated serially, the effect is not unusually dissonant, which is the result of the row, the permutations of the row, and the intervallic relationships of tones and rhythmic simplicity in which the row is initially presented. The rhythmic arrangement of the original set starts with an eighth-note figure and is followed by simple eighth-note, quarter-note, half- and whole-note patterns in the upper voices and terse dissonant harmonies in the supporting French horns and trombones.

The percussion instruments are used sparingly in the first section, but establish the following motive takes on a more vital role as the piece develops.

The first section of Somersault (mm. 1-16) is conservative in its use of melodic and rhythmic materials by avoiding the extreme registers of the instruments, numerous accents, dynamics, and pitch intervals which would impose serious technical problems for high school students. Perhaps the most arduous task would be to make the students aware of the fact that the entire first section was developed from the linear arrangement and transpositions of the row introduced by the flutes and clarinets in the opening three and a half measures.

Section 2 (mm. 16-44). The second section of Somersault is in $\frac{6}{8}$ meter and begins at rehearsal mark 1 with a retrograde transposition (R.O.2. 5th level of the transposition) of the original row in measure sixteen. The ordering of the complete retrograde transposition consists of the following pitch intervals: F#, Ab, C#, B, Eb, E, G, F, C, D, and Bb.

A technique Smith appears to favor throughout the development of this section is to begin a new musical idea with the last note of the previous row which results in a kind of overlapping of row transpositions. This device can be observed in the following example in which the E concert in the second and fourth French horn parts is the last note of the preceding row, and the F# concert in the first and third French horns is the first note of the retrograde (R.2.) transposition. This technique is not new, but it is worthwhile mentioning to acquaint student musicians with some of the compositional techniques Smith and other composers use in this genre.

Between measures eighteen and twenty, a retrograde inversion (R.I.2.) is stated by the cornets and trumpets for the first six tones and by the trombones, cornets, trumpets, and oboes for the last six tones of the row. The row (R.I.2.) includes the following pitches: C, Bb, F, G, Eb, D, B, C#, F#, E, Ab, A.

In measure twenty-one, the texture of the music becomes thicker due to the full complement of the band, dissonant harmonies, repeated syncopated rhythms, frequent textural gradations, and timbral contrasts which are derived from alternating groups of brass and woodwind instruments. The tone row expressed in measure twenty-one is a retrograde (R.O.3.) of the original row. The initial five notes of the row appear in blocked chords (see measure twenty-one) and the remaining seven notes are contained in a descending trumpet passage which commences in measure twenty-three and ends in measure twenty-four.

Beginning at measure twenty-seven, the oboes, clarinets, and glockenspiel are assigned five notes of the retrograde (R.O.2.) transposition in a fast eighth-note passage above an ascending chord pattern in the lower brasses and woodwinds which employs the tones of F#, G, and F. They are apparently randomly selected pitches from the retrograde (R.2.) tone row.

Between measures thirty-two and fifty-two, Smith achieves various levels of intensity by manipulating a series of dynamic graduations, dissonant harmonies which alternate between various groups of instruments, syncopated figures in the brasses, unison passages in the woodwinds, and restrained, but appropriate, activity in the percussion instruments to enhance the dynamic and timbral qualities of the music. However, in measure forty-two, three notes of the original row are played by the baritone horn and trombones and later by the French horns before developing into an ascending and descending eighth-note passage. Smith specifies the exact number of players to be assigned to each part (see measures forty-nine and fifty, rehearsal mark C).

Section 3 (mm. 53-84). The third section of Somersault is marked poco meno mosso (♩ = ca. 84) and opens with a permutation of the initial series in syncopated chords which consist of the odd numbers of the row

1	3	5	7	9	11
Ab,	Bb,	F,	C#,	B,	E

in the brasses and lower woodwinds and the even numbers

0	2	4	6	8	10
G,	C,	Eb,	D,	A,	F#

in the upper woodwinds.

It is interesting to note that the rhythmic pattern which was first introduced in measures thirteen, fourteen, and fifteen in the percussion section is now used as the garminating element in this rather explosive section, and features such techniques as wide intervals in the upper voices, diminution, permutations of row tones, and the repetition of dissonant block chords in contrasting rhythmic figures. In the seventy-fourth measure of rehearsal mark D, the texture is decreased in density and continues to rrehearsal mark E (measure seventy-nine) where the flutes, oboes, and Bb clarinets play the last seven notes of the row almost serially in an imitative passage.

Transition Section (mm. 85-90). The transition section features a pedal point (F# concert) starting in measures eighty-six in the first French horn. Above the F# pedal point, the first and second clarinets introduce a passage which consists of successive seconds and sevenths between the two parts. The texture in the transition section is comparatively thin when compared with some of the preceding material which utilizes larger groups of instruments. However, the transition material is perhaps more dissonant due to the use of seconds and sevenths in the upper voices and the elimination of percussion parts which have a tendency to mask the timbral and textural qualities of music.

Coda. The concluding section of Somersault commences at measure ninety-one, rehearsal mark G, with a retrograde (R.O.1.) transposition of alternating passages between groups of brass and woodwinds in unison to measure ninety-three. Increasing levels of loudness occur more frequently in this section as well as fast recurrences of short imitative passages, swift harmonic changes, an occasional tritone, and the use of the high registers by the woodwinds.

In measure ninety-three of the coda a retrograde inversion (R.I.1.) is employed which leads to measure ninety-five where the first hexachord of the (0.6) series is stated and followed by the first hexachord of the (0.1) series in strident syncopated blocked chords beginning in measure ninety-seven. The syncopated chords emphasized in measures ninety-seven, 103, 108, and 110 are separated by angular horizontal lines in the woodwinds and upper brasses. The reiteration of initial material at this point indicates that the piece is rapidly coming to a close after what appeared to be a certain amount of indecision.

Beginning in measure 104, Smith achieves brilliant timbres of juxtaposing various permutations of the (R.O.2.) series above a sustained F# pedal tone in pyramid style which resolves into a terse dissonant chord in measure 108. The piece concludes with repeated chords in various $\frac{6}{8}$ rhythmic figures accompanied by propulsive rhythmic activity in the percussion parts in measure 114.

Conclusion

Somersault was written for the purpose of introducing young instrumental students to some of the basic concepts and compositional devices employed in twelve tone music. It was an attempt on the part of the composer to bring to the rehearsal period explanations and examples of the materials used in this genre, and a series of listening, theoretical, and performance activities which would lead to a better perception and knowledge of certain techniques composers have used in serial composition. The composer has indicated in the score and the parts the transpositions which are used in various sections of the piece and the instruments assigned the most prominent parts. Thus, Somersault is an important piece for high school bands because it is one of the few serial pieces written for the specific purpose of developing in high school students an understanding of some of the basic principles of the twelve tone method.

The author is aware of the fact that most high school instrumental music teachers are limited in the amount of time they can afford during the regular class period to devote to the instruction of twelve tone techniques, but informed musicians are of the opinion that a good musician knows about many kinds of music, periods, styles, and, as a result, tends to be quite cosmopolitan. This implies, of course, that he can appreciate and understand music of different cultures as well as contemporary idioms.

Twelve tone music is an extension of the musics which evolved in past centuries; and since we are products of the twentieth century and charged with the responsibility of preparing students to become more receptive, more knowledgeable and appreciative of diverse kinds of music, it is our responsibility to inform students that twelve tone music is an extension and important part of the total music learning process. And like any other art form, music is subject to change philosophically and tonally to meet the needs of man and his society.

There is a tendency for some uninformed musicians to dislike certain kinds of contemporary music simply because it sounds strange and makes them a little hostile because they suspect that they are being hoaxed by some charlatan (occasionally they may be right), but the important point to be made is that there are many different ways that music can function in different societies and the good musician, while he may not appreciate all of the music he hears, will attempt to understand the music he hears and place each in its proper frame of reference.

Dimensions

Pitch. The pitch intervals in Somersault are selected from the various transpositions (forty-eight) of the original tone row, and the music is developed from various linear and horizontal arrangements of its row formations. Each pitch interval is given equal importance without subservience to a tonal center, and each row can be used to enhance the continuity, structure, and progression of the music.

Rhythm. Rhythm is an important dimension in all music, but is perhaps more of a germinating element in twelve tone music. The swift harmonic changes which occur through the manipulation of row-forms necessitate the use of rhythm as a unifying element in the development of contrasting musical phrases and ideas.

Texture. The texture in Somersault varies between thin and dense textures depending on the number of voice parts or musical lines presented in various sections and parts of the music; e.g., in the first two measures (see Example 64) the clarinets and flutes introduce a unison passage which employs eleven tones of the initial row. Obviously, this short passage would be called monophonic because only one line is featured. In measures three and four the French horns and trombones thicken the texture by providing a supportive harmony for flutes, clarinets, and oboes in a passage which features the last sic notres of the initial row. The above thematic and harmonic arrangement of musical lines or voice parts can be called an example of homophony.

At letter D, measures 53-64, there is an example of polyphony which infers the simultaneous interaction and equality of several musical lines. Texture is determined to a degree by the timbre of the sound-producing medium and is an important factor in the hierarchy of musical dimensions.

Form. Somersault is divided into four sections with a six-measure transition occurring between the third and fourth sections. The form of each section is not traditional but appears to possess its own internal logic. The sections achieve contrast between themselves through changing meters, smooth voice-leading in the upper parts, and a limited use of complex rhythmic patterns and virtuoso passages in the instrumental parts.

Student Objectives

After experiencing various encounters with some of the basic serial devices employed in the writing of Somersault, the student should be able to:

1. Show evidence of having achieved a better knowledge of terms such as the original tone row, inversion, retrograde, and retrograde inversion.

2. Show evidence of understanding how pitch intervals of different row formations are transposed for different groups of brass and woodwind instruments and how they are used to extend the length of a musical work.

3. Identify aurally the different textures and timbres which emanate from mixed and homogeneous groups of instruments.

4. Differentiate between linear unison passages and harmonic passages.

5. Develop an awareness of changing meters, dynamics, symmetry, and compositional techniques such as augmentation and diminution.

6. Show evidence of the ability to identify in other music similar serial devices.

7. Perform the music in Somersault with greater perception, proficiency, and comprehension.

8. Develop an interest in or at least tolerance for music of this genre.

Teaching Materials

1. Music pads and pencils.

2. Individual band parts and overlay tranparencies of selected measures from the score.

405

3.   Record player and recording equipment.

4.   12 x 12 matrix sheets.

5.   Blackboard, chalk, and erasers.

Teaching Strategies

1.   In order to develop an understanding of row transpositions, it is necessary for the band director to spend a portion of several band rehearsal periods demonstrating and explaining brass and woodwind transpositions. The students will be expected to master the transposition of their own instrument and then the transpositions of Eb, Bb, and F instruments. (This, of course, assumes that the student possesses an understanding of treble clef and bass clef notation.) They will then proceed to transpose the original tone row of Somersault from any of the three keys mentioned to concert pitch and vice versa. One of the important skills a student needs to develop during his or her musical development is the ability to transpose pitch intervals for various groups of instruments because this skill is essential for participation in performing groups and especially when there is some doubt as the the accuracy of the original concert pitch in serial compositions.

2.   Distribute a copy of the 12 x 12 matrix to each student and review the 12 x 12 matrix.

3.   For those students who are interested in writing a short twelve tone piece, assist them in a piece which employs the use of the original tone row, the inversion, the retrograde, and retrograde inversion.

4.   After the student has completed a short twelve tone piece, have him score the piece for a brass or woodwind ensemble with percussion parts.

5.   For those students who encounter difficulty learning the transpositions of various instruments, make a chart showing the transpositions and the corresponding concert pitches for Eb, Bb, and F instruments. At a later time, explain why the instruments sound higher or lower than the concert pitches.

6.   Assign several students the responsibility of making reports on other band selections which use the twelve tone system.[15]

7.   It is possible for some reader to question the value of having high school students attempt to learn the basic rules of the twelve tone music. Perhaps the answer lies in the importance of students' knowing something about the music of the twentieth century and the musicians who have made and are making contributions in this idiom. Also, an understanding of the twelve tone method will be of great significance for those students who elect to pursue a music career on the college or university levels.

Consummation

By Thad Jones

General Information about the Composer

Thad Jones is recognized by professional musicians in the jazz field as one of the outstanding composers, arrangers, and co-leaders of contemporary big bands. He is perhaps best known in music circles for his imaginative solos on Count Basie's recording of April in Paris. Even though Jones has arranged and composed a large number of selections for Count Basie, Harry James, and other musical groups, it was not until Thad Jones and Mel Lewis combined their musical talents in 1965 to form the dynamic Thad Jones-Mel Lewis big band that his recognition as a composer became internationally established.[18] This is not meant to imply that he was not recognized by his contemporaries for his skill and creativity, but it so happens that few band members achieve the recognition or status of band leaders.

Instrumentation

The instrumentation of most stage band arrangements consists of the following: 5 saxophones, 4 trumpets, 4 trombones, and a rhythm section consisting of a piano, bass, guitar, and drums.   In some instances, an electric piano along with amplified bass, guitar, and drums, are substituted for more conventional instruments.

In Consummation, the music is scored for first Eb alto saxophone doubling on flute, second Eb alto saxophone doubling on Bb clarinet, first and second Bb tenor saxophones doubling on clarinets, and the Eb baritone saxophone doubling on bass clarinet. The brass instrumentation calls for Bb flugelhorn, 4 Bb trumpets, 4 trombones, 4 French horns, and tuba. The rhythm section employs the usual complement of piano, bass, guitar, and drums.

An interesting feature of the instrumentation in this selection is the use of reed parts that require each player to double on another instrument and the use of French horns, flugelhorn, and tuba. Although doubling on a second or third instrument is common among professional musicians, it could pose a serious problem for high school musicians. A solution to the doubling problem can be resolved by bringing in the necessary players from the regular school band to perform parts not effectively played by the stage band members. Also, it is strongly recommended that band directors encourage high school reed players to study more than one instrument if they plan to pursue a career in music education or compete for jobs in the professional market.

Descriptive Analysis of Consummation

Consummation opens with a four-measure introduction that features a choir of muted French horns, tuba, and rhythm section. The metronome marking is ♩ = 60 for the first two measures and ♩ = 66 for the remainder of the piece.

After the introduction, a solo theme is introduced by the flugelhorn at rehearsal mark A, measure five, with accompaniment played by the French horns and tuba but later reinforced with woodwinds in unison and trombones in bucket mutes. The use of muted brasses is a favorite practice of big band arrangers and in this instance is appropriate because mutes modify the volume of the brass instruments and create soft textured harmonic lines to accompany the expressive flugelhorn solo.

Example 2

Jones: Consummation, mm. 1-7

During the early part of the twentieth century, the flugelhorn was included as part of the standard military band instrumentation, but for some reason it lost its popularity. In recent years jazz musicians have revived the popularity of the flugelhorn and it is not uncommon to find a considerable number of high school students studying the flugelhorn as a second instrument. The tonal quality of this instrument is less piercing than the trumpet and it has a soft melodic sound which often is the ideal instrument to play in small commercial rooms.

At rehearsal mark B, the solo theme continues in a modified version of the material stated at rehearsal mark A, but with the reeds in harmony rather than unison. The reed players are assigned flute, clarinet, and bass clarinet parts to vary the timbre, texture, and to enhance the musical interest of the supportive parts.

Beginning at rehearsal mark C, or what is commonly called the bridge or channel in jazz selections, the French horns are assigned the melody to create an effective change in the timbre of the melody and to heighten its intensity above supportive lines in the trombones and rhythm section.[20] A short dialogue occurs between the french horns and flugelhorn between measures twenty-one and twenty-five but eventually gives way to an imitative figure played by the trumpets and French horns in measures twenty-six and twenty-seven.

Throughout rehearsal mark C the trumpets are less consequential, but become more prominent as the music reaches higher levels of volume and textural density. Beginning at rehearsal mark D, we can observe the use of extreme high registers in the trumpet and trombone parts along with lip slurs, shakes, sixteenth note patterns, syncopated rhythms, terse harmonies in the French horns and trombones, and a greater use of dynamics in the percussion section. It may be of interest for the reader to know that in most large band arrangements, the full band ensemble is brought into play in the final chorus of the piece. In Consummation, the full ensemble appears at rehearsal mark D, or the last eight measures of the first chorus.

An interesting feature in the structural scheme of Consummation is the use of a four-measure interlude which appears after the first chorus (mm. 37-40) to set the mood for a piano solo commencing at rehearsal mark F, measure forty-one. Interludes vary between four and eight measures and are employed to break the monotony of a rather rigid harmonic sequence, to create interest, and to achieve a degree of asymmetry between different sections of the music.

Example 3

Jones: Consummation, mm. 29-35

The second chorus (rehearsal mark F) is a harmonic
repetition of the first chorus featuring a piano solo
with drum, guitar, and bass viol accompaniment. The
practice of reducing the size of the ensemble to three
or four instruments is comparable to techniques used in
the Baroque concerto grosso. Although it is not
certain that the composer was concerned with Baroque
practices, it is not uncommon to find works in the jazz
idiom which utilize the concept of tutti versus
concertino. In all probability, the composer was perhaps more interested in textural contrast, timbre, and
dynamics. However, the use of the harmonies expressed
in the measures of the piano part are comparable to the
figured bass system employed in secular and sacred
Baroque music.

Example 4

Jones: Consummation, mm. 36-42

At rehearsal mark G, the piano solo is accompanied by a choir of saxophones and rhythm instruments. The background of the saxophones is of a dance-like character for three measures (mm. 49-51) and then moves to a rather pensive mood where a series of seventh chords are used to effect different levels of contemplative timbral and harmonic embellishments.

In measure fifty-five of rehearsal mark G, the tuba, combined with trombones, French horns, and trumpets, provides an atmosphere of intensity from a variety of syncopated rhythms and dissonance harmonies. The music in this section (mm. 55-64) prepares for the recurrence (Dal segno al Coda) of the tutti material introduced at rehearsal mark D. The trumpets are assigned harmon mutes and the trombones cup mutes for tonal diversity. They are removed in measure fifty-nine so that the players can have sufficient time to prepare for full force of the ensemble. After the Dal segno, a coda is used to conclude the piece in a quiet manner with the French horns reiterating an altered version of the thematic material introduced at rehearsal mark C.

Dimensions as They Relate to Consummation

Pitch. The pitch intervals of the melodic lines are basically diatonic with rapid changing harmonic progressions in the supporting voices. Dissonant intervals result from the linear movement of the voices and the use of sequential dominant seventh chords within the tonic key.

Timbre. The timbre of Consummation is interesting because of the use of various woodwind and brass instruments such as flutes, clarinets, French horns, and tuba. The use of brass and woodwinds other than the traditional saxophones, trumpets, and trombones adds a timbral quality quite different from the regular popular band instrumentation.

Example 5

Jones: Consummation, mm. 58-64

Rhythm. The rhythm in stage band pieces is the most prominent feature because of its continuous and repetitious pulsation within a given metronome marking. Musical interest is achieved within a metronome marking by the juxtaposition of various musical ideas above a rhythmic scheme which usually begins and ends in the same tempo. However, some musicians argue that the tempo varies according to the dictates of the music, which, in the opinion of the writer, is true, but tempo for the most part is determined by the intent of the composer or arranger. If the piece is written for dancing, the tempo does not vary too much from the original tempo; but if the selection is performed for listening, e.g., a concert, the piece may well be played at a faster tempo and with more tempo changes.

Example 6

Jones: Consummation, mm. 65-70

Texture. In most stage band selections, the texture is usually thick because of the ever-present rhythm section and because most melodic ideas are accompanied by woodwind, brass, or a combination of both. Also, since the number of instruments is quite large and since the parts are written for four or five different instruments in each choir, the texture tends to be thick.

Form. The form of Consummation is framed in an A B A scheme with coda.

Student Objectives

After a variety of experiences with some of the basic devices employed in the performance of Consummation, the student should be able to:

1. Show evidence of having achieved a greater appreciation for the skill and technique required to peform in a stage band ensemble.

2. Show evidence of having developed an awareness of the stylistic and rhythmic configurations used in the writing and performance of jazz pieces.

3. Differentiate aurally between muted timbre and open or unmuted timbre used by brass players in various sections of Consummation.

4. Become aware of the need to develop proficiency on more than one reed instrument.

5. Be able to identify sections in Consummation that employ embellishments such as the shake, the smear, and the glissando.

6. Develop an interest in theory by learning to improvise on various harmonic progressions used in the jazz idiom.

Materials for Classroom Instruction

1. Individual band parts and overlay transparencies of selected passages from the score.

2. Music pads and pencils.

415

3. Record player and a recording of Consummation.

4. Blackboard, chalk, and erasers.

5. Recordings of other big band selections, such as Ellington's The Best of Duke and Count Basie's The Chairman of the Board.

Teaching Strategies

1. Play a recording of Consummation and have the students listen to the embellishments and stylistic traits of the music and determine if the melody is played as written or altered by the flugel horn player.

2. Rehearse the entire piece several times and call attention to dynamics, rhythm, texture, timbre, and form.

3. Ask them to improvise on the harmonic progressions of Consummation and decide if the composers uses the same harmonic progressions in each chorus of the piece.

4. After several rehearsals, ask the students to identify the measures in which the texture is homophonic as opposed to those which are polyphonic.

5. Ask the students to identify the element that has the strongest effect on the character of the piece. Also, identify some of the dynamics used to intensify the effect of the music at rehearsal mark C.

Conclusion

Since the late 1950's there have been serious accusations by some music educators that the instrumental music programs on the secondary level are chiefly public relations devices for the school and community. They complain that the music performed is trivial and selected for entertainment rather than educational values. They complain that too much time is spent on fund raising projects, after school rehearsals, and public activities. They complain that the instrumental music program is too expensive and that most students seldom, if ever, play their instruments after graduating from high school.

Perhaps most of these accusations are true, but the same thing is being said about certain other areas in public education; e.g., most students do not develop reading and writing skills during their formative years in school.

For these reasons and others, the author has made an attempt to improve music pedagogy on the secondary level by developing strategies which can be used by the instructor to further the development of music comprehension during the regular band rehearsal period. The information contained in this chapter is one approach which can be used by the teacher to help students in large and small ensemble groups gain a better understanding of the diverse and varied aspects of music in a comprehensive manner.

The strategies are designed to progress from rather simple dimensions of music to more complex areas of form and style through selected instrumental works. In addition, the student is afforded numerous opportunities to revisit the dimensions in various genres, which is one method of reinforcing music concepts. Also, strategies are designed to provide the student an opportunity to progress at his own pace or within a specified group.

The curriculum is not truly innovative, but it is logical. It is logical because each selection reveals some exemplary features which are evident in music of different periods, forms, and styles, and because it deals with those constructs which are essential in the development of musical concepts.

The musical selections and strategies used in this chapter do not preclude by any means the numerous problems confronting instrumental music teachers, but as John Muller stated:

> In spite of "progressive" theories enunciated during recent decades, one's measure of the value of education is its enrichment for mature life. The various values of music education are, therefore, not restricted to the school itself, but are planned with the view of carryover into adult activities, for which the school is merely the prelude.[21]

Harry Broudy made an excellent summation of the above when he stated in the following:

> The claim of music for a place in general education as a required subject in the curriculum should be based on the assertion that musical experience when cultivated by training gives rise to a special type of interest and enjoyment, similar to that engendered by connoisseurship in any field of human endeavor. The claim should rest on the promise to make the experiences of the pupil more musical in terms of performing, listening, knowledge of and about music, and that growth in these dimensions can be observed before the instruction is completed.[22]

In the final analysis, the most important outcome of any music program is that the learner should leave the program knowing more about music in terms of its musical dimensions, i.e., in terms of rhythmic, harmonic, and melodic patterns of sound, than he did before entering the program.

We may conclude by saying that a comprehensive music program must be designed to provide musical experiences for students which will enable them to develop greater knowledge, skill, and sensitivity in dealing with the dimensions of sound, moving in time.

NOTES FOR CHAPTER 19

1. The initial program of the Contemporary Music Project established in 1959 was known as the Young Composers Project (YCP). It was not until 1962 when MENC submitted a proposal to the Ford Foundation to continue the program that the name was changed to the Contemporary Music Project.

2. Reston Virginia: MENC Journal, May 1973, pp. 35-45.

3. Ibid., p. 39.

4. David Willoughby, "Contemporary Educational Thought and Comprehensive Musicianship," Comprehensive Musicianship and Undergraduate Music Curricula (CMP₆) (Washington, D.C.: Music Educators National Conference, 1971), pp. 24-42.

5. Casey, op. cit., p. 71.

6. Robert Casey's dissertation, "Serial Composition in Works for the Wind Band" (Doctoral dissertation, Washington University, 1971), is an excellent source for those interested in studying some of the serial techniques employed by composers who have written works in the twelve tone method. Several works have been analyzed and can be used by the instructor during the rehearsal period to identify tone rows and permutations of the tone rows.

7. David Reck, Music of the Whole Earth, (New York: Charles Scribner's Sons, 1977), p. 36.

8. George Wiskirchen, Developmental Techniques for the Jazz Ensemble Musician, (Boston: Berklee Press Publications, 1961), p. 2.

9. Jones decided to withdraw as co-leader of the Thad Jones-Mel Lewis band to pursue other musical activities.

19. Assorted mutes are important in the performance of jazz selections to effect different timbres. Each brass player is expected to possess a harmon mute, cup mute, straight mute, bucket, and plunger. French horn players usually mute their instruments by cupping the palm of the right hand in the bell of the instrument, but there are transposing and non-transposing mutes.

20. A channel or bridge is usually an eight-measure section employed in jazz selections to vary the harmonic scheme, add diversity, and prepare for the recapitulation of the initial theme.

21. John H. Muller, "Music in Education: A Sociological Approach," Basic Concepts of Music Education: The Fifty-seventh Yearbook of the National Society for the Study of Education, Part 1, ed. Nelson B. Henry (Chicago: The University of Chicago Press, 1958), p. 121.

22. Harry S. Broudy, "A Realistic Philosophy of Music
     Education,"   Basic Concepts of Music Education:
     The Fifty-seventh Yearbook of the National
     Society for the Study of Education, Part 1, ed.
     Nelson B. Henry (Chicago: The University of
     Chicago Press, 1958), p.80.

BIBLIOGRAPHY FOR CHAPTER 19

Baker, David. Jazz Improvisation. Chicago: John
     Maher Publications, 1969.

Boyle, David J., ed. Instructional Objectives in
     Music: Resources for Planning Instruction and
     Evaluation Achievement. Vienna, Va.: Music
     Educators National Conference, 1974.

Berry, Wallace. Form in Music. Englewood Cliffs,
     N.J.: Prentice-Hall, Inc., 1966.

Christ, Delone, and Allen Winold. Involvement with
     Music. New York: Harper's College Press, 1975.

Comprehensive Musicianship: An Anthology of Evolving
     Thought.   Washington, D.C.:   Music Educators
     National Conference, April, 1965.

Contemporary Music Project. Report of the Seminar on
     Comprehensive Musicianship.   Washington, D.C.:
     Music Educators National Conference, 1965.

Henry, Nelson B., ed. Basic Concepts in Music
     Education. Fifty-seventh Yearbook of the National
     Society for the Study of Education, Part I.
     Chicago: 1958:

Hindemith, Paul. Craft of Musical Composition. New
     York: Schott Music Corp., Fourth Edition, 1970.

Kennon, K. Wheeler. Counterpoint. Rev. ed. Englewood
     Cliffs, N.J.: Prentice-Hall, Inc., 1972.

Labuta, Joseph H. Teaching Musicianship in the High
     School Band.   New York: Parker Publishing
     Company, Inc., 1972.

LaPorta, John. Developing the School Jazz Ensemble.
    Boston: Berklee Press Publications, 1965.

Perle, George. Serial Compostion and Atonality. Rev.
    ed. Los Angeles: University of California Press,
    1977.

Thomas, Ronald B. A Study of New Concepts, Procedures
    and Achievements in Music learning as Developed
    in Selected Music Education Programs.
    Manhattanville   College,   USOE   No.   V-008,
    September, 1966.

Willoughby, David. Comprehensive Musicaianship and
    Undergraduate Music Curricula. Washington, D.C.:
    Music Educators National conference, 1971.

Wiskirchen, George. Developmental Techniques for the
    Jazz Ensembles Musician. Boston: Berklee Press
    Publications, 1961.

CHAPTER 20

COMTEMPORARY CHORAL MUSIC OF BLACK AMERICAN
COMPOSERS SUITABLE FOR THE HIGH SCHOOL CHOIR

Effie T. Gardner

With the exodus of the middle class and more affluent of our population to surburbia, today's urban public schools have become highly ethnic. The ethnic groups comprisimg our schools have needs of identity, not only with themselves and their heritage but with others around them. Efforts at integration have fostered multicultural situations that demand more insight with regards to teaching materials and approaches to teaching.

Within the multiculture of American life, a large Black sub-culture exists that has exerted an enormous amount of influence on American music. Less is known or taught about music that has been composed by Blacks than any other non-white culture, with the possible exception of American Indian music. Black music has made a tremendous impression, but little is known about it.

While choral music of the Black American composer is being performed with some frequency in the repertoires of high school choral groups, the compositions performed have been those works of well established Black choral arrangers such as William Dawson, Nathaniel Dett, Harry Burleigh, Hall Johnson, Jester Hairston and others. The main thrust of these composers can be called nationalistic, for their choral output has been based on arrangements of spirituals and the folk idiom of the early black man. These compositions most certainly have their place in the scheme of high school choral education in America and most continue to be performed. Now, however, there is a group of young composers whose styles utilize the more progressive techniques of twentieth century writings and whose source of inspiration does not come from the nationalistic idiom, but from sacred and secular themes not influenced by early black life.

It is particularly significant that the choral repertoire of large cities, whose school populations are 40 to 50 percent black, use comparatively little literature by composers such as Arthur Cunningham,

Ulysses Kay, or Hale Smith. Part of the problem may be that many choral conductors in secondary schools do not feel comfortable using contemporary compositions with their choirs. Undergraduate choral training is usually devoted to the music of the common practice periods with not enough emphasis on the writings and problems in conducting compositions of the last eighty years. Some conductors are attempting to perform twentieth century compositions, but invariably, their repertoire is taken from White American and European composers. How much more relevant would a piece by one of the numerous Black Composers be to the inner city population of student?

*The list of Black composers of contemporary music is an impressive one. Included are such artists as Howard Swanson, Olly Wilson, Steven Chambers, Adolphus Hailstork, Dorothy Rudd Moore, George Walker, Arthur Cunningham, Noel da Costa, Ronald Roxbury, Ulysses Kay, Coleridge-Taylor Perkinson, William Fisher, John Carter, David Baker, James Furman, Robert Harris, Julia Perry, Roland Carter, Thomas Kerr, Arthur Evans, Roque Cordero, Hale Smith, and Thomas Jefferson Anderson.

Because contemporary music draws upon the musical devices from previous periods, problems encountered in early music will apply to contemporary choral writing, plus some that are new and unique. Rapid articulation and dynamic changes, chords with more than four separate members melodies that skip into dissonances, nonvocal sounds and non-notated tone clusters, quartal and quintal approaches to building chords all present new choral music problems which have been encountered before but not in such profusion or in such combinations.

The suggestions given below have been found to be effective in the rehearsal of cntemporary choral music. It should be mentioned that because the Black-American composers who are the subjects of this chapter are using twentieth century compositional devices, problems encountered in their music would be no different than those problems of other compositions using those same techniques.

---

*A representative listing of twentieth century choral works by Black composers which will form a core of compositions upon which the reader may build can be found in appendix B.

1. Read and discuss the text. If possible, get other poetry by the author and become more familiar with this style of writing. To illustrate certain accents and rhythms, have students speak the entire text.

2. Contrary to the efforts of young people, the softer they sing, the easier it is to hear parts in music with different harmonic structures. A forced, loud tone usually creates a vibrato or wobble of some kind. A well-constructed, soft tone straightens out such problems. Sometimes the suggestion of a woodwind sound will evoke the quality that is desirable from the singers.

3. For problems in singing rapid words, begin by having the entire chorus speak the words slowly, distinctly and with every sound in every word present. As tempo is increased, be careful of the tendency to drop some sounds. There is no short-cut in learning to speak and then sing the words.

4. Be faithful to the score. Tidy up those small mistakes in rhythm or intervals. Sing the notes as written.

5. Where precise glissandi are required, begin by having the voices sing only the notes of the opposite extreme with proper accents. Then have them do a slow glissando gradually increasing the tempo. The long glissando is difficult for amateur singers to time. Most want to hold on to notes until the last instant and then slide very quickly to the next note. The proper method is to begin sliding as soon as the tone in established.

6. If your chorus is new at this style of music, don't push it at the first few rehearsals. Ten minutes a day may be enough until the singers begin identifying with the style.

7. Try working a designated problem at the beginning of a day's rehearsal. Reading contemporary music at sight is almost out of the question for high school students.

8. Some works are conceived sectionally. It may be wise to rehearse in reverse several times; that is, sing the final section, then the final two

sections, then the final three sections, etc. This emphasizes the last section and makes sure the chorus is going toward familiar material. In a difficult or unusual work, the choir may work on earlier sections to the detriment of the last parts. Rehearsing in reverse gives them the needed work on the last section.

9. If the composition is a linear one and somewhat dissonant, consider beginning with part rehearsals before attempting a complete run-through. Trying to read at sight may give a false impression of the difficulty. Learning the lines singly or in duets will gradually introduce your choir to the sound of the work without drowning them in the noise of the full piece.

The decision of where to begin in rehearsing contemporary music is one of the conductor's biggest concerns. Rehearsals of this kind of music requires adherence to a logical succession of tasks, just as is observed in the rehearsing of any other style of music.

With the high school student, it is important that we not only teach notes and work towards a finished performance, but that we make the music, the style, and the composer relevant to the singers. Comments about the composer and his contribution to American music are certainly in order, not only for the predominantly Black high school chorus, but for the White and multi-racial chorus as well. Misconceptions still exist concerning the Black American musician's contribution to music other than the more popular, less formal styles.

A second stage of the logical succession is "to assume that the composer and the publisher (if the piece is not in manuscript form) have some faith in the work as an artistic entity."[1] It is important that you as conductor believe in the composition or your communication to the students, and final product (if you persist in rehearsing it) will not be convincing or rewarding.

Next, analyze the text to determine whether you and your singers can identify with the words. Is the text used by the composer for "the purpose of communicating a literary idea or as a source of musical sounds. This determination is necessary or you will spend useless time in rehearsal trying to get a clearly understood text when the composer couldn't care less whether the words are understandable or not."[2]

The fourth step is to determine whether the primary concern is with individual melodies as complete entities or whether the most obvious element should be the sequence of chords. Knowing this will give an indication as to where emphasis should be placed at a given time and will make for a more worthy use of rehearsal time.

Emphasizing the articulation and dynamic markings on the score should by considered next. Contemporary music sometimes contains accents, sudden dynamic changes, non-word sounds such as whistles, sighs, clicks, as well as peculiar tone qualities and word fragmentations.

Finally, list the elements: melody, harmony or the proper intonation of various lines of music, articulation, and the text and its meaning, in order of importance for rehearsing the choral work. With traditional tonal music, the most common approach is to begin rehearsing the pitches. This may or may not be the right method with a contemporary composition. If the piece, for instance, has an intricate rhythmic structure but simple pitches, it would be more correct to begin with rhythmic and articulation problems.

Comtemporary music is no more difficult to rehearse and to make happen than traditional tonal music. It only requires a specialized preparation and a logical rehearsal schedule. The compositions of the Black American that are written using twentieth century idioms and compositional devices can provide the high school choral director with a wide range of styles within the contemporary idiom. The compositions range from extended serious works of a most provocative nature to lighter pieces of a simpler style; from easy pieces suitable for the inexperienced singer to more difficult settings which could be challenging to the most experienced high school choir. Much of the music is harmonically conservative and only mildly dissonnant. Other compositions utilize rapidly shifting atonal centers that seem to pull towards atonality and still others make use of more recent twentieth century innovations such as choral sprechstimme and passages of sound with clear pitch focus. The consideration and use of the choral music of the Black American composer as a part of the high school repertoire will prove to be a rewarding and challenging experience for both conductor and choir.

Musical Sketches

Arthur Cunningham has written in both tonal and atonal harmonic approaches, making use of traditional western scales and of modal and serial techniques. Chorally, his works tend to draw from the black experience and frequently uses jazz idioms!

Noel da Costa's music moves toward all the possibilities of harmonic, melodic, and rhythmic features of the comtemporary era. However, definite linear qualities predominante, with intervallic tendencies planned where tertain chords might otherwise be.

The music of Robert Harris shifts from tonal to absolute atonality and use of free harmonies is based on both the tertian and quartal system of chord building. Rhythmically his music is uncomplicated but has a feeling of movement and motion. His choral output, thus far, has dealt with sacred texts.

Lena McLin has developed a new form of music which she calls "art rock." Her music is basically tonal and very rhythmic. Many of her works are arrangements of spiritals and a large portion are written in the "art rock" idiom focusing on the ideas and thoughts of youth.

George Walker's writing show a strong affinity for modal lines. Time signatures change frequently but generally the established note unit will remain constant throughout. Harmonies are frequently non-tertian and give in many cases a strong quartal sound.

Ronald Roxbury is unique as a composer. His endeavors have taken him not only into traditional practices of compositions but consist of experimentation with graphic notation and idiomatic uses of the voice. His works are predominantly sacred and give a strong gregorian feeling harmonized with contemporary sonorities.

The choral works of Hale Smith are very linear and jazz influences have contributed considerably not only to the harmonic structure of his works, but to his rhythmic development as well.

427

James Furman is a composer with immense divertsity of style. His works present techniques ranging from gospel to dodicaphonic idioms. When composing without adherence to a tonal center, the works are linearly conceived and dissonant intervals occur as a result of moving horizontal lines. In his tonal works, homophony is usually the rule because these compositions are gospel or spiritual arragements and lend themselves to this texture. He includes non-traditional sounds and effects that are usually reserved for instrumental music.

Ulysses Kay has written choral works that can be used with choirs with very little experience and those with considerable musical difficulty. His earlier works tend to be more tonal and even later works,though highly chromatic, contain voice parts that are only mildly dissonant.

Roland Carter is a young composer who thus far has chosen the black experience as his source of inspira-ation. His works are generally tonal, very lyrical, and extremely effective in concert literature.

BIBLIOGRAPHY

Jack Boyd, Rehearsal Guide for the Choral Director, Champaign, Illinois: Mark Foster Music Co., 1977, p. 169.

Ibid, p. 170

Suggested Projects and Questions
for Discussion

1. Recall your own high school choral repetoire. What representation of twentieth century composers was included? Of These composers, which were Black Americans? Do not include arrangers of spirituals.

2. Does vocal tone quality change with the perform-ance of twentieth century music when compared with

compared with other period music? Would there be
a change in tonal concept in the performance of
the choral music of Black American composers?

3. Examine one or more compositions listed in this
chapter. Do the overall characteristics indicate
that the piece would have been in the performance
realm of your high school ensemble. What makes
each piece unique?

4. Begin a card file using the following example or
one which is more suitable to your needs. Examine
ten compositions by five different composers
mentioned in this chapter and add them to your
existing file or use them as a beginning to a file
that will grow with time and experience.

Title_____Publisher_____

Composer/Arranger_____Key_____

   Difficult_____   Range

   Medium_____

   Easy_____

                S   A T   B

Accompaniment_____

Comments:_____

_____

Continue on back of card.

6. Of those compositions mentioned in this chapter
which would be good introductions to music of the
twentieth century. Discuss reasons for your
choice.

BIBLIOGRAPHY for FURTHER READINGS

A Comprehensive Source Book on Black Derived, Music, Books and Related Materials Submitted by Music Companies and Individuals. Organized and Compiled by Camille C. Taylor, New York, N.Y.: The National Black Music Caucus of MENC, 400 Central Park West, 1981.

Jack, Boyd, Rehearsal Guide for the Choral Director, Champaign, IL: Mark Foster Music Co., 1970.

Eileen Southern, ed., The Black Perspective in Music, Cambria Heights, N.Y.: The Foundation for Research in the Afro-American Creative Arts, Inc., Selected Issues.

Alice, Tischler, Fifteen Black American Composers, Detroit, MI: Detroit Studies in Music Bibliography Information Coordinators, Inc., 1980.

Evelyn Davidson White, Selected Bibliography of Published Choral Music by Black Composers, Metuchen, N.J.: Scarecrow Publishers, 1981.

The Music of Black American Composers, New York, N.Y.: Belwin, Inc.

Chapter 21

THE CHURCH MUSIC PROGRAM

Jimmie James, Jr.

INTRODUCTION

Although there have been numerous studies and a great deal of money put into programs designed to help underachieving poor students in urban schools, there haven't been any "real" solutions. The problems have been universal, ranging from lack of finances to dissatisfied students to bureaucratic failures. A decrease in school funding usually means that all (so called) non-academic courses, such as music and art, are cut from the curriculum. This fact is elaborated on by Klotman who says that:

> Local school systems throughout our
> nation are being squeezed in an ever
> more acute fiscal bind. This is the
> product of declining enrollments,
> increasing local tax payer resistance
> to rising local property taxes and the
> inexorable pressure of inflation on a
> personal intensive activity. There is
> strong pressure to reduce the education
> program to the prescribed legal
> minimum. Frequently, that minimum
> includes no obligation to provide
> instruction in the arts.[1]

In an early report, Allen Ornstein discusses other factors which accounted for monetary cutbacks in funds for urban schools.

> As 1971 drew to an end, millions of
> students in both large and small cities
> as well as suburban areas faced the
> prospects of extended winter and spring
> vacations, and especially an early
> summer recess. Large cities such as
> Chicago, Cleveland, New York, and
> Philadelphia, smaller cities such as
> Dayton, Gary, and Newark, and suburban
> schools in Clovis, California;
> Malverne, New York; and Mansfield, Ohio
> are each in the red for exceedingly
> large sums-ranging from several million

dollars in each of the large cities to
several hundred thousand dollars in the
suburbs.[2]

School districts across the country were caught in
a squeeze between operating costs and teacher demands
for increased salaries vs. citizen revolts against
further tax increases and inflationary spending. In
order to stay open, some schools borrowed against the
next year's school budget, froze teacher salaries,
reduced teacher health benefits, reduced the teaching
staffs between 5 percent and 10 percent, limited
school repairs, reduced compensatory programs, increased class sizes, and reduced the work week of
janitors and other ancillary personnel. Of course the
same thing is happening today in many places throughout
our nation.

Many of the reductions in teaching staff were
music teachers and in most instances the cut back in
financial support affected music programs, especially
in the heavily populated urban areas where minorities
are predominant. This has caused considerable attention relative to the problem of accountability in our
music programs.

In some area the church has played a major role in
giving the children in urban area an opportunity to
receive music education. History indicates that the
black church has come to the rescue of the community
when they were denied participation in social, economic
and political life of the white American Community.
LeRoi Jones, in Blues People, reports the following:

> For Black folk...the church was at once
> a religious temple, a school for
> children and adults, a social center, a
> training ground for potential leaders
> of the race and, like the Catholic
> Church of early Europe, a patron of the
> arts--particularly music. Signifi-
> cantly, since their beginnings in the
> 18th century, black churches have
> occupied an important place in the
> lives of black folk; many black leaders
> have been ministers, and many black
> musicians have begun their careers in
> church choirs.[3]

Religious music has played a major role in the
history of black people, in terms of affirming their

432

rights as human beings. In a pioneer study of Black folk songs, Odum and Johnson made no mention of songs of protest.[4] Early observers likewise found Black songs to be comparatively free of protest and discontent, although more contemporary treatments have pointed to the protest elements of hymns and spirituals. Glazer and Fowke have voiced this opinion, pointing to a spiritual such as "Go Down Moses": In the trials and tribulations of the children of Israel, they saw a pattern of their own bondage. Thus they could do full justice to one of the great Bible stories of liberation -- the story of Moses who stood up to Pharoah and said, "Let my people go."[5]

Shortly after the end of World War I, social movements began to take interest in the black spiritual. Marcus Garvey's Universal Negro Improvement Association employed a hymn as the base for its official anthem:

Advance, advance to victory
Let Africa be free
Advance to meet the foe
With the might
Of the red, the black and the green.[6]

The Civil Rights movement rarely used songs not based on church hymns. To illustrate, nearly every selection found in the song "We Shall Overcome" has a religious base. The use of spirituals by southern Negroes, however, was more a function of familiarity and heritage than of imitation or parody. Robert Sherman, in describing "freedom songs" noted:

The freedom songs are heard everywhere in the South now--

at mass meetings, on the picket lines,
during street demonstrations. They are
sung in jails and often composed in
jails. They are dramatic emblems of the
struggle and mighty weapons in it.
Their steady, surging rhythmns, their
lilting melodies (taken usually from
familiar hymns or spitituals already
well known to the Negro community), and
their simple, inspirational words,
repeated over and over again, generate
a fervor that can only be described as
religious in its intensity."[7]

433

Within the civil rights movement "freedom songs" served to create unity and solidarity in the rank-and-file membership. The inner-directedness of the songs in great measure explains the use of hymns, since religion for the Black person was a keystone of his culture and social structure. As the late Dr. Martin Luther King suggested "There are so many difficult moments when individuals falter and would almost give up in despair. These freedom songs have a way of giving new courage."[8]

The utilization of religiously based songs gives the message an aura of sacredness, which further legitmizes the authority of leaders and the sanctity of the cause. Songs stating the justness of the cause tend to unify that entity, especially when employed an idiom familiar to the people. The use of religious music adds an appeal to tradition which social movements require. Movements, by their very nature of pleading social change, are not usually tied to tradition. Hymns appear to tie the movement to a common heritage, regardless of the programs they advocate. Finally, group singing encourages the individual to feel himself a part of the group or movement, and therefore important, allowing the participant to carry on.

One can see that music has been a vital part of Black history. Music can be just as important in the contemporary urban church. Music can be an aid to worship in the form of organ music, anthems, and responses and can become a means of worship in the singing hymns and doxologies and in congregational chants and responses. Music in the church can also serve to fill in the gap which is lacking in schools.

These and other factors reflect a need for a well-coordinated church music program to supplement the urban music education program. In considering such a program, certain areas need to be emphasized, including: the need for objectives, the music program offerings; planning the program; budgeting and financing it; public relations; scheduling; and music activities that can be shared between the church and the school. The remainder of this chapter will be concentrated on objectives and offerings of the music program.

ESTABLISHING OBJECTIVES

A successful church music program that is properly organized can certainly be advantageous to the urban student who is consideing a career in music education. It can also serve the needs of adult parishioners while at the same time help urban youngsters to become better music consumers when they reach adulthood.

Music in the church, however, is to be judged in its relationship to worship, and depends on the attitude of each person who shares in the praise of God. The minister must support the choir director, organist, soloists, and choirs in co-operation with the music committee. These people also have the responsibility of assisting volunteer lay leaders who are often unfamiliar with the potential of church music.

The church music director's job includes a variety of duties and responsibilities. In the urban church, there will be a need for him to plan a program that will successfully meet the needs of all concerned, especially if it is designed to offer assistance to students who are enrolled in urban music programs.

The church program, just as the school music program, should seek to develop the aesthetic potential of each individual involved to the highest possible level. There should be both general and specialized experiences. The general experiences could be gotten in a course given once a week, similar to a broad-based general music course in school which would involve acquaintance with a variety of music, listening and performance skills, as well as other broad experiences. On the other hand, the specialized experiences would be gotten in the various choirs, small ensembles and instrumental groups.

It is necessary for the music program to have a definite set of objectives. "Objectives assure the proper relation of the music program to the broader aims of the the governing body when based upon music's value to the individual and to society. These objectives determine the teacher's choice of musics, subject matter and methods. The effectiveness of the music program is evaluated on the basis of its objectives." The church music educator should be concerned with two levels of objectives - program and instructional. Program objectives are concerned with the program's development, organizing the musical activities, and the selection of experiences. Instructional objectives give direction to daily (or weekly) teaching in the rehearsal sessions. They should be based on the program objectives.

An effective church music program is one that is quite diverse, offering a number of experiences to meet the needs of local parishioners and other community participants. There should be experiences in listening and performance with a great deal of emphasis on a general music approach that will reach all persons involved; since, the intention is to supplement the "weak" school program as well as to provide the congregation with a wide variety of sacred music experiences.

OFFERINGS IN THE CHURCH MUSIC PROGRAM

Althugh a church's music program can be as large and varied as the budget, interest and personnel allow , this chapter will concern itself with music programs in terms of the congregation, christian education, the adult choir, the children's and youth choir and instruments.

The Congregation   In the order of a church worship service, the congregation is not an audience which comes to see a performance. Every person in the congregation has his own unique role in the act of worship. The main responsibility of the congregation is hymn singing, and they sing because of what God has done for them in Christ. In order for the congregational responses to be effective, correct attitudes and goals must be established in their minds.

Hymns can be used for expressing joy, teaching the truths, expressing prophecy or admonishing. Religious music appreciation is therefore a necessary part of the church music program. Although it is easy to say that the congregation ought to sing and appreciate good hymns, it is often a problem to find ways and means of training and helping a congregation to take its rightful place in terms of worship in song. The problem boils down to several factors:

1. It is nearly impossible for the congregation to do two things at once -- read music and listen for the tune.
2. Hymn singing depends upon interest, which must be aroused by some means.

436

3. New hymns must be related to familiar hymns, scripture, or ideas -- moving from the known to the unknown. Obviously, what is required is education and a formal learning experience, and the worship service is hardly the place for informal teaching.⁹

Some churches have tried music training during fellowship or family night supppers. Others have tried it at prayer meetings, Sunday evening services, men's women's or youth meetings, or at the close of the service. Different means could be employed dependent on congregational interest.

Christian Education is one of the ministries by which the church seeks to fulfill its nature and perform it mission. It is an integral part of the total work of the church, which includes many aspects such as worship, the sacraments and ordinances, pastoral counseling, parish administration, evangelism, missions, stewardship, social action, and teaching. These are not mutually exclusive functions but overlap and interpenetrate in many ways. Each aspect ultimately involves all the others, each utilizes educational procedures and each helps to achieve the aims of the church. Hence, the objectives of Christian Education are one way of stating what the church is seeking to do in its total life and ministry.

This is the area in which music instruction would probably have its greatest impact on the youth. It would be most beneficial to us choir members or other church members with training as aides in the Sunday School departments who would work closely with the other teachers to help teach and use music in the classrooms. Music should be an integral part of the teaching process and should prepare the children in the techniques of music. In this way, their response in church life as well as in other settings would become more meaningful.

It is necessary for the music teacher to integrate the songs with the curriculum used for the children in their church school classes. Teachers must select songs for the appropriate age level. The material in the songs should not contain concepts which would have to be unlearned at a later time.

The vocabulary should be meaningful to the children, and should help them use their imagination. The songs contain theological truths, and avoid talking down to them. Furthermore, some texts should be chosen from the church hymnal so that the children will feel comfortable in worship services.

In terms of melody, the lines should be pleasant and in the vocal range of the children who are to sing it. It should have rhythmic vitality and variety, and a sound harmonic structure. The children should be taught "good" music.[10]

One should not forget other musical activities such as musical games, rhythms, actions, instruments, and recordings. For many black children, music is called "sounds," and the art is participation in some direct way with sound so that the individual can get the "feeling" of the music. In African and Afro-American music it is essential that students share a steady feeling of time within which sounds are placed. An awareness of the density referent and the ability to use it form the basis for the entrance of sounds and patterns which help students understand various types of black music.[11]

The opportunities for music in Christian educaion are unlimited. Knowledgeable personnel is the first requirement for a quality music program.

Adult Choir The choir can be an enriching experience since it enables the participants to sing and hear good music. By working together as a group, ignoring individual differences and personal likes and dislikes for the greater good, choir members have the opportunity to develop into finer adults.

The choir's major role in the church service is to bring the congregation's focus to the sense of worship. Secondly, the choir can provide the church with meaningful music, and its members can work throughout other areas in the church to hasten the church's musical growth.

Children's and Youth Choir This program enables every child in the church to have an "opportunity to participate in a musical activity maintained on a level that will satisfy his musical, emotional, and spiritual needs."[12] A junior choir offers vocal, musical instruction that either supplements or takes the place

438

of that in the school. It also gives the child a healthy extracurricular activity and experience in a cooperative groups situation.

> "A well disciplined unison choir can add a uniquely beautiful dimension to the musical experience of the church. There is a unique literature of sacred song which can be most effectively sung by a unison choir: plainsong, melodic chorales, and psalm tunes; songs and arias of the great classic composers; folk songs from the world around. Unison singing is the basis of all choral art. The most complex choral scores are merely combinations of many unison voice lines. A unison choir seems a logical place to teach singing, the most essential of choral skills."[13]

Many of the objectives here are the same as those for the christian education programs or adult choir, and will not be re-iterated here.

Instruments The use of band and orchestra instruments should be encouraged in the church. Many times directors may feel that they do not have the expertise in instrumental music to adequately organize and develop the program. Others feel that the instrumental ability of their members is too limited to be successful. However, the opportunities for the use of instruments are such that a great number of youth and adults could regularly be utilized in the service.

There are numerous ways of beginning an instrumental music program. One way to begin is by getting a complete and accurate view of the present situation regarding these items:

1. Who in the church are presently capable of playing an instrument?

2. Who have played instruments at some time in the past?

3. Who have never learned to play an instrument but would like to learn?

4. Of those who are potential instrumentalist in the church, who owns, or are able to obtain

439

instruments"[14]

One way of securing the needed information is to survey members of the congregation by having them complete a questionnaire. These could be distributed to all Sunday school classes as well as to persons that attend the morning and evening worship services. An effort should be made to obtain a completed questionnaire from virtually every person in the church. All persons interested in the program, regardless of the level, should be included. This calls for a diverse program with opportunities for performance during the regular worship services and for other "lesser" occassions.

Instruments will need to be provided for many of the players. Some will own personal instruments while others wll need assistant in securing an instrument. Students that participate in the school band or orchestra should be encouraged to secure permission to use their instruments for church performances. There are two ways to deal with larger instruments such as a tuba and timpani. One way is for church authorities to seek permission from the school administration to use these larger instruments when they are needed. Another way is for the church to purchase the larger instru- ments. This is the best method if the church music budget is large enough since there would be no problem securing the instruments when they are needed. Many times the school music director will readily cooperate because he will be happy that his students are getting additional experience.

There are many occasions to use instruments in the church music program. The writer has had success in using brass, woodwind, string and percussion instru- ments during the morning and evening services as well as for special occasions such as provided accompani- ment for cantatas, oratorios and concert performances.

Brass or woodwind choirs or string ensembles are quite effective in a variety of ways when to provide the prelude, postlude or a special selection during the worship service. Brass choirs are even more effective when combined with organ and percussion. Handbell choirs have become quite popular in many churches. They are purchased in matched sets and are very expensive. It is suggested that the music director seek the assistance of talented high school and college students in helping to tutor instrumentalists enrolled in the church music program.

> "Elaborate instrumental resources are not always available in many small churches. They are not always required for effective choral accompaniments. A single instrument appropriately scored, can make the difference between a memorable performance and an ordinary one."[15]

An ongoing relationship should be developed between the church music director and the school music teacher. Cooperative programs should be organized and presented periodically. It is possible that the local band or orchestra director will assist the church music director in his attempts to include instruments in the church program. A simple telephone call or letter inviting the school director to become involved is often all that is needed. Once the program is organized, regardless of the level, a definite schedule should be placed in the hands of the instrumentalists and announced in the church bulletin.

As can be seen by this brief outline, a fully developed church music program has the best opportunity to help the urban child grow in musical appreciation, and ability and can help him live some of his heritage and provide a framework for growth.

DISCUSSION QUESTIONS

1. How can the church and school music directors works in a cooperative effort to improve the music program of both church and school?

2. What is the role of music in the church? Is it the same in the school? Explain

3. How can today's media and especially the T.V. Ministry aid in helping individuals to understand the unique role music play in church, school, home and community?

4. The Black Church according to Rev. Charles G. Adams, "is the preserver of our culture, the

guardian of our humanity, the incubator in the development of our leaders, the seed bed of racial solidarity, and the genesis of our school." In what ways are these statements true in our churches today?

5. By what standards do we use to judge the quality of the church music program?

6. What role has religious music played throughout history in the struggle of human beings to obtain rights, call attention to moral and social issues and for nationalistic purposes?

7. What are the necessary ingredients for a well-balanced church music program?

NOTES FOR CHAPTER 21

1. Robert H. Klotman, President of MENC, An address Delivered in an appearance before the House Appropriation Sub-committee for Interior and Related Agencies, April 21, 1977.

2. Allan C. Ornestein, Urban Education: Student Unrest, Teacher Behaviors, and Black Power, Columbus, Ohio: Charles E. Merrill Publishing Co., 1972.

3. LeRoi Jones, Blues People.

4. Howard W. Odum and Guy B. Johnson, The Negro and His Songs (Chapel Hill: Univerity of North Carolina Press, 1925).

5. Joe Glazer and Edith Fowke, Songs of Work and Freedom, (Chicago: Roosevelt University Press, 1960) p. 169.

6. Serge Denisoff, Sing a Song of Social Significance, (Bowling Green: Bowling Green University Popular Press, 1972), p. 53

7. Ibid.

8. Robert Sherman, "Sing a Song of Freedom," in DeTurk and Poulin, eds. The American Fold Scene

(New York: Dell Publishing Co., 1966) pp. 173-174.

9.   Austin C. Lovelace and William C. Rice,
     Music and Worship in the Church (Nashville:
     Abingdon Press, 1976) pp. 159, 160.

10. Ibid.

11. Barbara Reeder, "Getting Involved in Shaping the
     Sounds of Black Music," Music in World Cultures
     (Washington D.C.:   Music Educators National
     Conference, 1927) p. 64.

12. Lovelace and Rice, p. 106.

13. Dayton W. Nordin. How to Organize and Direct the
     Church Choir. (West Nyack, N.Y.:   Parker
     Publishing Co., Inc., 1973) p. 28.

14. Harold Pottenger. Instrumental Handbook. Kansas
     City, MO: Becon Hill Music, 1971 p. 12.

15. Jimmie James. Organizing and Administering the
     A.M.E. Church Music Program. Savannah: Atlantic
     Communications, Inc., 1977 p. 36.

BIBLIOGRAPHY

Adorno, Theodor W. Introduction to the Sociology
     of Music. New York: Seabury Press, 1976.

Brandt, William E. The Way of Music. Boston: Allyn
     and Bacon, 1968.

Brocklehurst, J. Brian. Response to Music: Principles
     of Music Education. London: Routledge and K.
     Paul, 1971.

Denisoff, Serge. Sing a Song of Social Significance.
     Bowling Green: Bowling Green Univerity Popular
     Press, 1972.

Glazer, Joe and Fowke, Edith. Songs of Work and
     Freedom. Chicago: Roosevelt University Press,
     1960.

Chapter 22

CAREER OPTIONS IN MUSIC EDUCATION

Charles E. Hicks, Donald Jones

and

Ed Bland

Career education has come of age since its inception in the early 1970's. This issue is one that has received national attention in recent years. Institutions in many states have printed career education information, allocated funds by legislative act, and mandated in-service training for public school personnel. Several states have appointed career education consultants at the state level to coordinate the many activities of the department. These efforts have meant the incorporation of career and consumer types of programs in the public schools from elementary school to graduate school.

Career and consumer education is an important dimension of the nursery through adult curriculum which provides for students in a comprehensive continuum of experiences through which each individual may develop a more realistic awareness of his/her abilities and prepare students to enter and re-enter the world of work.

Prior to 1970, many school music educators have only focused attention on preparing music students to become public school and college teachers. Since approximately less than 20 percent of school music students attend college to study music, it seems that the musical resources could be better used if career music education was more emphasized in the school music program. By the year 2000, it is estimated that approximately two-thirds of the children in kindergarten now will fill jobs not yet in existence. This notion offers to those responsible for the education of America's Youth some fascinating alternatives and an opportunity for bold and courageous leadership.

Careers in Music

There is a growing trend in urban public schools toward emphasizing vocational and career educational opportunities for students. Unless music educators keep pace with changing trends, music is likely to occupy the bottom rung of the priorities totem pole.

We have felt for a number of years that one of the tragedies of school music programs is the large number of students who enjoy performing in vocal and instrumental groups, but no longer use those skills upon graduating from high school. Many of these students would like to make music a career but cannot because of the small (less than 5 percent) number of musicians who make their living solely as performers.

These are the students who should be afforded career offerings in the various support areas of music. The music industry is the eighth largest industry in America and there are several courses which could be taught in vocational oriented schools which play a vital part in preparing students for careers in music industry.

The following are some examples of courses which could be taught, enabling students to re-direct and broaden their vocational skills:

Instrumental Repair - such a course could provide theoretical and practical instruction and experience for repairing brass, woodwind, string and percussion instruments. We can envision many school systems providing their own repair services for school-owned instruments.

Piano Turning, Maintenance and Repair - this course could cover the tuning of acoustic and electric pianos, adjusting and replacing parts and even, possibly, woodworking and refinishing.

Music Copying - this course could include notation and its application to preparing music for live performances and for recordings.

Basic Recording Techniques - included in this course could be theory and experience in editing, mike set-ups, mixing and general knowledge of recording equipment.

Electronic Instrument Repair - there has been an increasing use of electronic instruments in all facets of music in the past decade. Such instruments include electric pianos, guitars, microphones, synthesizers, speakers and amplifiers.

The Business of Music - Many secondary students form their own performing groups and perform at a variety of functions, often being exploited in the process. This course could provide students with a basic understanding of such topics as: contracts, union regulations, managers, booking agents, publishers and producers.[1]

These courses, all related to the various technical support areas of music, will provide students with possible alternative non-performing careers in music and music education. Such alternatives are particularly needed in urban schools since a large percentage of students by virtue of a late start or poor training have little chance for performing careers.

At least two school systems have already made significant strides in this direction. In Boston, Massachusetts, the "new" Boston High School of Music opened in the Fall of 1976. The school is designed so that students will be able to concentrate in music while still fulfilling all required academic courses.

In Denver, Colorado, the "Career Education Center," is a separate high school in the Denver school system, offering a broad range of courses including a full music curriculum. Students are drawn from the system's other nine high schools and courses are designed so that any student with professional aspirations could acquire a solid foundation in courses such as instrument repair, piano tuning, sound and recording.

For a more comprehensive listing of career opportunities in music consult Downbeat magazine's "handbook 77." In that publication is an excellent article by Charles Suber entitled "Guide to Music Careers." One other excellent source is "Careers in Music" published by the Music Educators National Conference. It is a comprehensive listing of many potential careers in music which all music educators should be aware of. Also the March, 1977 Music

Educators Journal devotes the entire issue to music and music careers.

Ed Bland, a practicing music Career Consultant includes many of the above mentioned careers in his list of nine (9) "career options for music students." Each of these options focuses attention on skill areas and/or music support areas as opposes to the endeavors which lead to "Musical Stardom." In addition to music copyists and instrumental manufacture and repair, the Bland Options include:

1.   Composer - A good background in traditional harmony, counterpoint, form and analysis, orchestration and composition, coupled with background and practice with the jazz and/or commercial syntax will prepare one for composing careers in: (a) advertising commercials -a highly competitive field but one in which it's relatively easy to get a foothold; (b) industrial shows - songwriting ability and orchestrative and arranging abilities will stand one in good stead for this area. Industrial shows are put up by many manufacturers, and they travel throughout the country; (c) children's music - this is an area to be exploited by those with the special skill to appeal to children musically through kids' records, television and music publishing houses; (d) composers capable of composing a quantity of quality music for educational use in high school and college bands and orchestras can earn a steady income.

2.   Music Editor - Music publishing houses, both classical and popular, need music editors to correct and proofread music to be published.

3.   Studio Musician - Those students who have a great deal of flexibility, i.e., who can double on many instruments, have a good playing knowledge of the various current popular styles and who can sight read and transpose at sight, have an excellent opportunity of becoming studio musicians in one of the large recording centers. Wages can range from $30,000.00 to $200,000.00 yearly.

4. Arranger/Orchestrator - There is work for arranger/orchestrators with good training and background in the jazz and/or commercial syntax and traditional music in Big Band writing, Act Music, Broadway shows, film writing and recording sessions.

5. Record Producer - A basic knowledge of music plus knowledge of basic recording techniques and the record industry marketplace, including trends and a history of pop music, is needed to pursue this career. This is a hard field to break into. The best opener is to approach a record company with something that you've produced.

6. Music Director - This is a mixture of administrative, budgeting and creative duties (composing, arranging and orchestrating). Music Directors are needed for (1) traveling shows in which cases the music diretor is also conductor; (2) film; (3) television; and (4) Broadway shows. Music directors are also needed in the larger advertising agencies' creative departments.

7. Music Critic - This career is for those who have a basic musical knowledge and a flair for journalism. There are numerous magazines and newspapers to break into. A student should try his or her university newspaper to get his/her feet wet as a critic.

8. Music Editor (Film) - Films need music tracks to be put in place against the visual and other tracks. Film editors who specialize in this are called music cutters. A knowledge of film editing, some knowledge or sense of music, and a talent for marrying the right music with the right visuals are necessary.

9. Instrumentalist - Aside from recording work, many instrumentalists earn a living through freelancing in various ensembles for concert and night club work in addition to teaching. It's best to pursue such a career in New York, Los Angeles, Chicago or Nashville.

Because the decade of the eighties is likely to be more crucial for music education and the arts some predictions from The Bureau of Labor Statistics emphasize the importance of career education in music.

The Job Market in Ten Years

The Department of Labor's new Occupational Outlook
Handbook has predicted both good and bad news for those
who will be preparing themselves for a job during the
next decade. What is important in the Bureau of Labor
statics forecast, is not how many individuals will be
out of work in the 1980's but rather which occupations
will need the most workers and provide the greatest
opportunities for possible career employment. The following is a list of the best and worst prospect for
jobs during the next decade:

Best Prospects

Airplane mechanics, assemblers, computer program-
mers, cashiers, cooks and chefs, dental assistants,
draftsmen, emergency medical technicians, geologists,
health service administrators, industrial-machinery
repairmen, life scientists, lithographers, local
truck-drivers, machine-tool operators, nursing aides
and orderlies, operating engineers, personnel and la-
bor-relations specialists, petroleum engineers, physi-
cians and osteopaths, plumbers and pipefitters, police
officers, receptionists, registered nurses, social
workers, statisticians, systems analysts, wastewater
treatment-plant engineers, and waiters/waitresses.

Worst Prospects

Aerospace engineers, bookkeepers, college teachers, compositors and typesetters, flight attendants,
historians, Kindergarten teachers, elementary teachers, long-distance truck-drivers, mathematicians,
newspaper reporters, physicists, school counselors,
secondary school teachers, and stenographers.

As grim as this news might sound, it's even worse
to have no skill at all. According to statisticians
the number of unskilled jobs available new will dwindle
to almost nothing in ten years. Even though these are
only predictions of what may occur, it is important to
note that in past years the predictions from the BLS
have been surprisingly accurate.

For those of us in education the job is twofold.
First, providing realistic alternatives in career and
consumer education for the majority of our students who
do not have the desire nor proper orientation for col-

lege. Secondly, we must begin to package our educational resources for an older clientele. By the year 2000 over half our population will be approximate-ly fifty years and older. These implications are frightening for a society who has fashioned its educational programs for the young. For music educators we must begin now with all deliberate speed to including career education as a major component in the music curriculum.

Notes for Chapter 22

1. S.S. Holdsworth, "Career Education Center", Music America, Vol. 1, No. 1 (November 1976), pp. 16-19.

BIBLOGRAPHY

Bland, Ed, Music Career Options (New York: Ed Bland Agency, 107 Green Street, New York, NY 10012, (212) 431-5058).

Boyce, Tommy. How to write a Song and sell it (Songwriter, P.O. Box 3510, Hollywood, CA 90028.

Careers in Music. 20 to 30 Minute tapes on Ten Careers in music (New York: Alfred Publishing Company Inc., 1978).

Cornell, Richard. Your Career in Music: Arco's College Guidance Series (New York: Arco Publishing Co., Inc., 1979).

Csida, Joseph. The Music/Record Career Handbood (First Place Music Publishers, Inc., 12754 Ventura Blvd., Studio City, CA 91604).

Hansen, Charles. Harry Dexter's Harmony Theory Pocket Book (Hansen Education Music and Books, 1860 Broadway, New York, NY 10023).

Harris, Herby and Lucien Farrar. How to Make Money in Music: A Guide for Success in Today's Music Businesss (Arco Publishing Co., Inc., 219 Park Avenue South, New York, NY 10003).

Murphy, James F. Music: Advanced Test for the G.R.E.
     (Arco Publishing Co., Inc.).

Music Educators Journal, "Careers and Music" (Reston,
     VA: Music Education National Conference, 63:7,
     March 1977, Entire issue).

Pincus, Lee. The Songwriter's Success Manual (Music
     Press, Inc., Box 1229, Grand Central Station, New
     York, NY 10017).

Rogers, Milt. Learning to Sight-Sing (Charles Hansen
     Education Music and Books).

Shemel, Sidney, and M. William Krasilovsky. The
     Business of Music (Cincinnati, Ohio: Bilboard
     Book Division).

SOURCES OF INFORMATION

A letter to any of the leading trade publications
can be very helpful. If you have specific questions,
they will often provide you with answers and direct you
to other sources they know about.   In your letter
include a stamped, self-addressed envelope if you want
a speedy reply. In addition, ASCAP, BMI, AGVA, AFTRA,
SESAC, and others issue periodicals and communications
which are usually free and serve to help keep you on
top of conditions and changes in the industry. They
are all eager to encourage serious and talented people.
Chaeck libraries, schools, and colleges in your area to
see if they offer courses or information which can
benefit you.

The following list of sources will help you get
started and lead to other sources too numerous to be
included here.

PERIODICALS

Billboard
Billboard Publications
One Astor Plaza
New York, NY 10036

Cashbox
119 West 57th Street
New York, NY 10019

Guitar Player
Box 615
Saratoga, CA 95070

Modern Recording
Cowan Publishing Corporation
14 Vanderventer Avenue
Port Washington, NY 11050

Record World
1700 Broadway
New York, NY   10019

(Note: These orga-
nizations publish
annual directory
and buyer's guides
and other industry
publications.)

Accent
1418 Lake Street
Evanston, IL   60204

Backstage Publications,
    Inc.
165 West 46th Street
New York, NY   10036

Downbeat
222 West Adams Street
Chicago, IL   60606

Rolling Stone
78 East 56th Street
New York, NY   10022

Show Business
136 West 44th Street
New York, NY   10036

Songwriter Magazine
900 Sunset Boulevard, Suite
    1510
Los Angeles, CA   90069

Songwriter Review
1697 Broadway
New York, NY   10019

Songwriter's Magazine
P.O. Box 3510
Hollywood, CA   90028

Timesmith
P.O. Box 3839
Hollywood, CA   90028

Variety
154 West 46th Street
New York, NY   10036

ASSOCIATION PROVIDING MUSIC

CAREER INFORMATION

EDUCATION

American Music
  Conference
Kalamazoo, MI   49002

College Band Directors
  Association
c/o University of
  California Bands
59 Student Center
Berkeley, CA   94720

College For Recording
  Arts
655 Harrison Street
San Francisco, CA   94107

Music Educators National
  Conference
1902 Association Drive
Reston, VA   22090

National Association For
  Music Therapy
P.O. Box 15
Lawrence, KA   66044

National Association of Jazz
  Educators
Box 724
Manhattan, KA   66502

National Association of
  Schools
11250 Roger Bacon Drive
Reston, VA   22090

National Band Association
Box 2454
West lafayette, IN   47906

Tennessee College For
  Recording Arts
904 Rayner Street
Memphis, TN   38114

TRADE ASSOCIATIONS

Actor's Equity
  Association
1500 Broadway
New York, NY   10036

Afro-American Arts
  Institute
109 North Jordan
Bloomington, IN   47401

American Federation of
  Musicians (AFM)
1500 Broadway
New York, NY   10036

American Guild of Authors
  Composers (AGAC)
40 West 57th Street
New York, NY   10019

American Guild of Musical
  Artists, Inc.
1841 Broadway
New York, NY   10023

American Guild of Organist
630 Fifth Avenue
New York, NY   10020

American Federation of
Television and Radio
(ADTRA)
1350 Avenue of the
Americas
New York, NY 10019

American Guild of Variety
Artists (AGVA)
1540 Broadway
New York, NY 10036

UNIONS

American Society of
Composers, Authors,
and Publishers
(ASCAP)
One Lincoln Plaza
New York, NY 10023

National Association of
Recording Merchandisers
(NARM)
Trianon Building
Suite 703
Bola Cynwyd, PA 19004

Artists' Representatives
Association, Inc.
1270 Avenue of the
Americas
New York, NY 10020

National Entertainment
Conference
P.O. Box 11489
Capitol Station
Columbia, SC 29211

Associated Actors and
Artistes of America
New York, NY 10036

Piano Technicians' Guild
P.O. Box 1813
Seattle, WA 98111

Broadcast Music,
Incorporated (BMI)
40 West 57th Street
New York, NY 10019

Recording Industry
Association of
America, Inc. (RIAA)
9200 Sunset Boulevard,
Suite 1005
Los Angeles, CA 90069

Country Music
Association, Inc.
1511 Sigler Avenue
Nashville, TN 37203

Screen Actors Guild, Inc.
7750 Sunset Boulevard
Nashville, TN 37203

Fraternity of Recording
Executives (FORE)
828 East 22nd Street
Bronx, NY 10047

Society of European Stage
Authors and Composers
(SESAC)
10 Columbus Circle
New York, NY 10019

National Academy of
Recording Arts and
Sciences (NARAS
Institute
505 North Lake Shore
Drive
Chicago, IL   60611

National Association
of Broadcasters
485 Madison Avenue
New York, NY   10022

National Association
of Music Merchants
35 East Wacker Drive,
Suite 3320
Chicago, IL   60601

Songwriter's Resources and
Services
6381 Hollywood Boulevard
Suite 503
Hollywood, CA   90028

Chapter 23

NATIONAL ASSESSMENT MEASURES MUSIC LEARNING:

BLACKS AND ·HISPANICS PERFORM BELOW THE NATION

AT ALL AGE LEVELS

Charles E. Hicks

The National Assessment of Education Progress (NAEP) has conducted two assessments of the music education of American students. The first assessment occured during the 1971-72 school year and the second, during the 1978-79 school year. In each assessment 9-13-, and 17-year-olds were administered exercises designed to measure some of their cognitive abilities and some of their experiences with music. The music exercises were designed to measure students' achievement on learning goals considered important by a cross-section of American Music Educators. The goals were formulated into five major objectives:

I. Value music as an important realm of human experience

II. Perform music

III. Create music

IV. Identify the elements and expressive controls of music

V. Identify and classify music historically and culturally

RESULTS OF SECOND ASSESSMENT DATA

Results of the second assessment show that about three-fourths of the students at each age level appear to have positive feelings about music and appear able to make simple judgments about it. Many students have some knowledge of the elements and expressive controls of music. On 45 exercises concerning this area, the average percentage of success for 9 -year olds was 52 percent; on 50 exercises, the average for 13-year olds was 61 percent; and on 49 exercises, the average for 17-year olds was 57 percent. Students appear strongest at identifying the elements and controls and weakest at identifying the relationships among them in a given music selection.[2] Fewer 9 and 17-year-olds were successful in answering their respective exercises in the 1978-79 assessment than in the 1971-72 assessment. The decline between assessments for 9-year-olds was 3.3 percent; for 17-year-olds, it was 2.5 percent. The percentage of 13-year-olds able to respond correctly to music exercises was about 41 percent in both assessments.[3]

Achievement results on objectives indicated that, fewer 9-year and 17-year-olds in the second assessment were successful on exercises that required knowledge of the elements and expressive controls of music than in the first assessment. The decline between assessments was 3.4 percent for 9-year-olds and 4.9 percent for 17-year-olds. Students knowledge about music history and style did not decline between assessments among 9-, 13-, or 17-year-olds. Among the findings, Blacks and Hispanics who did not decline significantly between assessments, but who remained below the nation, are the following: (1) Black students, at age 13 and 17, (2) Hispanic students, at ages 9, 13, and 17, and (3) students at age 9, and 13 who attended schools in disadvantaged-urban communities.

Table 23:1

Average Percentages of Correct Responses for
Selected Groups on Music Items, Age 9, 1972 and 1979

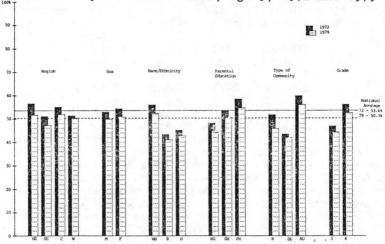

Average Percentages of Correct Responses for
Selected Groups on Music Items, Age 13, 1971 and 1978

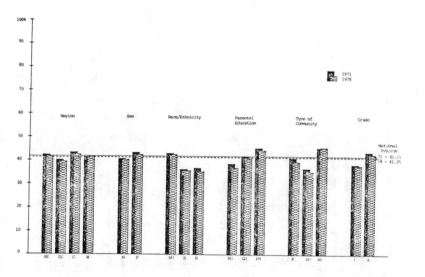

Knowledge about music history and style is less
widespread: on 18 exercises assessing these areas, the
average percentage of success for 9-year olds was 58
percent; on 55 exercises, the average percentage for
13-year olds was 36 percent; and on 61 exercises for
17-year olds, the average percentage of success was 39
percent.

Table 23:3

Average Percentages of Correct Responses for Selected Groups on Music Items, Age 17, 1972 and 1979

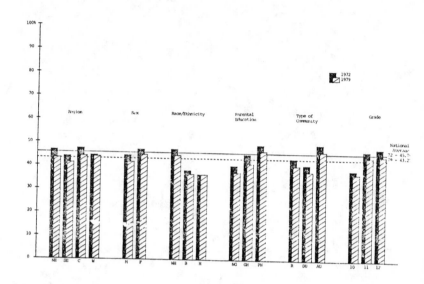

Table 23:4

National Mean Percentages and Changes in Correct Responses for 9-, 13- and 17-Year-Olds in Two Music Assessments

	Mean % Correct 1971-72	Mean % Correct 1978-79	Change in Mean % Correct 1971-72, 1978-79
Age 9, total exercises — 25	53.6	50.3	−3.3*
Age 13, total exercises – 69	41.8	41.3	−0.5
Age 17, total exercises — 80	45.7	43.2	−2.5*

* Asterisk indicates percentages statistically significant at the .05 level.

Some exercises from the first assessment were readministered to students in the second assessment so that changes in music achievement could be measured. Results on these exercises are shown in Table 23:4. Some groups' position relative to national levels of achievement did not change significantly, there were a marked decline in achievement between the two assessments. For example, students in disadvantaged urban areas both Black and Hispanic ages 9 and 13 slipped even further below the national average. While17 yr. old Hispanic students remained the same for both assessments. Table 23:8 provides a more comprehensive listing of groups' results.

MUSIC ACTIVITIES OUTSIDE SCHOOL

NAEP also gathered data on the music training background of students. All students participating in the 1978-79 music assessment were asked the same questions about their exposure to musical activities outside of school. The date revealed that more 13--and 17-year-old than 9-year-olds listen to music, sing just for fun and sing with friends for fun. However, percentages for 9- and 13-year-olds are more similar to each other than to percentages for 17-year-olds who sing with friends for fun. Conversely, more 9--year-olds than 13-or 17-year-olds indicated that they sing in a church or community music group. Percentages of 9-, 13-, or 17-year-olds who do at least one of the singing activities are very similar. More 13-, and 17-year-olds than 9-year-olds play a musical instrument alone for fun, while more 9-year-olds than 13-or 17-year-olds indicated that they play a musical instrument in a community group. In addition, more 9-year-olds than 13- or 17-year-olds indicated at least one activity involving playing an instrument. More 9-year-olds than 13- or 17-year-olds take music lessons and make up their own music.

MUSIC ACTIVITIES WITHIN SCHOOL

Seventy-four percent of the 9-year-olds indicated that they "listen to music"; 45 perent indicated that they "sing just for fun"; nearly 30 percent indicated that they "play a musical instrument just for fun"; and nearly 14 percent indicated that they "play a musical instrument in a special music group" in a school music class. The nine-year-olds who indicated that they had been taught music in school for two years (1977-78/1978-79) performed about 4 percentage points better on all music exercises than those who had been taught music in school for only one year and 6 percentage points better than those who had not been taught music in school in either year.[5]

Table 23:5 shows the results of 9-year-olds on exercises designed to measure objective 1. Students were asked "which one of the following things would you rather do if you had one free period a day in school?" An analysis performed to compare the selection of music-related activities (numbers 1, 4 and 6) to non-music-related activities (numbers 2, 3, 5 and 7). Twenty-nine percent (29.4 percent) of the 9-year-olds chose music-related activities, while more than two-thirds of them (67.3 percent) chose non-music-related activities." Significantly more Blacks and Hispanos students who reported that neither parent graduated from high school and youths who attended school in disadvantaged-urban communities chose music-related activities over 9-year-olds nationally. Significantly more White Students chose nonmusic-related activities than 9-year-olds nationally."[6]

Table 23:5

Responses for 9-Year Olds: Which ONE of the Following Things Would You Rather Do If You Had One Free Period a Day in School?

		Region				Race/Ethnicity			Sex		Parental Education			Type of Community †		
Nation	NE	SE	W	C	WH	B	H	M	F	NG	GH	PH	R	DU	AU
1. Play a musical instrument															
14.4%	14.0%	16.3%	14.0%	13.4%	13.4%*	18.9%*	20.1%	14.7%	14.1%	17.2%	14.7%	15.3%	13.5%	17.6%	13.9%
2. Draw or paint															
34.0	33.8	32.9	35.1	33.8	34.9*	29.3*	30.7	35.2	32.8	29.0	35.1	31.7	32.7	30.1	35.0
3. Write a story															
9.0	8.3	8.6	10.0	9.1	8.7	10.5	10.9	7.9	10.2	10.9	9.1	9.4	9.9	11.9	7.7
4. Sing in a musical group															
4.5	5.1	4.4	4.5	4.1	3.8*	7.2*	7.8	3.3*	5.8*	6.7	4.6	3.9	4.5	7.9*	3.6
5. Learn a foreign language															
13.9	12.9	13.5	13.3	15.7	14.5*	11.9	10.5	12.6	15.2	12.0	14.3	16.3*	13.4	10.5	16.5
6. Listen to music															
10.5	10.4	11.7	10.0	10.0	10.4	9.9	10.5	9.7	11.3	12.4	10.4	10.2	12.1	10.5	9.4
7. None of these															
10.4	11.8	9.2	9.9	10.7	11.3*	7.2*	4.8*	13.2*.	7.5*	7.0*	9.4	10.9	10.7	6.1*	11.7
Preferences for above:															
Music related (1, 4, 6)															
29.4#	29.5	32.5	28.4	27.6	27.6*	36.1*	38.4*	27.7	31.2	36.3*	29.8	29.4	30.1	36.1*	27.0
Nonmusic related (2, 3, 5, 7)															
67.3#	66.9	64.2	68.2	69.3	69.5*	58.8*	56.9*	68.8	65.7	58.9*	67.9	68.3	66.7	58.6*	70.8

* Asterisk indicates percentages statistically significant at the .05 level.
† This population group represents about one-third of the sample.
# Figures may not total 100% due to rounding.

462

Thirteen-and-17-year-olds also were asked a series of questions to explore their participation in school musical activities. More 13- and 17-year-olds indicated participation in general music classes than in choir, band or orchestra. However, approximately 28 percnt of the 13-year-olds and 18 percent of the 17-year-olds have never taken a general music class or music appreciation. Forty-eight percent of the 13-year-olds and 46 percent of the 17-year-olds have never taken choir, chorus or glee club; 50 percent of the 13-year-olds and nearly 52 percent of the 17-year-olds have never taken band or instrumental music; and a bit more than 90 percent of the 13- and 17-year-olds have never taken orchestra. In terms of race/ethnicity, Table 23:1 revealed that Black 9-year-olds from disadvantaged urban-areas scored below their White and Hispanic counterparts. This same Table shows that those disadvantaged Blacks who live in the Southeast part of the United States were below the same age group category from other regions of the nation. In Tables 23:2 and 23:3 data for 13- and 17-year-olds on the music items showed that the Southeast part of the country ranked lowest. Blacks and Hispanics in the 13 and 17-year-olds groups ranked about the same, both group scores showed a decline from the first assessment. Students in all age groups from disadvantaged urban areas ranked lowest in all categories.[7]

Table 23:6

Group Results, 126 Music Exercises, Age 17, 1979[8]

	Mean % Correct	Mean Group Differences#
Nation	49.98	
Region		
Northeast	49.75	−0.23
Southeast	48.12	−1.85*
Central ‡	50.86	0.89*
West ‡	50.92	0.95
Sex		
Male	48.16	−1.82*
Female	51.69	1.72*
Race/ethnicity		
White	51.18	1.20*
Black	43.41	−6.56*
Hispano	43.74	−6.24*
Parental education		
Not graduated high school	44.36	−5.62*
Graduated high school	47.84	−2.14*
Post high school	53.35	3.38*
Type of community †		
Rural	47.62	−2.36*
Disadvantaged urban	45.06	−4.92*
Advantaged urban	53.21	3.24*
Grade		
10	44.10	−5.87*
11	50.88	0.90*
12	51.57	1.60*

Figures may not total due to rounding.

* Asterisk indicates percentages statistically significant at the .05 level.

‡ A smaller difference (.89) for the Central region is statistically significant, while a larger difference (.95) for the West is not significant because there is a larger sample size in the Central region and also some sampling error in estimates of variations.

† This population group represents about one-third of the sample.

Table 23:7

Group Results by Objectives, Age 17, 1979[9]

	Objective I 16 Exercises	Objective IV 49 Exercises	Objective V 61 Exercises
Nation	71.16	57.06	38.73
Region			
Northeast	−1.81*	−1.55	1.22
Southeast	2.67*	−3.14*	−2.04*
Central	−0.56	1.97*	0.39
West	−0.05	2.30*	0.10
Sex			
Male	−2.96*	−2.71*	−0.78
Female	2.79*	2.62*	0.69
Race/ethnicity			
White	−1.02	1.90*	1.16*
Black	6.62*	−10.29*	−7.02*
Hispano	1.95	−10.38*	−5.09
Parental education			
Not graduated high school	1.37	−8.54*	−5.14*
Graduated high school	−1.11	−2.88*	−1.83*
Post high school	0.69	4.74*	2.92*
Type of community†			
Rural	0.45	−1.91	−3.46*
Disadvantaged urban	2.09	−7.15*	−4.97*
Advantaged urban	1.30	3.57*	3.49*

* *Asterisk indicates percentages statistically significant at the .05 level.*
† *This population group represents about one-third of the sample.*

465

Table 23:8

Group Results In Two Music Assessments,[10] 1971-72 And 1978-79

Group Results, 25 Music Exercises, Age 9, 1972, 1979#

	Mean % Correct		Change in Mean % Correct 1972-79	Mean Group Differences		Change in Mean Group Differences 1972-79
	1972	1979		1972	1979	
Nation	53.61	50.33	-3.28*			
Region						
Northeast	56.49	51.67	-4.82*	2.88*	1.35	-1.53
Southeast	51.04	47.17	-3.87*	-2.57*	-3.15*	-0.58
Central	55.05	51.95	-3.10*	1.44*	1.62	0.18
West	51.33	50.35	-0.98	-2.27*	0.03	2.30
Sex						
Male	52.85	49.88	-2.97*	-0.76*	-0.45	0.31
Female	54.32	50.79	-3.53*	0.71*	0.46	-0.25
Race/ethnicity						
White	55.95	52.33	-3.62*	2.34*	2.01*	-0.33
Black	43.29	41.03	-2.26*	-10.32*	-9.30*	1.02
Hispano	45.10	42.77	-2.33	-8.51*	-7.56*	0.95
Parental education						
Not graduated high school	48.12	44.25	-3.87*	-5.49*	-6.08*	-0.59
Graduated high school	53.54	50.49	-3.05*	-0.06	0.17	0.23
Post high school	58.39	54.64	-3.75*	4.78*	4.31*	-0.47
Type of community†						
Rural	51.68	45.76	-5.92*	-1.93	-4.56*	-2.63
Disadvantaged urban	43.38	41.95	-1.43	-10.22*	-8.38*	1.84
Advantaged urban	59.76	55.98	-3.78*	6.15*	5.66*	-0.49
Grade						
3	46.81	44.31	-2.50*	-6.80*	-6.02*	0.78
4	56.07	52.53	-3.54*	2.46*	2.20*	-0.26

Figures may not total due to rounding.
* Asterisk indicates percentages statistically significant at the .05 level.
† This population group represents about one-third of the sample.

Summary

Results from the NAEP Music Assessment seem to confirm what many music educators had expected; "most young Americans are attuned to the sounds of music, but they're a bit off key when it comes to knowledge about music and music history." Between assessments, data revealed a decline for nine and seventeen-year-olds, while thirteen-year-olds were holding their own. The second assessment showed that nearly all teenagers (90 percent at age 13 and 98 percent at age 17) listen to music; but a much smaller percentage of nine, thirteen and 17-year-olds respectively have taken a class in general music, while almost a third of that same group participated in vocal or instrumental music at least one year.

Blacks and Hispanics did not show very well, scoring below the national average at all grade levels. Students who attended school in disadvantaged-urban areas scored lower than their rural and advantaged-urban counterparts on all measures. Data also showed an absence of ethnic and non-western music being taught in the music classrooms of this nation on the level suggested by the Tanglewood Symposium and other such conferences. This latest assessment proves what many music educators have suspected for sometime; large numbers of American Youths are involved in music, but outside of the school music classroom. Until the music profession get serious about and start including rock, pop, jazz and other culturally based music in schools, our youths will continue to stay away from the school music classes.

Discussion

The results of the national assessment in music points to the fact that public schools are not educating Blacks and minorities. The schools are not done its job in teaching Blacks to read, to write, do math and learn music. Why?

As one who have worked in urban schools for more than sixteen (16) years, I have some thoughts about why Blacks and minorities are not being educated in numbers in our urban schools. One possible reason might be the following: The cultural differences and other problems associated with minority groups have created less expectation from teachers. The "deprived" child syndrome, the attempt to legitimatize non-standard

(Black) English, Bi-lingual educational programs for non-english speaking students, after school reading programs and other programs all have translated into excuses for not expecting these groups of children to live up to their potential. Social promotion and yes, low IQ scores have caused teachers, counselors and administrators to accept less from these children. Consequently, at each level in their education teachers have expected less, and that is what they're got, and the viscious circle continues.

This chapter could be correctly sub-titled Testing and the Miseducation of Minorities. Who should be held accountable for the education of children in schools today? The state, the school district, or the parents. The buck stops at the state and local school level. The schools have failed in its mission; if it does not educate all of its students. However, the Parent (taxpayer) must continue to expect, demand and hold our public schools accountable for educating their sons and daughters. If this is not done, Blacks and minorities children will continue to receive an inferior education, not only in music but other subjects as well.

No longer can Blacks and the minority poor of this nation allow school officials to use their nowhere in this nation and around the world are there differences made for Blacks, Hispanics, in jobs. Do Black doctors use a different type of medicine, Do Black athletes get by with only playing eight innings in baseball, or three quarters of basketball or do they get to use a different ball from the other competitors? Standard English is used in all tests, if minority children are to compete with the rest of the world, they too must be able to handle standard English. They too must be able to read, write and do math and Music like anyone else. The schools can no longer make excuses for these groups of children and parents can no longer accept these excuses a valid.

NOTES FOR CHAPER 23

1.   National Assessment of Education Progress, Music 1971-79; Results from the Second National Music Assessment (Denver: Education Commission of the States), p. 4.

2.   Ibid. p. xiii

3.   Ibid.

4.   Ibid. pp. 10-18

5.   Ibid. pp. 10-18

6.   Ibid. pp. 12-14

7.   Ibid. pp. 6-9

8.   Ibid. p. 53

9.   Ibid. p. 56

10. Ibid. p. 57.

BAKER'S BLACK GOSPEL ANALYSIS MODEL

Artist(s): _____   Date of Record: _____
Record Title: _____   Index Number: _____
Label and Number: _____   Source: _____

SOUND

Components	Description	Element(s) Present
Voices(s)	1. Soprano I 2. Soprano II 3. Alto I 4. Alto II 5. Contralto 6. Tenor I 7. Tenor II 8. Baritone 9. Bass 10. Quartet 11. Quintet 12. Group 13. Chorus 14. Ensemble 15. Other _____	_____ _____ _____ _____ _____ _____ _____ _____
Vocal Devices	1. Nonharmonic tones: a. upper neighboring tones b. lower neighboring tones c. passing tones d. anticipation 2. Fill-in tones 3. Portamento 4. Vibrato: a. terminal b. tremolo 5. Octave leap 6. Substitute intervals 7. Scat singing 8. Moan 9. Growl/Scream 10. Hum 11. Explosive release 12. Falsetto 13. Worrying 14. Bend 15. Lining out 16. Turn 17. Off-beat phrasing 18. Strong-beat phrasing 19. Vocal stops 20. Syncopation 21. Other _____	_____ _____ _____ _____ _____ _____ _____ _____ _____ _____ _____ _____ _____ _____
Vocal Styles	1. Doo-wah 2. Falsetto emphasis 3. Spoken introductions/ interludes 4. Echo effects	_____ _____ _____

(c) 1978

Components	Description	Element(s) Present
	5. Responsorial 6. Inverted voicing 7. Blues 8. Jazz 9. Chorale 10. Lining out 11. Other _____	_____ _____ _____ _____

Instrument(s)
| | 1. Piano 2. Organ 3. Guitar: a. acoustic b. amplified c. bass d. lead 4. Drums: a. set b. congo/bongo 5. Strings: a. violin b. viola c. cello d. bass 6. Woodwinds: a. flute b. oboe c. clarinet d. bassoon 7. Brass: a. trumpet b. saxophone c. trombone d. horn 8. Celeste 9. Xylophone 10. Tambourine 11. Body Percussion: a. hand clap b. foot pat c. thigh pat 12. Other _____ | _____ _____ _____ _____ _____ _____ _____ _____ _____ _____ _____ |

Instrumental
Devices
| | 1. Bend 2. Glissando 3. Fill-in notes 4. Fill-in chords 5. Vibrato: a. terminal 6. Worrying 7. Octave leap 8. Upper neighboring tones 9. Lower neighboring tones 10. Passing tones 11. Tremolo 12. Arpeggio 13. Syncopation 14. Ostinato 15. Echo effects 16. Other _____ | _____ _____ _____ _____ _____ _____ _____ _____ _____ |

Instrumental
Styles
| | 1. Simple chordal accompaniment 2. Elaborate arrangements 3. Keyboard styles: 'a. boogie woogie b. blues c. classical d. jazz e. polarized f. responsorial g. syncopatedd chordal style 4. Other _____ | _____ _____ _____ _____ _____ _____ _____ |

471

Components	Description	Element(s) Present
Texture	1. Contrasting Sections 2. Monophonic 3. Homophonic 4. Polyphonce 5. Other ————————	———— ———— ———— ————
Dynamics	1. Terraced 2. Graduated a. b. c. d. e. f. g. 3. Level 4. Other ————————	———— ———— ———— ———— ————

RHYTHM

Tempo	1. Fast 2. Slow 3. Mixed 4. Rubato 5. Free 6. Other ————————	———— ———— ————
Meter	1. Regular 2. Irregular/ Asymmetrical 3. Polymetric 4. Hemiolic 5. Syncopation 6. Other ————————	———— ———— ———— ————
Density	1. Polyrhythmic 2. Homorhythmic 3. Mixed 4. Other ————————	———— ————
Melodic Rhythm	1. Syllabic 2. Melismatic 3. Neumatic 4. Active 5. Static 6. Other ————————	———— ————
Harmonic Rhythm	1. Slow 2. Moderate 3. Fast 4. Other ————————	———— ————

MELODY

Contours	1. Ascending 2. Descending 3. Level 4. Swatoothed 5. Wave form 6. Other ————————	———— ———— ———— ————

472

Components	Description	Element(s) Present
Motion	1. Disjunct 2. Conjunct 3. Mixed 4. Other _____	_____ _____
Range	1. Narrow 2. Wide	_____
Tessitura	1. High 2. Low 3. Moderate	_____

HARMONY

Tonality	1. Atonal 2. Tonal 3. Modal 4. Quartal 5. Quintal 6. Pentatonic 7. Consonant 8. Dissonant	_____ _____ _____ _____
Modulations	1. None 2. Few 3. Many	_____
Final Cadences	1. Full 2. Half 3. Deceptive	_____
Chord Progessions	1. Diatonic 2. Chromatic 3. Modal 4. Traditional 5. Transitional 6. Contemporary	_____ _____ _____

FORM

Repetition with Contrast	1. Two-part song form. 2. Three-part song form 3. Rondo	_____ _____
Repetition with Variation	1. Theme and Variation 2. Strophic Variation 3. Extended Chorus 4. Other _____	_____ _____ _____

473

Components	Description	Element(s) Present
Free Forms	1. Through-composed 2. Other	
	_____	

TEXT

Religious
Characterization
        1. Blessings 2. Sorrows
        3. Trials 4. Tribulations
        5. Joy 6. Jubilation 7. Faith
        8. Hope 9. Father 10. Mother
        11. Grace 12. Death 13. Heaven
        14. Patience 15. Optimism
        16. Other _____

Textual
Interpolations
        1. Petitions 2. Commands
        3. Questions 4. Support
        5. Vocables: a. my Lord
        b. well c. oh d. yes e. ooh
        6. Testimony 7. Shouts
        8. Other _____

EXTRA-MUSICAL ELEMENTS

Congregational
Response   1. Shouts 2. Screams
        3. Unmetered clap 4. Yells
        5. Moans 6. Chants 7. Other

        _____

Personal   1. Witnessing 2. Testifying
Testimony   3. Other _____

UNIQUE/UNUSUAL FEATURE

1. Active melodic rhythm - three (3) or more melodic rhythmic patterns within a single phrase.

2. Anticipation - a tone that does not belong to a chord, but will be a part of the subsequent one.

3. Ascending melodic contour - the general tendency of a melodic line to a move in an upward direction, and end on a pitch higher than the beginning pitch.

4. Asymmetrical - uneven, unbalanced metric pulse.

5. Atonal - absence of a tonal center.

6. Bend - slight raising or lowering of a pitch less than a semitone.

7. Blessings - generally undeserved good works from God.

8. Blues style - in the manner of the blues. This style is generally characterized by the use of the blues form (twelve-or sixteen-bar pattern) divided into three (3) call-and-response sections, the blues scale with lowered third, fifth, and seventh, and a harmonic pattern of I-IV-I-V(IV)I. No attempt to identify specific blues styles has been made.

9. Boogie-woogie piano style - a blues piano style characterized by a continuing rhythmic ostinato, sometimes outlining a seventh chord, and often using eight notes to the bar.

10. Chorale - four part harmony (SATB) with the melody in the top voice.

11. Chorus - large group of singers, usually more than fifteen (15).

12. Chromatic harmony - chords based on the chromatic scale (twelve equal one-half steps between an octave.

13. Classical keyboard style - piano technique based on the classics of the Western piano literature

from Mozart through contemporary keyboard composers.

14. Commands - interpolations into the text that order or direct the listener to obey (i.e., "Listen to me church," "Pray with me").

15. Conjunct melodic motion - successive degrees of the scale moving in ascending or descending motion.

16. Consonant tonality - absence of dissonant quality in music.

17. Contemporary chord progression - complex diatonic and chromatic cord movements where the chord size is expanded to include 9ths, 11ths and 13ths, as well as diminished and augmented intervals.

18. Contrasting sections - varied sound combinations achieved by reducing, adding, or changing the performing forces thus creating contrasts in the sound and the appearance of the score.

19. Deceptive cadences - when the tonic is replaced by another chord, most often the VI, in a cadential progression.

20. Descending melodic contour - the general tendency of a melodic line to move in a downward direction and end on a pitch lower than the beginning pitch.

21. Diatonic chord progressions - chords based on the natural scale (five whole steps and two 1/2 steps) as it is produced on the white keys of the keyboard, excluding chromatic tones.

22. Disjunct melodic contour - the line produced by melodic movement that forms intervals larger than a second; moves by skip rather than step.

23. Dissonant tonality - characterized by tension and irregularity in music.

24. Doo-wah vocal style - characterized by sustained chords on syllables such as "doo, ah, oh, and ooh." Very popular in the '50's as a vocal accompaniment style.

25. Echo effects - are produced by vocal and instrumental accompaniments when a word, phrase, or motive is imitated in exact repetition, thus producing an echo effect.

26. Elaborate arrangement- one that is written out, rehearsed, and/or includes instruments from either the string, the woodwind, or the brass families.

27. Ensemble - group of several (usually more than two but often less than fifteen) singers.

28. Explosive release - percussive accent on consonants (for example: "t, d, ch").

29. Extended chorus - a special, added on section of a Black gospel song that allows the soloist and chorus to improvise more extensively.

30. Faith - inner belief in the unseen; substance of things hoped for.

31. Fall - the downward or descending movement of a pitch at the release of a sustained pitch.

32. Falsetto - refers to male singers who are able to use their "head register" or high notes above their ordinary voice range. The tone is usually lighter and softer than tones sung using the "chest register."

33. Fast harmonic rhythm - three or more different chords per measure.

34. Fast tempo - Maezel metronome markings ♩ = 74-200.

35. Father - the Father is usually God; father is the natural parent.

36. Few modulations - one key change in one piece.

37. Fill-in chords - chords that are played or sung to literally "take up space" in a line and provide continual motion to the accompaniment; usually occurring on long, sustained melodic notes.

38. Fill-in notes - notes that fill-in or connect an interval larger than a third.

39. Free tempo - without tempo markings, and often sung in the style of recitative.

40. Glissando - the execution of rapid scales by a sliding movement on an instrument.

42. Graduated dynamics - the measure increase or decrease of volume.

43. Group - refers to two to six singers.

44. Growl - usually a throaty, husky sound.

45. Half cadence - cadences that have the third or fifth of the tonic chord in the soprano voice; cadences that occur at the end of the first half of a musical phrase; cadences that occur in transposition of the dominant.

46. Hemiolic meter - refers to time values that are in the relationship of 3:2.

47. High tessiture - largest number of notes fall in the upper half of the scale.

48. Homophonic texture - chordal style with the top voice having the melody.

49. Homorhythmic density - uniform rhythmic patterns in all instrumental parts.

50. Hope - expectation based on faith.

51. Inverted voicing - often refers to the tenor line sung an octave above where it is written by the soprano voice often resulting in the $\frac{6}{4}$ inversion.

52. Irregular meter - asymmetrical, uneven metric pulses.

53. Jazz style - characerized by improvisation of melody, rhythm, harmony and structure. A common element of all jazz is "swing," created by "unexpected hesitations and anticipations (rubato) and/or inflections of tone; placing naturally accented beats or phrases in sudden contrast to syncopated notes or phrases; by unexpected changes of phrasing and rhythmic figures; changes of dynamic level on the same tone or series of tones; altering phrase lengths; and

478

creating tension and relaxation through the use of these devices.[27]

54. Jesus - refers to Lord, the Son of God.

55. joy - happiness.

56. Jubilation - rejoicing.

57. Level melodic contour - indicated by pitches that are relatively stationary and end and begin on the same pitch.

58. Lift - the upward or rising movement at the release of a sustained tone.

59. Lining out - a style of singing where the words are presented by a solo singer in a parlando style (similar to sprechstimme).

60. Low tessiture - largest number of notes fall in the lower half of the scale.

61. Lower neighboring tones - a descending tone occurring between two notes of the same pitch, creating a 1/2 step down and then back up to the original note.

62. Many modulations - two or more key changes in one piece.

63. Melismatic - several notes and groups of notes sung to one syllable.

64. Mixed rhythmis denisty - a combination of poly-rhythmic and homorhythmic patterns in one piece.

66. Moan - characterized by a soft, pitched wail in a modal tonality.

67. Modal tonality - harmonic and melodic formations based on the church modes (dorian, phrygian, lydian, mixolydian, and aeolian).

68. Moderate harmonic rhythm - two different chords per measure.

69. Moderato tempo- Maezel metronome markings=61.73.

70. Monophonic texture - single line of solo melody.

71. Mother - usually refers to the natural mother.

72. Narrow range - short distance (a fifth or less) between the lowest and highest notes of a melody.

73. Neumatic melodic rhythm - group of two to four notes per syllable.

74. Octave leap - a move upward or down the interval of an octave. The upward move is sometimes sung in falsetto by male singers.

75. Off-beat phrasing - see Weak-beat phrasing.

76. Optimism - the belief that things will be better; anticipating the best possible outcome.

77. Organ - refers to the electric organ; the Hammond organ is perhaps the most popular, followed by the electric Baldwin.

78. Ostinato - a clearly defined melodic pattern that is repeated consistently throughout a piece or a section of a piece, often forming a rhythmic ostinato.

79. Passing tones - notes that occur between two pitches that are intervals of a third or a second.

80. Patience - the ability to wait; to bear pain or trials calmly without complaint.

81. Pentatonic tonality - harmony built on the tonal five-tone scale that has no half steps. In gospel music this scale is usually played using only the black keys on the piano.

82. Petitions - earnest requests of God.

83. Polorized piano - a keyboard style that incorporates low, deep left-hand octaves and high, treble chords simultaneously.

84. Polymetric - contrasting rhythms involving a conflict of meter.

85. Polyphonic - each voice has independent part; countrapuntal.

86. Polyrhythmic denisty - contrast of instrumental rhythms within the same meter; cross-rhythms.

87. Portamento - a vocal device where the singer glides gradually from one tone to the next through all the intermediate pitches. The corresponding instrumental practice is called glissando.

88. Quartal harmony - harmony based on the fourth as opposed to the present common system of tertian harmony, based on the third.

89. Quartet - usually four singers, but occasionally groups of five will still refer to the group as a quartet.

90. Quintal harmony - based on the interval of a fifth as compared to tertian (based on the third).

91. Quintet - usually refers to a group of five singers.

92. Regular meter - metric pattern where note values and accents remain unaltered throughout a section or entire piece.

93. Responsorial style - characterized by a musical statement and response, question and answer, or call and response pattern. Instrumentally, the response is an appropriate motive. Vocally, the response can be an answer to a question, or a musical response to a motive.

94. Rondo - a five-part song form characterized by the return of the A section at least three times.

95. Rubato - elasticity and flexibility of tempo consisting of unexpected hesitations and anticipations.

96. Scream - an emotional, non-pitched yell.

97. Shout - a movement made by an individual in expressing his personal emotion resembling a shuffle dance with unpredictable, jerky movements accompanied by screams, moans, chants, and singing that is peculiar to the individual at a particular moment.

98. Simple chordal accompaniment - characterized by root position, first, and second inversion chords.

99. Slol harmonic rhythm - one chord per measure.

100. Slow tempo - Maezel metronome markings ♩ = 44-60.

101. Sorrow - sadness sometimes associated with death, burdens, or pain.

103. Static melodic rhythm - nearly uniform melodic rhythm.

104. Strong-beat phrasing - characterized by phrases that end on strong beat.

105. Strophic variation - a piece written in verse form where the melody is varied by improvised vocal ornamentation and embellishments each time it returns.

106. Two-part song form - musical form in two parts (A and B) that follows the key relationship of Tonic to Dominant in part A, and Dominant to Tonic in part B. There may also be an introduction or a coda. Additionally, two-part form is considered to be a verse plus a chorus, regardless of key relationships.

107. Unmetered clap - one that lacks any metrical pattern or scheme.

108. Upper neighboring tones - an ascending tone occurring between two notes of the same pitch creating a whole or half step up from the original note.

109. Vocables - syllables and short words interjected into the gospel song.

110. Vocal stop - the placing of rests and/or breathing between words or syllables in words.

111. Vibrato - the natural wavering of vocal and instrumental tone.

112. Weak-beat phrasing - often called off-the-beat phrasing because the phrase ends on a weak beat, or on a part of the strong beat that is not

expected.

113. Wide melodic range - an interval of a sixth or more between the lowest and highest notes of a melody.

114. Worrying - characterized by repeating a melodic motive or a particular word or phrase at a quick pace.

CONTEMPORARY CHORAL MUSIC OF
BLACK AMERICAN COMPOSERS SUITABLE
FOR THE HIGH SCHOOL CHOIR

Composer	Title	Voicing	Publisher
Arthur Cunningham			
	Honey Brown	TTBB	TP
	Harlem Suite	SATB, SA	TP
	Two Players	SATB	TP
	He Met Her At The Dolphin	SAATB	R
	Night Song	SATB	TP
	Sunday Stone	SATB	TP
	Timber	SATB	TP
	Amen	SATB	
	Hymn of Our Lord	SATB	
	In The Year Seventeen	SATB	
	Ring Out Wild Bells	SATB	
	Fruitful Trees More Fruitful Are	SATB	
	When I Was One and Twenty	SATB	
	Fifty Stars	SA	
	The Gingerbread Man	TTBB	
Noel da Costa			
	Little Lamb	SATB	
	O God of Light and Love	SATB	
	Counterpoint	SATB	
	I Have A Dream	SATB	
Robert Harris			
	For the Beauty of the Earth	SATB	
	Glory to God	SATB	JB
	Let us Break Bread Together	SSA	JB
	A Collect for Peace	SATB	
	Benedictus	SSAA	
	Kyrie and Gloria	SATB	
	May the Grace of Christ Our Savior	SATB	
	O Come, Let Us Sing Unto the Lord	SATB	
	Rejoice Ye Pure In Heart	SATB	
	Canticle: The Hungry Angels	SATB	MF
Lena McLin			
	Challenge	SATB	GWM

Composer	Title	Voicing	Publisher
Lena McLin (cont.)			
	All The Earth Sing Unto The Lord	SATB	GWM
	What Will You Put Under the Christmas Tree	SATB	GWM
	Friendship	SATB	GWM
	For Jesus Christ Is Born	SATB	NK
	Free At Last (A Portrait of Martin Luther King)	SATB	GWM
	Sanctus and Benedictus	SATB	GWM
	Winter, Spring, Summer, Autumn	SATB	GWM
	Memory	SATB	GWM
	The Love of God	SATB	GWM
	In This World	SATB, soil Rock Combo	GWM
	Gwendolyn Brooks, A Musical Portrait	SATB	GWM
	The Colors of the Rainbow	SATB	PA
	Give Me That Old Time Religion	SATB	GWM
	Cert'nly Lord, Cer'ny Lord	SATB, soil	GWM
	Done Made My Vow To The Lord	SATB	GWM
	Eucharist of the Soul Glory, Glory, Hallelujah	SATB	GWM
	If They Ask You Why He Came	SATB	GWM
	I'm So Glad Trouble Don't Last Always	SATB	GWM
	Let The People Sing Praise Unto the Lord	SATB	GWM
	Lit'le Lamb, Lit'le Lamb	SATB	GWM
	The Litle Baby	SATB	GWM
	My God Is So High	SATB	GWM
	New Born King	SATB	GWM
	Since He Came Into My LIfe	SATB	GWM
	Te Deum Laudamus	SATB	GWM
	This Land	SATB or Unison	GWM
	The Torch Has Been Passed	SATB	GWM
	Written Down My Name	SATB	GWM
Julia Perry			
	Song of Our Savior	SATB	G
	Carrilon Heigh-Ho	SATB	CF
Dorothy Rudd Moore			
	In Music Be the Food of Love	SAR	

485

Composer	Title	Voicing	Publisher

Dorothy Rudd Moore (cont.)

	Passing By	SSA	R
	Ride on, King Jesus	SATB	R
	This Little Light of Mine	SATB	R
	Wiegenlied	SSA	R

Frederick C. Tillis

	Freedom: Memorial For Dr.		
	Martin Luther King Jr.	SATB	SMP
	Allelulia	SATB	

Coleridge-Taylor Perkinson

	Fredom-Freedom	SATB	TMC

George Walker

	Gloria In Memorian	SSA	
	Stars	SATB	AMP
	O Lord God of Hosts	SATB	GMP
	Sing Unto the Lord	SATB	GMP
	Give Thanks Unto The Lord	SSA	GMP
	O Praise The Lord	SATB	GMP
	Priase Ye The Lord	SATB	GMP
	With This Small Key	SATB	GMP
	A Babe Is Born	SATB	
	Three Lyrics for Chorus	SATB	GMP
	The Bereaved Maid		
	Take, O, Take Those Lips Away		
	O Western Wind		

Ronald Roxbury

	There Is No Rose of Such		
	Vertu	SATB	WMC
	Ave Maria	SATB	WMC
	As Dew In Aprille	SATB	WMC
	That Yonge Child	SATB	WMC
	Ave Verum	ATTBB	
	Regina Coeli	TTBB, w soli	
	Virgo Virginum	TTBB	
	Ave Maria Stella	TTBB, w soli	
	Missa Brevis	SATB	
	Ma Bell	SSA	

Hale Smith

	In Memoriam -		
	Beryl Rubinstein	SATB	HP
	Comes Tomorrow	SATB	EBM
	Two Kids	SATB	EBM

Composer	Title	Voicing	Publisher
Hale Smith (cont.)			
	I'm Coming Home	SATB	EM
	Toussaint L'Ouverture	SATB	
James Furman			
	Let Us Break Bread Together	SATB	
	Trampin'	SATB	
	I Keep Journeyin' On	SATB	
	The Threefold Birth	SATB, Boys Voices	
	The Quiet Life	SATB	
	Fanfare and Pastorale		
	Quiet By Day		
	Sound Sleep By Night		
	Thus Let Me Live		
	Some Glorious Day	SATB	SF
	Go Tell It On The Mountain	SATB	SF
	Ave Maria	SSAATTBB	
	Come, Thou Long Expected Jesus	SATB	LG
	Four Little Foxes	SATB	OUP
	Speak Gently		
	Walk Softly		
	Go Lightly		
	Step Softly		
	Hold On	SATB	
	Hehlehlooyah, A Joyful Expression	SATB	HM
	Salvina Regina		
Ulysses Kay			
	Christmas Carol	SSA	PIC
	Come Away, Come Away Death	TBB	PIC
	Dedication	SATB	
	A Lincoln Letter	SATB, solo	CFP
	Triumvirate	TTBB	PIC
	A Wreath for Waits	SATB	AMP
	Noel		
	Lully, Lully		
	Welcome Yule		
	What's In A Name?	SSATB	LM
	How Stands the Glass Around	SSATB	AMP
	A New Song	SATB	CFP
	Sing Unto the Lord		
	Like As A Father		
	O Praise the Lord		
	Grace to You and Peace	SATB	CFP
	Hymn-Anthem on the Tune		

Composer	Title	Voicing	Publisher
Ulysses Kay (cont.)			
	"Hanover"	SATB	CFP
	Tears, Flow No More	SSAA	
	The Epicure	SATB	LM
	Flowers in the Valley	SATB	CFP
	To Light That Shines	SAB	
	Emily Dickinson Set	SSA	
	Two Dunbar Lyrics	SATB	MCA
	O Come, Emanuel	SATB	MCA
	Lo, the Earth	SATB	MCA
	God, The Lord	SATB	MCA
	Love Divine, All Love Excelling	SATB	MCA
	The Birds		
	The Great Black Crow	SA	
	The Skylark	SA	
	The Peacock	SSA	
	The Throstle Answer to a Child's Question	SA	
	Triple Set		DMC
	Ode: To The Cuckoo	TB	
	Had I A Heart	TB	
	A Toast	TBB	
	Pentagraph		
	Epigrams and Hymn	SATB	PMC
	Two Folksong Settings	SATB	JCP
	Sally Ann		
	Blow, Ye Winds in the Morning		
Roland Carter			
	I Want To Die Easy	SATB, solo	MV
	Hold Fast To Dreams	SATB, solo	
	A Hampton Portrait	SATB, solo	
	Give Me Jesus	SATB	
	Ride on, Jesus	SATB	
	Rise, Shine, For the Light Is A'Comin'	SATB	
	Lord, I Don't Feel No Ways Tired	SATB	
	Done Made My Vow To The Lord	SATB	
	Great Day	SATB	
	You Must Have That True Religion	SATB	
	Steal Away	SATB	
	I Heard The Preaching of de Elders	SATB	
	Five Choral Responses	SATB	MV

Composer	Title	Voicing	Publisher

Roland Carter (cont.)

	Hampton	SSAATTBB	
	Lift Every Voice and Sing	SATB	MV
	Precious Lord, Take My Hand	SATB, soli	
	In Bright Mansions Above		
	Ode To The Woman Who's Black		
	Tis The Ol' Ship of Zion		

PUBLISHERS OF CHORAL MUSIC

AMP   Associated Music Publishers
8666 Third Avenue
New York, N.Y.   10022

CF   Carl Fisher, Inc.
62 Cooper Square
New York, N.Y.   10003

CFP   C. F. Peters
373 Park Avenue South
New York, N.J.   10015

DMC   Duchess Music Corporation
c/o MCA - Music Corporation of American

EBM   Edward B. Marks
1790 Broadway
New York, N.Y.   10019

GWM   General Words and Music
c/o Neil A Kjos Publishers

GMP   General Music Publishing
Hasting-On-Hudson, New York

G   Galaxy Music Corporation
2121 Broadway
New York, N.Y.   10023

HP   Highgate Press
Galaxy Music Corp.
2121 Broadway
New York, N.Y.   10023

HM   Hinshaw Music, Inc.
P.PO. Box 470
Chapel Hill, N.C.   27514

JB   Joseph Boonin, Inc.
Hackensack, New Jersey

JCP   J. C. Penny Project

LM   Leeds Music Publishers
c/o MCA - Music Corporation of American

LG   Lawson-Gould Publishers
      c/o G. Schirmer
      860 Third Avenue
      New York, N.Y.   100222

MCA   Music Corporation of American
      435 Hudson Street
      New York, N.Y.   10014

MF   Mark Foster Publishers
      Box 4012
      Campaign, Illinois

MV   Mar-Vel Music Publishers
      P. O. Box 6411
      Hampton, Virginia   23668

NK   Neil A. Kjos Music Co.
      525 Busse Highway
      Park Ridge, Illinois   60068

OUP   Oxford University Press
      200 Madison Avenue
      New York, N.Y.   10016

PIC   Peer International Corp.
      c/o Southern Music Publishing Co.

PMC   Pembroke Music Co.
      c/o Carl Fisher

PA   Pro Art Publications, Inc.
      Westbury, L. I,. New York

R   Rudmor Publishing Company
      33 Riverside Drive
      New York, N.Y.   10023

SMP   Southern Music Publishing Co.
      1740 Broadway
      New York, N.Y.   10019

SF   Sam Fox Music Publishers
      1540 Broadway
      New York, N.Y.   10036

TP   Theodore Presser Co.
      Presser Place
      Bryn Mawr, Pennsylvania

491

TMC   Tosci Music
        122 Boylston St.
        Boston, Mass. 02116

WMC   Walton Music Corporation
        17 West 60th Street
        New York, N.Y. 10023

ADDRESSES OF COMPOSERS

Robert A. Harris
Director of Choral Organizations
Northwestern University
Evanston, Illinois

George Walker
Professor of Piano and Composition
Rutgers University
Newark, New Jersey

Ronald Roxbury
248 West 17th Street
New York, N.Y. 10011

Hale Smith
Professor of Music
University of Connecticut

James Furman
Associate Professor of Music
Western Connecticut State College
Danbury, Connecticut

Roland Carter
Director of Choirs
Hampton Institute
Hampton, Virginia 23668

Noel da Costa
Rutgers University
Newark, New Jersey

INDEX OF SONGS

495

498